Theory of Knowledge
for the IB Diploma

Richard van de Lagemaat

Cambridge University Press's mission is to advance learning, knowledge and research worldwide.

Our IB Diploma resources aim to:

- encourage learners to explore concepts, ideas and topics that have local and global significance

- help students develop a positive attitude to learning in preparation for higher education

- assist students in approaching complex questions, applying critical-thinking skills and forming reasoned answers.

CAMBRIDGE
UNIVERSITY PRESS

CAMBRIDGE UNIVERSITY PRESS
Cambridge, New York, Melbourne, Madrid, Cape Town,
Singapore, São Paulo, Delhi, Mexico City

Cambridge University Press
The Edinburgh Building, Cambridge CB2 8RU, UK

www.cambridge.org
Information on this title: www.cambridge.org/9781107669963

First published 2005
Full-colour edition 2011
4th printing 2012

Printed and bound in the United Kingdom by the MPG Books Group

A catalogue record for this publication is available from the British Library

ISBN 978-1-107-66996-3 Paperback

Cambridge University Press has no responsibility for the persistence or
accuracy of URLs for external or third-party internet websites referred to in
this publication, and does not guarantee that any content on such websites is,
or will remain, accurate or appropriate.

This material has been developed independently by the publisher and the
content is in no way connected with nor endorsed by the International
Baccalaureate Organization.

According to the philosopher Martin Heidegger, 'in all teaching, the teacher learns the most'. This book is dedicated to the countless students and teachers I have met whose ideas have informed, inspired and delighted me.

Contents

Acknowledgements

The author and publishers are grateful for the permissions granted to reproduce materials in either the original or adapted form. While every effort has been made, it has not always been possible to identify the sources of all the materials used, or to trace all copyright holders. If any omissions are brought to our notice, we will be happy to include the appropriate acknowledgements on reprinting.

p. 19 From *White Noise* by Don DeLillo, copyright © 1984, 1985 by Don DeLillo. Used by permission of Viking Penguin, a division of Penguin Group (USA) Inc., and Pan Macmillan, London Copyright © Don DeLillo 1986; p. 21 Edward Harrison © New Scientist Magazine; p. 40 from *The Tao of Physics* by Fritjof Capra, published by HarperCollins, by permission of David Higham Associates; p. 42 from *The Life of Galileo* by Bertold Brecht, translated by John Willett © Bertold Brecht and Methuen Drama, an imprint of A&C Black Publishers Ltd; p. 83 Peter Popham © The Independent 1996; p. 105 Laura Spinney © New Scientist Magazine; pp. 108, 253 © Hilary Lawson, Director of the Institute of Art and Ideas; p. 141 by Deborah Tannen, from The New York Times, 14 Jan 1994 © 1994 The New York Times. All rights reserved. Used by permission and protected by the Copyright Laws of the United States. The printing, copying, redistribution, or retransmission of this Content without express written permission is prohibited; p. 143 extract from *Cultural Anthropology: A Perspective on the Human Condition* by permission of the authors Emily Schultz and Robert H. Lavenda, published by West Publishing Company; p. 169 'Rethinking thinking' from The Economist 16 Dec 1999 © The Economist; pp. 172, 356 from *How the Mind Works* by Steven Pinker. Copyright © 1997 by Steven Pinker. Used by permission of W.W. Norton & Company Inc. and Penguin Group UK; p. 213 Michael Lemonick; p. 215 Ian Stewart © New Scientist Magazine; p. 250 Excerpt from "Crystalline Truth and Crystal Balls" from *A Devil's Chaplain: Reflections on Hope, Lies, Science and Love* by Richard Dawkins. Copyright © 2003 by Richard Dawkins. Reprinted by permission of Houghton Mifflin Harcourt Publishing Company; p. 283 by Jared Diamond (UCLA) published in Discovery Aug 1987; p. 286 'Is Economics a Science?' by Arthur Williamson and a reply by Seamus Hogan from Chemistry NZ; p. 322 *Nineteen Eighty Four* by George Orwell (Copyright © George Orwell, 1949) by permission of Bill Hamilton as the Literary Executor of the Estate of the Late Sonia Brownell Orwell and Secker & Warburg Ltd; p. 325 'History as "Some Kind of a Novel"' by George F. Kennan printed with permission of the American Academy of Arts and Letters, New York City; p. 361 "Whose side are you on?' by Lewis Wolpert, The Observer 10 March 2002, reprinted with permission of the author; p. 401 Jim Holt New York Times, 20 June 2004; p. 431 Ian Sample, © Guardian News & Media Ltd 2005; p. 435 from *The Mind of God* by Paul Davies, copyright © 1992 by Orion Productions, all rights reserved, reprinted with the permission of Simon & Schuster Inc.; p. 463 from *Zen and the Art of Motocycle Maintenance* by Robert Pirsig, published by the Bodley Head. Reprinted by permission of The Random House Group Ltd., Copyright © 1974 by Robert M. Pirsig, reprinted by permission of HarperCollins Publishers; p. 465 Lynch, Michael P., *True to Life: Why Truth Matters*, 1365 word excerpt, © 2004 Massachusetts Institute of Technology, by permission of The MIT Press

The publishers would like to thank the following for permission to reproduce illustrations:

p. vii © International Baccalaureate Organisation, 2011; p. 7 *The Betrayal of Images: `Ceci n'est pas une pipe'*, 1929 (oil on canvas), Magritte, Rene (1898-1967) / Los Angeles County

Introduction

This book is designed to be used with the Theory of Knowledge course in the International Baccalaureate Diploma Programme. (It is, however, not an official guide to the IB Theory of Knowledge syllabus and is not connected with the IBO in any way.) The book may also be useful for students following other critical thinking courses.

The main question in Theory of Knowledge (TOK) is 'How do you know?' The course encourages you to think critically about the subjects you are studying rather than passively accepting what you are taught. Critical thinking involves such things as asking good questions, using language with care and precision, supporting your ideas with evidence, arguing coherently, and making sound judgements. You are, of course, encouraged to thinking critically in every subject that you study. TOK is designed to help you to reflect on and further develop the thinking skills you have acquired in your other classes.

You can get an overview of the main elements of the Theory of Knowledge course by considering the diagram below:

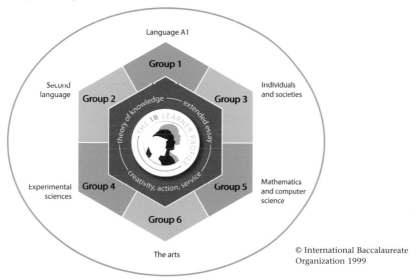

© International Baccalaureate
Organization 1999

In line with the above diagram, this book consists of three main parts and a conclusion:

1 Knowers and knowing
2 Ways of knowing
3 Areas of knowledge.

1 *Knowers and knowing*   Since TOK is concerned with the question 'How do you know?', we naturally need to spend some time talking about the nature of knowledge. We will be concerned with this in Part 1 and again in Part 4 of this book. Among the questions we shall be asking are: What is knowledge? How does knowledge differ from belief? What is the difference between knowledge, information and wisdom? Should we seek the truth at any price, or are there some things it would be better not to know?

2 *Ways of knowing* In TOK, we say there are four main ways of acquiring knowledge about the world: perception, language, reason and emotion. Take any thing that you claim to know and ask yourself how you know and you can trace it back to one of these four sources: either you saw it, or you heard it or read it, or you reasoned it out, or you have a gut-feeling that it is true. Despite their value, none of these ways of knowing is infallible. In fact, they are all *double-edged* in the sense that they can be both a source of knowledge and an obstacle to it. For example, many of our knowledge claims are based on perception, but our senses sometimes deceive us. Much of our knowledge is communicated to us 'second-hand' by other people, but the language they use may mislead us. We pride ourselves on being rational animals, but we often make errors in our reasoning and jump too quickly to conclusions. Finally, we sometimes appeal to feelings and intuitions to justify our knowledge claims, but they are not infallible guides to the truth. In Part 2, we will look at each of these knowledge tools and consider the extent to which they can be relied on in trying to make sense of the world.

3 *Areas of knowledge* In Part 3 we go on to look at the various areas of knowledge – mathematics, the natural sciences, the social sciences, history, the arts, ethics and religion. (Although religion does not appear in the above diagram, it is an important enough area to deserve its own chapter.) In each area of knowledge we raise the question 'How do you know?', and consider the role played by perception, language, reason and emotion in the subject in question. We will also touch on some of the 'big questions' that lie at the frontiers of knowledge. For example:

> Why is mathematics so useful?
> Does science prove things?
> What makes human beings different?
> Can the past be known?
> Do we have free will?
> Are there any universal values?
> Is everyone selfish?
> What is the purpose of art?
> Does life have a meaning?

We will also consider the similarities and differences between the above areas of knowledge and raise various interdisciplinary questions that will help you to think about how different subjects are related to one another and to develop a more coherent and inclusive picture of the world.

The chapters in this book are arranged to be consistent with the above diagram, but they do not have to be read in the order in which they are presented. Each chapter begins with a page of quotations and ends with a summary of key points, terms to remember, some suggestions for further reading, and linking questions. The reading resources at the end of all each chapter give you the opportunity to explore some of the topics covered in greater depth.

The vast majority of the questions raised in this book do not have definite answers, but this does not make them any less important. My aim in writing this book is not to save you the effort of thinking about these issues, but to provoke you to think about them for yourself. My hope is that you will be able to relate what I have written to your own experience and that this book will help you to find your way to your own conclusions.

PART 1

Knowers
and knowing

1 The problem of knowledge

'The greatest obstacle to progress is not the absence of knowledge but the illusion of knowledge.'
Daniel Boorstin, 1914–2004

'The familiar is not understood simply because it is familiar.'
Georg Wilhelm Friedrich Hegel, 1770–1831

'By doubting we are led to enquire, and by enquiry we perceive the truth.'
Peter Abélard, 1079–1142

'All men have opinions, but few think.'
George Berkeley, 1685–1753

'What men really want is not knowledge but certainty.'
Bertrand Russell, 1872–1970

'A very popular error – having the courage of one's convictions; rather it is a matter of having the courage for an attack upon one's convictions.'
Friedrich Nietzsche, 1844–1900

'Common sense consists of those layers of prejudice laid down before the age of 18.'
Albert Einstein, 1879–1955

'It is the customary fate of new truths to begin as heresies and to end as superstitions.'
T. H. Huxley, 1825–95

'There are two ways to slide easily through life: to believe everything, or to doubt everything; both ways save us from thinking.'
Alfred Korzybski, 1879–1950

'We know too much to be sceptics and too little to be dogmatists.'
Blaise Pascal, 1623–62

'Man is made by his belief. As he believes, so he is.'
Bhagavad Gita, 500 BCE

'To know one's ignorance is the best part of knowledge.'
Lao Tzu, c. 600 BCE

'To teach how to live without certainty, and yet without being paralysed by hesitation is perhaps the chief thing that philosophy in our age can still do for those who study it.'
Bertrand Russell, 1872–1970

Introduction

We live in a strange and perplexing world. Despite the explosive growth of knowledge in recent decades, we are confronted by a bewildering array of contradictory beliefs. We are told that astronomers have made great progress in understanding the universe in which we live, yet many people still believe in astrology. Scientists claim that the dinosaurs died out 65 million years ago, yet some insist that dinosaurs and human beings lived simultaneously. Apollo 11 landed on the moon in 1969, but it is rumoured in some quarters that the landings were faked by NASA. A work of art is hailed as a masterpiece by some critics and dismissed as junk by others. Some people support capital punishment, while others dismiss it as a vestige of barbarism. Millions of people believe in God, yet atheists insist that 'God is dead'. Faced with such a confusion of different opinions, how are we to make sense of things and develop a coherent picture of reality?

Given your school education, you might think of knowledge as a relatively unproblematic commodity consisting of various facts found in textbooks that have been proved to be true. But things are not as simple as that. After all, if you had attended school one hundred or five hundred years ago, you would have learned a different set of 'truths'. This suggests that knowledge is not static, but has a history and changes over time. Yesterday's revolution in thought becomes today's common sense, and today's common sense may go on to become tomorrow's superstition. So what guarantee is there that our current understanding of things is correct? Despite the intellectual progress of the last five hundred years, future generations may look back on our much-vaunted achievements and dismiss our science as crude, our arts as naive, and our ethics as barbaric.

When we consider ourselves from the perspective of the vast reaches of time and space, further doubts arise. According to cosmologists, the universe has been in existence for about 15 billion (15,000,000,000) years. If we imagine that huge amount of time compressed into one year running from January to December, then the earliest human beings do not appear on the scene until around 10.30 p.m. on 31 December, fire was only domesticated at 11.46 p.m., and the whole recorded history occupies only the last ten seconds of the cosmic year. Since we have been trying to make sense of the world in a systematic way for only a minute fraction of time, there is no guarantee that we have got it right. Furthermore, it turns out that in cosmic terms we are also pretty small. According to astronomers, there are ten times more stars in the night sky than grains of sand in *all* the world's deserts and beaches. Yet we flatter ourselves that we have discovered the laws that apply to *all* times and *all* places. Since we are familiar with only a minute fraction of the universe, this seems like a huge leap of faith. Perhaps it will turn out that some of the deeper truths about life, the universe and everything are simply beyond human comprehension.

Common sense

Most people do not think that there is a problem of knowledge and they see knowledge as nothing more than organised common sense. While there may be something to be said for this view, the trouble is that much of what passes for common sense consists of little more than vague and untested beliefs that are based on such things as prejudice, hearsay and blind appeals to authority. Moreover, many things that at first seem obvious to common sense become less and less obvious the closer you look at them.

Yet we need some kind of picture of what the world is like if we are to cope with it effectively, and common sense at least provides us with a starting point. We all have what might be called a **mental map** of reality which includes our ideas of what is true and what is false, what is reasonable and what is unreasonable, what is right and what is wrong, etc. Although only a fool would tell you to rip up your mental map and abandon your everyday understanding of things, you should – at least occasionally – be willing to subject it to critical scrutiny.

To illustrate the limitations of our common-sense understanding of things, let us make an analogy between our mental maps and real geographical maps. Consider the map of the world shown below, which is based on what is known as the Mercator Projection. If you were familiar with this map as you grew up, you may unthinkingly accept it as true and be unaware of its limitations.

Figure 1.1 The Mercator Projection

1 Think of as many different ways as you can in which the world map shown in Figure 1.1 is:
  a inaccurate
  b based on arbitrary **conventions**
  c culturally biased.
2 Do you think it would be possible to make a perfect map of a city? What would such a map have to look like? How useful would it be?

Among the weaknesses of the above map are the following:

1   It distorts the relative size of the land masses, so that areas further from the equator seem larger than they are in reality. The distortion is most apparent when we compare Greenland to Africa. According to the map they are about the same size, but in reality Africa is fourteen times bigger than Greenland.

2   It is based on the convention that the northern hemisphere is at the top of the map and the southern hemisphere at the bottom. Although we are used to this way of representing things, the reality is, of course, that the world does not come with a label saying 'This way up'!

3   The map is eurocentric in that it not only exaggerates the relative size of Europe, but also puts it in the middle of the map.

Now compare the Mercator Projection with another map of the world, known as the Hobo-Dyer Equal Area Projection.

Figure 1.2 Hobo-Dyer Projection

This projection accurately reflects the relative sizes of the land masses (although it distorts their shape); it has the southern hemisphere at the top and the northern hemisphere at the bottom; and it is centred on the Pacific rather than Europe. The fact that most people find this map disorienting illustrates the grip that habitual ways of thinking have on our minds and how difficult it is to break out of them.

The point of this excursion into maps is to suggest that, like the Mercator Projection, our common-sense mental maps may give us a distorted picture of reality. Our ideas and beliefs come from a variety of sources, such as our own experience, parents, friends, teachers, books and the media, and since we don't have time to check up on everything to make sure that it is true, there are likely to be all kinds of inaccuracies, half-truths and falsehoods woven into our mental maps. Furthermore, it can be difficult for us to think outside the customs and conventions with which we are familiar and see that there may be other ways of looking at things. Finally, there may be all kinds of cultural biases built into our picture of the world. If you ask an English person to name the greatest writer and greatest scientist of all time, they will probably say Shakespeare and Newton. If you ask the same question to an Italian, they are more likely to say Dante and Galileo.

One final point to draw out of this discussion is that, while different maps may be more or less useful for different purposes, there is no such thing as a perfect map. A *perfect* map of a city which included every detail down to the last brick and blade of grass would have to be drawn on a scale of 1:1. Such a map would, of course, be useless as a map, and would in any case quickly become out of date. We might call this the **paradox of cartography**: *if a map is to be useful, then it must of necessity be imperfect*. There will, then, always be a difference between a map and the underlying territory it describes. To sum up in a well-known slogan that is worth keeping in mind throughout this book: ***'the map is not the territory'***.

Activity 1.2

1 What relevance do you think the slogan 'the map is not the territory' has to our search for knowledge?
2 Look at the painting below by the Belgian surrealist René Magritte (1898–1967) called *The Treason of Images* (1928–29). What do you think of the title of the painting? What has this got to do with our discussion?

Figure 1.3 Magritte: *The Treason of Images*

Certainty

If there are problems with our common-sense picture of the world, perhaps we should abandon our everyday understanding of things and limit ourselves to what is certain. For it has often been thought that certainty is what distinguishes knowledge from mere belief. The idea here is that when you know something you are certain it is true and have no doubts about it; but when you merely believe it, you may *think* it is true, but you are not certain. At first sight, this seems reasonable enough; but when you start to look critically at the things we normally claim to know, you may begin to wonder if any of them are completely certain!

Activity 1.3

List in order the five things in life that you are most certain of. Compare your list with someone else's. Can you come to any agreement?

Consider, for example, the following four statements:

1 I know that Neil Armstrong landed on the moon in 1969.
2 I know that strawberries are red.
3 I know that if *a* is bigger than *b* and *b* is bigger than *c*, then *a* is bigger than *c*.
4 I know that murder is wrong.

I imagine you would say that all of the above statements are true. But how do you know? You might say that you know that Neil Armstrong landed on the moon in 1969 because you read about it in an encyclopaedia; you know that strawberries are red because you can see that they are red; you know that if *a* is bigger than *b* and *b* is bigger than *c*, then *a* is bigger than *c* because you can reason it out; and you know that murder is wrong because it is intuitively obvious. However, if you ask yourself whether you are 100 per cent certain that these statements are true, doubts may begin to creep in. A quick look at each of the four **ways of knowing** – language, perception, reason and emotion – suggests that they cannot simply be taken at face value.

1 Language

Language enables us to acquire knowledge from other people, and we claim to know a great many things because we have been told them or we have read them somewhere. However, the authority of other people is not always a reliable source of knowledge, and even the so-called experts sometimes 'get it wrong'. If you are into conspiracy theories, you might ask how we can be sure that the alleged American moon landings were not an elaborate CIA-inspired hoax.

2 Perception

Much of our knowledge is based on personal experience, but our senses sometimes deceive us. For example, if you are colour blind, you might not see strawberries as red. We shall have more to say about this in Chapter 4. For the time being, you might like to consider Figure 1.4.

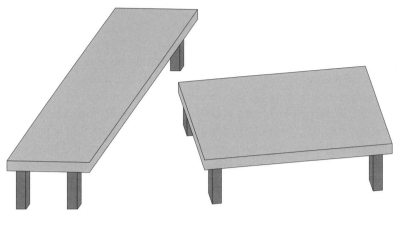

Figure 1.4

Believe it or not, the two table tops above are exactly the same shape and size. This suggests that we should not blindly trust our perception and assume that it gives us certainty.

3 Reason

Statement 3 above might seem less open to doubt than the others, and some philosophers have claimed that reason gives us greater certainty than perception. In practice, however, people do not seem to be very good at abstract reasoning and they are liable to make all kinds of errors. To illustrate, assuming that some dentists are drunkards and no cyclists are drunkards, does it follow that some cyclists are dentists? The answer is that it does not – but we may well struggle to see that this is true.

4 Emotion

Some of the things that we claim to know strike us as intuitively obvious or are based on our gut feelings. The trouble is that what is intuitively obvious to me may not be intuitively obvious to you, and gut feelings are far from being a sure guide to the truth. You only have to consider debates about such things as abortion or capital punishment to see the extent to which people may have conflicting intuitions on important issues. And it would surely be arrogant simply to assume that my intuitions are right and yours are wrong. Emotions may provide us with the energy to pursue knowledge, but it is far from clear that they are infallible guides to the truth.

Radical doubt

So far, we have raised some preliminary doubts about knowledge that is derived from language, perception, reason and emotion. But, following the French philosopher René Descartes (1596–1650), there is perhaps one statement that you think is *absolutely* certain – namely that 'I exist'. Surely that is something that cannot sensibly be doubted?

Well, if pushed, I might say that I am not even sure about that! In the movie *The Truman Show* a character called Truman Burbank lives on an island called Seahaven and leads an apparently ordinary life. As the movie progresses, we learn that Truman's entire life is being filmed 24 hours a day and broadcast live on TV, and that his wife, family, friends and acquaintances are all paid actors. Truman himself is unaware of this and he mistakes his illusory world for reality. So how can you be certain that you are not living a Truman-Show-type life and that the people around you are not simply actors? Some philosophers have even speculated that the whole of life might be a dream. Perhaps you will awake in a few minutes and realise that you have been having the strangest dream in which you were a creature called a human being, living on a planet called Earth. Although such a radical supposition does not prove that you do not exist, it *does* suggest that your life might be completely different from what you thought.

Activity 1.4

1 Do you think it is seriously possible that you could be dreaming right now?
2 Do you think that some areas of knowledge are more certain than others?

Relativism

Sometimes people react to this lack of certainty by swinging to the opposite extreme and embracing a position known as **relativism**. According to relativism, there is no such thing as absolute truth that exists in an objective way independent of what anyone happens to *believe* is true. Instead, truth is relative and may be different for different individuals or for different cultures. So rather than say that something is true or false in an unqualified way, the most we can do is say that it is 'true for me' or 'false for you'. Since there are no grounds for saying that one opinion is better than another, we must therefore conclude that all points of view are of equal value.

Since there are disputed questions in all areas of knowledge, relativism might at first seem an attractive position. Rather than insist that I am right and you are wrong, it is surely more attractive to say that one and the same knowledge claim can be true for me and false for you?

Despite its attractions, relativism leads to as many difficulties as equating knowledge with certainty. Consider the question of whether or not the earth is round. According to a relativist we would have to say it is true for me and false for a member of the flat-earth society. But surely there is an objective fact of the matter independent of what I or anyone else may happen to think? After all, the earth cannot be both round *and* flat. In view of this, I think that what people really mean when they say that something is 'true for them' is that they *believe* it is true. You are, of course, entitled to believe what you like, but the mere fact that you believe that something is true doesn't mean that it actually *is* true. A young child might believe that Santa Claus exists, but it only confuses the issue to say that it is 'true for the child'. For, no matter what the child believes, Santa Claus does not in fact exist.

The fact that we take seriously the idea that someone might be wrong in their beliefs suggests that relativism is false. Indeed, it could be argued that the statement 'All truth is relative' is self-contradictory. For if we ask ourselves about the status of the statement itself, we seem to run into difficulties – as can be seen from the dialogue in Figure 1.5. On the one hand, if it is absolutely true that all truth is relative, then there is at least one absolute truth – namely the truth that all truth is relative. On the other hand, if it is only relatively true that all truth is relative, then if a consistent relativist meets someone who says 'It is *not* true for me that all truth is relative', they are hardly in a position to argue with them.

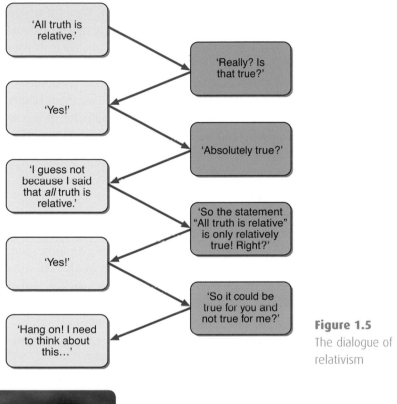

Figure 1.5
The dialogue of relativism

Activity 1.5

Read the dialogue taken from a novel *White Noise* by Don DeLillo (see Reading resources, page 19). What doubts does Heinrich cast on his father's claim that it is raining? Which, if any, of these doubts do you think are reasonable?

What should we believe?

We have seen that neither common sense, nor certainty, nor relativism can give us a quick solution to the problem of knowledge. So what should we believe? There is no simple answer to this question, and TOK is, in any case, more concerned with *how* you believe something than with *what* you believe. Whatever you believe, you should, for example, try to support your beliefs with evidence and be able to consider and respond to criticisms of your views.

The role of judgement

Since we live in a world in which there are few black and white certainties, you will probably have to rely more on **judgement** than proof in deciding what to believe. One important aspect of good judgement is the ability to balance scepticism with open-mindedness. Take the claim that aliens have visited the earth at some time in the past – something which opinion polls suggest is believed by around one-third of Americans. We should be sceptical enough to question some of the flimsy evidence that has been put forward to support this claim, but open-minded enough to allow that it is possible that a technologically advanced civilisation may have evolved and sent envoys to our planet. We must then engage in the difficult task of assessing the balance of evidence and coming to a provisional conclusion.

The great marketplace of beliefs in the so-called information age is, of course, the Internet. Surfing around, you can quickly find websites devoted not only to a whole range of academic subjects, but also to a dizzying array of paranormal phenomena, conspiracy theories and urban legends. Since we live in a credulous age, we should cultivate a healthy scepticism as an antidote to intellectual – and financial – gullibility. (If you are too gullible, you will find plenty of charlatans and hucksters out there who will be only too willing to relieve you of your money.)

The danger of gullibility

Now, you may personally believe in some or other paranormal phenomenon or conspiracy theory, and at some point it may even be shown to be true. However, no one is willing to believe *everything* they read on the Internet, and we all have limits beyond which we conclude that a belief is absurd. I very much doubt that you would take seriously any of the following headlines from the *Weekly World News*, which styles itself as 'America's wildest and zaniest supermarket tabloid':

'Amazing New Proof of Life After Death' (11 January 1999)
'Faith Healer Cures Sick Pets with the Power of Prayer' (13 August 1999)
'US Scientists Bring Mummy Back to Life' (27 August 1999)
'Washington Think Tanks are Riddled with Space Aliens' (1 October 1999)
'First Marriage Between Human and Space Alien Still Going Strong'
(8 October 1999)
'Dog Reincarnation: Five Ways to Tell if Your Dog was a Human in a Past Life'
(12 November 1999)
'Top Psychic Warns: Hitler is Coming Back' (21 January 2000)
'Top Scientist says Sicko Space Aliens are Stealing Our Women and Turning them into Prostitutes' (6 April 2000)
'Your Dead Pet's Ghost May be Peeing on Your Carpet' (16 May 2000)

The danger of scepticism

Despite the above comments, there is also a danger in being *too* sceptical; for you may then close your mind to new ideas that challenge the conventional wisdom. There are many examples of ideas that were ridiculed when they first appeared but were later shown to be true. For example, until the early nineteenth century, scientists dismissed the idea that stones could fall from the sky as superstition; but we now take the existence of meteorites for granted. Similarly, when Alfred Wegener (1880–1930) suggested the theory of continental drift in 1912, it was rejected by his contemporaries; but it was resurrected in the 1960s as part of the theory of plate tectonics. The moral of the tale is that just because an idea does not fit our currently accepted theories does not necessarily mean that it is wrong. For it is always possible that it is our theories that need to be changed. Thus if we are too sceptical the danger is that intellectual progress will grind to a halt and knowledge stagnate.

So we need to find a balance between being open to new ideas that challenge our current way of thinking, and keeping in mind that human beings are credulous animals who are sometimes willing to believe strange things on the basis of slender evidence.

"For goodness sake, man, SNAP OUT OF IT...!!! We're NOT aliens from outer space!!
We're PIXIES! from your GARDEN..!! IS THAT SO DIFFICULT TO UNDERSTAND...?!?"

Figure 1.6

Activity 1.6

Comment on the following quotation, and explain why you either agree or disagree with it: 'My view is that there is such a thing as being too open-minded. I am *not* open-minded about the earth being flat, about whether Hitler is alive today, about claims by people to have squared the circle, or to have proven special relativity wrong. I am also not open-minded with respect to the paranormal. And I think it is wrong to be open-minded with respect to these things, just as I think it is wrong to be open-minded about whether or not the Nazis killed six million Jews in World War II.' [Douglas Hofstadter]

Reasonable knowledge

In trying to determine whether or not a knowledge claim is reasonable, two preliminary criteria may serve as useful guides: (1) evidence and (2) coherence.

1 Evidence

For a belief to be reasonable there should be some positive evidence in support of it. Imagine someone claiming that there are little green men living on Mars. When you challenge them to support their belief, they say 'Well, you can't prove that there aren't.' This is a bad argument because the person has given no positive evidence to support their belief; and although it is difficult to prove that there are definitely not little green men on Mars, this simply reflects the fact that it is always difficult to prove a negative. The fact that you can't prove that something *isn't* true does nothing to show that it *is* true. The fallacy of thinking that it does is called **argument *ad ignorantiam*.**

Activity 1.7

1 Which of the following is an example of argument *ad ignorantiam*?
   a Since many people claim to have seen ghosts, it is likely that they exist.
   b Many members of the Society for the Paranormal believe in ghosts.
   c Ghosts must exist because no one has proved that they do not.
   d It is true for me that ghosts exist.
2 Make up three examples of your own to illustrate the fallacy of argument *ad ignorantiam*.
3 How would you go about trying to prove that a species has become extinct? What has this got to do with our discussion?

We should look not only for evidence in favour of our beliefs, but also for evidence that would count against them. For, according to psychologists, we have a disturbing tendency, known as **confirmation bias**, to notice only evidence that supports our beliefs. For example, if you believe in astrology, you will tend to notice the times your horoscope is right and overlook the times it is wrong. To counter this tendency, you should keep a record not only of how often the horoscope is right but also of how often it is wrong.

2 Coherence

A second criterion for deciding whether or not a belief is reasonable is whether it coheres, or fits in, with our current understanding of things. Despite appearances, I don't think that this criterion contradicts what we said earlier about the need to question common sense. When it comes to examining our beliefs, our position is like that of a sailor who has to rebuild his ship while still at sea. If he dismantles the ship completely and tries to rebuild it from scratch, he will drown. His only option is to rebuild it piece by piece. Similarly, we cannot cast doubt on all of our beliefs at the same time. The best we can do is examine them one at a time against the background of our other beliefs. If we don't want to drown, there is simply no other way to proceed.

What this criterion implies is that, although we should be open to new ideas, the more unlikely something is relative to the current state of knowledge, the stronger the evidence in its favour should be before we take it seriously. Consider, for example, the claims of people such as Uri Geller – 'the world's most famous paranormalist' – to be able to bend spoons using only mental energy. Given our current knowledge of the way the world works, it seems unlikely that a spoon can be bent through non-physical means simply by focusing one's mind on it. So before accepting such a belief we should demand good evidence in support of it. As far as I know, no such evidence currently exists.

Activity 1.8

1 According to the astronomer Carl Sagan (1934–96), 'extraordinary claims require extraordinary evidence'. Explain what he meant by this. Do you agree?

2 Explain, with reasons, which of the following statements you think is less likely to be true.
   a The Loch Ness monster exists.
   b Some mystics are able to levitate.

3 In a book entitled *The Appalling Fraud* (*L'effroyable imposture*), the French author Thierry Meyssan makes the extraordinary claim that a passenger jet did not hit the Pentagon on 11 September 2001, and that the explosion was instead caused by a truck load of explosives. Using the criterion mentioned above, how much evidence would you need in order to be convinced of the truth of Meyssan's claim?

Who cares?

At this point, you might ask whether it really matters what we believe. We may laugh at some of the crazy ideas people hold, but what harm do they do? Don't people have the right to believe what they like? I am as in favour of freedom of belief as the next person, but I think it matters what you believe; and although it may sound undemocratic I think some beliefs are more worthy of respect than others.

One reason why your beliefs and opinions matter is that they are an important – perhaps defining – part of who you are as a person. So if you want to be something more than a 'second-hand self' who mindlessly repeats the opinions of other people, you need to make your beliefs and opinions genuinely your own by subjecting them to critical scrutiny. Socrates (470–399 BCE) once famously said that 'The unexamined life is not worth living.' Although it would make little sense to be *constantly* examining your beliefs, I think that if you *never* examine them you end up leading a life that is not genuinely your own.

A second reason why beliefs matter is that people's beliefs affect their actions; and, in some cases at least, beliefs can literally be a matter of life and death. For example, between the fifteenth and seventeenth centuries in Europe, an estimated half a million people were burnt to death because they were believed to be guilty of the 'crime' of witchcraft. Fortunately, we no longer burn people to death for witchcraft; but there is no shortage of dangerous and misguided beliefs in circulation. Here are two examples:

1   A former chief executive of Philip Morris once claimed that cigarettes are no more addictive than gummy bears candy. But the statistical evidence suggests that every cigarette you smoke shortens your life by about the amount of time it takes to smoke it.

2   In 1997, the leader of an American religious cult called 'Heaven's Gate' persuaded his followers that if they 'shed their bodies' they would be beamed on board a spaceship behind the Hale-Bopp comet and taken to a new world. Thirty-nine people committed suicide as a result.

Activity 1.9

1   Do you think we should respect the beliefs of a racist or sexist person? Give reasons.
2   Find some examples of beliefs that you think are both misguided and dangerous.

The French philosopher Voltaire (1694–1778) once said that 'People who believe absurdities will commit atrocities.' Although most people who hold eccentric beliefs show no interest in massacring their neighbours, I think there is an element of truth in Voltaire's comment. A society in which 'anything goes' is a fertile breeding ground for fanatics and extremists of all kinds. Some historians have observed that the rise of Hitler in Germany was accompanied by a growing interest in various kinds of pseudo-science. The psychologist Viktor Frankl (1905–97), who was a survivor of a Nazi concentration camp, sees a direct link between the two: 'I am absolutely convinced that the gas chambers of Auschwitz, Treblinka, and Maidanek were ultimately prepared not in some ministry or other in Berlin, but rather at the desks and in the lecture halls of nihilistic scientists and philosophers.' If there is any truth in this claim, then each of us has the responsibility, at least occasionally, to take a critical look at our own beliefs and prejudices.

Conclusion

At the beginning of this chapter, we saw that it is difficult to form a coherent picture of reality in the modern world. The way we see the world is shaped by our history, and by culture and psychology; and since in cosmic terms we have not been around very long, we may wonder if we have any privileged access to the truth. We then looked at three possible solutions to the problem of knowledge – common sense, certainty and relativism – and we saw that none of them is entirely adequate. Since the problem of knowledge has no easy solution we must use our judgement in trying to decide what to believe.

I hope that at this stage you will agree that there is a problem of knowledge and that it is worth spending some time thinking about it. What we now need to do is look in more detail at what we mean by the word 'knowledge'. That is the task of Chapter 2.

- The world is a confusing place in which we find a bewildering variety of different opinions.
- Our common-sense picture of reality probably contains inaccuracies and biases that we are not aware of.
- We acquire knowledge about the world through language, perception, reason and emotion, but none of these ways of knowing can give us certainty.
- According to relativism, truth is relative to the individual; but the fact that we take seriously the idea that someone may be wrong in their beliefs suggests that relativism is false.
- Since there are few black and white certainties in the world, we have to rely more on judgement.
- An important aspect of good judgement is finding the right balance between scepticism and open-mindedness.
- Two preliminary criteria for deciding whether a knowledge claim is plausible are evidence and coherence.
- Since we are what we believe and our beliefs affect our actions, if we want to be authentic and responsible we should occasionally subject our beliefs to critical scrutiny.

Terms to remember

argument *ad ignorantiam*	evidence	paradox of cartography
certainty	gullibility	paranormal phenomena
coherence	judgement	relativism
common sense	mental map	scepticism
confirmation bias	open-mindedness	ways of knowing

Further reading

André Comte-Sponville, *The Little Book of Philosophy* (Heinemann, 2004), Chapter 5: 'Knowledge'. A beautifully written chapter on knowledge, scepticism and certainty. Since it is written by a philosopher, it is quite challenging, but it is worth reading, thinking about, and then reading again!

Carl Sagan, *The Demon Haunted World* (Ballantine, 1997). This classic text written from a scientific and sceptical point of view contains many thought-provoking chapters. Try Chapter 12, 'The Fine Art of Baloney Detection', Chapter 17, 'The Marriage of Skepticism and Wonder', and Chapter 19, 'No Such Thing as a Dumb Question'.

Perception
How trustworthy are our senses?

Language
Does some knowledge lie beyond language?

Reason
How can we justify logic?

Religion
Can we know what the meaning of life is?

Emotion
How reliable are our feelings and emotions?

Ethics
Are values objective or subjective?

Some problems of knowledge

Mathematics
How does mathematics relate to the world?

The arts
Do the arts give us knowledge?

Natural sciences
How certain is scientific knowledge?

History
Can history be unbiased?

Human sciences
Can human behaviour be predicted?

SCIENCE'S FINEST HOUR

The following dialogue is taken from a novel called *White Noise* by Don DeLillo. A father is driving his 14-year-old son, Heinrich, to school. Heinrich begins the conversation.

'It's going to rain tonight.'

'It's raining now', I said.

'The radio said tonight.' ...

'Look at the windshield', I said. 'Is that rain or isn't it?'

'I'm only telling you what they said.'

'Just because it's on the radio doesn't mean we have to suspend belief in the evidence of our senses.'

'Our senses? Our senses are wrong a lot more often than they're right. This has been proved in the laboratory. Don't you know about all those theorems that say nothing is what it seems? There's no past, present or future outside our own mind. The so-called laws of motion are a big hoax. Even sound can trick the mind. Just because you don't hear a sound doesn't mean it's not out there. Dogs can hear it. Other animals. And I'm sure there are sounds even dogs can't hear. But they exist in the air, in waves. Maybe they never stop. High, high, high-pitched. Coming from somewhere.'

'Is it raining', I said, 'or isn't it?'

'I wouldn't want to have to say.'

'What if someone held a gun to your head?'

'Who, you?'

'Someone. A man in a trenchcoat and smoky glasses. He holds a gun to your head and he says, "Is it raining or isn't it? All you have to do is tell the truth and I'll put away my gun and take the next flight out of here."

'What truth does he want? Does he want the truth of someone traveling at almost the speed of light in another galaxy? Does he want the truth of someone in orbit around a neutron star? Maybe if these people could see us through a telescope we might look like we were two feet two inches tall and it might be raining yesterday instead of today.'

'He's holding the gun to your head. He wants *your* truth.'

'What good is my truth? My truth means nothing. What if this guy with a gun comes from a planet in a whole different solar system? What we call rain he calls soap. What we call apples he calls rain. So what am I supposed to tell him?'

'His name is Frank J. Smalley and he comes from St Louis.'

'He wants to know if it's raining *now*, at this very minute?'

'Here and now. That's right.'

'Is there such a thing as now? "Now" comes and goes as soon as you say it. How can I say it's raining now if your so-called "now" becomes "then" as soon as I say it?'

'You said there was no past, present, or future.'

'Only in our verbs. That's the only place we find it.'

'Rain is a noun. Is there rain here, in this precise locality, at whatever time within the next two minutes, that you choose to respond to the question?'

'If you want to talk about this precise locality while you're in a vehicle that's obviously moving, then I think that's the trouble with this discussion.'

'Just give me an answer, okay, Heinrich?'

'The best I could do is make a guess.'

'Either it's raining or it isn't', I said.

'Exactly. That's my whole point. You'd be guessing. Six of one, half dozen of the other.'

'But you see it's raining.'

'You see the sun moving across the sky. But is the sun moving across the sky or is the earth turning?'

'I don't accept the analogy.'

'You're so sure that's rain. How do you know it's not sulfuric acid from factories across the river? How do you know it's not fallout from a war in China? You want an answer here and now. Can you prove, here and now, that this stuff is rain? How do I know that what you call rain is really rain? What is rain anyway?'

'It's the stuff that falls from the sky and gets you what is called wet.'

'I'm not wet. Are you wet?'

'All right', I said. 'Very good.'

'No, seriously, are you wet?'

'First-rate', I told him. 'A victory for uncertainty, randomness and chaos. Science's finest hour.'

'Be sarcastic.'

'The sophists and the hairsplitters enjoy their finest hour.'

'Go ahead, be sarcastic, I don't care.'

THE UNCERTAINTY OF KNOWLEDGE

According to this article, written in 1987 by Edward Harrison, a professor of physics and astronomy at the University of Massachusetts, contemporary scientists stand no closer to the ultimate 'truths' than their forebears did.

Perhaps you have noticed that few people are speechless when it comes to answering the burning questions. The person without answers is a nobody. In our writings, lectures, conversations and pronouncements over the dining table we tell one another that life would be much better if only people were more educated, had more faith in religion, devoted greater effort to the cure of diseases, supported more vigorously social reform, dieted, exercised more, flossed their teeth and voted for this or that political party. On every side can be heard the clamour of voices claiming to know what must be believed and what must be done.

With a sigh of relief we escape from this confusion of beliefs into the quietness and certainty of the natural sciences. Here, in this lofty museum of secure knowledge... may be found the right answers on display for all to see and examine. Exhibits and working models reveal the truth with the utmost clarity. Some of the latest exhibits, naturally, are not quite ready for public view and require finishing touches. Some display cases – but not many – still remain empty: but judging by the activity around them, they will not stay empty for long. Soon the screens will be pulled aside, unveiling to the public view answers that will explain what the Universe is all about.

Visitors come away feeling convinced that the end of the search for knowledge in the natural sciences is now in sight. The final pieces in the cosmic jigsaw puzzle are about to take their place. Even the staff seem convinced. One or two subatomic particles remain to be tracked down, a few items – such as quantising gravity to make us universally wise and controlling DNA to make us physiologically perfect – remain to be developed, and then everything fundamental, genuinely worth knowing, will be revealed for us to see, as it was, is and will be, forever and ever, amen.

Confronted with this inspiring challenge, the humanities, arts, social sciences and professions, not relishing the idea of being left far behind, are hastening to make their own contributions to the wisdom of the 20th century. At last, after groping our way in the darkness for millennia, we see light at the end of the tunnel.

It all sounds terribly familiar. The pages of history are covered with equivalent certainties and crystalline clarities. Yet all have vanished into thin air like the celestial-angelic spheres of medieval astronomy and the luminiferous ether of Victorian physics. Human beings of all societies in all periods of history believe that their ideas on the nature of the real world are the most secure, and that their ideas on religion, ethics and justice are the most enlightened. Like us, they think that final knowledge is at last within reach. Like us, they pity the people in earlier ages for not knowing the true facts. Unfailingly, human beings pity their ancestors for being so ignorant and forget that their descendants will pity them for the same reason.

Light always gleams ahead. The end to the search for true knowledge always looms in sight. The one invariant characteristic of rational inquiry is the imminence of final knowledge.

Dare I say – contrary to the popular belief – that secure knowledge can never be found? That our boundless ignorance explains why we feel so confident of success in bounded knowledge? That each discovery creates in the long run more mystery than it solves? That we stand no closer to the ultimate 'truths' than did our forebears? And that we are no better intellectually and morally than the people who lived a thousand and even ten thousand years ago?

We have this overwhelming belief that we are rapidly filling in the detail of the cosmic picture. Unfortunately, the picture keeps changing. One landscape with figures melts away and a new landscape with figures emerges requiring fresh paintwork. The picture keeps growing bigger and we cannot help occasionally noticing how gaps on the canvas are spreading faster than dabs of paint.

Let me say how I view the uncertainty of knowledge. Knowledge must forever change otherwise it withers. The quest for knowledge is endless and its greatest joy is constant surprise. We forever reshape the scheme of things nearer to the heart's desire. Permanent enlightenment cannot be secured by bringing down from the mountaintop infallible laws engraved in stone. We project our desires and figure our designs on the face of the inscrutable, and the inscrutable, which includes us, seems patient of endless interpretation. We represent reality seeking to understand itself.

I feel liberated by this philosophy. I find comfort in the thought that the creative mind fashions the world in which we live. For it means that the mind and reality are more profound than we normally suppose.

2 The nature of knowledge

'A man with only one theory is a lost man.'
Bertolt Brecht, 1898–1956

'The will to a system is a lack of integrity.'
Friedrich Nietzsche, 1844–1900

'Science is the belief in the ignorance of experts.'
Richard Feynman, 1918–88

'Knowledge is the small part of ignorance that we arrange and classify.'
Ambrose Bierce, 1842–1914

'Man is a credulous animal, and must believe something; in the absence of good grounds for belief, he will be satisfied with bad ones.'
Bertrand Russell, 1872–1970

'We must rise above the obsession with quantity of information and speed of transmission, and recognize that the key issue for us is our ability to organize this information once it has been amassed – to assimilate it, find meaning in it.'
Vartan Gregorian, 1934–

'Information is acquired by being told, whereas knowledge can be acquired by thinking.'
Fritz Machlup, 1902–83

'It is the mark of an educated man to look for precision in each class of things just so far as the nature of the subject admits; it is evidently foolish to accept probable reasoning from a mathematician and to demand from a rhetorician scientific proofs.'
Aristotle, 384–322 BCE

'The average man's opinions are much less foolish than they would be if he thought for himself.'
Bertrand Russell, 1872–1970

'If 50 million people say a foolish thing, it is still a foolish thing.'
Anatole France, 1844–1924

'If the world should blow itself up, the last audible voice would be that of an expert saying it can't be done.'
Peter Ustinov, 1921–2004

'Knowledge is of two kinds. We know a subject ourselves, or we know where we can find information upon it.'
Samuel Johnson, 1709–84

'The more connections and interconnections we ascertain, the more we know the object in question.'
John Dewey, 1859–1952

Introduction

Having looked at the problem of knowledge, we now need to say something about the nature of knowledge. The word 'knowledge' is what might be described as a *thick concept* in that it is not exhausted by a short definition and can only be understood through experience and reflection. Indeed, the whole of this book is, in a sense, a reflection on the meaning of the word 'knowledge'. Having said that, a definition can still give us a useful preliminary hook for thinking about the meaning of a word. So we shall begin by exploring a definition of knowledge as *justified true belief*. But it is important to keep in mind that this should be the starting point for reflection rather than its finishing point.

Knowledge as justified true belief

Taking our preliminary definition of knowledge as *justified true belief*, let us consider the three elements that make it up.

Truth

The most obvious thing that distinguishes knowledge from belief is truth. If you know something, then what you claim to know *must* be true, but if you merely believe it, then it may be true or it may be false. This is why you cannot *know* that Rome is the capital of France, or that pigs have wings, or that the earth is flat.

Truth is another thick concept, which we shall have a lot to say about in Chapter 14. For the time being we can say that, as traditionally understood, truth is independent of what anyone happens to believe is true, and that simply believing that something is true does not make it true. Indeed, even if *everyone* believes that something is true, it may turn out to be false. For example, during the Middle Ages, everyone thought they knew that there were seven 'planets' orbiting the earth (Sun, Moon, Mercury, Venus, Mars, Saturn and Jupiter). They were wrong: we now know that there are nine planets orbiting the sun.

This raises the question of how can we ever be sure that what we think we know really is true. Perhaps in the future they will discover a tenth planet, and what we thought we knew will turn out to be false. Since we are fallible beings, this is indeed possible. But, as we saw in Chapter 1, this simply shows that knowledge requires something less than certainty. In practice, when we say that something is true, we usually mean that it is 'beyond reasonable doubt'. Since we are willing to imprison – and in some cases execute – people on the basis of evidence that is beyond reasonable doubt, this is surely an acceptable criterion for saying that we know something.

Belief

If you know something, then what you claim to know must not only be true, but you must also *believe* it to be true. We might say that, while truth is an objective requirement for knowledge, belief is a subjective requirement for it. If you have no conscious awareness of something, then it makes little sense to say that you know it. That is why encyclopaedias do not *know* that Paris is the capital of France, and pocket calculators do not *know* that $2 + 2 = 4$.

Since the time of Plato (428–348 BCE), some philosophers have argued that when you know something you are in a completely different mental state to when you merely believe it. For when you know something you are certain of it, and when you merely believe it you are not. However, we shall adopt a less demanding standard of knowledge. Rather than think of knowledge as being completely different from belief, it may make more sense to think in terms of a belief–knowledge continuum, with unjustified beliefs at one end of the continuum, beliefs for which there is some evidence in the middle, and beliefs which are 'beyond reasonable doubt' at the other end.

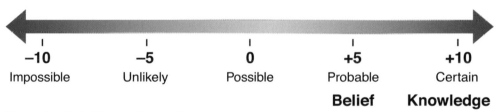

Figure 2.1 Belief–knowledge continuum

Here are three examples of various kinds of belief:

- *A vague belief* I may vaguely believe that eating tomatoes helps to reduce the risk of heart disease, but have no idea where I came across this idea and readily abandon it in the light of counter-evidence.
- *A well-supported belief* I may believe that Smith killed Jones, and be able to give evidence for my belief, but still be unwilling to say that I know that this is the case.
- *A belief that is beyond reasonable doubt* I may find the evidence which supports the claim that the Americans landed on the moon in 1969 so convincing and the counter-evidence of conspiracy theorists so flimsy that I am willing to say that I know the Americans landed on the moon.

Given this way of looking at things, the question of exactly where we should draw the line between belief and knowledge does not strike me as a very interesting one. It is like asking where, in a spectrum of shades running from black to white, black ends and white begins. The important thing, surely, is to try to develop as reasonable and well-supported a set of beliefs as possible.

Activity 2.2

Where on the belief–knowledge continuum, running from –10 to +10, would you put the following propositions?

a Christopher Columbus 'discovered' America in 1492.

b If A is bigger than B and B is bigger than C, then A is bigger than C.

c Human beings are descended from apes.

d Murder is wrong.

e Aliens have visited the earth at some time during its history.

f All metals expand when heated.

g Human beings have an immortal soul.

h It is possible to construct a square with the same area as a given circle.

Justification

You might think that true belief is a sufficient condition for knowledge, and that if you believe something and your belief is true, then you can be said to know it. However, something more is in fact required – your belief must also be justified in the right kind of way. Imagine that someone claims to know that there are nine planets in the solar system. When you ask how they know, they reply that there is an analogy between the 'microcosmos' of the human body and the 'macrocosmos' of the solar system, and that, just as there are nine 'windows' in the temple of the body – two nostrils, two ears, two eyes, a mouth, and two windows in the lower portion of the body – so there must also be nine planets in the solar system. This person believes that there are nine planets in the solar system, and his belief is true, but we would not want to say that he *knows* this because his belief has not been justified in the right kind of way. To us it makes no sense to talk of an analogy between the 'windows' in the human body and the planets in the solar system.

The point, in short, is that in order to be able to say that you know something you must be able to justify your belief, and your justification must be of the right kind. We usually justify our knowledge claims by appealing to one of the four ways of knowing. If someone asks you how you know, you might reply:

'Someone told me' (language)
'I saw it' (perception)
'I worked it out' (reason)
'It's intuitively obvious' (emotion)

With respect to our planetary example, you might be said to *know* that there are nine planets in the solar system if you are part of a team of astronomers that have made the relevant observations, or if you came across this fact in a reputable encyclopaedia or science magazine.

Now, you might ask why some kinds of justification, such as perception, are usually considered acceptable, while others, such as telepathy, are not. Imagine that a psychic asks you to think of an animal, and then correctly says that you are thinking of a zebra. When you ask her how she knew, she replies that she read your mind. I think that most people would not find this an acceptable justification, and would say that the psychic did not really *know* that you were thinking of a zebra, but simply made a lucky guess.

The key thing that distinguishes acceptable from unacceptable justifications seems to be *reliability*. Although it is not infallible, perception is a generally reliable source of knowledge. Telepathy, by contrast, is unreliable, and the scientific evidence to date suggests that psychics do no better than chance when it comes to trying to read other people's minds. The sceptic and magician James Randi has offered a prize of $1 million to anyone who can demonstrate psychic powers. At the time of writing, the prize remains unclaimed. This does not prove that telepathy is false, but it does suggest that it cannot be appealed to as a reliable justification for our knowledge claims.

Figure 2.2

Whether or not you are justified in saying that you *know* something also depends on context. For example, you might claim to know that Mr Thompson is in his office because you just saw him go in, and you can hear his voice through the wall. But if, for some extraordinary reason, the future of the planet depended on whether or not Mr Thompson really is in his office, you might begin to feel less sure. Perhaps what you saw was only an actor who looked like Mr Thompson, and perhaps what you can hear is only a recording of his voice. This is the stuff of Hollywood dramas, and you are never likely to find yourself in such a situation. Since life is too short to raise sceptical doubts about everything you see, you have to make a judgement about when doubt is appropriate and when it is inappropriate. While *indiscriminate* scepticism has little to commend it, you would probably be more cautious about saying 'I know' in a court of law than you would in everyday life.

When you say you *know* something you are, in a sense, taking *responsibility* for its being true. If, for example, you say that you *know* the bridge across the chasm will support my weight, there is a sense in which you are responsible for what happens to me if I cross it. And if you say you *know* that Apollo 11 landed on the moon, you are implying that if other people look at the evidence with an open mind they *ought* to come to the same conclusion. Although we tend to think of facts as being completely different from values, this suggests that there is an ethical element built into the pursuit of knowledge.

Levels of knowledge

There is a lot more we can say about knowledge than simply that it is justified true belief. For a start, there are also different levels of knowledge. You may, for example, have a superficial grasp, a good understanding, or complete mastery of a subject. When five-year-old Jimmy says 'My mum's a doctor' his understanding of what this means is clearly not the same as his mother's. Much of what we claim to 'know' is in fact second-hand knowledge that we have acquired from other people and do not understand in any great detail. You might, for example, struggle to explain to another person what gravity is, or why the sky is blue, or how a mobile phone works. Young children who are continually asking 'Why?' are sometimes irritating precisely because they bring to light the superficial nature of our understanding.

Figure 2.3

If you study a subject in depth, your understanding of it is likely to grow and develop over time. For example, if you study the *theory of relativity* in your physics class, revisit it as a university student, specialise in it when studying for a doctorate, and finally teach courses on it as a university professor, your knowledge of the theory as a university professor will be deeper and more sophisticated than it was as a first-year physics student. You may already have had the experience of revisiting a topic several years after you first studied it and realising how superficial your previous understanding of it was!

Knowledge and information

At this point, we should make a distinction between *knowledge* and *information*. Imagine sitting a child down one afternoon and teaching them some disconnected facts: 'nine times seven is sixty-three'; 'the chemical formula for water is H_2O'; 'aardvarks live in Africa'; 'the heroine in *Pride and Prejudice* is called Elizabeth Bennett', and so on. By the end of the afternoon, the child may be said to have acquired some knowledge in the limited sense of information. After all, each of these statements is true, the child (we assume) believes they are true, and she is justified in taking them as true because you are a reliable authority. However, if the child does not know how to multiply, knows nothing about atoms and molecules, does not know where Africa is, and has never read *Pride and Prejudice*, there is clearly something missing from her knowledge. Drilling random facts into someone's mind may be good for quiz shows, but it does not lead to genuine understanding.

A person with genuine knowledge of a subject does not merely have information about it, but understands how the various parts are related to one another to form a meaningful whole. To clarify with an analogy, we might say that information is to knowledge as bricks are to a building. While you cannot have a building without bricks, a building is more than just a heap of bricks. Similarly, while you cannot have knowledge without information, an area of knowledge is more than just a heap of information. The point is that when you study a subject you are not simply taught endless lists of facts, but you also learn various background assumptions, theories and informing ideas that help you to make sense of the facts.

So, if you wish to understand something, it is not enough to merely acquire information about it – you also need to think about the information and see how it hangs together. In a well-known *Sherlock Holmes* story, the famous detective and his trusty assistant, Dr Watson, are at the scene of a murder surveying the evidence. Holmes turns to Watson and says 'I see it all now, I know who did it.' Watson says with astonishment 'My dear Holmes, I've examined this same room with you and I see nothing at all!' To which Holmes replies 'No Watson, you "see" everything, but you "observe" nothing.' While Watson has at his disposal exactly the same information as Holmes, he cannot see the pattern which has allowed Holmes to solve the crime. What this story shows is that you can sometimes acquire knowledge simply by reflecting on the information you already have at your disposal rather than by looking for more information. This is a point worth keeping in mind in the Internet age when many people have access to vast amounts of information.

Activity 2.3

1 Have you ever passed an exam by cramming the week before, but felt that you did not really understand the subject? What does this suggest to you about the difference between knowledge and information?

2 What is the difference between knowing in the sense of understanding and knowing in the sense of being able to recite the relevant facts and theories without understanding them?

Second-hand knowledge

The search for knowledge is not only an individual enterprise, but also a communal one, and one of our main sources of knowledge is other people. Since we can share our experiences through language, we are able to know a great deal more about the world than if we had to rely on our own resources. If Smith goes north and Jones goes south, and Bloggs goes east and Brown goes west, and they then come together and share their knowledge, they will do much better than if they each try to discover everything for themselves.

Activity 2.4

How much do you think you could know about the world if you *never* trusted what anyone else told you, or anything that you read?

Our ability to communicate with one another also means that we are able to pass on our beliefs and practices from one generation to another in the form of **culture**. The existence of culture means that, rather than constantly reinventing the wheel, we can make progress by building on the accumulated achievements of past generations. The scientist Isaac Newton (1642–1727) once remarked: 'If I have seen further it is by standing on the shoulders of giants.' His point was that he was able to make his discoveries only because he was building on the contributions of other brilliant minds.

Despite the advantages of accepting knowledge 'second-hand' from other people, we must be careful that we do not fall into **authority worship** and blindly accept what we are told without thinking about it. For hundreds of years people believed that the earth was the centre of the universe, that everything was made up of four elements – fire, water, earth and air – and that some people were natural slaves – but they were wrong. As this example shows, the mere longevity of a belief is no guarantee of its truth.

Second-hand knowledge is also known as **knowledge by authority**, or **knowledge by testimony**. Among the main sources of such knowledge are:

- cultural tradition
- school
- the Internet
- expert opinion
- the news media.

While each of these can be a valuable source of knowledge, they are not infallible, and we should be aware of their limitations.

Cultural tradition

The culture we grow up in has a strong influence on the way we see the world, and is likely to determine our intellectual default settings. For we have a natural attachment to our own beliefs and practices, and they provide a point of reference for what we consider to be 'normal' or 'reasonable'. To see the power of traditional ways of thinking, you only have to look at the clock face in Figure 2.4. While it might seem more rational to divide a day into ten equal hours, most people would not want to decimalise time simply because they are used to dividing a day into two 12-hour periods, and it therefore feels right.

Since a cultural tradition embodies 'the inherited wisdom of the community', we should, I think, approach different traditions with respect, and be open to the fact that we may have something to learn from them. At the same time, we need to keep in mind that *living* traditions change and develop over time, and we do not have to be imprisoned by what we have inherited from the past. A person living in Britain in the nineteenth century might have argued that it was a long British tradition, sanctified by time, to exclude women from political power. Fortunately, some people were willing to question this inherited belief. If we are to make progress in any area of knowledge, we need to find the right balance between respecting traditional ways of thinking and being willing to question them.

Figure 2.4 Ten-hour clock

Activity 2.5

1 Which of the following is natural and which is simply a matter of tradition or convention?
   a A seven-day week
   b A 365-day year
   c A base 10 number system
   d The value of pi
   e Reading from left to right
   f Wearing clothes

2 Which of the following would you be unwilling to eat or drink? Give reasons:
   a Cows
   b Pigs
   c Dogs
   d Snails
   e Cockroaches
   f Alcohol
   g Sulphuric acid

3 To what extent do you think our beliefs about what is disgusting are determined by the culture we grow up in? What, if anything, is considered disgusting in every culture?

School

Since the introduction of universal education, schools have played a key role in the transmission of knowledge from one generation to the next. The roughly 14,000 hours you spend at school are supposed not only to give you mastery of various subjects, but also to prepare you for life. Since it is impossible to teach literally everything, any school curriculum will inevitably be selective and cover only a limited number of topics. This raises questions not only about how we should decide what to include in the curriculum, but also about the difference between education and **indoctrination**. Some people would argue that the difference between the two concerns not so much *what is taught as the way it is taught*, and that the hallmark of a good school is one that – no matter what the curriculum – encourages you to question things and think for yourself.

Activity 2.6

1 The philosopher Bertrand Russell (1872–1970) once observed that 'In most countries certain ideas are recognized as correct and others as dangerous. Teachers whose opinions are not correct are expected to keep silent about them.' What opinions, if any, are teachers in your country expected to keep silent about, and to what extent can this be justified?

2 What qualities would you look for if you were appointing a new teacher to your school? How far would they vary according to the subject that was to be taught?

3 If you were asked to design a curriculum for students aged 14 to 18 living in a colony on the moon, what would you include in the curriculum and why?

4 How would you rate the International Baccalaureate as an educational programme? To what extent do you think it is genuinely international and to what extent do you think it is culturally biased?

The Internet

When you have school work to do, the first place you look for information is probably the Internet. The advantage of the Internet is its speed and accessibility. The disadvantage is that there is no quality control. Hence it can be a source not only of information, but also of disinformation. Here are three examples of **urban legends** which circulated widely on the Internet and have no basis in fact:

- American astronauts conducted sex experiments while orbiting the earth in the space shuttle in 1996.
- Nostradamus predicted the attack on the World Trade Center.
- Waterproof sun-screen can cause blindness in children.

In theory, we all know that we should not believe everything we read on the Internet, but in practice we sometimes judge the reliability of a website by its appearance and believe the information on a website if it looks good. There are clearly better ways of deciding what to believe!

1 Find two articles from the Internet, one that you believe and one that you do not believe. Give reasons.

2 What criteria would you use for distinguishing generally trustworthy websites from generally untrustworthy ones?

3 Do some research and try to determine which of the following commonly held beliefs is true.

   a The dinosaurs went extinct because they were slow-moving and stupid.

   b The Inuit have hundreds of different words for snow.

   c We use only 10 per cent of our brains.

   d Human beings are the only animals that kill their own kind.

   e Christopher Columbus' contemporaries believed that the earth was flat.

Expert opinion

One important consequence of the explosive growth of knowledge over the last hundred years is that it is no longer possible for even a very bright person to be a 'universal genius' and know everything. In an increasingly specialised world, we have to rely on expert opinion to justify many of our knowledge claims. For example, I am willing to say that I *know* that the sun is 93 million miles (150 million kilometres) from the earth even though I have only the vaguest idea of how to prove this myself. But I could, if necessary, refer you to an astronomer who could support this knowledge claim with a wealth of evidence. At a practical level, we show our confidence in other people's expertise every time we get on a plane, visit a doctor or call a plumber.

Despite the obvious value of relying on expert opinion, we should keep in mind two things about it:

a *Experts are fallible and sometimes get it wrong.* For example, from 1923 until 1955 it was widely agreed by experts that human beings had twenty-four pairs of chromosomes. This was known to be true because a Texan biologist called Theophilus Painter (1889–1969) had counted them under a microscope. Unfortunately, Painter miscounted and no one got round to checking his data for more than thirty years! (We in fact have twenty-three pairs of chromosomes.)

Another well-known example of the fallibility of experts concerns the 'Piltdown Man' hoax. When the skulls of 'Piltdown Man' were discovered in 1913, anthropologists thought they were the 'missing link' between human beings and apes; but in 1953 chemical tests proved that the fossils were frauds.

Experts are particularly fallible when it comes to predicting the future. In 1894, the eminent American physicist Albert Michelson said 'It seems probable that most of the grand underlying principles [of physical science] have been firmly established.' Eleven years later, Albert Einstein burst onto the scene and changed the nature of physics forever. In 1933 another famous physicist, Ernest Rutherford (1871–1937), said 'Anyone who expects a source of power from the transformation of... atoms is talking moonshine.' Twelve years later atomic bombs were dropped on Hiroshima and Nagasaki. And while I am as worried about global warming as the next person, it is worth noting that as recently as the 1970s some climatologists were predicting a new ice age!

b *Experts have a limited range of competence.* There is no reason to believe that an expert has any privileged insight into things outside his own area of competence. The physicist Richard Feynman (1918–88) once said: 'I believe that a scientist looking at non-scientific problems is just as dumb as the next guy.' His point was that while you might take Albert Einstein as an authority in physics, he is not necessarily a competent guide in areas such as politics, ethics and religion.

Activity 2.8

1 Which of the following would you consider to be a reasonable appeal, and which an unreasonable appeal, to expert opinion? Give reasons.

   a My maths teacher said Fermat's Last Theorem has recently been proved by someone called Andrew Wiles.

   b *Gosh*, a popular men's magazine, quotes the pop star Hank Johnson as saying that for good dental hygiene you should floss your teeth three times a day.

   c The Oxford historian Dr Trevor Packard says that the newly discovered Hitler Diaries are genuine; but this is disputed by fellow historian Dr Suzanne Ferguson of Cambridge.

   d There is broad agreement among art critics that Pablo Picasso was one of the greatest painters of the twentieth century.

   e According to Dr Daniel Clarke, head of scientific research at Cigarettes R Us, the health hazards associated with tobacco have been greatly exaggerated.

   f Mona Jakes, a well-known astrologer, says that Derek and Jane will be happy together because they have compatible star signs.

2 Advertisers sometimes appeal to the authority of science in order to sell their products. Find and analyse two such examples.

3 Can we speak of expert opinion in all areas of knowledge, or only in some of them? Give reasons.

The news media

The news media play a key role in shaping our picture of the world. Despite the aura of objectivity surrounding a television news bulletin, we are all aware that there is some bias in both the selection and presentation of news stories. You will, for example, get a very different slant on a story presented by Fox News to one presented by al-Jazeera!

There seem to be three common criteria for deciding what to put into a news bulletin.

a *Bad news.* Most news bulletins focus on bad news and usually consist of a long catalogue of crimes, wars and natural disasters. Some people have argued that this creates a **bad news bias**, which gives people an unduly pessimistic view of the state of the planet, and helps to create and sustain a climate of fear.

b *Extraordinary news*. Someone once said that if a dog bites a man then it isn't news, but if a man bites a dog – that's news. News broadcasts tend to focus far more on extraordinary rather than ordinary events. One consequence of this is that gradual changes that may have a significant effect on people's lives tend to get little coverage. For such stories cannot be squeezed into the short time-slot available and packaged in the dramatic way favoured by TV news.

c *Relevant news*. A news story is usually considered to be relevant if it concerns domestic citizens. If a plane crashes in dense fog in a distant country killing everyone on board, the coverage it gets on British news will probably depend on how many British people are on the flight.

Figure 2.5

Some years ago a radio station had as its slogan, 'Don't trust anyone – not even us!' This was doubtless designed to encourage listeners to think critically about the news. But if you are going to find out what is going on in the world then you have to trust *someone*. The question is 'whom?' Despite the existence of bias, some news outlets are surely more objective than others. The trouble is that most people who follow current affairs choose outlets that reflect their pre-existing prejudices. If people on the left buy left-wing newspapers and people on the right buy right-wing newspapers, it is hardly surprising that both sides find their beliefs confirmed by reports of what is happening in the world. Perhaps we should occasionally select a news outlet that reflects a political view that is the opposite of our own. At least, this would encourage us to question our assumptions and not take our own way of looking at things for granted.

Activity 2.9

1 On a day when a major news story breaks, compare and contrast the way that different newspapers cover the story. To what extent is it possible to establish the underlying facts of the matter?

2 How objective do you think television news is in your country? How could it be improved?

3 There are various other sources of second-hand knowledge in addition to those we have mentioned. Discuss the reliability of two other sources.

The limitations of second-hand knowledge

Despite its importance, second-hand knowledge – whether it comes from your cultural tradition, school, the Internet, expert opinion, or the news media – can never be an *original* source of knowledge. For example, I may claim to know that Napoleon was defeated at the battle of Waterloo on 18 June 1815 because I read it in a textbook; and the writer of the textbook may claim to know it because he read it in some other book. But sooner or later this chain must terminate in the account of an eye-witness who was at Waterloo on that fateful day.

Since authority is not an original source of knowledge, our knowledge claims must ultimately be justified by such things as perception, reason and intuition. Nevertheless, problems can arise if you rely exclusively on your own judgement in trying to determine the truth. For if you do not test your beliefs and opinions against those of other people you may end up simply believing what you want to believe rather than believing what is true. This is particularly apparent in the case of our beliefs about ourselves; for most of us tend to overestimate our strengths and underestimate our weaknesses. Talking to people with different opinions may help us to improve our self-knowledge and develop a more balanced picture of the world.

Activity 2.10

1 When, if ever, would you be willing to trust the authority of other people rather than the evidence of your own senses?

2 Have you ever done a science experiment and got a result that differed from the textbook? If so, which did you trust – your own result, or the textbook? Why?

Conclusion

We began this chapter by defining knowledge as justified true belief, and then suggested that the difference between knowledge and belief is one of degree rather than kind. We then saw that knowledge consists of more than a jumble of isolated facts, and that its various parts are related to one another in a systematic way. You only have to think of the way in which a textbook is organised to see that this is the case. This suggests that, in order to gain a deeper understanding of an area of knowledge, you need a mixture of *detail* and *context*. (If the mind is like a camera, we could say that you need both a zoom and a wide-angle function.) Finally, we have seen that a great deal of knowledge comes to us second-hand on the authority of other people. While such a division of intellectual labour makes obvious sense, it raises the problem of which sources of knowledge to trust and which not to trust. As usual, there is no easy answer to the question, and we need to find the right balance between taking knowledge on authority and relying on our own resources. If you lack the courage, resources or confidence to think things out for yourself, then you are condemned to take all your beliefs second-hand from other people. But, if you are never willing to test your ideas against those of other people in dialogue and debate, you may end up with a distorted and fantasy-ridden picture of the world.

The task in Part 2 of this book is first to take a closer look at language, which is the medium through which we acquire knowledge from other people, and then to consider the three personal ways of knowing – perception, reason and emotion.

- A good preliminary definition of knowledge is to say that it is justified true belief.
- According to the traditional picture, truth is independent, and simply believing that something is true does not make it true.
- Rather than say that belief and knowledge are two completely different things, it may make more sense to think of there being a belief–knowledge continuum.
- Knowledge is more than true belief, for your belief must be justified in the right kind of way.
- The main thing that seems to distinguish an acceptable from an unacceptable justification is reliability.
- Whether or not you are justified in saying you know something depends on context.
- When you say you know something you are in a sense taking responsibility for its truth.
- There are different levels of knowledge ranging from a superficial grasp of a subject to complete mastery of it.
- The difference between knowledge and information is that knowledge is information organised into a meaningful whole.
- The fact that we can share our knowledge means that we can all know a great deal more than if we relied purely on our own resources.
- Despite the advantages of accepting knowledge second-hand from other people, the danger is that it can lead to authority worship.

Terms to remember

authority worship	information	primary knowledge
context	justified true belief	second-hand knowledge
culture	knowledge by authority/	sufficient condition
expert opinion	testimony	thick concept
indoctrination	news media	urban legend

Further reading

Stephen Law, ***The Philosophy Gym*** (Hodder, 2003), Chapter 19: 'What is Knowledge?' Law helps you to exercise your intellect by considering some problems with the definition of knowledge as justified true belief and considering an alternative which also runs into problems. Such is TOK!

Charles van Doren, ***A History of Knowledge*** (Ballantine, 1992). A fascinating book to dip into; van Doren weaves a coherent narrative of the people and events that advanced knowledge from ancient times up to the present.

Linking questions

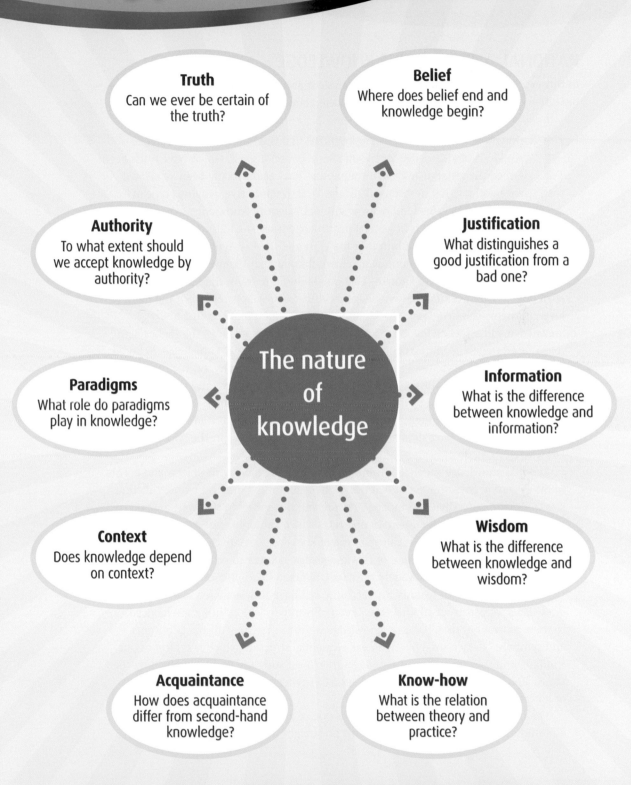

Truth
Can we ever be certain of the truth?

Belief
Where does belief end and knowledge begin?

Authority
To what extent should we accept knowledge by authority?

Justification
What distinguishes a good justification from a bad one?

Paradigms
What role do paradigms play in knowledge?

The nature of knowledge

Information
What is the difference between knowledge and information?

Context
Does knowledge depend on context?

Wisdom
What is the difference between knowledge and wisdom?

Acquaintance
How does acquaintance differ from second-hand knowledge?

Know-how
What is the relation between theory and practice?

RATIONAL AND INTUITIVE KNOWLEDGE

In this extract from *The Tao of Physics*, the physicist and philosopher Fritjof Capra discusses the difference between Western and Eastern ideas about the nature of knowledge.

Throughout history, it has been recognized that the human mind is capable of two kinds of knowledge, or two modes of consciousness, which have often been termed the rational and the intuitive, and have traditionally been associated with science and religion, respectively. In the West, the intuitive, religious type of knowledge is often devalued in favour of rational, scientific knowledge, whereas the traditional Eastern attitude is in general just the opposite. The following statements about knowledge by two great minds of the West and the East typify the two positions. Socrates in Greece made the famous statement 'I know that I know nothing', and Lao Tzu in China said, 'Not knowing that one knows is best.' In the East, the values attributed to the two kinds of knowledge are often already apparent from the names given to them. The *Upanishads*, for example, speak about a higher and a lower knowledge and associate the lower knowledge with various sciences, the higher with religious awareness. Buddhists talk about 'relative' and 'absolute' knowledge, or about 'conditional truth' and 'transcendental truth'. Chinese philosophy, on the other hand, has always emphasized the complementary nature of the intuitive and the rational and has represented them by the archetypal pair *yin* and *yang* which form the basis of Chinese thought. Accordingly, two complementary philosophical traditions – Taoism and Confucianism – have developed in ancient China to deal with the two kinds of knowledge.

Rational knowledge is derived from the experience we have with objects and events in our everyday environment. It belongs to the realm of the intellect whose function it is to discriminate, divide, compare, measure and categorize. In this way, a world of intellectual distinctions is created; of opposites which can only exist in relation to each other, which is why Buddhists call this type of knowledge 'relative'.

Abstraction is a crucial feature of this knowledge, because in order to compare and to classify the immense variety of shapes, structures and phenomena around us we cannot take all their features into account, but have to select a few significant ones. Thus we construct an intellectual map of reality in which things are reduced to their general outlines. Rational knowledge is thus a system of abstract concepts and symbols, characterized by the linear, sequential structure which is typical of our thinking and speaking. In most languages this linear structure is made explicit by the use of alphabets which serve to communicate experience and thought in long lines of letters.

The natural world, on the other hand, is one of infinite varieties and complexities, a multidimensional world which contains no straight lines or completely regular shapes, where things do not happen in sequences, but all together; a world where – as modern physics tells us – even empty space is curved. It is clear that our abstract system of conceptual thinking can never describe or understand this reality completely. In thinking about the world we are faced with the same kind of problem as the cartographer who tries to cover the curved face of the Earth with a sequence of plane maps. We can only expect an approximate representation of reality from such a procedure, and all rational knowledge is therefore necessarily limited.

The realm of rational knowledge is, of course, the realm of science which measures and quantifies, classifies and analyses. The limitations of any knowledge obtained by these methods have become increasingly apparent in modern science, and in particular in modern physics which has taught us, in the words of Werner Heisenberg, 'that every word or concept, clear as it may seem to be, has only a limited range of applicability.'

For most of us it is very difficult to be constantly aware of the limitations and of the relativity of conceptual knowledge. Because our representation of reality is so much easier to grasp than reality itself, we tend to confuse the two and to take our concepts and symbols for reality. It is one of the main aims of Eastern mysticism to rid us of this confusion. Zen Buddhists say that a finger is needed to point at the moon, but that we should not trouble ourselves with the finger once the moon is recognized; the Taoist sage Chuang Tzu wrote:

> 'Fishing baskets are employed to catch fish; but when the fish are got, the men forget the baskets; snares are employed to catch hares; but when the hares are got, men forget the snares. Words are employed to convey ideas; but when the ideas are grasped, men forget the words.'

In the West, the semanticist Alfred Korzybski made exactly the same point with his powerful slogan, 'The map is not the territory.'

What the Eastern mystics are concerned with is a direct experience of reality which transcends not only intellectual thinking but also sensory perception. In the words of the *Upanishads*,

> 'What is soundless, touchless, formless, imperishable,
> Likewise tasteless, constant, odourless,
> Without beginning, without end, higher than the great stable –
> By discerning That, one is liberated from the mouth of death.'

Knowledge which comes from such an experience is called 'absolute knowledge' by Buddhists because it does not rely on the discriminations, abstractions and classifications of the intellect which, as we have seen, are always relative and approximate. It is, so we are told by Buddhists, the direct experience of undifferentiated, undivided, indeterminate 'suchness'. Complete apprehension of this suchness is not only the core of Eastern mysticism, but is the central characteristic of all mystical experience.

The Eastern mystics repeatedly insist on the fact that the ultimate reality can never be an object of reasoning or of demonstrable knowledge. It can never be adequately described in words, because it lies beyond the realm of the senses and of the intellect from which our words and concepts are derived.

BRECHT'S GALILEO

The following is an extract from Bertolt Brecht's play *Life of Galileo*, which explores the question: Should knowledge be based on authority or the evidence of the senses?

GALILEO *at the telescope*: As your highness no doubt realises, we astronomers have been running into great difficulties in our calculations for some while. We have been using a very ancient system which is apparently consistent with our philosophy but not, alas, with the facts. Under this ancient, Ptolemaic system the motions of the stars are presumed to be extremely complex. The planet Venus, for instance, is supposed to have an orbit like this. *On a board he draws the epicyclical orbit of Venus according to the Ptolemaic hypothesis*. But even if we accept the awkwardness of such motions we are still unable to predict the position of the stars accurately. We do not find them where in principle they ought to be.

What is more, some stars perform motions which the Ptolemaic system just cannot explain. Such motions, it seems to me, are performed by certain small stars which I have recently discovered around the planet Jupiter. Would you gentlemen care to start by observing these satellites of Jupiter, the Medicean stars?

ANDREA *indicating the stool by the telescope*: Kindly sit here.

PHILOSOPHER: Thank you, my boy. I fear things are not quite so simple. Mr Galileo, before turning to your famous tube, I wonder if we might have the pleasure of a disputation? Its subject to be: Can such planets exist?

MATHEMATICIAN: A formal dispute.

GALILEO: I was thinking you could just look through the telescope and convince yourselves?

ANDREA: This way please.

MATHEMATICIAN: Of course, of course. I take it you are familiar with the opinion of the ancients that there can be no stars which turn round centres other than the earth, nor any which lack support in the sky?

GALILEO: I am.

PHILOSOPHER: Moreover, quite apart from the very possibility of such stars, which our mathematician – *he turns towards the mathematician* – would appear to doubt, I would like in all humility to pose the philosophical question: are such stars necessary?... The universe of the divine Aristotle, with the mystical music of its spheres and its crystal vaults, the orbits of its heavenly bodies, the slanting angle of the sun's course, the secrets of the moon tables, the starry richness catalogued in the southern hemisphere and the transparent structure of the celestial globe add up to an edifice of such exquisite proportions that we should think twice before disrupting its harmony.

GALILEO: How about your highness now taking a look at his impossible and unnecessary stars through this telescope?

MATHEMATICIAN: One might be tempted to answer that, if your tube shows something which cannot be there, it cannot be an entirely reliable tube, wouldn't you say?

GALILEO: What d'you mean by that?

MATHEMATICIAN: It would be rather more appropriate, Mr Galileo, if you were to name your reasons for assuming that there could be free-floating stars moving about in the highest sphere of the unalterable heavens.

PHILOSOPHER: Your reasons, Mr Galileo, your reasons.

GALILEO: My reasons! When a single glance at the stars themselves and my own notes makes the phenomenon evident? Sir, your disputation is becoming absurd.

MATHEMATICIAN: If one could be sure of not over-exciting you one might say that what is in your tube and what is in the skies is not necessarily the same thing.

PHILOSOPHER: That couldn't be more courteously put.

FEDERZONI: They think we painted the Medicean stars on the lens.

GALILEO: Are you saying I'm a fraud?

PHILOSOPHER: How could we? In his highness's presence too.

MATHEMATICIAN: Your instrument – I don't know whether to call it your brainchild or your adopted brainchild – is most ingeniously made, no doubt of that.

PHILOSOPHER: And we are utterly convinced, Mr Galilei, that neither you nor anyone else would bestow the illustrious name of our ruling family on stars whose existence was not above all doubt....

MATHEMATICIAN: Let's not beat about the bush. Sooner or later Mr Galilei will have to reconcile himself to the facts. Those Jupiter satellites of his would penetrate the crystal spheres. It is as simple as that.

FEDERZONI: You'll be surprised: the crystal spheres don't exist.

PHILOSOPHER: Any textbook will tell you that they do, my good man.

FEDERZONI: Right, then let's have new textbooks.

PHILOSOPHER: Your highness, my distinguished colleague and I are supported by none less than the divine Aristotle himself.

GALILEO *almost obsequiously*: Gentlemen, to believe in the authority of Aristotle is one thing, tangible facts are another. You are saying that according to Aristotle there are crystal spheres up there, so certain motions just cannot take place because the stars would penetrate them. But suppose these motions could be established? Mightn't that suggest to you that those crystal spheres don't exist? Gentlemen, in all humility I ask you to go by the evidence of your eyes.

MATHEMATICIAN: My dear Galileo, I may strike you as very old-fashioned, but I'm in the habit of reading Aristotle now and again and there, I can assure you, I trust the evidence of my eyes.

GALILEO: I am used to seeing the gentlemen of the various faculties shutting their eyes to every fact and pretending that nothing has happened. I produce my observations and everyone laughs: I offer my telescope so they can see for themselves, and everyone quotes Aristotle.

FEDERZONI: The fellow had no telescope.

MATHEMATICIAN: That's just it.

PHILOSOPHER *grandly*: If Aristotle is going to be dragged in the mud – that's to say an authority recognized not only by every classical scientist but also by the chief fathers of the church – then any prolonging of this discussion is in my view a waste of time. I have no use for discussions which are not objective. Basta.

GALILEO: Truth is born of the times, not of authority. Our ignorance is limitless: let us lop one cubic millimeter off it. Why try to be clever now that we at last have a chance of being just a little less stupid? I have had the unimaginable luck to get my hands on a new instrument that lets us observe one tiny corner of the universe a little, but not all that much, more exactly. Make use of it.

PHILOSOPHER: Your highness, ladies and gentlemen, I just wonder where all this is leading.

GALILEO: I should say our duty as scientists is not to ask where truth is leading.

PHILOSOPHER *agitatedly*: Mr Galilei, truth might lead anywhere!

PART 2

Ways
of knowing

3 Language

'Speech is but a broken light upon the depth/ Of the unspoken.'
George Eliot, 1819–80

'Man is an animal suspended in webs of significance he himself has spun.'
Clifford Geertz, 1923–2006

'The word is half his that speaks, and half his that hears it.'
Michel de Montaigne, 1533–92

'Language was given to man to disguise his thoughts.'
Talleyrand, 1754–1838

'Almost all education is language education.'
Neil Postman, 1931–2003

'Who does not know another language does not know his own.'
Goethe, 1749–1832

'"When I use a word", Humpty Dumpty said in rather a scornful tone, "it means just what I choose it to mean – neither more nor less". "The question is", said Alice, "whether you can make words mean so many different things". "The question is", said Humpty Dumpty, "which is to be master – that's all."'
Lewis Carroll, 1832–98

'Language is not merely a reproducing instrument for voicing ideas but rather is the shaper of ideas... We dissect nature along lines laid down by our native languages.'
Benjamin Whorf, 1897–1941

'Language was the real innovation in our biological evolution; everything since has just made our words travel faster or last longer.'
Steven Pinker, 1954–

'Philosophy is a battle against the bewitchment of our intelligence by means of language.'
Ludwig Wittgenstein, 1889–1951

'If your language is confused, your intellect, if not your whole character, will almost certainly correspond.'
Sir Arthur Quiller-Couch, 1863–1944

'Thought is not merely expressed in words; it comes into existence through them.'
L. Vygotsky, 1896–1934

'Man is the animal that speaks. Understanding language is thus the key to understanding man.'
Thomas Szasz, 1920–

Introduction

Like the air we breathe, language is something that so completely surrounds us that we rarely think about it or are consciously aware of it. Yet it has a central function in human life. We use language for a variety of purposes, such as describing things, expressing our feelings, persuading people, telling jokes, writing literature and speculating about the meaning of life.

Language is relevant to the theory of knowledge because it is one of the main ways in which we acquire knowledge about the world. By communicating with one another, we are able to break out of the small circle of our own experience and tap into the collective experience of the community. As we saw in Chapter 2, this makes possible an 'intellectual division of labour' which has been a key factor in our success as a species.

> **Activity 3.1**
>
> How much could you know about the world if you had no language or means of communicating with other people?

Despite its importance, language is not a perfect medium of communication, and it has drawbacks as well as benefits. One problem is that what one person means when they say something may not be what another person understands when they hear it. (How often have you found yourself saying to someone 'No, that's not what I meant at all'?) Furthermore, language is sometimes used to deliberately deceive and manipulate people – as, for example, in propaganda. So we cannot simply take language for granted, but must look in more detail at what it is and how it affects our knowledge of the world.

What is language?

Since language is a complex phenomenon, we should begin by saying more about its nature. In what follows, we shall consider three key features which might be said to distinguish it from non-language.

1. Language is rule-governed.
2. Language is intended.
3. Language is creative and open-ended.

Language is rule-governed

When you learn another language, one of the main things you have to learn is grammar. Grammar gives the rules for how to combine words in the correct order, and it helps to determine the meaning of a sentence. For example, if someone asks who did what to whom in the sentence 'Jill hit Jack', we can say that Jill is the active 'hitter', and Jack the passive 'hittee'. How do we know this? Well, in English there is a rule which says that the noun before the verb is the subject, and the noun after the verb is the object. There is no deep reason why the rule is the way it is, and English might have evolved so that the noun before the verb is the object and the noun after the verb the subject. All that really matters is that everyone agrees on the rules.

The other main element in language – vocabulary – is also governed by arbitrary rules. For a native English speaker, it feels as if there is a natural – almost magical – connection between the word 'dog' and the animal it stands for. But there is of course no deep reason why this noise should be associated with *that* animal. It could just as well be *quan* (Chinese), *koira* (Finnish), *chien* (French), *Hund* (German), *kutta* (Hindi), *inu* (Japanese), *gae* (Korean), *sobaka* (Russian), *perro* (Spanish), or *köpek* (Turkish). For communication to work, it does not matter what noises or squiggles we correlate with objects, so long as there is general agreement within the tribe.

Activity 3.2

Take any familiar word of your choice, such as 'table' or 'chair', and repeat it twenty times. What happens? What does this suggest to you about the relation between words and things?

Language is intended

Although language is a form of communication, not all communication is language. To see the difference between the two, consider the following two situations.

- You are bored in class and, while the teacher is writing on the board, you catch someone's eye across the room and make a yawning gesture by putting your hand to your mouth.
- You are trying to look interested in what someone says and to your horror find yourself starting to yawn.

While both of these yawns communicate information – and might loosely be called **body language** – only the first can really be described as language. This is because the first is intended and the second is not. This suggests that a key thing that distinguishes the subset of communication that is language from other forms of communication is that the former is intended while the latter is not.

Figure 3.1 Body language

1 How would you interpret the body language in the two pictures at the foot of page 49? What do you think is being communicated?

2 How easy is it to misunderstand the body language of someone from a different culture?

There are many situations in which information is communicated, but no one would describe it as language. For example, if you put a dollar in a vending machine and press the button which says 'coffee white with sugar', you get coffee white with sugar. Although information has clearly been communicated, you would not say the vending machine *understood* that you wanted a cup of coffee. Vending machines – and other mechanical devices – are simply not in the business of understanding things.

Language is creative and open-ended

A final distinguishing feature of language is that the rules of grammar and vocabulary allow us to make an almost infinite number of grammatically correct sentences. We are able to create and understand sentences that have never been written or said before. For example, you have probably never seen the following sentence before, 'The wise cow seeks shelter when it snows at dusk', but you have no problem understanding what it means and conjuring up a mental picture corresponding to it. The creative resources of language are, in fact, staggering. The psychologist Steven Pinker (1954–) has calculated that there are at least 10^{20} grammatically correct English sentences up to twenty words long. (This is a huge number: if you said one sentence every five seconds, it would take you one hundred trillion, 10^{14}, years to utter them all – that's 10,000 times longer than the universe has been in existence!)

Moreover, languages are not static entities, but change and develop over time. William Shakespeare (1564–1616) introduced many new words into the English language, such as 'dwindle', 'frugal' and 'obscene'. As well as inventing new words, languages also borrow words from one another. English is full of such borrowed words: 'algebra' is Arabic, 'Kindergarten' is German and 'chutzpah' Yiddish. Other new words arrive on the back of technology.

1 Make up a meaningful – though not necessarily true – English sentence which to the best of your knowledge has never in the history of the universe been written before.

2 Give some examples of words that have entered the English language as a result of the computer revolution.

3 Do you think animals have language? Read the 'Dialogue on Animal Language' in the resource file at the end of this chapter. Who do you think gets the better of the argument – Dolly or Guy?

One thing that comes out of our discussion is that, although we usually associate language with meaningful sounds or squiggles, it could in principle express itself in any medium. The sign language used by deaf people is a language in the full sense of the word because it has rules (grammar and vocabulary), is intended and is creative and open-ended. Indeed, if we could emit distinct sequences of smells by controlling our sweat glands, then we could develop a scent language!

"Although humans make sounds with their mouths, and occasionally look at each other, there is no solid evidence that they actually communicate with each other."

Figure 3.2

The problem of meaning

Since much of our knowledge comes to us in the form of language, we need to be clear about the meanings of words if we are to understand the information that is being communicated to us.

Activity 3.5

Read the following passage, attributed to Judy Lanier, which is called 'The Montillation of Traxoline', and answer the questions below.

'It is very important that you learn about traxoline. Traxoline is a new form of zionter. It is montilled in Ceristanna. The Ceristannians gristeriate large amounts of fevon and then bracter it into quasel traxoline. Traxoline may well be one of our most lukized snezlaus in the future because of our zionter lescelidge.'

1 What is traxoline?
2 Where is traxoline montilled?
3 How is traxoline quaselled?
4 Why is it important to know about traxoline?

You probably had no difficulty in answering the above questions – traxoline is a new form of zionter, it is montilled in Ceristanna, and so on. However, you have not really learned anything from this passage because you have no idea what words such as 'montillation' and 'traxoline' mean. (In fact, they don't mean anything!)

The above example shows that if you do not know what the key words in a passage mean you will not understand it. This raises the question of what it is to know the meaning of a word. Meaning is important in our search for knowledge because *you must know what a sentence means before you can decide whether it is true or false.* You can repeat parrot-fashion that traxoline is montilled in Ceristanna, but if you do not know what 'traxoline' and 'Ceristanna' refer to, you will have no idea whether the statement is true or false.

We tend to assume that pinning down meaning is a relatively straightforward business, and that every word has a fixed meaning that is understood and accepted by everyone. While life might be easier if this were true, I want to suggest that there is a *problem of meaning* and that words are often ambiguous and open to a variety of interpretations.

Theories of meaning

We will briefly look at three theories of what distinguishes meaningful words from meaningless ones. The first theory says that meanings are to be found in dictionaries, the second that they are found in the world, and the third that they are found in the mind.

1 Definition theory

The most obvious way of trying to resolve confusions about what a word means is to consult a dictionary. However, coming up with a good definition of a word can be more difficult than it seems.

Activity 3.6

1 Define as precisely as you can the following three words:
   a triangle   b table   c love.
2 How would you try to explain to a blind person what the word 'red' means? What does this suggest to you about the limitation of definitions?

If you tried the above exercise, you probably had no difficulty in defining a triangle. 'Three straight lines that define an area' might do it. When it comes to the word 'table', things are more difficult. Perhaps you came up with something similar to the following dictionary definition: 'a piece of furniture with a flat top and one or more legs, providing a level surface for eating, writing, working at, playing games etc.' That seems fairly good, but it is not difficult to think of borderline cases and counter-examples. What about a flat surface that is built into an alcove and doesn't have any legs, or a flat surface that is suspended by chains from the ceiling? Where exactly does a table end and a desk begin? What if you regularly use an old tea chest as a table – does that make it a table? A good response to these questions might be: who cares? Life is surely too short to worry about exactly where tables end and non-tables begin!

Love is probably the most difficult of the three words in the above exercise to define. My dictionary says it is 'an intense feeling of deep affection or fondness for a person or thing' (although it also offers 'zero score in games such as tennis'). The trouble with a word such as 'love' is that it seems to have depths that cannot be captured in a few well-chosen words. If Angie turns to Jake and says 'I don't think you really know the meaning of the word "love", you are not going to solve Jake's problem by handing him a dictionary!

What seems to come out of this discussion is that the only words that we can define in a clear and unambiguous way are mathematical ones, such as 'triangle', 'circle', 'straight line', etc. When it comes to other words, they have a fuzziness at their borders that is hard – if not impossible – to eliminate.

Criticisms

The main problem with the idea that the meaning of a word is its dictionary definition is not simply that most definitions are vague and imprecise, but, more fundamentally, that they only explain the meanings of words by using other words. If we are to avoid being trapped in an endless circle of words, language must surely connect with the world.

2 Denotation theory

According to the denotation theory what distinguishes a meaningful word from a meaningless one is that the former stands for something while the latter does not. Thus 'France' means something because it stands for the country in Europe that is north of the Pyrenees and west of the Rhine, while 'jumblat' is meaningless because there is nothing in the world that corresponds to it. Since the following lines from the opening of Lewis Carroll's (1832–98) poem 'Jabberwocky' do not refer to anything, they are considered nonsense poetry:

> Twas brillig, and the slithy toves
> Did gyre and gimble in the wabe:
> All mimsy were the borogroves,
> And the mome raths outgrabe.

Criticisms

While the denotation theory might work in the case of names such as 'France' or 'Socrates', it seems to fall down in the case of abstract words – such as 'multiplication', 'freedom' and 'wisdom' – which do not seem to stand for any *thing*. Admittedly, you may be able to point to examples of wisdom, but you cannot point to wisdom itself.

On reflection, problems arise even in the case of proper names. The meaning of a name such as 'Socrates' cannot literally be Socrates – for otherwise the word would have become meaningless when Socrates died. If we took the denotation theory literally, then people would be unable to talk about you after you were dead.

3 Image theory

According to the image theory, the meaning of a word is the mental image it stands for, and you know the meaning of a word when you have the appropriate concept in your mind. For example, you know what the word 'freedom' means when you associate it with the concept of freedom – being able to do what you like, not being imprisoned and so on. This view also has something to be said for it. For the difference between my speaking English and a parrot 'speaking English' is surely that, while my speech is accompanied by the appropriate mental activity, the parrot quite literally does not know what it is talking about. Rather than *speaking* English, the parrot is merely making noises that *sound* like the noises made by an English speaker.

Criticisms

The problem with the image theory is that if meanings are in the mind then we can never be sure that someone else understands the meaning of a word in the same way that we do – or, indeed, that they understand it at all. For you can never get into another person's mind and find out what is going on in it.

Activity 3.7

1 To what extent is your use of language accompanied by images? Does every word conjure up an image or only some of them?
2 How do you know that what we both call 'red' I don't experience as what you would call 'green' if you were looking out of my eyes, and what we both call 'green' I don't experience as what you would call 'red' if you were looking out of my eyes?
3 What difference, if any, would it make in real life if the above were the case?

Figure 3.3 We sometimes fail to understand what someone else is saying to us

Meaning as know-how

Rather than think of meanings as something that can be found in dictionaries, or in the world, or in the mind, perhaps it would be better to say that meaning is a matter of *know-how*, and that you know the meaning of a word when you know how to use it correctly. For example, if you can use the word 'red' appropriately when discussing such things as traffic lights, red peppers and Rudolf the red-nosed reindeer, you must surely know what it means. At the same time, it is hard to resist the idea that there must be something appropriate going on in our heads when we mean and understand things.

Activity 3.8

Do you think a robot could use and respond appropriately to language? What difference, if any, would it make in real life if this were the case?

Problematic meaning

When we consider how language is used in practice, things start to get complicated. We often use language in all kinds of non-literal ways. As the poet Robert Frost (1874–1963) observed, we rarely say exactly what we mean, for 'we like to talk in parables and in hints and in indirections – whether from diffidence or some other instinct'. In what follows, we will consider five kinds of problematic meaning that can be found in everyday language: vagueness, ambiguity, secondary meanings, metaphor and irony.

1 Vagueness

Many words, such as 'fast' and 'slow', are intrinsically vague, and their meaning depends on context. For example, 'fast' means something different to a long-distance runner than to a Formula 1 driver. And, even in a specific context, people may have quite different ideas of what a vague word implies.

Activity 3.9

1 Without thinking too much about it, write a figure down for each of the following:
   a John lives close to his school. How near does he live?
   b Janet is a heavy smoker. How many cigarettes does she smoke a day?
   c Mr Smith is middle-aged. How old is he?
   d Nafisha's mother earns a lot of money. What is her annual income?
2 Do you think that communication would be improved if we got rid of vague words, or do you think they sometimes serve a useful purpose?
3 'It is easy to be certain – one only has to be sufficiently vague' (Charles Sanders Peirce, 1839–1914). What do you think Peirce meant by this? Give examples.

Despite their disadvantages, vague words are in fact very useful; for, although they may fail to pin things down, they can at least point us in the right direction. It is, in any case, impossible to make words completely precise. Ask yourself, for example, how little hair a man must have before you can describe him as bald? Does the loss of one particular hair change him from being non-bald to bald? The answer is, of course, that the concept is inherently vague. Some men are balder than others, but it is impossible to say exactly where non-baldness ends and baldness begins. Many other concepts are similarly vague – even ones that might appear quite precise. For example, if you say that an object is exactly 4 centimetres long, the vagueness comes in when we ask to how many decimal places you made the measurement.

2 Ambiguity

Many words and phrases are ambiguous. For example, 'The duchess cannot bear children' can mean either that the duchess is unable to have children, or that she cannot stand them. 'The author lives with his wife, an architect and amateur musician in Hampshire' would usually be taken to mean that the author lives with his wife *who* is an architect and amateur musician; but it could also mean that the author lives with his wife *and* an architect *and* an amateur musician.

Activity 3.10

1 Each of the following sentences is ambiguous. Give two different meanings for each of them:
   a Flying planes can be dangerous.
   b They saw Mrs Jones and the dog sitting under the table.
   c Bob tickled the man with a feather duster.
   d Refuse to be put in the basket.
   e Mia wanted to hear the pop star sing very badly.
   f Visiting relatives can be boring.
   g Many poor students are on scholarships.
   h Johnny ate the bacon on the sofa.
   i I didn't sleep with my spouse before we were married. Did you?
   j As Imran came in to bowl I saw her duck.
2 To what extent can punctuation help to reduce the ambiguity of a sentence?
3 Many jokes are based on ambiguity. Give some examples and analyse them.

Ford: You should prepare yourself for the jump into hyperspace; it's unpleasantly like being drunk.
Arthur: What's so unpleasant about being drunk?
Ford: Just ask a glass of water.
[From *The Hitchhiker's Guide to the Galaxy* by Douglas Adams (1952–2001)]

While ambiguity is sometimes amusing, it can also be used to mislead people. A politician might deliberately exploit an ambiguous sentence so that it is understood in different ways by different listeners. For example, 'I am opposed to taxes which damage incentives' could be taken to mean 'I am opposed to all taxes because they damage incentives' or 'I am opposed only to those taxes which damage incentives.'

Context can again help us to determine the meaning of an ambiguous sentence. In (b) above the most reasonable interpretation of the sentence is 'They saw Mrs Jones and *the-dog-sitting-under-the-table*' rather than 'They saw *Mrs-Jones-and-the-dog* sitting under the table'. This is because people do not usually sit under tables with dogs.

3 Secondary meaning

Words have not only a primary meaning or **denotation**, but also a secondary meaning or **connotation**. The denotation of a word is what it refers to, the connotation is the web of associations that surrounds it. While the denotation of a word is public, its connotations vary from person to person. Words such as 'love', 'death', 'school' and 'priest' may have different connotations for different people. Sometimes we use **euphemisms** for harsh words because they have more acceptable connotations. For example, 'passed away' is a euphemism for 'died'. Both expressions have the same denotation, but 'passed away' brings with it associations of peace and serenity that 'died' lacks.

Activity 3.11

1 When Bill Clinton entered the White House in 1993, his wife Hillary Rodham Clinton wanted to be known not as the 'First Lady' but as the 'Presidential Partner'. What is the difference in connotation between 'First Lady' and 'Presidential Partner'?

2 If Hillary Clinton ever became president of the USA, what do you think would be an appropriate title for her husband?

3 Explain the different connotations of each of the following sets of words:
   a slender, skinny, thin
   b stubborn, steadfast, firm
   c praise, flatter, commend
   d energetic, spirited, frenzied
   e stench, smell, fragrance

4 Think of as many different words or expressions for each of the following. What is the difference in their connotations?
   a Vomit
   b Drunk
   c Stupid

4 Metaphor

We use language not only literally, but also metaphorically. You might say that 'Miranda has got her *head in the clouds*', or 'Marvin is a *pillar* of the community', or 'Agnes has *put her roots down* in Canada'. Despite being literally false, each of these sentences might still be metaphorically true. Miranda does not have an unusually long neck, but she may walk around in a dreamlike state; Marvin is not made of stone, but he may be an important figure in his community; Agnes has not grown roots, but she may have settled permanently in Canada.

When trying to decide whether a sentence is meant literally or metaphorically, we might get a hint from the context. Compare, for example, the following two sentences:

(1) 'My brother is a butcher.'
(2) 'My dentist is a butcher.'

Most people would interpret (1) literally and (2) metaphorically. For while your brother may well make his living as a butcher, I don't know of anyone who divides their professional life between dentistry and butchery.

In practice it can be difficult to determine where literal meaning ends and metaphorical meaning begins. For ordinary language is riddled with *dead metaphors*. Consider, for example, the following expressions: 'night*fall*'; '*sharp* tongue', '*brilliant* mind', 'chair *leg*', '*in love*'. All of these phrases are, strictly speaking, metaphorical, but they are so familiar that we have forgotten their metaphorical origin.

Activity 3.12

1 Explain the difference between the following two sentences. Is either of them true? If so, in what sense?
  a 'No man is an island'
     (John Donne, 1572–1631)
  b 'No man is a banana'
     (Richard van de Lagemaat, 1958–)
2 Take a paragraph from a newspaper or magazine, and identify as many metaphors in it as you can. Try to rewrite the piece without using any metaphors.
3 Birds fly and planes fly. Since fish swim, why don't we say that submarines also swim? What do submarines do?

5 Irony

Irony – the saying of one thing in order to mean the opposite – shows just how problematic language in action can be. Despite the oddity of using a sentence which literally means X in order to suggest not-X, irony is something that is found in all cultures. If the weather forecast predicted sunshine and it is pouring with rain outside, you might look out of the window and say 'Nice weather, heh?' Or if your friend makes a dumb suggestion, you might say 'Any more bright ideas, Einstein?' Irony means that we cannot necessarily take a statement at face value, and it adds another layer of ambiguity to language.

Meaning and interpretation

We could perhaps summarise our discussion of problematic meaning in three words: *language is ambiguous*. For vagueness, secondary meaning, metaphor and irony can all be seen as different kinds of ambiguity. The implication is that there is an element of *interpretation* built in to all communication. Although language is governed by rules, and you cannot make words mean anything you like, many of the rules are quite loose and there is often more than one way of interpreting a sentence. As we have seen, *context* may help you to decide what someone 'really means'. If a friend says 'It was so funny that I nearly died laughing', you do not ask if they were rushed to intensive care or chalk it up as another near-death experience. But you cannot always rely on context. If someone says 'I am so angry I could kill him', you would probably not alert the police; but perhaps this time they really mean it!

Rather than think of meaning as an all-or-nothing concept – either you understand it or you don't – it might make better sense to think in terms of levels of meaning. As we said in Chapter 2, a physics professor is likely to have a much clearer idea of what 'the theory of relativity' means than a non-physicist. And a forty-year-old adult is likely to have a more sophisticated understanding of what 'love' means than a six-year-old child.

Activity 3.13

What problems are there in trying to interpret the following sentences?
a 'If John works hard, he should do himself justice in the final exam.'
b 'It is as difficult for a rich man to enter the kingdom of heaven as it is for a camel to pass through the eye of a needle.'
c 'After he had said this, he left her as on the previous evening.'
d 'What's up?'
e '$E = mc^2$'

Why should we care about the meanings of words?

We have spent some time talking about the problem of meaning, but you may wonder why should we care about it. Does it really matter if we cannot pin down the meaning of a word? In some cases, I think it does. For an accused person, the difference between 'murder' and 'manslaughter' may be literally a matter of life and death. And if you want a war on terrorism, you need to be clear about what you mean by 'terrorist'.

It probably comes as no surprise to you that politicians sometimes manipulate the meanings of words in order to deceive the public. If you want to reduce poverty in a country the most painless way of doing it is to redefine what you mean by the word 'poverty'. Unemployment too high? Simple! Just change what the word means. Want to raise taxes without anyone noticing? Try calling it 'revenue enhancement'! So if we want our politicians to be genuinely accountable, it pays to keep an eye on the way they use language.

"Congratulations, Dave! I don't think I've read a more beautifully evasive and subtly misleading public statement in all my years in government..."

Figure 3.4

Another group of people who exploit vague language are tricksters who claim to have psychic powers or to be able to predict the future. In the 1940s, the eminent psychologist B. R. Forer gave each of his students the following 'individualised' horoscope, and asked them to rate how well it described their character:

> You have a strong need for other people to like you and for them to admire you. At times you are extroverted, affable, and sociable, while at other times you are introverted, wary, and reserved. You have a great deal of unused energy which you have not turned to your advantage. While you have some personality weaknesses, you are generally able to compensate for them. You prefer a certain amount of change and variety and become dissatisfied when hemmed in by restrictions and limitations. You pride yourself on being an independent thinker and do not accept other opinions without satisfactory proof. You have a tendency to be critical of yourself. Some of your aspirations tend to be pretty unrealistic.

Almost all of Forer's students rated the description as 'good' or 'excellent'. Forer concluded that 'people tend to accept vague and general personality descriptions as uniquely applicable to themselves without realising that the same description could be applied to just about anyone'. If we are not to be taken in by tricksters and charlatans, it is worth keeping this example in mind.

Language and translation

Up until now we have been speaking about 'language' as if there were only one such thing, but there are, of course, many different languages in the world. (The most commonly quoted figure is 3,000, but they are disappearing fast.)

Each of us has a privileged relation to our own native language, and we tend unthinkingly to assume that it fits reality like a glove. According to one apocryphal story, the US senate was once debating whether the constitution should be amended to state that English is the official language of the United States. A senator who supported the amendment allegedly finished his speech with the rousing words, 'And if English was good enough for Jesus, then it's good enough for me!' Whether or not the story is true, it illustrates the dangers of unthinking linguistic chauvinism. As well as enabling you to communicate with other people, one of the benefits of learning a second language is that it gives you a perspective on your own.

Activity 3.14

1　What would be the advantages and disadvantages if everyone in the world spoke a single common language? What would be gained by this, and what would be lost?

2　'Who does not know another language does not know his own' (Goethe, 1749–1832). What can you learn about your own language by studying a second language?

3　In what other ways does learning a second language contribute to, and expand, your knowledge of the world?

When you learn a second language, one of the things you discover is that different languages divide the world up in different ways. If words were simply labels we stuck on objects and the only difference between languages was that they used different words to refer to these objects, then translation would be a relatively straightforward matter. But it does not work like that. If you make a word-for-word translation from one language to another, you will not get a workable translation but gobbledygook. That is why translation is more of an art than a science.

Problems of translation

There are three problems that arise in translating something from one language to another that are particularly worth mentioning: context, untranslatable words and idioms.

Context

The meaning of a word in a language is partly determined by its relation to other words. For example, to understand what the word 'chat' means in English, you also need to be aware of related words such as 'talk', 'gossip' and 'discuss', each of which has a different shade of meaning. When we move from one language to another, such subtle differences can easily get lost in translation.

Untranslatable words

Every language contains words that have no equivalent in other languages, and can only be translated by a lengthy and inelegant paraphrase. For example, the English word 'quaint' has no very precise equivalent in other languages. Here are some examples from other languages:

- *Schlimmbesserung* (German), 'an "improvement" that actually makes things worse'
- *Aware* (Japanese), 'the feeling engendered by ephemeral beauty'
- *Rojong* (Indonesian), 'the relationship among a group of people committed to accomplishing a task of mutual benefit'
- *Puijilittatuq* (Inuktitut, Canadian Arctic), 'he does not know which way to turn because of the many seals he has seen come to the ice surface'
- *Mamihlapinatapai* (Terra del Fuegan), 'to look at each other, each hoping the other will offer to do something which both parties much desire done but which neither is willing to do' (According to *The Guinness Book of Records*, this is the most succinct word in the world.)

Translation problems can even arise at a relatively simple level. For example, German and French – together with many other languages – have two forms of 'you' – *du* and *Sie*, and *tu* and *vous*. When both are translated into English as 'you', something is clearly lost.

Idioms

An idiom is a colloquial expression whose meaning cannot be worked out from the meanings of the words it contains: for example, 'I was over the moon'; 'Don't beat about the bush'; 'He was born with a silver spoon in his mouth.' Such idiomatic expressions are particularly difficult to translate from one language to another. According to one story, when the sentence 'Out of sight is out of mind' was translated into Russian, and then re-translated into English, it came back as 'invisible idiot'. And 'The spirit is willing, but the flesh is weak' came back as 'The vodka is agreeable, but the meat is inferior.'

Activity 3.15

1 Give some examples of words in your own language, or your second language, which have no precise English equivalent.

2 How would you go about trying to translate the following idioms into another language?

   a 'David is barking up the wrong tree.'

   b 'Tina threw a spanner in the works.'

   c 'Samuel was only pulling your leg.'

   d 'Daniela is resting on her laurels.'

3 Give some examples of idiomatic expressions in other languages that are difficult to translate into English.

4 What kinds of text do you think are easiest to translate from one language to another and what kinds of text do you think are most difficult to translate?

There are many amusing anecdotes about mistranslations. When Pepsi Cola ran an advertising campaign in Taiwan, they translated the slogan 'Come Alive with Pepsi' into Chinese. The campaign was a flop. When the slogan was translated back into English, it read 'Pepsi brings your ancestors back from the dead!', understandably a failure. And the Swedish company Electrolux were no more successful when they tried to advertise their vacuum cleaners in the United States with the slogan 'Nothing sucks like an Electrolux'. Here are some other entertaining examples of mistranslations:

'The manager has personally passed all the water served here.' [Mexican hotel]

'The lift is being fixed for the next day. During that time we regret that you will be unbearable.' [Romanian hotel]

'Ladies may have a fit upstairs.' [Hong-Kong tailor shop]

'You are invited to take advantage of the chambermaid.' [Japanese hotel]

'Ladies, leave your clothes here and spend the afternoon having a good time.' [Italian laundry]

'Visitors are expected to complain at the office between the hours of 9:00 a.m. and 11:00 a.m. daily.' [Athens hotel]

'Take one of our horse-driven city tours – we guarantee no miscarriages.' [Czech tourist agency]

'We take your bags and send them in all directions.' [Danish airline ticket office]

'Ladies are requested not to have children in the bar.' [Norwegian cocktail lounge]

Lost in translation

Perhaps not surprisingly, most linguists would say that there is no such thing as a perfect translation and that something is always lost when we move from one language to another. As an Italian saying has it, *Traduttore traditore* – 'the translator is a traitor'. (Something is lost even in this translation!) So what makes one translation better than another? There are three commonly agreed criteria:

- *Faithfulness* – the translation should be faithful to the original text.
- *Comprehensibility* – the translation should be comprehensible.
- *Back translation* – when we retranslate a translation back into its original language, it should approximate to the original.

To take some simple examples, consider how one might translate the following sentences:

  a '*Guten Tag.*' (German → English)

  b '*S'il vous plaît.*' (French → English)

  c 'How do you do?' (English → any language)

The literal translation of '*Guten Tag*' is 'Good day', but people in Britain do not usually say 'Good day' (although it is more common in Australia). So a better translation might be 'Good morning', 'Good afternoon', or 'Hello'. Similarly, we do not translate '*S'il vous plaît*' as 'If it pleases you', but as 'Please'. Finally, 'How do you do?' would sound absurd in German and French if translated literally – how do you do what? Perhaps it is best translated as '*sehr erfreut*' and '*enchanté*'.

These examples show in microcosm the tension between going with the letter and going with the spirit of a text when you are making a translation. The more faithful you are to the letter – or literal meaning – of the text, the stranger the translation is likely to sound in the target language. The more natural the translation sounds in the target language, the more likely you are to have strayed from the literal meaning of the original text.

Poetry raises particular problems for the translator. When some of his poems were translated into French, the Chilean poet Pablo Neruda (1904–73) commented: 'If I had been a French poet, I would not have said what I did in that poem, because the value of the words is so different. I would have written something else.' And Spanish and French are closely related languages. Imagine how difficult it would be to translate one of Neruda's poems into Chinese!

Activity 3.16

Find a copy of Lewis Carroll's poem 'Jabberwocky' and translate it into another language. What difficulties are involved in doing this? How would you decide that one translation was better than another?

Although we should not get carried away with the problem of translation, it could in fact be said that there is an element of translation involved in all communication. For even when native speakers are talking together, they understand one another's words in slightly different ways. Indeed, getting to know another person could be said to be partly a matter of getting to know how they use language.

Labels and stereotypes

Our discussions about language, meaning and translation in the previous three sections have focused on the problematic nature of human communication and shown that we cannot simply take the meanings of words for granted. I now want to look at the way in which language affects the way we see and think about the world. In this section, we will look at labels and stereotypes; and we will then go on to consider how language affects the way we think and the kinds of value-judgements that we make about things.

Language consists of two main kinds of words: proper names and general words. We give proper names to such things as people, places and pets. But the vast majority of words in a language – such as 'reticent', 'rhinoceros', 'riddle', 'river' and 'run' – do not describe one unique thing, characteristic or action, but are general in nature. For this reason, we can think of language as being essentially a labelling system.

Labels

Putting labels on things has advantages and disadvantages. On the plus side, using labels is efficient and economical. If, for example, there was no general word for 'sand' and we were standing on a beach and had to baptise each individual grain with a proper name, communication would quickly become impossible. A good label enables you to predict how the object in question will behave. For example, if you take an object from a box labelled apples, you can be confident that it will look, smell and taste like an apple, and that it will nourish rather than poison you.

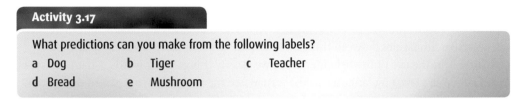

Activity 3.17

What predictions can you make from the following labels?

a Dog   b Tiger   c Teacher
d Bread   e Mushroom

On the negative side, labelling creates the danger that you mislabel things. If you treat similar things as if they were different, or different things as if they were similar, you are likely to run into trouble. Imagine, for example, that there are three glasses, A, B and C; filled with liquid; A and C are colourless, and B is red (Figure 3.5); and you are asked which liquid is the odd one out.

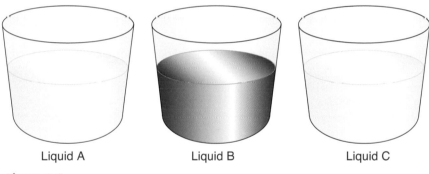

Liquid A   Liquid B   Liquid C

Figure 3.5

You might naturally say that liquid B is the odd one out. But not if you are thirsty, and liquid A is water, liquid B is water coloured with a harmless red vegetable dye, and liquid C is hydrochloric acid! This shows that if you classify things on the basis of superficial resemblance, you may overlook important underlying differences between them.

Since it is always possible to find similarities or differences between things, there are in fact many different ways of labelling or classifying a group of objects. Consider, for example, luggage at an airport: you can classify it according to shape, size, weight, colour, material, make, owner, country of origin, destination, etc. The most useful way of classifying luggage is likely to vary with context. A designer is likely to classify it in one way, a baggage handler in another way, and a traveller in a third way.

Since there are many different ways of classifying things, you might ask why we classify things the way we do. According to one view the labels we use reflect natural classes of things that exist 'out there'. According to another, labels are essentially social constructions that we impose on the world. While the first view says that labels are *natural* and there are objective similarities between things, the second says that labels are *cultural* and that similarity is in the eye of the beholder. Since we classify things using words, what is at issue here is the role played by language in the way we see the world. To what extent do our labels passively describe reality, and to what extent do they actively structure it?

The idea that our labels reflect the natural order of things is supported by the fact that there really do seem to be elements – such as gold and silver – and species – such as dogs and cats – out there corresponding to our categories. However, other labels – especially those used to classify human beings – might seem to be more cultural than natural.

Stereotypes

One danger with putting labels on people is that our labels can easily harden into stereotypes. A stereotype arises when we make assumptions about a group of people purely on the basis of their membership of that group. The use of stereotypes is particularly apparent in the case of nationality. Since Giovanni is Italian, he must love wine, pasta and ice cream, throw his hands around when he talks, and enjoy opera. And since Fritz is German, he must love beer, sausages and sauerkraut, work hard, and be very serious.

Despite the dangers of stereotyping people, some generalisations contain an element of truth in them. If you visit a restaurant in Rome and one in Berlin, you will notice a difference in atmosphere and the way people typically behave. According to one quip, students go to international schools with prejudices about other cultures and leave realising they are all true!

What, then, distinguishes damaging stereotypes from harmless generalisations? Typically, a stereotype is a caricature which exaggerates the negative features of a group and assumes they are possessed by *all* members of the group. Furthermore, it is usually based on prejudice rather than fact and is difficult to change in the light of contrary evidence. For example, if a racist who believes that all immigrants are lazy is shown an example of a hard-working immigrant, he will probably insist that the example is not typical, and quickly forget it.

Activity 3.20

1 What stereotypes, if any, do you think exist in your culture concerning the following groups?

   a Americans   b Islamic fundamentalists

   c Feminists   d Environmental activists

   e Lawyers   f Buddhists

   g Scientists   h Computer hackers

2 What other common stereotypes exist in your culture? To what extent do you think they affect the way people see things?

3 Which of the following pairs of sentences sounds normal, and which sounds a bit strange? What does this have to do with stereotypes?

   a1 'She's a mother, but she isn't a housewife.'

   a2 'She's a mother, but she is a housewife.'

   b1 'He's a father, but he doesn't work.'

   b2 'He's a father, but he does work.'

4 In your culture, which of the following adjectives are associated more with men and which are associated more with women? How much truth do you think there is in these stereotypes?

   a Emotional   b Reckless

   c Active   d Aggressive

   e Sensitive   f Tough

   g Affectionate   h Cautious

5 Some believers in astrology say that Leos and Cancers are incompatible – i.e. if you are a Leo, there is no point in dating a Cancer, and vice versa. To what extent could this be seen as the astrological equivalent of racism?

What comes out of our discussion of labels and stereotypes is that we need to be aware of the disadvantages as well as the advantages of using general words to label things. Despite their obvious value, labels can trap us into one particular way of looking at things. Moreover, it is difficult – if not impossible – to capture the uniqueness and individuality of things in words. If you try to describe one of your friends to someone who does not know them, you will see how hard it is to paint a verbal portrait of them. It is equally difficult to capture the taste of a strawberry, or the colour of the sea, or falling in love in the butterfly net of language. Reality, it seems, always spills beyond any description that we are able to give of it.

Language and thought

We must now consider the extent to which language affects the way we think about the world.

The Sapir–Whorf hypothesis

According to the **Sapir–Whorf hypothesis**, language determines our experience of reality, and we can see and think only what our language allows us to see and think. To give a well-known example, the Inuit are said to have many different words for snow, and their sophisticated snow vocabulary helps them to make finely grained snow discriminations. As a result, they see and experience snow-covered landscapes quite differently from the rest of us. According to Edward Sapir (1884–1939), one of the proponents of the hypothesis:

> The 'real world' is to a large extent unconsciously built upon the language habits of the group. No two languages are ever sufficiently similar to be considered as representing the same social reality. The worlds in which different societies live are distinct worlds, not merely the same world with different labels attached... We see and hear and otherwise experience very largely as we do because the language habits of our community predispose certain choices of interpretation.

Benjamin Whorf (1879–1941), the other proponent of the hypothesis, studied the difference between the language of the Hopi Indians of North America and European languages, and came to the surprising conclusion that the Hopi language contains 'no words, grammatical forms, constructions or expressions that refer directly to what we call "time", or to past, present, or future, or to enduring or lasting'. Since the Hopi have no words for it, Whorf came to the conclusion that they have no concept of abstract time. In his fascinating book *The Language Instinct*, Steven Pinker gives several examples of Whorf's translations of Hopi language:

> 'He invites people to a feast' → 'He, or somebody, goes for eaters of cooked food.'
> 'The boat is grounded on the beach.' → 'It is on the beach, pointwise as an event of canoe motion.'

Activity 3.21

1 Could the above examples simply be bad translations? To test this idea, translate something word-for-word from a foreign language into English. Does the result sound equally bizarre?
2 If you are fluent in more than one language, to what extent do you think differently when you switch between languages?

Since the Sapir–Whorf hypothesis claims that language determines the way we think, it can be described as a form of **linguistic determinism**. A well-known fictional example of this can be found in George Orwell's (1903–50) dystopian novel, *1984*. Orwell imagines a totalitarian government called *Ingsoc* which seeks to control, not only how people behave, but also what they think, by inventing a new language called Newspeak:

The purpose of Newspeak was not only to provide a medium of expression for the world-view and mental habits proper to devotees of Ingsoc, but to make all other modes of thought impossible. It was intended that when Newspeak had been adopted once and for all and Oldspeak forgotten, a heretical thought – that is, a thought diverging from the principles of Ingsoc – should be literally unthinkable, at least so far as thought is dependent on words. Its vocabulary was so constructed as to give exact and often very subtle expression to every meaning that a Party member could properly wish to express, while excluding all other meanings and also the possibility of arriving at them by indirect methods. This was done partly by the invention of new words but chiefly by eliminating undesirable words and by stripping such words as remained of unorthodox meanings, and so far as possible of all secondary meanings whatever. To give a single example. The word 'free' still existed in Newspeak, but it could only be used in such statements as 'This dog is free from lice' or 'This field is free from weeds'. It could not be used in its old sense of 'politically free' or 'intellectually free', since political and intellectual freedom no longer existed even as concepts, and were therefore of necessity nameless. Quite apart from the suppression of definitely heretical words, reduction of vocabulary was regarded as an end in itself, and no word that could be dispensed with was allowed to survive. Newspeak was designed not to extend but to diminish the range of thought, and this purpose was indirectly assisted by cutting the choice of words down to a minimum.

Testing the hypothesis

Several attempts have been made to test the Sapir–Whorf hypothesis. In his book *Word Play: What Happens When People Talk* the anthropologist Peter Farb (1929–80) discusses an experiment which used as test subjects bilingual Japanese women who had married American servicemen and were living in the USA.

The women spoke English to their husbands, children, and neighbours, and in most everyday speech situations; they spoke Japanese whenever they came together to gossip, reminisce, and discuss the news from home. Each Japanese woman thus inhabited two language worlds – and according to the predictions of the hypothesis, the women should think differently in each of these worlds. The experiment consisted of two visits to each woman by a bilingual Japanese interviewer. During the first interview he chatted with them only in Japanese; during the second he carried on the same discussion and asked the same questions in English. The results were quite remarkable; they showed that the attitudes of each woman differed markedly, depending upon whether she spoke Japanese or English. Here, for example, is the way the same woman completed the same sentences at the two interviews:

When my wishes conflict with my family's...
... it is a time of great unhappiness. [Japanese]
... I do what I want. [English]

Real friends should...
... help each other. [Japanese]
... be very frank. [English]

Clearly, major variables in the experiment had been eliminated – since the women were interviewed twice by the same person in the same location of their homes, and they discussed the same topics – with but one exception. And that sole exception was language. The drastic differences in attitudes of the women could be accounted for only by the language world each inhibited when she spoke.

Despite the above evidence, some people are not convinced by the Sapir–Whorf hypothesis. According to critics, the fact that the Inuit have many different words for snow does not show that language determines reality, but instead suggests that reality determines language. For the Inuit presumably developed their snow vocabulary in response to their environment. The reason there are not many words for 'snow' in English is that it doesn't snow very often in England. But when people such as skiers require a more discriminating snow vocabulary, they don't have much difficulty in inventing words, or borrowing them from other languages. To say that the Inuit have a different experience of reality because they have lots of different words for snow is surely no more plausible than saying that printers have a different experience of reality because they have lots of different words for print fonts.

Furthermore, although the Sapir–Whorf hypothesis says that language determines thought, there is in fact evidence to suggest that thought is possible without language:

1   Psychologists have discovered that babies and animals are able to think without the benefit of language. Some clever experiments have shown that babies as young as five months can do a simple form of mental arithmetic. And pigeons have been trained to recognise general classes such as trees, human beings, bodies of water, dogs and fish.

2   Some creative people claim that language plays only a secondary role in their thinking and that their ideas first come to them in images. Albert Einstein once observed:

> The words of a language as they are written and spoken do not seem to play any role in the mechanisms of my thought. The physical entities which seem to serve as elements in thought are certain signs and more or less clear images which can be voluntarily reproduced and combined. The above mentioned elements are, in my case, of visual, and some of muscular type. Conventional words or other signs have to be sought for laboriously only in a secondary stage.

3   We sometimes struggle to find the right words to express thoughts that feel as if they are already there. You have probably had the experience of saying something, and then adding in frustration 'No, that's not quite what I want to say', and then trying to express yourself with greater clarity. This suggests that our thoughts are there prior to language and that we are simply trying to find the right words with which to express them.

4   If language determines thought, it is unclear how new words ever enter a language, or, indeed, how language could have arisen in the first place. The most obvious explanation is that some kind of pre-linguistic thought is possible for which we later find words.

While the above points count against a strong version of the Sapir–Whorf hypothesis, you might still find plausible a weaker version of the hypothesis, which says that language *influences* rather than *determines* thought. For complex thinking does seem to be closely connected to language. A baby may have a basic concept of number before it can talk, but it is hard to see how someone could do multiplication if they did not have the appropriate mathematical vocabulary. The American cultural critic Neil Postman (1931–2003) gave a good example to illustrate the point:

> The process by which words and other symbols give shape and substance to our thoughts can be suggested by your trying to multiply 495 by 384. Except in this instance you must use only Roman numerals. I think you will find the operation quite impossible to do. Without access to the symbol 0 and a system of positional notation, the answer is literally inconceivable, i.e., you cannot think it.

More generally, it might be hard to have various abstract ideas if you did not have the appropriate vocabulary. Admittedly, we sometimes think in images and then struggle to find the appropriate words, but we usually know what we think only after we have put it into language. While language may not determine thought, it might be said to predispose it, in the sense that we tend to think along the lines of our linguistic categories. This is not to say that we are trapped in our own language. For, as we saw earlier, it is always possible to borrow words from another language. Nevertheless, to come up with a new way of thinking usually requires the development of a new vocabulary – and this is one of the hallmarks of genius.

> ...As imagination bodies forth
> The forms of things unknown, the poet's pen
> Turns them to shapes, and gives to airy nothing
> A local habitation and a name.
> [William Shakespeare, 1564–1616, *A Midsummer Night's Dream*, V, i]

Language and values

We use language not only to describe the world, but also to persuade and influence one another. When we gossip, for example, we don't just tell stories about people, but negotiate with one another about how to describe them. Would you say that John is a good storyteller or a liar? Is Maurice a fluent conversationalist or a wind-bag? Do you see Melissa as self-confident or arrogant? Is Paul's refusal to show emotion a sign of inner strength or of insensitivity? Which of these competing descriptions you settle on is likely to affect the way you think about the person in question.

Advertisers have long been aware of the power of language to influence and persuade. Here are two examples:

- It was a stroke of marketing genius on someone's part to brand water with bubbles in it as '*sparkling* water'. If it had been marketed as 'gassy water', it would probably never have become so popular.

- Since airlines have something called 'first class', it would be natural to think that the next two classes should be called 'second class' and 'third class'. Wrong! It's 'business class' and 'economy class'. Now even 'economy class' is becoming unfashionable. If you travel economy, British Airways now describes you as a 'world traveller'. Although this may sound impressive, but it makes no difference to the quality of the food or the leg room.

Using language to influence and persuade

To explore the connection between language and values further, let us consider four ways in which language can be used to influence and persuade people.

1 Emotionally laden language

Some words have not only a descriptive meaning, but also an **emotive meaning**. Emotive meaning can be defined as 'the aura of favourable or unfavourable feeling that hovers about a word'. While some words such as 'hero', 'peace' and 'democracy' have positive connotations, others such as 'thief', 'liar' or 'pervert' have negative ones. That is why everyone claims to be in favour of peace, and no one likes to be labelled a liar.

Activity 3.24

1 Analyse the way language is being used in each of the following pairs of expressions:
 a Terrorist / freedom fighter.
 b Pro life / pro choice.
 c Genetically modified food / Frankenstein food.
 d Free speech / hate speech.
 e 'Blocking your child's access to objectionable material on the Internet is not called CENSORSHIP, it is called PARENTING' (Al Gore).
2 In 1947 the United States Department of War was renamed the Department of Defense. What difference, if any, do you think this makes? What is the corresponding department of state called in your country?

Euphemisms, which substitute mild or neutral sounding words for a negative sounding one, are a widely used form of emotive language. We sometimes resort to euphemisms in order to avoid taboo subjects, or to protect people's feelings. Thus, we may speak of the 'rest room' rather than the toilet. In addition to such benign uses, people sometimes use euphemisms to deliberately mislead people. For example, the timber industry no longer speaks of 'clear cutting' – an ugly sounding expression – when it cuts down old-growth forest, but of 'landscape management'. This may serve to hide the reality of what is happening and make an unacceptable practice sound acceptable.

Although the influence of emotionally laden language is a matter of continuing debate, there is evidence to suggest that how people respond to survey questions depends on how they are phrased. In one US survey, when people were asked if more money should be spent on 'assistance to the poor', 68 per cent replied 'yes'; but when they were asked if more money should be spent on 'welfare', the number dropped to 24 per cent. In another survey, people were far more willing to spend money on 'national defence' than on the 'military'.

2 Weasel words

Weasel words are words such as 'many', 'should' and 'probably' which people slip into sentences to give themselves an escape route. For example, a manufacturer might say, 'Our product will work for you if you simply follow the instructions carefully.' You buy the product; it doesn't work; and when you phone up to complain, you are told that you clearly didn't follow the instructions *carefully enough*.

Activity 3.25

Explain how weasel words are used in each of the following cases:
1 'Our product can restore up to 25% of lost hair.'
2 'Probably the best lager in the world.'
3 'Dentifresh toothpaste helps fight tooth decay.'
4 'If Timothy works hard, he should do himself justice in the final exam.'

3 Grammar

Grammar can also affect the way people see things. For example, the passive voice may be used to cover up someone's responsibility for something. Compare the following two sentences:

(a) 'Many villages were bombed.'
(b) 'We bombed many villages.'

While the first sentence makes the bombing sound like a natural disaster, the second puts the spotlight on the perpetrators.

4 Revealing and concealing

Language can be used not only to *reveal* certain aspects of reality, but also to conceal other aspects by diverting attention away from them. Consider, for example, the following four descriptions:

(a) 'I have invited an attractive blonde to the party.'
(b) 'I have invited a cellist to the party.'
(c) 'I have invited a marathon runner to the party.'
(d) 'I have invited a lesbian to the party.'

Each description carries with it a different set of connotations, but it is possible that they all refer to the same person. Which description we use is likely to affect the way other people see the person in question.

Activity 3.26

1 According to a well-known children's rhyme, 'Sticks and stones may break my bones, but names will never hurt me.' Do you agree or disagree with this? Give reasons.
2 Find out something about the political correctness (PC) movement, which seeks to use language to change attitudes to the oppressed or disadvantaged. What arguments are there in favour of political correctness and what arguments are there against it?

"You see Thag..? Names CAN break your bones. Especially when those names are carved on ROCKS."

© www.CartoonStock.com

Figure 3.6

Language at war

The fact that language is not innocent and can be used to manipulate the way we see things is particularly apparent in times of war. Military training camps have long been aware that to get 'our boys' to kill their troops, *they* need to be dehumanised. During the Vietnam war, enemy soldiers were known as 'Gooks' by US servicemen. And in the first Gulf War (1991), an American pilot described firing on Iraqi soldiers as a 'turkey shoot'. Whatever your views about the rights and wrongs of these military campaigns, you would probably agree that it is psychologically easier to kill 'gooks' and 'turkeys' than human beings. Here are some more examples of 'warspeak', which is often used to cover up the reality on the ground.

Warspeak	Real meaning
security assistance	arms sales
neutralise	kill
no longer a factor	dead
take out	destroy
inoperative combat personnel	dead soldiers
pacification	bombing
service a target	dropping bombs on a target
collateral damage	bombed cities
friendly fire	accidentally firing on your own troops
strategic redeployment	retreat
liberate	invade
reporting guidelines	censorship
pre-emptive	unprovoked
ethnic cleansing	genocide

Language is power

While opinions differ about the relation between language and values, the fact that political parties and businesses invest so heavily in media consultants and spin doctors suggests that they, at least, think that it plays an important role in shaping our attitudes. At the limit, the seductive eloquence of demagogues such as Adolf Hitler (1889–1945) reminds us that language can be used not only to educate and enlighten, but also to fuel the flames of hatred. So we would be well-advised to take seriously the slogan that 'language is power'.

Conclusion

Since much of our knowledge comes to us in words, our discussion of language in this chapter is clearly relevant to our quest for knowledge. Perhaps the key thing we have discovered is that language is not as simple or straightforward as we first thought. We need to know what a statement means before we can decide whether it is true or false, but in practice it is difficult to pin down the meanings of words with complete precision.

As a final point, let us conclude by briefly considering two different views about the relationship between language and knowledge. On one side, some people claim that in order to know something you must be able to put it into words, and that 'if you can't say it then you don't know it' (Hans Reichenbach, 1891–1953). Such a robust view suggests that the only way to demonstrate your understanding of something is to put it into words. Against this, other people insist that some of our knowledge lies beyond words, and that 'I know more than I can say' (Michael Polanyi, 1891–1976). Advocates of this view argue that our knowledge of things with which we are acquainted spills beyond our ability to describe them. This takes us back to the slogan mentioned in Chapter 1: 'the map is not the territory'.

Interestingly, mystics in all the great world religions have held that the deepest truths cannot be expressed in language. The Taoist sage Lao Tzu (*c.* 600 BCE) observes that 'Those who speak do not know; those who know do not speak'; the Buddhist *Lankaatara Sutra* tells us that 'Truth is beyond letters and words and books'; and in Judaism the Talmud says that 'If silence be good for the wise, how much the better for fools.'

One thing, however, is certain: if the deepest truths about life, the universe and everything do lie beyond words, then there is nothing we can say about them! With that in mind, I leave the last word to the philosopher Ludwig Wittgenstein (1889–1951) who at the end of his great book *Tractatus Logico-Philosophicus* wrote: 'What we cannot speak about we must pass over in silence.'

- A great deal of our knowledge comes through language and this makes possible an intellectual division of labour.
- Language is a subset of communication and is rule-governed, intended and creative.
- We need to understand what a sentence means before we can decide whether it is true or false.
- Since the definition, denotation and image theories of meaning all have shortcomings, perhaps we should say that meaning is a matter of know-how.
- A great deal of language is ambiguous and there is an element of interpretation built into all communication.
- Since different languages divide the world up in different ways translation is more of an art than a science.
- We use language to label and classify and this brings with it the danger that we misclassify or stereotype things.
- Although language may not *determine* our experience of reality, as claimed by the Sapir–Whorf hypothesis, it seems likely that it *influences* it.
- We use language not only to describe, but also to influence and persuade – and sometimes *manipulate* the way people see things.
- Whether or not there are some truths that lie beyond language is a matter of continuing debate.

ambiguity	denotation	linguistic determinism
back translation	emotive meaning	metaphor
body language	euphemism	Sapir–Whorf hypothesis
classification	grammar	stereotype
communication	idiom	weasel words
connotation	irony	

Further reading

Donna Jo Napoli, *Language Matters* (Oxford University Press, 2003). Written by a professor of linguistics, this short, accessible and entertaining book has chapters on such things as how we acquire language, whether animals have language, translation, and the relation between language and thought.

George Lakoff and Mark Johnson, *Metaphors We Live By* (University of Chicago Press, 1980). According to the authors, metaphors pervade our language and often shape our thinking without our being aware of it. If you only dip into Chapters 1 and 2 you will already get a sense of the power of such metaphors as 'argument is war' and 'time is money'.

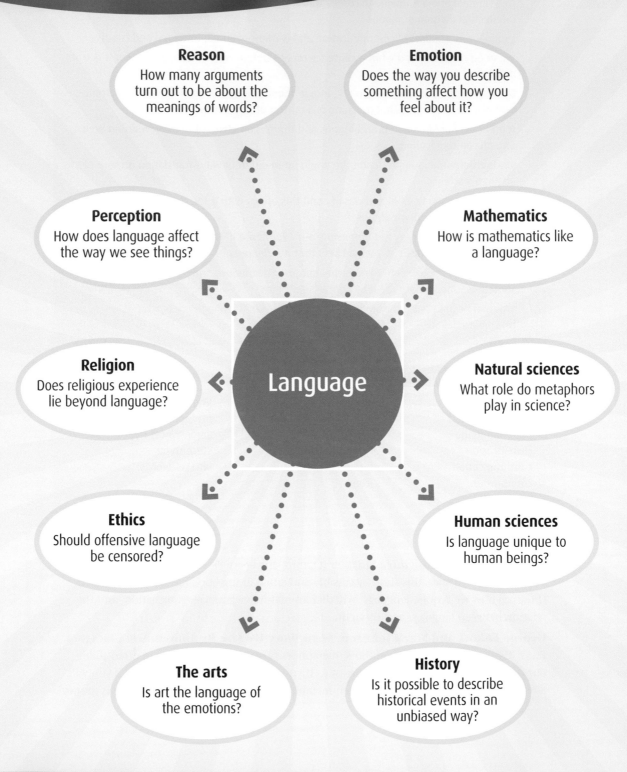

Reason
How many arguments turn out to be about the meanings of words?

Emotion
Does the way you describe something affect how you feel about it?

Perception
How does language affect the way we see things?

Mathematics
How is mathematics like a language?

Religion
Does religious experience lie beyond language?

Language

Natural sciences
What role do metaphors play in science?

Ethics
Should offensive language be censored?

Human sciences
Is language unique to human beings?

The arts
Is art the language of the emotions?

History
Is it possible to describe historical events in an unbiased way?

DIALOGUE ON ANIMAL LANGUAGE

The following dialogue by Richard van de Lagemaat explores the question of whether or not any animals can be said to possess language.

DOLLY: I have just been to the zoo, and I was wondering: do you think that animals have language?

GUY: Animals? Hmm ... Well, as it stands that is a badly formulated question.

DOLLY: What do you mean?

GUY: The word 'animal' covers a spectrum of living beings, ranging from amoebae and worms at one end to apes and human beings at the other. When you ask, 'Do animals have language?', I could answer that since we are animals, and since what we do is *by definition* language, then it is trivially true that animals have language. Nevertheless, I doubt that amoebae have a lot to say for themselves.

DOLLY: Well, apart from human beings, you would surely agree that most animals communicate with each other in one way or another – either through noises, or scents, or bodily movements. To take a well-known example, bees perform a 'dance' to convey information about the distance and direction of nectar sources to their fellow workers. And that surely is a rudimentary form of language.

GUY: I think we need to make a distinction here between language and communication. I would say that while bees certainly communicate with one another, they do not have language.

DOLLY: What is the difference?

GUY: Well, language is a *subset* of communication, and while all language is a form of communication, it is not the case that all forms of communication are language.

DOLLY: I would have said that the words 'language' and 'communication' are pretty much synonymous.

GUY: No! There are many forms of communication that no one would call language. For example, when you turn your car key in the ignition, the car starts, but no one would say the car *understands* that you want it to start. While information is certainly communicated, the communication in question is purely mechanical and has nothing to do with language.

DOLLY: As sometimes happens, our disagreement here seems to be about the meanings of words. My understanding of the word 'communication' is derived from the *Encyclopaedia Britannica* which defines it as 'the exchange of meanings between individuals through a common system of symbols.' You seem to be using it in a much broader sense to include purely mechanical communication.

GUY: Well, let's not get bogged down in semantics. My point is that bees respond to one another in an essentially mechanical way. In any case, since all they can 'talk' about is nectar, it would, to say the least, be misleading to describe their dance as a form of language.

DOLLY: But how do you know that nectar is all they can talk about?

GUY: Well, given that bees have only primitive brains, I think it's a safe bet that they don't spend much time discussing the meaning of life.

DOLLY: OK. To move the discussion forward, why don't we focus on higher animals, such as monkeys? Do you think that monkeys have language?

GUY: No! I believe that language is unique to human beings.

DOLLY: But given that we evolved from chimpanzees and share 99% of our genes with them, we should surely take seriously the idea that they might have abilities similar to our own?

GUY: The fact that we share 99% of our genes with chimpanzees doesn't tell us anything – the remaining 1% could make all the difference. Moreover, our brains account for a much bigger proportion of our body weight than do chimp brains, and a bigger relative brain size is a good indication of greater intelligence.

DOLLY: Well, let's take a look at some of the scientific evidence. Take the case of vervet monkeys. Scientists have discovered that their alarm calls vary according to the predator that threatens them. The leopard alarm call, eagle alarm call, and snake alarm call are all different from each other, and elicit different responses from members of the group. When the monkeys hear the leopard alarm call they climb into the trees, when they hear the eagle alarm call they hide in the undergrowth, and when they hear the snake alarm call they look around in the grass. This surely proves that they have *words* for 'leopard', 'eagle', and 'snake', and that they understand what these words mean.

GUY: It proves no such thing! What your example shows is that vervet monkeys can communicate with one another about matters that are important for their survival. Rather than attribute understanding to them, I think their behaviour is best explained in terms of stimulus and response. Just as Pavlov's dogs were conditioned to salivate whenever they heard a bell ring, so the monkeys are reacting automatically to various alarm calls. Understanding does not come into it – it is simply a matter of a particular call triggering a particular response.

DOLLY: OK, so what about the various experiments in which chimpanzees have been taught American sign language? One of the first stars of such experiments was a chimp called Washoe who successfully learnt more than a hundred words of sign language.

GUY: Well, from what I've read about this experiment, Washoe's main concern was with getting food and being tickled. Drilling a chimpanzee in a few bits of sign language doesn't seem so very different from training a hungry rat to press a lever that releases food.

DOLLY: You are not doing justice to the remarkable linguistic abilities shown by these chimps. For example, their ability to talk about absent objects shows that they are not simply reacting automaton-like to things in their immediate environment. Similarly, the fact that they sometimes tell lies in order to mislead their trainers suggests that rather than responding instinctively to various cues, they are using signs intentionally. Perhaps most impressive of all, they demonstrate genuine creativity by inventing new combinations of signs. To give a few examples, Washoe came up with the constructions 'open food eat' for a refrigerator, 'hot metal blow' for a cigarette lighter, and 'listen drink' for Alka-Seltzer. Such creativity proves that far from responding mechanically, Washoe had a genuine understanding of the meanings of these signs.

GUY: I think you will find that more recent research has cast doubt on the validity of these experiments. According to some observers, Washoe's trainers became so emotionally involved with their subject that they lost the ability to be objective and were often simply *projecting* sign language onto Washoe's random hand movements. In the view of Steven Pinker of MIT, Washoe may actually have known as few as 20 signs. Compare that with human beings whose vocabularies consist of literally thousands of words.

DOLLY: Your talk about lack of objectivity shows that you don't really understand how social science works. You simply cannot study apes with the same dispassionate objectivity with which you can study rocks – at least, not if you want to teach them language. If you were trying to teach your child language, how far do you think you would get if you tried to do it objectively and without emotional involvement? Not very far, I'll bet! It's the same with apes. You can only teach them language if you have some kind of emotional rapport with them.

GUY: Perhaps you are right about that; but my point is that once you have made an emotional connection with an ape, you may be too keen to attribute skills to it that it does not really possess. Just as I think parents are not the best judges of their children's intelligence, so I doubt that someone who has spent years working with an ape can look at what is happening dispassionately.

DOLLY: You know, I'm beginning to think that you do not really have an open mind on this topic, that you have already decided that chimps do not have language, and that you are not willing to accept any evidence that goes against your belief.

GUY: Not at all! I am sceptical about the claims concerning primate language because I know that people have a tendency to project human qualities on to animals and that they find it difficult to be objective about them.

DOLLY: Well, let's take the more recent experiments conducted by Sue Savage-Rumbaugh on bonobo chimps. Rather than sign language, she taught her chimps to communicate using a keyboard with more than 200 symbols on it, each representing a particular word; and she has achieved results with her star pupil, Kanzi, at least as impressive as those of Washoe. Since replacing signs with a keyboard gets rid of any ambiguity about how we interpret what is going on, I don't think you can dismiss this evidence so easily.

GUY: But what exactly does it prove?

DOLLY: It proves that Kanzi has a grasp of semantics and understands the meanings of words. When his trainers say to him things like, 'Please go to the office and bring back the red ball', he does just that. What's that if it is not understanding?

GUY: Once again, I would say that it is the ability to respond to signals as the result of training.

DOLLY: Listen, they set up an experiment in which Kanzi was given 600 sentences *he had never heard before*, and he was able to respond correctly to them in over 75% of cases. That is as good as what is achieved by a two-and-a-half-year-old child. You can't explain that away in terms of mere training.

GUY: Even so, there is still a huge gulf between what a two-year-old child can do, and what a mature user of the language can do.

DOLLY: Well, at least you seem to be admitting that these chimps have a rudimentary form of language similar to that possessed by children.

GUY: I am admitting no such thing! Look, I don't think you have grasped my main point. Sure, these chimps are clever, and their trainers are dedicated; but basically they've just been taught a bunch of party tricks that don't have a whole lot to do with language. All they are doing is responding to cues from their trainers in order to get rewards. Language proper has something called syntax – rules for joining words together to form complex sentences – words like 'but', 'and', 'or', 'not' and 'because' which enable us to articulate complex thoughts. Animals don't have language because they don't have syntax. When we use language, we don't just talk about our immediate desires or objects in our environment. We can formulate abstract thoughts, talk about the distant past and future, and meditate on the meaning of life. Even the people who work with chimps and gorillas readily admit that their subjects can do none of these things.

DOLLY: You know, you keep raising the bar. You said vervet monkeys were just reacting to signs, so I gave the example of Washoe and his creative use of language. You questioned the validity of that evidence, so I then gave you the example of Kanzi where the evidence is beyond question. Now you suddenly redefine what you mean by language. I am not claiming that what the chimps can do is the same as what you and I can do: I am claiming that it is *sufficiently similar* to deserve the name of language.

GUY: Sufficiently similar? I don't think so! To describe what these chimpanzees do as a form of language is like describing what champion long jumpers do as a form of flight. The best athletes may be able to jump more than 8 metres, but no matter how hard they train – or how many illegal drugs they take – they will never be able to fly like an eagle flies. And just as human beings are not built for flight, so chimpanzees are not built for language.

DOLLY: I think your analogy is misleading and simply confuses the issue. As I said earlier, my impression is that you have decided in advance of the evidence that animals do not have language, and this makes me wonder about your motives. Perhaps you will feel more comfortable about exploiting animals if you can convince yourself that there is an unbridgeable gulf between human beings and the rest of the animal kingdom.

GUY: Listen, I, too, am opposed to the exploitation of animals and I believe in animal rights. However, the reason that animals have rights derives from the fact that they are able to feel pain, and it has nothing to do with whether or not they have language. So instead of trying to project human qualities onto animals, why don't you just accept that they are different from us?

DOLLY: Well, perhaps you should remember what you said at the beginning of the discussion – namely, that we, too, are animals. In any case, this particular animal is getting tired. Perhaps it is time to stop.

THE DAY A LANGUAGE DIED

Peter Popham, the *Independent*, London

Another language died one day in January. Carlos Westez, more widely known as Red Thunder Cloud, the last speaker of the Native American language Catawba, died of a stroke at the age of 76. With him passed away the Catawba language.

Anyone who wants to hear the war songs, the hunting songs, and the religious chants of the Catawba can apply to the Smithsonian Institution in Washington DC where, back in the 1940's Red Thunder Cloud recorded a series of them for posterity. But Catawba as something that lived and breathed and developed organically is gone for good.

All of us have been alerted over the past 20 years to the damage that modern industry can inflict on the world's ecology. Less obvious, but no less powerful, is the impact of a homogenizing monoculture upon our languages and ways of life. We are witnessing the spread of English, carried by American culture, delivered by Japanese technology. We also are witnessing the hegemony of a few great transnational tongues: Chinese, Spanish, Russian and Hindi. With their rise as tools of culture and commerce have come the deaths of hundreds of other tongues that are the losers in the competition for linguistic survival.

Scholars believe that there are some 6,000 languages around the world. The richest linguistic life is close to the equator, where the fecundity of nature means that tribes can survive in smaller areas in relative isolation beyond the reach of the outside world, keeping their culture and language intact. But most of these languages are spoken by very small numbers of people, and many of them could die out within the next 100 years.

Aore is the language native to Vanuatu in the Pacific. But its fate is sealed: Like Catawba (until January), it is spoken by the island's only remaining native inhabitant. So it, too, is bound to die out. Many other languages will share its fate: A large proportion of the languages of Ethiopia are used by tiny numbers of people. Two speakers of the Ethiopian language Gaat were fine until a well-intentioned language researcher took them out of their native jungle, whereupon they caught cold and died.

One of the world's richest language banks is Papua New Guinea, where more than 100 languages are threatened with extinction. The link between this and the destruction of the natural habitat by foreign commercial exploitation is glaringly obvious. In the Americas 100 languages, each of which has fewer than 300 speakers left, are on their last legs.

That is why Red Thunder Cloud's death made news around the world: Native Americans face a peculiarly keen and formidable threat to their languages and Red Thunder Cloud was one of the first to recognize this and try to do something about it.

What does it mean for the rest of us when a language disappears? When a plant or insect or animal species dies, it is easy to understand what has been lost. But language is merely a product of the mind, an arrangement among the different parts of different people's nervous systems. What the rest of us lose when a language dies is the possibility of a unique way of perceiving and describing the world.

Speaking a language is a complex accomplishment. Understanding how we do it has produced a vast literature in philosophy, semiotics, and the neuro-sciences. The earliest theories of language were that words and ideas stood for sensations and feelings. It was only in the 20th century that theories of language became more complex and proliferated. Noam Chomsky, the American academic, made a reputation for himself with the claim that we can speak languages only because our brains have an innate capacity to understand the underlying structure of a language.

To learn a language that is extremely remote from English, such as Japanese, is to take on a radically new identity. In Japanese, there are immense opportunities for vagueness and great difficulties in being precise. There are many different ways of saying thank you and sorry, half a dozen different ways of expressing formality or intimacy, humility or arrogance, without saying anything of substance at all.

Yet one would not, except out of great perversity or scholarly zeal, learn a language that is close to extinction. If the language is only a sort of trophy, used for ceremonies, toasts, or greetings, it has already ceased to exist in a meaningful sense and is already on the road to extinction.

There is an escape clause, however: If the language has been written down (as Catawba was not), there remains at least the theoretical possibility of reviving it. The only truly miraculous example in modern times is what has happened to Hebrew in Israel: Long replaced as the language of the Jews by the tongues dominant wherever they happened to find themselves during the Diaspora, its only remaining purpose was in the synagogue. In Israel, however, it is now the universal language of everyday life, born of the necessity of forging a nation out of disparate ingredients. Language is the only thing that can have that sort of binding function.

English played a similar role in binding together the polyglot, multicultural elements of the empire and making a self-conscious entity of them. But while the engine of colonialism long ago ran out of steam, the momentum of its languages is still formidable and it is against their tyranny that the smaller languages fight to survive.

4 Perception

'It's not what you look at that matters, it's what you see.'
Henry David Thoreau, 1817–62

'Two thirds of what we see is behind our eyes.'
Chinese proverb

'A fool sees not the same tree that the wise man sees.'
William Blake, 1757–1827

'The greatest calamity that can befall people is not that they should be born blind, but rather that they should have eyes and yet fail to see.'
Helen Keller, 1880–1968

'Whilst part of what we perceive comes through our senses from the object before us, another part (and it may be the larger part) always comes out of our own mind.'
William James, 1842–1910

'Things do not seem the same to those who love and those who hate, nor to those who are angry and those who are calm.'
Aristotle, 384–322 BCE

'The greatest thing a human soul ever does is to see something, and to tell what it saw in a plain way... To see clearly is poetry, prophecy and religion – all in one.'
John Ruskin, 1819–1900

'It is only with the heart that one can see rightly; What is essential is INVISIBLE TO THE EYE.'
Antoine de Saint–Exupéry, 1900–44

'Every man takes the limits of his own field of vision for the limits of the world.'
Arthur Schopenhauer, 1788–1860

'If the doors of perception were cleansed, everything would appear to man as it is – infinite.'
William Blake, 1757–1827

'You can't depend on your eyes when your imagination is out of focus.'
Mark Twain, 1835–1910

Introduction

Perception can be defined as the awareness of things through our five senses – sight, sound, touch, taste and smell. These are 'the gates and windows' of the mind – channels of communication between ourselves and the outside world, which effortlessly present us with the rich, and often pleasurable, variety of the world: the beautiful colours of a New England autumn, the sound of waves breaking on a shore, the tickle of a feather, the taste of hot soup on a cold day, the smell of freshly cut grass.

Activity 4.1

If for some reason you had to sacrifice one of your senses, which would you be most willing to lose and which would you be least willing to lose? Give reasons.

When people are asked this question, the great majority say that they would be most willing to lose their sense of smell, and least willing to lose their sight. This is not very surprising; indeed we are such visually oriented creatures that vision is sometimes identified with knowledge. For example, we say that seeing is believing rather than smelling is believing; when we understand someone we say 'I see what you mean', not 'I smell what you mean'; and we speak of someone having in*sight* not in*smell*.

Activity 4.2

Can you give any other examples of figures of speech in English, or any other language, that connect knowledge and the senses?

Smell, by contrast, is the poor relation of the senses, and it is sometimes called the mute sense. For, while we have many different words for colours, our smell vocabulary does not extend much beyond 'smells good', 'smells bad' and 'smells like'. Despite its lowly status, we are in fact able to distinguish more than ten thousand different odours. And our sense of smell has a more direct route to our brains than any of our other senses. This may explain why evocative smells can sometimes trigger powerful emotional memories, and why the perfume industry is worth millions of dollars a year.

Allowing that there may be differences in the relative importance we attach to each of our senses, most people would agree that our five senses are important sources of knowledge. Indeed, according to one major school of philosophy, known as **empiricism**, *all* knowledge is ultimately based on perceptual experience. This may be too extreme, but perception clearly plays a key role in almost all subject areas, ranging from the sciences through history to the arts. Think, for example, of the role played by observation in biology, or eye-witness accounts in history, or the ability to see things with new eyes in the visual arts.

As a preliminary point of reference, let us consider the position known as **common-sense realism**. According to this, perception is a passive and relatively straightforward process which gives us an accurate picture of reality. Colours and sounds and smells exist 'out there', and the act of observation does not affect what is observed. This view of the relation between perception and the world is probably adequate for dealing with the practical demands of everyday life; for if our senses were not generally reliable, we would probably not have survived as a species.

Nevertheless, in what follows I shall argue that there is more to perception than meets the eye, and that it is a more active process than common-sense realism allows. Rather than our senses passively reflecting an independent reality, our experience of the world is affected not only by what is 'out there', but also by the structure of our sense organs and our minds.

Perceptual illusions

Despite the ease with which we perceive the world, perception is a complex process in which many things are going on 'under the bonnet' of conscious awareness. Simplifying somewhat, I think it can usefully be thought of as consisting of two distinct elements:

- *sensation*, which is provided by the world, and
- *interpretation*, which is provided by our minds.

In everyday life, we are not usually aware of our minds interpreting the sensations that flood into our senses, and we simply experience the familiar world of tables and chairs and cats and dogs and family and friends. A good way of becoming explicitly aware of such interpretations is to look at some visual illusions. In what follows we will look at four kinds of visual illusion, all of which arise not from sensations as such, but from the interpretation we put on them.

Figure 4.1

Context

The way we see something depends partly on the context in which we see it. Look at the three men in Figure 4.1. While the figure on the right looks a lot bigger than the figure on the left, the reality is that they are both the same size. How can we explain this illusion? Well, it has something to do with perspective. Relative to the background, the man on the left is small and the man on the right is big.

In everyday life, we are constantly making such contextual judgements without being consciously aware of it. If you look at Figure 4.2 and focus on the figure on the left and the figure in the middle, they appear to be two normal-sized people, one some distance away and the other in the foreground. However, the two-dimensional 'reality' is that the figure originally on the left is much smaller than the one in the middle – as can be clearly seen when it is moved to the right of the picture.

What both of the above illusions illustrate is that we usually judge the size of an object by looking at the overall context.

Figure 4.2

Figure and ground

When we look at something, we tend to highlight certain aspects of what we see ('figure'), and treat other parts of it as background ('ground'). For example, when you look at a page of writing, the black parts stand out and you pay no attention to the white background. Sometimes we can make different aspects of what we see stand out as the figure. This is best illustrated by the well-known Rubin face/vase illusion. Figure 4.3 can be interpreted either as a beautiful symmetrical vase, or as two identical silhouettes looking at one another.

Figure 4.3

There are many examples of ambiguous figures which rely on the figure–ground phenomenon. If you try slightly blurring your vision, you should be able to find two different interpretations of each of the pictures below.

Figure 4.4 Young man–old man

Figure 4.5 Young woman–old woman

Visual grouping

We have a natural tendency to look for meaning in what we see and to group our perceptual experiences together into shapes and patterns. If you look at Figure 4.6, you have no difficulty in seeing a dog. What is striking is how little information is actually given to us – just a few patches of black. But our minds have no difficulty in filling in the missing parts to create a meaningful picture.

In some cases, however, it can be more difficult to find any meaning in what we see. The first time people see Figure 4.7 they are usually unable to make any sense of it. (If you want to know what this is, look at page 102).

Figure 4.6

Figure 4.7

Expectations

Our expectations can also influence how we see things. For example, in a well-known experiment, people were asked to identify playing cards that were briefly flashed before them. However, irregular cards, such as a red six of Spades or a black nine of Diamonds were included in the pack. When people saw an irregular card, most of them misperceived it in accordance with their expectations. For example, the red six of Spades was seen as either a regular six of Diamonds or a regular six of Spades.

You might think *you* would not make such a mistake, but look at Figure 4.8 and read the message contained in it.

If you have not seen this before, you probably read 'Paris in the spring', but it actually says 'Paris in the *the* spring'. When you look again you may think to yourself 'How could I have missed that second "the"?' The reason, of course, is that, since you did not expect to see two 'the's in a row, your mind simply blanked out one of them. If you think how difficult it is to spot your own typing errors, then you can see that this kind of perceptual error is far from uncommon.

While we can experience many other kinds of illusion, the examples of the role played by context, figure–ground, visual grouping and expectations should be enough to convince you that there is an important element of interpretation built into our perception of the world.

Figure 4.8

The role of the unconscious

According to psychologists, many of the interpretations we routinely make about the world happen at an unconscious level. When you look at something what actually appears on your retina are two small inverted two-dimensional images. Yet, without any conscious effort on your part, you see one life-size right-way-up three-dimensional world.

In an interesting psychology experiment, which illustrates the power of unconscious interpretation, subjects were asked to put on spectacles which inverted their image of the world. For the first few days they were completely disoriented and saw everything as being upside down. But, interestingly, their brains soon flipped the images round so that they saw the world the right way up again. When the spectacles were removed at the end of the experiment they again experienced everything as upside down for a while until their vision returned to normal.

In fact, we are constantly making all kinds of unconscious inferences about what we experience. For example, your image in the bathroom mirror is actually about half the size of your head; but when you stumble out of bed in the morning and look at yourself in the mirror, you never have the impression that your head has shrunk in the night. It always *looks* the right size. Similarly, if someone walks towards you from the other end of a corridor, the image on your retina steadily expands, but you do not see them as slowly inflating like a balloon. As far as you are concerned, they remain the same size.

More generally, although vision is simply a matter of light of various wavelengths falling on your retina, you do not experience the world as so many blobs of colour. You never, for example, have to think to yourself 'Ah, those patches of colour over there must be a desk, and these patches must be someone's face.' You just see the world of familiar everyday objects. Sadly, however, some people who have suffered brain damage experience a condition known as **visual agnosia** in which they lose the ability to interpret what they see. To find out more about this condition, read the reading resource on pages 108–110.

Selectivity of perception

Apart from visual illusions, another reason for being cautious about what our senses tell us is that perception is *selective*. A vast amount of data is constantly flooding in to our senses, and our minds would overload if we were consciously aware of everything. So we only notice some things in our perceptual field and overlook others. The selectivity of perception can be seen as a generalisation of the figure–ground phenomenon mentioned above. Certain aspects of a situation engage our attention and 'stand out', and the rest fade away into a more or less indeterminate background. For example, if we are having a conversation at school, I may notice your facial expression, yet have no conscious awareness of the picture on the wall behind you; or I may hear what you are saying, yet be oblivious to the ticking of the clock, or the quiet hum of the computer. While the light reflected from the picture affects my eyes, and the air vibrations caused by the clock and the computer hit my ears, my conscious mind treats these things as the background against which what I am interested in stands out.

If we ask what kind of stimuli we usually notice, intensity and contrast are two important factors. The ticking clock may sometimes go unheard, but you would hear if a bomb exploded in the building next door. Drop a small object on a patterned carpet and it can sometimes be hard to find again; but a tiny drop of blood on a white carpet will be immediately apparent. For good evolutionary reasons, we are also sensitive to moving objects. If you work at a desk by a window, your attention may suddenly be caught by something which makes you look up without quite knowing why – only to realise a second later that there is a distant bird passing over the trees. Since it may be moving towards you, such an object represents a potential threat and you therefore notice it.

What you see also depends on various subjective factors such as interest and mood. Your interests can be thought of as filters which determine what shows up as you scan the world around you. If three friends go for a walk in the countryside, one may focus mainly on nature and the variety of the wildlife; a second may attend to what his friends are wearing and talking about; and a third may notice very little because her mind is on something else. The following question, which I owe to an anonymous colleague, shows how our perspective on something affects the way we see it.

Activity 4.5

Take one of the following phenomena and describe how it might be seen through the eyes of the following people:
a A child dying in poverty as seen by a doctor, an economist, a social worker, the child's father.
b A sunset as seen by a religious figure, a physicist, a painter, a farmer.
c A tree as seen by a biologist, a logger, an environmentalist, a native American.

As the pattern of our interests changes, so does what we perceive. It is striking that if your family buys a new car you will probably start seeing cars of the same model and colour everywhere. Similarly, if a woman becomes pregnant, she begins noticing pregnant women wherever she goes.

Our feelings and emotions also shape and colour our perceptions, and when you are in a good mood you see the world in quite a different way to when you are in a bad mood. While an optimist sees a glass as half-full, a pessimist sees the same glass as half-empty. An emotion such as love can have a particularly strong effect on our perception. When you fall in love with someone you may unconsciously project your dreams and fantasies onto them so that they seem to possess every imaginable perfection. If you later fall out of love, you may look at your 'ex' and wonder what you ever saw in them. Perhaps not surprisingly, it has been said that at the beginning of a relationship you tend to notice the things you have in common with someone, and at the end of a relationship you tend to notice the things that make you different. Our perception can also be distorted by fear. If you are alone on a dark and stormy night you may be frightened by sounds that you wouldn't normally notice. As a Persian proverb has it, 'He who has been bitten by a snake fears a piece of string.'

1 Take one of the following and explain how education and training can affect what we perceive:
   a A biologist looking down a microscope
   b A dentist looking at an X-ray
   c A professional wine taster
   d A lifeguard
   e An artist
2 To what extent do you think that the culture you come from affects the way in which you see the world?
3 In what emotional state do you think we see the world with the greatest clarity and objectivity?

Seeing and believing

At the start of this chapter, I quoted the saying that 'seeing is believing' but, since our beliefs and expectations can affect the way we see things, it might sometimes be more accurate to say that 'believing is seeing'. Here are three examples from different subject areas of the way in which our beliefs can affect our perception.

- *Science.* In the nineteenth century some scientists speculated that an undiscovered planet – which they christened Vulcan – existed between Mercury and the sun. With this belief in mind, some astronomers claimed to have seen Vulcan through their telescopes. But it turned out that no such planet exists.

- *History.* 'Bloody Sunday' is an infamous day in the history of Northern Ireland. On 30 January 1972 there was a violent confrontation between British troops and Catholic demonstrators which left thirteen Catholics dead. According to the British soldiers, they came under attack from terrorist elements and returned fire. But Catholic witnesses said the army opened fire on a peaceful demonstration without provocation. Perhaps one of the two sides was lying; but it is equally possible that, as a result of the 'fog of battle', each side genuinely believed its own version of events.

- *Art.* In the visual arts, people have a tendency to draw and paint, not what they see, but what they think is there. For example, in antiquity some artists portrayed horses with eyelashes on the upper and lower lids of their eyes even though horses in fact have eyelashes only on their upper lids.

We are all very good at seeing only what we want to see. Can you give some examples of the way in which our beliefs affect the way we see things?

Eye-witness testimony

The fallibility of perception not only is of theoretical interest but also has important implications in the real world. In criminal trials, juries tend to put a great deal of faith in eye-witness testimony, and such evidence can determine whether or not a person is found guilty. However, according to psychologists the uncorroborated evidence of a single witness should be treated with great caution. In recent years, a number of cases have come to light of people convicted of crimes on the basis of eye-witness accounts that subsequent DNA testing showed they could not have committed. To see just how unreliable eye-witnesses can be, read the article called 'Blind to change' in the reading resources at the end of this chapter.

What emerges from recent research is that the eye is not a camera and visual memories are not photographs that can be universally relied on to give an accurate record of what we have seen. In fact, it might be more accurate to say that every time we remember something, we *reconstruct* it.

Furthermore, it is easy to confuse the *source* of your memories. For example, if you think back to your childhood, you may be unsure whether some of your memories are really memories of the events in question, or whether your parents have told you some stories so many times that you *think* you remember them. Similar confusions can undermine the reliability of eye-witness evidence. Studies have shown that witnesses who have previously been shown mugshots of possible suspects are more likely to pick one of these people out in an identity parade than witnesses who have been shown nothing beforehand.

Activity 4.8

Imagine you witness a violent crime and get a brief but clear glimpse of the assailant. What confidence would you have that you could correctly identify one of the following three men?

Figure 4.9 Suspects

Distinguishing appearance from reality

Although perception is an important source of knowledge, our discussion has shown that there are at least three reasons for treating it with caution:

1 we may misinterpret what we see
2 we may fail to notice something
3 we may misremember what we have seen.

However, we must not get carried away with sceptical doubts and conclude that we can *never* trust our senses. After all, we take some things to be illusions only relative to other things that we assume to be true. For example, I can say that the three men in Figure 4.1 are *really* the same height only because I trust my senses when I measure them. If I were uniformly suspicious, I could not even trust the evidence which tells me that some of my perceptions are illusions.

How, then, do we distinguish between appearance and reality in everyday life?

Confirmation by another sense

One way to distinguish appearance from reality is to use a second sense to confirm the evidence of a first. If something looks like an apple and tastes like an apple, then it seems reasonable to conclude that it really *is* an apple. If, on the other hand, there is a conflict between two of our senses, then we may suspect that we are experiencing an illusion. For example, if a pencil is half-immersed in a beaker of water it appears bent to the eye, but if you run your hand along it you can feel that it is straight. So you are likely to conclude that the pencil is not *really* bent but merely *looks* bent.

If you want to be awkward, you might ask why in this example we have privileged our sense of touch over that of sight. Why not say instead that when I half-immerse a pencil in water, it bends, but I suffer a peculiar tactile illusion that makes me think it is still straight? The answer is that, as a matter of brute fact, touch takes priority in determining the reality of something. If you are unsure whether the wall in front of you is real or an illusion, try banging your head against it. If you think that you may be hallucinating the fire in the hearth, try putting your hand in it. For common sense at least, pain is proof enough of the reality of an object. In short, if it hurts then it is real.

Coherence

A second way of distinguishing appearance from reality is in terms of coherence. If you see something that does not 'fit in' with your overall experience of the world, then the chances are that you are mistaken. If a drunk sees a pig flying over the rooftops one evening, he is unlikely to believe what he saw when he is sober again. Since pigs lack the aerodynamic wherewithal to fly, it makes more sense to dismiss a flying pig as an alcohol-induced hallucination.

Coherence also explains why in the pencil example it makes more sense to say that we suffer a visual rather than a tactile illusion. The point is that, while the hypothesis that objects bend every time you half-immerse them in water contradicts the known laws of physics, we can explain why they appear to bend in terms of physical theories about the refraction of light.

Independent testimony

A final criterion for distinguishing appearance from reality is the testimony of other people. We saw above that the evidence of a single eye-witness cannot always be taken at face value; but the credibility of such evidence is greatly increased if it is confirmed by other people. If dozens of independent witnesses claim to have seen a plane crash into a building, then, unless you are in the grip of a conspiracy theory, there is a high – 'beyond reasonable doubt' – probability that such testimony is true.

To summarise our discussion, we can say that, while our senses are liable to error, we are in many cases able to correct our mistakes by appealing to such things as a second sense, coherence and the testimony of other people. Of course, we can never be certain that we are right but, as we saw in Chapter 2, knowledge requires something less than certainty. Perception may be fallible, but in many cases it is a reliable enough foundation on which to base our knowledge claims.

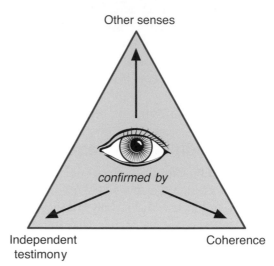

Figure 4.10 Checking evidence

Ultimate reality

The final topic we need to look at in this chapter is a philosophical one concerning the extent to which perception gives us knowledge of ultimate reality. Since this is quite an abstract topic, let us begin by saying something more about the psychology of perception.

Psychology of perception

While our five senses give us valuable information about the world, they each have a limited range of sensitivity, and capture only certain kinds of data in their net. For example, our eyes are sensitive only to light of a certain wavelength, and we are unable to see such things as ultraviolet and infrared which lie beyond the visible spectrum. Similarly, our ears can detect only certain kinds of sound and our noses only certain kinds of smell; and dogs can hear and smell things that we are completely unaware of. Some animals even have senses that are completely different from our own. For example, bats navigate by a system of echo-location, which gives them what might be called 'acoustic vision'. They emit high-frequency sounds and are then able to determine the shape, size and distance of surrounding objects by the echo that is reflected back to their ears.

"And only you can hear this whistle?"

Figure 4.11

With the above points in mind, imagine if we had evolved so that our eyes were sensitive to light in a different range of wavelengths, or that we used echo-location rather than vision. Our experience of the world would presumably be very different from what it is now. This may lead us to wonder what reality is like once we strip away the interpretation that our sense-organs impose on it.

What is really out there?

To explore the question of what is really 'out there', let us consider the following three examples.

1 Pain, taste and colour

If by accident you burn your hand in a fire, you think of the resulting pain as being in your hand rather than in the fire. You do not think that the pain is somehow in the fire independent of your experience of it. The pain that you feel is surely nothing more than the subjective experience that results from the interaction between your hand and the fire.

Take another example: if you drink a can of cola it tastes sweet. Does the sweetness exist in the cola, or does it exist only in your mouth? Well, again, you would probably agree that the sweetness is simply a subjective experience that results from the interaction between your taste buds and the cola.

Activity 4.9

Galileo (1564–1642) once said 'The tickle is not in the feather.' Explain what you think he meant by this. What relevance does it have to our discussion?

While you may be happy with the idea that pain and taste are merely subjective experiences, you probably feel less comfortable with this way of thinking when it comes to such things as colours. Surely the sky is blue and snow is white and grass is green? Well, for *us* all of these things are of course true. But if we apply the same reasoning that we used in the cola example, we seem forced to admit that the green is no more in the grass than the sweetness is in the cola or the pain is in the fire. The green that you see when you look at the grass is, once again, simply the result of the interaction between your eyes and the underlying structure of the grass. And if our eyes had evolved differently and were sensitive to light of a different wavelength we would not see grass as green at all. We seem to be pushed towards the unsettling conclusion that the world in itself has no colour at all – reality is colourless.

2 The tree in the forest

Consider the well-known question 'If a tree falls in a forest and there is no one there to hear it, does it make a sound?' The common-sense answer is to say that of course it makes a sound. Falling trees are noisy things. You may conjure up in your mind a picture of a huge tree falling and the tremendous crash it makes as it falls to the ground. But if you think that sound is nothing more than the effect of air vibrations on our ears, then it would seem to follow that if there are no ears in the neighbourhood, then the tree does not make a sound.

One way of trying to resolve the above puzzle is to make a distinction between two senses of the word 'sound'. Sound$_1$, we might say, is *physical* sound – i.e. the vibrations in the air that are caused by things like falling trees. Sound$_2$, by contrast, is *experienced* sound – the actual crash, bang, wallop that we hear when trees hit the ground. We can now say that if a tree falls in a forest and there is no one there to hear it, there is sound$_1$ but no sound$_2$.

This solves the problem, but it may leave you with a somewhat eerie feeling. For it means that, if the phone goes after everyone has left my apartment in the morning, there may be vibrations in the air, but there is no distinctive 'ring-ring' sound. The most we can say is that if I were in my apartment then I would hear the phone ring. More dramatically, this way of thinking means that, millions of years ago before the emergence of life on Earth, our planet was a silent place. Breaking waves and storms and volcanoes set up vibrations in the air, but there were no crashes or bangs or wallops. And if right now we were to surgically remove the ears from all sentient beings, the world would again revert to silence.

Now consider another question: if a rose flowers and dies in an uninhabited garden and there is no one there to see it, does it have a colour? We might again distinguish between physical and experienced colour, and say that in the former sense it has a colour, and in the latter sense it does not. This seems to lead us to the conclusion that, before there were any eyes in the world, the sky was not blue, and the roses were not red, and the grass was not green – at least not in the experiential sense of these words.

The examples we have considered above suggest that we cannot say that colours, sounds and tastes exist out there independent of our experience of them. So we may begin to wonder whether *anything* can be said to exist independent of our experience of it.

3 The tables in the classroom

As a final example, consider the tables in your classroom at school. After you leave the room at the end of the day, how do you know the tables are still there? If you had nothing better to do, you could sneak back to school in the evening and take a look. I am confident that you would find the tables quietly sitting there just as you left them. But how do you know the tables are still there when no one is looking at them? (This is similar to the child's question: 'How do you know the light goes out when you close the fridge door?')

This may sound like a stupid question, and common sense will of course say that unobserved tables look much the same as observed tables. But how do you *know*? Perhaps tables only behave like decent, law-abiding tables when we are there to keep an eye on them; and perhaps when no one is around they dance around the room and turn somersaults.

You might think that there is a conclusive way to put an end to such surreal speculations. All you have to do is set up a video camera in the classroom, switch it on before you go home for the evening, and leave it running overnight. You will produce the most boring movie ever made: *Tables! The Motion Picture* – a movie in which absolutely nothing happens. This surely proves that unobserved tables behave in the same way as tables that are observed. But in fact your use of the video has not solved the problem, but merely relocated it. For the question now arises: 'How do you know that the images stay on the film when you are not watching it?'

This discussion may confirm your suspicion that philosophers spend their time asking useless questions that have no practical value. Surely life is too short to worry about what tables do when there is no one around to see them? Who really cares? Although we may be unable to *prove* that tables behave in standard table-like ways when we are not around, perhaps all that really matters is that they behave like tables when we are around. Perhaps we should conclude that what tables do in their spare time is no concern of ours.

Theories of reality

There are three different theories about the relationship between perception and reality: (1) common-sense realism; (2) scientific realism; (3) phenomenalism.

1 Common-sense realism

This is the common-sense idea, mentioned at the beginning of this chapter, that the way we perceive the world mirrors the way the world is. However, since what we perceive is determined in part by the nature of our sense-organs, we have seen that there are good reasons for rejecting common-sense realism.

Activity 4.10

In your own words, outline the main arguments against common-sense realism.

---

2 Scientific realism

According to scientific realism, the world exists as an independent reality, but it is very different from the way we perceive it. The physicist Sir Arthur Eddington (1882–1944) once compared the common-sense description of a table with the scientific description of it. According to common sense, a table has extension and colour, and is comparatively permanent and substantial. But the scientific table is quite different:

> It does not belong to the world previously mentioned – that world which spontaneously appears around me when I open my eyes... My scientific table is mostly emptiness. Sparsely scattered in that emptiness are numerous electric charges rushing about with great speed; but their combined bulk amounts to less than a billionth of the bulk of the table itself. Notwithstanding its strange construction it turns out to be an entirely efficient table. It supports my writing paper as satisfactorily as [an ordinary table] for when I lay the paper on it the little electric particles with their headlong speed keep on hitting the underside, so that the paper is maintained in shuttlecock fashion at a nearly steady level. If I lean upon this table I shall not go through; or, to be strictly accurate, the chance of my scientific elbow going through my scientific table is so excessively small that it can be neglected in practical life.

> [*The Nature of the Physical World*, London: Dent, 1935]

This brief description draws attention to the strangeness of the scientific picture of reality. The familiar, comfortable, sensuous world of our everyday experience vanishes and is replaced by a colourless, soundless, odourless realm of atoms whizzing around in empty space.

3 Phenomenalism

At the beginning of this chapter, I mentioned a philosophical position known as empiricism according to which all knowledge must ultimately be based on experience. If we take this idea seriously, then we seem to arrive at a more radical position known as phenomenalism. According to this view, *matter is simply 'the permanent possibility of sensation'*, and it makes no sense to say that the world exists independent of our experience of it. A phenomenalist would take the statement 'There are tables in the classroom at school' to mean not that the tables are in some deep sense there but simply that if you go to the classroom you will have various table-experiences. The Irish philosopher George Berkeley (1685–1753) summed up the phenomenalist position with the famous slogan 'To be is to be perceived.'

Despite its counter-intuitive nature, phenomenalism seems to follow logically from the idea that all knowledge must ultimately be based on experience. For, if this is true, then we obviously cannot know what the world is like independent of our experience of it. This does not mean that the world does *not* exist independent of our experience of it – for that, too, is to make a claim that goes beyond the limits of experience. The point is rather that, beyond our experience of reality, there is simply nothing to be said. Understood in this way, phenomenalism could be seen as a call to humility; for it insists that we can only know the world from our distinctively human perspective and have no right to pontificate about the nature of ultimate reality.

1 If you believed in phenomenalism, what difference, if any, would it make to practical life?
2 Does it bother you to think that we cannot know anything about what the universe is like independent of our experience of it?

What should we believe?

The three theories of reality we have discussed can be summarised in the following three slogans.

Common-sense realism	'What you see is what is there'
Scientific realism	'Atoms in the void'
Phenomenalism	'To be is to be perceived'

One interesting thing that comes out of our somewhat surreal discussion about the nature of ultimate reality is that if you push empiricism to its limits you end up with counter-intuitive conclusions. At this point you have a choice. You can either stick with empiricism and insist that we can know nothing about ultimate reality, or reject strict empiricism and insist that there is a world out there independent of our experience of it.

I suspect that deep down most people are realists about the existence of the world. Despite the doubts we have raised about realism, there are perhaps two ways of trying to rescue it:

1 Although you cannot prove the existence of an independently existing reality, you might argue that it is the most reasonable hypothesis to account for the regularity of our experience. If, for example, you light a fire and return some hours later to find only a pile of ashes, the simplest way to explain what happened is to say that the fire was burning continuously in your absence.

2 The vast majority of people have a strong intuition that the world exists independent of our perception of it. As our discussion of scientific realism has shown, it may be very different from our everyday picture of it, but most scientists are intuitive realists and believe that they are making discoveries about an independently existing reality.

Conclusion

We began this chapter by stressing that perception is an important way of knowing which plays a key role in most areas of knowledge. However, as our discussion has progressed we have seen that there is more to perception than meets the eye, and that we cannot simply take the evidence of our senses for granted. For not only do they sometimes deceive us, but they are also selective and can be distorted by our beliefs and prejudices. In everyday life, there are ways of distinguishing between appearance and reality, and moving towards a more accurate picture of the world. We can, for example, use a second sense to check up on a first, or appeal to the testimony of other people.

"Don't you understand? This is <u>life</u>, this is what is happening. We <u>can't</u> switch to another channel."

Figure 4.12

At a practical level, you would be mad to simply ignore the evidence of your senses. If you want to survive when you cross the road, it pays to go with the hypothesis that if something looks and sounds like a 20 tonne truck speeding towards you then it really is a 20 tonne truck. As a general rule of thumb, it probably makes sense to doubt our senses only if there are good reasons for doing so. Admittedly, perception cannot give us certainty but, as we saw in Chapter 2, knowledge requires something less than certainty. If the perceptual evidence is consistent with other ways of knowing, such as reason and intuition, then it is probably a good enough foundation for reliable knowledge.

Figure 4.13 Face: the image of Figure 4.7, clarified

- Our five senses are an important source of knowledge about the world; but rather than passively reflect reality, they actively structure it.
- Perception consists of two elements, sensation and interpretation, but we are often not consciously aware of the latter element.
- Looking at visual illusions can help make us aware of the role that interpretation plays in perception.
- Perception is selective and what we notice in a given environment is influenced by factors such as intensity, contrast, interest, mood and expectations.
- The fallibility of perception is relevant to issues in the real world such as eye-witness testimony in criminal trials.
- We usually distinguish between appearance and reality by using a second sense to confirm the evidence of the first, or by appealing to coherence or the testimony of other people.
- The way we experience the world is partly determined by the structure of our sense-organs.
- If we accept that pain and taste are subjective, we might conclude that colour and sound are also subjective.
- There are three main theories about the relationship between perception and reality: common-sense realism, scientific realism and phenomenalism.
- Despite sceptical doubts, the existence of the external world is the most reasonable hypothesis to account for the regularity of our experience.
- Although perception cannot give us certainty, if the evidence of our senses is consistent with what reason and intuition tell us, it can still provide a good foundation for reliable knowledge.

Terms to remember

common-sense realism	phenomenalism	visual agnosia
empiricism	scientific realism	visual grouping
figure and ground	sensation	

Further reading

Diane Ackerman, *A Natural History of the Senses* (Vintage, 1995). In this book, Diane Ackerman takes us on a rich journey through each of the five senses. She skilfully weaves insights from the sciences, arts and personal experience into a fascinating synthesis.

V. S. Ramachandran, *Phantoms in the Brain* (Quill, 1999), Chapter 4: 'The Zombie in the Brain'. V. S. Ramachandran is a neuroscientist who has studied brain-damaged patients. In this chapter he focuses on a strange condition known as 'blindsight' to analyse and speculate about the nature of perception.

Linking questions

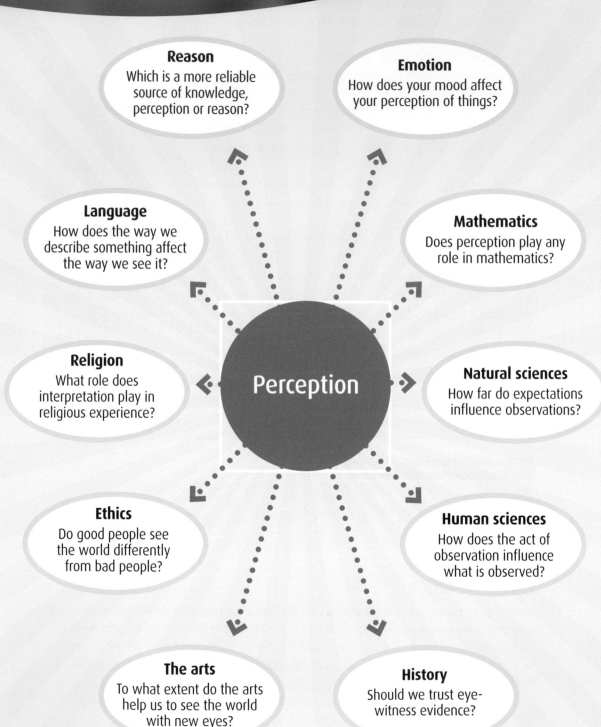

Reason
Which is a more reliable source of knowledge, perception or reason?

Emotion
How does your mood affect your perception of things?

Language
How does the way we describe something affect the way we see it?

Mathematics
Does perception play any role in mathematics?

Religion
What role does interpretation play in religious experience?

Perception

Natural sciences
How far do expectations influence observations?

Ethics
Do good people see the world differently from bad people?

Human sciences
How does the act of observation influence what is observed?

The arts
To what extent do the arts help us to see the world with new eyes?

History
Should we trust eye-witness evidence?

BLIND TO CHANGE

New Scientist, 18 November 2000

We all suffer from selective attention and sometimes fail to notice things that are in front of us. The article below suggests that such selective attention may be more common and more far-reaching than you might think.

How much of the world around you do you really see? You only take in a tiny piece of information at a time and that can have unnerving consequences, says Laura Spinney.

Picture the following, and prepare to be amazed. You're walking across a college campus when a stranger asks you for directions. While you're talking to him, two men pass between you carrying a wooden door. You feel a moment's irritation, but they move on and you carry on describing the route. When you've finished, the stranger informs you that you've just taken part in a psychology experiment. 'Did you notice anything change after the two men passed with the door?' he asks. 'No,' you reply uneasily. He then explains that the man who initially approached you walked off behind the door, leaving him in his place. The first man now comes up to join you. Looking at them standing side by side, you notice that the two are of different height and build, are dressed differently, have different haircuts and different voices.

It sounds impossible, but when Daniel Simons, a psychologist at Harvard University, and his colleague Daniel Levin of Kent State University in Ohio actually did this experiment, they found that fully 50 per cent of those who took part failed to notice the substitution. The subjects had succumbed to what is called change blindness. Taken with a glut of recent experimental results, this phenomenon suggests we see far less than we think we do.

Rather than logging every detail of the visual scene, says Simons, we are actually highly selective about what we take in. Our impression of seeing everything is just that – an impression. In fact we extract a few details and rely on memory, or perhaps even our imagination, for the rest. Others have a more radical interpretation: they say that we see nothing at all, and our belief that we have only to open our eyes to take in the entire visible world is mistaken – an illusion.

Until the last decade, vision researchers thought that seeing really meant making pictures in the brain. By building detailed internal representations of the world, and comparing them over time, we would be able to pick out anything that changed. Then in 1991, in his book *Consciousness Explained*, the philosopher Daniel Dennett made the then controversial claim that our brains hold only a few salient details about the world – and that this is the reason we are able to function at all.

We don't store elaborate pictures in short-term memory, Dennett said, because it isn't necessary and would take up valuable computing power. Rather, we log what has changed and assume the rest has stayed the same. Of course, this is bound to mean that we miss a few details. Experimenters had already shown that we may ignore items in the visual field if they appear not to be significant – a repeated word or line on a page of text, for instance. But nobody, not even Dennett, realised quite how little we really do 'see'.

Just a year later, at a conference on perception in Vancouver, British Columbia, John Grimes of the University of Illinois caused a stir when he described how people shown computer-generated pictures of natural scenes were blind to changes that were made during an eye movement. Dennett was delighted. 'I wish in retrospect that I'd been more daring, since the effects are stronger than I claimed,' he says.

Since then, more and more examples have been found that show just how illusory our visual world is. It turns out that your eyes don't need to be moving to be fooled. In a typical lab demonstration, you might be shown a picture on a computer screen of, say, a couple dining on a terrace. The picture would disappear, to be replaced for a fraction of a second by a blank screen, before reappearing significantly altered – by the raising of a railing behind the couple, perhaps. The picture flickers back and forth, and many people search the screen for up to a minute before they see the change. A few never spot it.

It's an unnerving experience. But to some extent 'change blindness' is artificial because the change is masked in some way. In real life, there tends to be a visible movement that signals the change. But not always. As Simons points out, 'We have all had the

experience of not noticing a traffic signal change because we had briefly looked away.' And there's a related phenomenon called inattentional blindness, that doesn't need any visual trick at all: if you are not paying attention to some feature of a scene, you won't see it.

Last year, with Christopher Chabris, also at Harvard, Simons showed people a videotape of a basketball game and asked them to count the passes made by one or other team. After about 45 seconds, a man dressed in a gorilla suit walked slowly across the scene, passing between the players. Although he was visible for five seconds, 40 per cent of the viewers failed to notice him. When the tape was played again, and they were asked simply to watch it, they saw him easily. Not surprisingly, some found it hard to believe it was the same tape.

Now imagine that the task absorbing their attention had been driving a car, and the gorilla-man had been a pedestrian crossing their path. According to some estimates, nearly half of all fatal motor-vehicle accidents in the US can be attributed to driver error, including lapses in attention. It is more than just academic interest that has made both forms of cognitive error hot research topics.

Such errors raise important questions about vision. For instance, how can we reconcile these gross lapses with our subjective experience of having continuous access to a rich visual scene? Last year, Stephen Kosslyn of Harvard University showed that imagining a scene activates parts of the visual cortex in the same way as seeing it. He says that this supports the idea that we take in just what information we consider important at the time, and fill in the gaps where the details are less important. 'The illusion that we see "everything" is partly a result of filling in the gaps using memory,' he says. 'Such memories can be created based on beliefs and expectations.'...

In the Simons-Levin experiment... even the object to which the person is attending – the stranger asking for directions – can be swapped without them noticing. Despite the fact that they were looking at him for around a minute, half the subjects encoded none of the details of his physical appearance that were later to change. It was not relevant that the stranger had a certain haircut or that his trousers were a certain colour. What was relevant was that he was a person in a certain location addressing them with a certain query. 'Paying attention to an object does not give you all of that object's properties for free,' says Simons. He points out that those who did notice the switch were students of about the same age as the 'strangers'. Being in the same social group, he and Levin speculated, they would be more inclined to take in individual details, whereas older subjects might categorise the stranger as 'student' and leave it at that.

The relationships between attention, awareness and vision have yet to be clarified. But there is one thing on which most researchers agree: because we have a less than complete picture of the world at any one time, there is the potential for distortion and error. And that has all sorts of implications, not least for eyewitnesses. If it is possible to stand less than a metre from a person and talk to them for a minute without taking in more than a few basic facts, how reliable is the testimony of a person who witnesses a scene from a distance, when they were oblivious to its significance and only later came to recall it?

'In my view, imagery plays a key role in many sorts of false memories,' says Kosslyn. 'One is "filling in" the gaps and later remembering not only what was attended to, but also what was filled in.' In retrospect, he says, we don't make any distinction between the two types of information.

For all our experience of a rich visual world, it seems that we take in no more than a handful of facts about the world, throw in a few stored images and beliefs, and produce a convincing whole in which it is impossible to tell what was real and what imagined. As Blackmore puts it: 'There is a world and a brain in it, which together are building a construction, a story, a great confabulation.'

A WORLD WITHOUT PATTERNS, FACES WITHOUT MEANING

This article by Hilary Lawson explores a disturbing state known as visual agnosia, which sheds light on the nature of perception.

It is a condition which has already been publicised in the book 'The Man who Mistook his Wife for a Hat'. The name for it is visual agnosia – an inability to recognise anything or distinguish perfectly ordinary objects. But what does that mean for the sufferers, and what can it tell us about 'normal' perceptions of the world?

John can't recognise himself in the mirror: 'I can see my face quite happily, I can see my ears and earlobes, I can see my lips moving as I speak to you... obviously I can see my glasses and my eyes behind them, but if you were to ask me who it is, I still wouldn't know.' He does not recognise his wife either, or his children or grandchildren. He is hopelessly lost a few yards from his own home. Yet he is highly intelligent and can see detail as well as the rest of us.

There is a name for John's condition: visual agnosia. But the name tells us little – like many medical categories, it merely describes what we already knew, in this case that John is unable to make sense of what he sees. The obvious question is, why? An answer would not only explain John's condition but would also throw light on the nature of perception, and possibly even the origin of consciousness.

During the war John was in the RAF, and until six years ago he and his wife, Iris, had a successful, typical middle-class lifestyle. John was the European manager of a thriving American company. But following a routine appendix operation all this changed. When John came round from the anaesthetic, he awoke to find himself in a strange and unknown place: an *Alice in Wonderland* world of alternatives, of myriad patterns each with a multitude of possible meanings. He could not distinguish between shadow and object, a person and a picture. He was unable to recognise anything around him. Not only did he not recognise Iris when she came to visit, but he failed to recognise her from one minute to the next. He could not even find his bed again once he had got out of it.

At first it was thought that he would improve and that these were temporary reactions. Doctors assured Iris that when she took him home, all would click into place. But when he did go home he did not recognise the street he lived in, his own house or even his own sitting-room. Standing outside the house he had lived in for twenty years, he could see the line of the roof against the sky, the frame of what he assumed to be the windows, the shape of the handle on the front door. But he had no idea whether this was his home or not. He had slipped into a world in which any single thing might turn out to be something else. Without certainty, John was left with fearful expectation:

'At that time, I didn't know, perhaps she had ideas of taking me to a loony-bin. As far as I was concerned we were going into completely unknown territory. Nothing made any sense. I was wildly suspicious of where she was taking me and what skulduggery she was up to to get rid of me for life.'

Gradually he was able to work out what objects were, so long as they were not in an unusual place and so long as they had some particular, distinguishing characteristic. He would do this not by seeing them as something, but by deducing what they were likely to be. John would know, for example, that he was in the sitting-room by what everyone was doing: it would be obvious from what they were saying. As a result, he would guess correctly that the large, flat object in front of him was likely to be the coffee-table. Similarly, in the dining-room, if the table were laid, he would be able to find the knives and forks. He would know that the fork had three or four prongs and would look for a shape that had a number of elongated points attached to a longer rod.

When you meet him, he appears quite normal and is entertaining in conversation, but unless he recognises your voice or you tell him who you are, he will probably never recognise you again. He will remember meeting you and what you discussed, but after the meeting he would have no hope of finding his way home on his own. John is as lost in his world as we might be in the depths of a rain forest.

How are we to explain John's difficulties? He is clearly not blind – he occasionally brings Iris tiny bits of fluff or dirt that he has found on the carpet, thinking that these might be something important. He does, however, have one problem with his sight: he has lost his colour vision. This, though, is no explanation of his condition, for we can all recognise black-and-white photographs perfectly well. Another obvious explanation would be that he has lost his memory – but he can remember his past perfectly well. He can describe what his house looks like: he simply can't recognise it when he is there. You might imagine that he had a problem with language, that he had forgotten what to call things, but he can easily give accurate dictionary definitions of objects that he fails to recognise.

John lives in a world of detail, of lines and shapes, but these lines and shapes are without order, without structure. John cannot make sense of what he sees because he is unable to impose order on his visual world – an order which we all need to impose to enable us to have experience at all. Although we think we see the world as it really is, we live in a world of our own making.

To see things, we have first to structure our sensations and give them brightness and orientation so that we can form lines and shapes. John's psychologists, Glynn Humphries and Jane Riddoch, believe that John's problem stems from damage at a fairly early state in the structuring and interpreting process. They argue that John can see detail but he is unable to put this detail together to form a global outline. As a result, he is then unable to attach meaning to this outline, so he is unable to have visual experience of things. At present there are competing theories about the workings of the brain, some of which suggest that the stages of processing are consecutive and others that they work in parallel. In either case, experience appears to require the active imposition of structure and interpretation on elementary sensation. To this extent, every animal inhabits a different world, and the human world is a world that owes its construction to the physical make-up of the brain and the categories we choose to impose.

It was the 18th-century philosopher Immanuel Kant who first argued that experience was not merely the product of sensation but the result of combining sensation and interpretation. Cases of visual agnosia seem to imply that he was right. Like John, we must all give the world form and order – only, for most of us, this is done so immediately and so easily that we are not even aware it has taken place. Whether scientist or poet, journalist or politician, artist or priest, we all seek to impose an order, a pattern that will enable us to make sense of the world.

The basic patterns we impose, the distinctions between objects, between light and dark, hot and cold, good and bad, are the patterns that help us survive. Without them we would not only be helpless, we would have no world to be helpless in. John has to struggle to make that world, to impose categories that we take for granted. Similarly, John's psychologists provide structures and theories to make sense of his condition. So do we all try to give order to our lives.

We may have the illusion that these categories and theories are more than just human inventions, but it seems that's all they are.

5 Reason

'You are not thinking. You are merely
being logical.'
Niels Bohr, 1885–1962 to Albert Einstein

'Logic is the beginning of wisdom,
Valeris, not the end.'
Spock, *Star Trek*

'The head is always fooled by the heart.'
La Rochefoucauld, 1613–80

'Two extravagances: to exclude reason,
to admit only reason.'
Blaise Pascal, 1623–62

'We are never more true to ourselves
than when we are inconsistent.'
Oscar Wilde, 1854–1900

'All generalizations are false – including
this one.'
Henry David Thoreau, 1817–62

'Critical reason is the only alternative
to violence so far discovered.'
Karl Popper, 1902–94

'You do not reason a man out of
something he was not reasoned into.'
Jonathan Swift, 1667–1745

'Reason is itself a matter of faith.
It is an act of faith to assert that
our thoughts have any relation to
reality at all.'
G. K. Chesterton, 1874–1936

'Man has such a predilection for
systems and abstract deductions
that he is ready to distort the truth
intentionally, he is ready to deny the
evidence of his senses only to justify
his logic.'
Fyodor Dostoevsky, 1821–81

'He that will not reason is a bigot; he
that cannot reason is a fool; and he
that dares not reason is a slave.'
William Drummond, 1585–1649

'My aim is not to be consistent with
my previous statements on a given
question but to be consistent with the
truth as it may present itself to me at
a given moment.'
Mahatma Gandhi, 1869–1948

'The madman is not the man who has
lost his reason. The madman is the
man who has lost everything but
his reason.'
G. K. Chesterton, 1874–1936

'Logic n. The art of thinking and
reasoning in strict accordance with
the limitations and incapacities of the
human misunderstanding.'
Ambrose Bierce, 1842–1914

Introduction

According to Sherlock Holmes, that most English of fictional detectives, 'crime is common, logic is rare'. Holmes prided himself on having made the 'faculties of deduction and logical synthesis' his 'special province'. In one mystery concerning the theft of an expensive race horse, a police officer asks Holmes if any aspect of the crime strikes him as significant. 'Yes', he says, 'the curious incident of the dog in the night time'. 'The dog did nothing in the night time', says the hapless police officer. 'That was the curious incident', replies Holmes. The solution to the crime hinges on the fact that the watchdog guarding the horse did not bark in the night, and from this Holmes deduces that the thief must have been known to the dog. Formally, we can lay out Holmes' reasoning process as follows:

> Watchdogs bark at strangers.
> The watchdog did not bark at the thief.
> Therefore the thief was not a stranger.

This is a good example of the way in which we can acquire new knowledge about the world by using reason. Although we may not have Sherlock Holmes' power of deduction, we are constantly using reason to go beyond the immediate evidence of our senses. You notice that the pavement is wet when you go out in the morning and conclude that it has been raining during the night. You know that you left your mobile phone either in your coat pocket or on your desk; it is not in your coat pocket, therefore it must be on your desk. You know that Lake Geneva is a fresh-water lake, and you know that sharks don't like fresh water; therefore there cannot be any sharks in Lake Geneva.

The benefits of this kind of reasoning are obvious. Take the last example: assuming that your initial assumptions are correct, you don't need to waste your time checking every freshwater lake you come across to see if it has any sharks in it. Reason tells you that you can safely swim in any freshwater lake happy in the knowledge that you will not be attacked by a shark. Similarly, Holmes did not need to base his knowledge that the dog knew the thief directly on sense experience, but was able to infer it from what he already knew.

One of the great attractions of reason as a source of knowledge is that it seems to give us certainty. To take a well-known example, given that all human beings are mortal, and given that Socrates is a human being, it *necessarily* follows that Socrates is mortal. There are no 'if's' or 'but's' about it, and it is not a matter of personal opinion or the culture in which you were brought up. Given the assumptions – which in logic are called **premises** – the conclusion *has* to follow. There is no way you can wriggle out of it. After discussing the fallibility of perception in the last chapter, this kind of certainty might seem refreshing, and it is perhaps not surprising that there is a school of philosophy, called **rationalism**, according to which reason is the most important source of knowledge.

The central tenet of rationalism is that we can discover important truths about reality through the use of reason alone. Rationalists are particularly impressed with areas of knowledge such as logic and mathematics, which seem to be both certain and useful; and, unlike their empiricist rivals, they are suspicious of knowledge based on perception on the grounds that our senses can all too easily mislead us. One of the most famous rationalists in history was René Descartes (1596–1650) who tried to build a system of philosophy on his famous, and allegedly self-evident, starting point, 'Cogito ergo sum' ('I think therefore I am'). Curiously enough, in one of his books Descartes tells us that the idea of building a rational system of philosophy first came to him in a dream!

Whether it is actually possible to build a system of philosophy based purely on reason may be doubted, but reason is clearly an important way of knowing. In what follows, we will look at three kinds of reasoning:

- deductive reasoning
- inductive reasoning
- informal reasoning.

In our discussion, we shall encounter a variety of well-known and commonly committed **fallacies** (i.e. invalid patterns of reasoning) that it is important to guard against. We will then try to come to a balanced assessment of the value and limitations of logic.

Activity 5.1

1 Which of our faculties do you think is more reliable – reason or perception? Give reasons.

2 The following text is taken from a Calvin & Hobbes cartoon and is an amusing exchange between Calvin and his father. Analyse what Dad says and determine whether or not it is internally consistent.

CALVIN: Dad, how come old photographs are always black and white? Didn't they have color film back then?

DAD: Sure they did. In fact, those old photographs are in color. It's just the world was black and white then.

CALVIN: Really?

DAD: Yep. The world didn't turn color until some time in the 1930s, and it was pretty grainy color for a while, too.

CALVIN: That's really weird.

DAD: Well, truth is stranger than fiction.

CALVIN: But then why are old paintings in color? If the world was black and white, wouldn't artists have painted it that way?

DAD: Not necessarily. A lot of great artists were insane.

CALVIN: But – but how could they have painted in color anyway? Wouldn't their paints have been shades of grey back then?

DAD: Of course, but they turned color like everything else did in the '30s.

CALVIN: So why didn't old black and white photos turn color too?

DAD: Because they were color pictures of black and white, remember?

Figure 5.1

Deductive reasoning

Deductive reasoning is any form of reasoning that moves from the general to the particular. For example:

> All dogs are mammals.
> Fido is a dog.
> Therefore Fido is a mammal.

As you can see, the argument moves from a general claim about *all* dogs to a particular conclusion about Fido.

Syllogisms

The above kind of deductive argument is known as a **syllogism**. A syllogism consists of the following items:

1 two premises and a conclusion
2 three terms, each of which occurs twice ('dogs', 'mammals' and 'Fido')
3 **quantifiers**, such as 'all', or 'some' or 'no', which tell us the quantity that is being referred to.

Truth and validity

Before looking at some more examples of syllogisms, we need to make a distinction between **truth** and **validity**. These two words are sometimes used interchangeably, but they do not mean the same thing. Truth is concerned with what is the case, validity with whether conclusions follow from premises; truth is a property of statements, validity of arguments. To avoid confusion, you should not say that an argument is true or false, but rather that it is valid or invalid.

More formally, we can say that an argument is valid if the conclusion follows logically – i.e. necessarily – from the premises. And it is invalid if the conclusion does *not* follow logically from the premises. The main point to grasp is that *the validity of an argument is independent of the truth or falsity of the premises it contains*. Consider, for example, the following syllogism:

> All panthers are pink.
> Che Guevara is a panther.
> Therefore Che Guevara is pink.

Both the premises and the conclusion of this argument are false, but *the argument itself is valid*. To see this, *imagine* a world – call it planet Zog – where all panthers are pink, and Che Guevara is a panther. You can immediately conclude that on planet Zog Che Guevara must be pink!

So, if you want to determine the validity of an argument, imagine that the first premise is true on planet Zog, and imagine that the second premise is true on planet Zog – it doesn't matter whether or not the premises are true on Earth – and then ask yourself whether, on planet Zog, the conclusion must necessarily be the case. If the answer is 'yes', then the argument is valid; if it is 'no', then the argument is invalid. What logic enables you to do is draw conclusions about planet Zog that may not have been obvious from the information you were initially given (the premises).

It is worth noting that an argument can be valid, not only when its premises and conclusion are false – as in the above example – but also when premises are false and the conclusion is true. For example:

> All ostriches are teachers.
> Richard is an ostrich.
> Therefore Richard is a teacher.

In fact, we can construct valid arguments for almost any combinations of true and false premises and conclusions. *The only situation that is impossible is a valid argument with true premises and a false conclusion.*

Activity 5.2

Make up your own valid syllogisms to illustrate each of the following.
1 Two true premises and a true conclusion
2 One true premise, one false premise and a true conclusion
3 One true premise, one false premise, and a false conclusion
4 Two false premises and a true conclusion
5 Two false premises and a false conclusion

The structure of arguments

As our discussion has suggested, pure logic is concerned only with the *structure* of arguments. It doesn't matter if the premises are false, or even meaningless. All that matters is that the conclusion logically follows from the premises. Consider, for example, the following syllogism:

> All blims are blams.
> Some blims are bloms.
> Therefore some blams are bloms.

Although 'blim', 'blam' and 'blom' are meaningless words, we can still say with total confidence that if all blims are blams and some blims are bloms, then some blams are bloms. What this means is that, once you have determined that the structure of an argument is valid (or invalid), you can say that any other argument with the same structure will also be valid (or invalid). The argument structure for the above syllogism is:

All *A*s are *B*s.
Some *A*s are *C*s.
Therefore some *B*s are *C*s.

We can substitute anything we like for *A*, *B* and *C* and the argument will always be valid.

Abstracting from the content of an argument and focusing on its structure can help to avoid the danger of **belief bias**. This refers to the tendency we have to believe that an argument is valid simply because we agree with the conclusion. Consider the following argument: 'Democrats are in favour of free speech, and since dictators are not democrats, they are obviously opposed to free speech.' Since you probably agree with the conclusion, you might be tempted to say that the argument is valid. But it is not. The point to take away from this example is *just because you agree with a conclusion does not mean that the argument for it is a good one.*

Using Venn diagrams

Trying to decide whether or not a syllogism is valid is no easy matter. A useful way to picture what is going on is to draw a **Venn diagram**. The example above can be represented in terms of three overlapping circles. To represent 'All *A*s are *B*s', put the circle of *A*s inside the circle of *B*s; and to represent 'Some *A*s are *C*s', have the circle of *C*s intersect the circle of *A*s. You can now see that to the extent that circles *A* and *C* intersect, circles *B* and *C* must also intersect. It therefore follows that 'Some *B*s are *C*s'. The argument is valid.

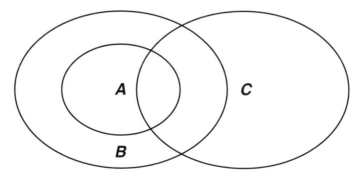

Figure 5.2

You can also use Venn diagrams to show invalid argument structures. For example, the following argument structure is invalid.

All *A*s are *B*s.
All *B*s are *C*s.
Therefore all *C*s are *A*s.

This can be pictured as follows:

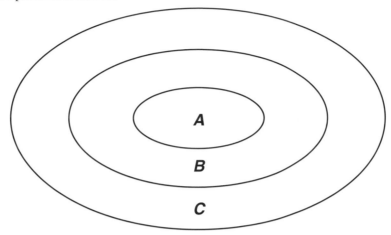

Figure 5.3

You can now see that just because the circle of *A*s falls inside the circle of *B*s, and the circle of *B*s falls inside the circle of *C*s, it does not follow that 'All *C*s are *A*s'. The argument is invalid.

Activity 5.3

How would you have to change the conclusion in the above example to make the argument structure valid?

If you use Venn diagrams to judge the validity of arguments, you need to be careful about the way you interpret them. Despite appearances, you cannot conclude from Figure 5.2 that 'Some *C*s are not *A*s'. Nor can you conclude from Figure 5.3 that 'Some *C*s are not *A*s'. (Can you see why in each case?) Using Venn diagrams, then, is no substitute for careful thinking; but it can still be a help in solving these kinds of problem.

Activity 5.4

Using Venn diagrams, state whether each of the following arguments is valid or invalid:

1 All Italians eat spaghetti.
   Giovanni Rossi eats spaghetti.
   Therefore Giovanni Rossi is an Italian.

2 No Martians have red noses.
   Rudolph has a red nose.
   Therefore Rudolph is not a Martian.

3 All bull-fighters are brave people.
   Some brave people are compassionate.
   Therefore some bull-fighters are compassionate.

4 Some monks are Tibetans.
   All Tibetans are good at yoga.
   Therefore some monks are good at yoga.

5 Some astrologers are frauds.
   Some frauds are not wealthy.
   Therefore some astrologers are not wealthy.

6 All bobos have dogs.
   No doctors have dogs.
   Therefore no bobos are doctors.

7 All rookies are red-heads.
   All red-heads are runners.
   Therefore all rookies are runners.

8 No alphas are betas.
   No gammas are betas.
   Therefore no gammas are alphas.

Figure 5.4

Deductive reasoning preserves truth

We have seen that the validity of an argument has nothing to do with the truth or falsity of its premises. So *just because an argument is valid, it does not follow that the conclusion is true*. To be sure that the conclusion of an argument is true, you must be able to answer 'yes' to both of the following questions:

1 Are the premises true?
2 Is the argument valid?

In practice, logic is most useful when we begin with true premises; for if we then reason validly we can be sure that the conclusion is true. Logical reasoning can therefore be seen as a technique for *preserving truth* in the sense that if you begin with truth you will end up with truth. (If, on the other hand, you begin with falsehood, you can end up with anything.)

When people argue in everyday life, they rarely set their arguments out in a formal way, and if a premise strikes them as obvious, they may simply assume it and not bother explicitly stating it. Such an incomplete argument is known as an **enthymeme**.

Activity 5.5

Supply the missing premise for each of the following enthymemes:
1 Jenny goes to Oxford University, so she must be very intelligent.
2 Drugs should be legalised because they only harm the addict.
3 Graham is a politician so he is probably lying.
4 Cheerleading should be an Olympic event because cheerleaders compete, train and have a high level of physical fitness.
5 Since it is natural to eat meat, there is nothing morally wrong with it.

We have seen that deductive reasoning is an instrument for the *preservation* of truth but this does not mean that it is a *source* of truth. If you go back to the syllogism about Socrates, the conclusion that 'Socrates is mortal' is true only if the premises are true. But how do you know that the premises are true? How, for example, can you be sure that 'All human beings are mortal'? Your knowledge that all human beings are mortal cannot be conjured out of logic, but is based on *experience*. This brings us to the topic of inductive reasoning.

Activity 5.6

How sure are you that some day you will die? What evidence do you have for your belief?

Inductive reasoning

While deductive reasoning goes from the general to the particular, another kind of reasoning, known as **induction**, goes in the opposite direction – from the particular to the general. With reference to the above example, my belief that all human beings are mortal is a generalisation from a vast number of particular instances. In history, every human being I know of eventually died, and I have never heard of a human being who *didn't* die. Therefore, I can say with confidence that 'All *observed* human beings have died.' But when we reason inductively we typically go further than this and generalise – or make an *inductive inference* – from the observed to the unobserved. Thus, in this example, we move from 'All *observed* human beings are mortal' to 'All human beings are mortal.'

Since inductive reasoning typically moves from the observed to the unobserved, it enables us to make generalisations about the world, and we are constantly using such reasoning in everyday life. Since apples have nourished me in the past, I assume that they will nourish me in the future. Since my neighbour's dog has been friendly to me in the past, I am confident that he will not bite me today. And since my chair has supported my weight in the past, I expect it to continue to do so in the future. In each of these cases past experience shapes our expectations about the (unobserved) future. If you think about it, you will see that you make literally thousands of such inferences every day, and that life would be impossible if you did not assume that most of the regularities that have held in the past will continue to hold in the future.

Indeed, there is a sense in which the whole of language is based on inductive generalisations. For, as we saw in Chapter 3, when we put labels, such as 'teacher', or 'dog' or 'table', on things we are implicitly organising them into general classes so that we can make predictions about them. If you call something a 'table' you have different expectations about its behaviour than if you call it a 'dog'. For example, tables aren't interested in being stroked, and dogs don't like having objects put on them. Thus language might be thought of as the inherited wisdom of the community about how the world is organised; and our tendency to look for regularities in our environment and put labels on them has obvious survival value.

Activity 5.7

1 If someone says, 'You should never generalise' there is a sense in which they are contradicting themselves. Why is this, and what conclusion do you draw from it?

2 My dog, Fido, gets excited when I get his leash out, and seems to know that he is about to go for a walk. Do you think he is using inductive reasoning to predict what is going to happen in the future? Does this mean that he is able to reason?

Science also uses inductive reasoning and typically formulates general laws on the basis of a limited number of observations. For example, if metal A and metal B and metal C expand when heated, at some point a scientist is likely to conclude that *all* metals expand when heated.

Activity 5.8

What percentage of the metal existing on our planet would you guess scientists have tested to see if it expands when heated? What does this suggest to you about the certainty or otherwise of scientific laws?

Deduction and induction compared

When we compare induction with deduction we can say that the former gives us more information in that it enables us to make generalisations about the world, but the latter is more certain. The difference between the two kinds of reasoning can be summarised in the table below.

Deduction	Induction
Definition	
Reasoning from general to particular	Reasoning from particular to general
Example	
All metals expand when heated. A is a metal. Therefore A expands when heated.	Metal *A* expands when heated; metal *B* expands when heated; metal *C* expands when heated. Therefore *all* metals expand when heated.
Value	
More certain, but less informative than induction	More informative, but less certain than deduction

In practice, however, deduction turns out to be no more certain than induction. This is because the premises on which deductive reasoning about the world is based must be derived from induction. To see this, go back to the example at the beginning of this chapter. The validity of Sherlock Holmes' conclusion that the thief was known to the dog depends on the truth of the premise that all watchdogs bark at strangers. And we can know that only by induction! Watchdogs *A, B, C, D, E,* … bark at strangers. Therefore all watchdogs bark at strangers. So Holmes' conclusion is only as certain as the inductive premises on which it is based.

How reliable is inductive reasoning?

Since induction goes beyond the immediate evidence of our senses, we cannot always rely on it. This is because we tend to make *hasty generalisations* and jump to conclusions on the basis of insufficient evidence. For example, if a tourist is served by a rude French waiter, he may conclude that all French people are rude; and if a female fighter pilot crashes a jet her male colleague may conclude that women are unfit to fly. Neither of these conclusions is justified by the evidence, and this kind of faulty reasoning can easily lead to racist or sexist attitudes. The trouble, as the psychologist Gordon Allport (1897–1967) observed, is that, 'Given a thimbleful of facts, we rush to make generalizations as large as a tub.'

Sometimes even well-established generalisations can let us down. With reference to the examples mentioned above, it is always possible that tomorrow apples make me sick, my neighbour's dog savages me, and my chair collapses. Europeans used to believe that all swans are white until they went to Australia and discovered that some swans are black. You might even question a well-established regularity, such as 'Water boils at 100 degrees centigrade.' After all, it is not true if you are at the top of a mountain!

The tendency to make hasty generalisations is made worse by a phenomenon known as **confirmation bias**. As we saw in Chapter 1, this suggests that people tend to remember only evidence that supports their beliefs and to forget evidence that goes against them. Thus once you have decided that the French are arrogant or that the English are cold, you may notice only examples that confirm your prejudice and overlook those that go against it. This may explain why it is so difficult to change the mind of someone who is in the grip of a prejudice.

Activity 5.9

1 Give three examples of your own of some hasty generalisations.
2 Why do you think that people are so quick to jump to conclusions?
3 What is the difference between a prejudice, a generalisation, and a scientific law?

To illustrate the extent to which we jump to conclusions on the basis of insufficient evidence, consider the following story, which was devised by the psychologist William V. Haney to illustrate precisely this point:

> A businessman had just turned off the lights in the store when a man appeared and demanded money. The owner opened a cash register. The contents of the cash register were scooped up, and the man sped away. A member of the police force was notified promptly.

Activity 5.10

Given the information in the story, respond to each of the 11 statements below by writing next to each one either 'T' if the statement is definitely true, 'F' if the statement is definitely false, and 'U' if the statement is unknown.

1 A man appeared after the owner had turned off his store lights.
2 The robber was a man.
3 The man did not demand money.
4 The man who opened the cash register was the owner.
5 The store owner scooped up the contents of the cash register and ran away.
6 Someone opened a cash register.
7 After the man who demanded the money scooped up the contents of the cash register, he ran away.
8 While the cash register contained money, the story does not state how much.
9 The robber demanded money of the owner.
10 The story concerns a series of events in which only three persons are referred to: the owner of the store, a man who demanded money, and a member of the police force.
11 The following events in the story are true: someone demanded money, a cash register was opened, its contents were scooped up, and a man dashed out of the store.

If you check your responses with the answers given at the end of this chapter, you may be surprised by the extent to which you jumped to various false conclusions on the basis of the information that was given to you.

What distinguishes good generalisations?

Since generalisations sometimes lead us into trouble, we need to think about how to distinguish good ones from bad ones. Here are some relevant general criteria:

1 *Number* You should look at a reasonable number of instances. If you see one example of a dog swimming, this is clearly not enough to conclude that 'all dogs can swim', and you should look at a lot more cases.

2 *Variety* You should look at a variety of circumstances. In the above example, you might look at different breeds of dogs, young dogs, old dogs, etc.

3 *Exceptions* You should actively look for counter-examples. You might, for example, ask if anyone has a dog that cannot swim. This will help to guard against confirmation bias.

4 *Coherence* You should demand more evidence to support surprising claims than unsurprising ones. It would take more to convince me that all dogs can walk on their hind legs than that all dogs can swim.

5 *Subject area* You should be aware of the subject area you are dealing with, and keep in mind that generalisations tend to be more reliable in the natural sciences than in the social sciences. For example, if you heat copper sulphate crystals they always turn from blue to white; but when you do experiments with dogs, the results are much less predictable. Indeed, according to the so-called Harvard law of animal behaviour, 'Under carefully controlled experimental circumstances an animal will behave as it damned well pleases.' And the behaviour of human beings – the most complex and contrary of animals – is, of course, the most difficult to predict of all. That is why there are a greater number of reliable generalisations in chemistry than in economics.

Although the above criteria can help us to distinguish between more and less reasonable generalisations, they are not precise rules. How many times should a team of scientists repeat an experiment before concluding that they have discovered a new law of nature? We can give some general advice, such as 'Many times if the experiments deal with complex phenomena or give unexpected results'. But there is not a number we can stipulate such as seven or twenty-three. All we can say is that the greater the number of confirming instances the more confident we can be about the generalisation.

Informal reasoning

In the last two sections, we looked at some fallacies associated with deduction and induction, such as invalid syllogisms and hasty generalisations. We will now consider some other fallacies that crop up frequently in arguments and discussions.

Post hoc ergo propter hoc

The fallacy of *post hoc ergo propter hoc* (literally, 'after this, therefore on account of this') consists of assuming that because one thing, *B*, follows another thing, *A*, then *A* must be the cause of *B*. For example, just because the murder rate in a country goes up after the abolition of capital punishment, it does not necessarily follow that capital punishment is an effective deterrent. The increase in the murder rate could be explained by other factors – such as a rise in poverty or the greater availability of guns. Notice that we said 'it does not *necessarily* follow that capital punishment is an effective deterrent'. The point is that while it *could be* the case, we cannot jump to this conclusion simply from the fact that the murder rate has gone up. We need more evidence.

Even when one event, *A*, is *regularly* followed by another event, *B*, it still does not necessarily mean that *A* is the cause of *B*. For example night is *regularly* followed by day, but night is not the *cause* of day. The evening weather forecast is *regularly* followed by the next day's weather, but the forecast does not *cause* the weather. The purchase of wedding rings is regularly followed by weddings, but the rings do not cause people to marry. In each of the above cases, the event in question is caused by some other factor – the rotation of the earth on its axis, pre-existing weather conditions, the decision to marry.

Activity 5.11

How would you explain the well-known observation – supported by statistical evidence – that as the number of churches in American cities increases, so does the number of prostitutes?

We need to be careful that we do not claim that this fallacy is being committed when in fact it is not. For example, for many years the American tobacco industry admitted that there was a statistical correlation between smoking and cancer, but denied that there was a causal connection. They implied that people who said 'Smoking causes cancer' were committing the *post hoc ergo propter hoc* fallacy. A clever ploy, but the fact is that, in addition to this statistical correlation, there is a large amount of other evidence that smoking causes cancer.

In general, we can say that a correlation between two things may be a *preliminary* indication that there is a causal connection between them. If, for example, I notice that the incidence of heart disease is lower in people who drink a glass of red wine every day than in the general population, it may be worth investigating this further. A fallacy is only being committed if we immediately jump to the conclusion that red wine prevents heart disease.

Ad hominem fallacy

The *ad hominem* fallacy (literally, 'against the man') consists in attacking or supporting the person rather than the argument. If, for example, you make an argument for world government, and are told that you are too young and idealistic to know what you are talking about, that is *ad hominem*. Rather than critiquing your argument, your opponent is simply attacking *you*. Similarly, if I make a case for higher salaries for teachers, and you reject what I say on the grounds that as a teacher I *would* say that, then that, too, is *ad hominem*. The fact that as a teacher I might have a **vested interest** in teachers getting higher salaries may, of course, make you *suspicious* of my argument, but it is not in itself a reason for rejecting it. You need to look at what I actually say.

Although the *ad hominem* fallacy is usually committed by *criticising* someone, it can also be committed by *supporting* them. For example, if you say 'Einstein was in favour of world government, so it must be a good thing', you are again focusing on the speaker rather than the argument. The same mistake arises when we appeal to what 'most people' or the 'vast majority' believe in order to justify something. Just because the vast majority of people believe something doesn't mean it is true. After all, there was a time when most people believed that it was acceptable to keep slaves and that women shouldn't be allowed to vote.

The above discussion raises the question of whether we are *ever* justified in taking an argument on trust from someone else. I suppose the ideal would be to always work everything out for ourselves; but in practice we lack the time and expertise to do this. Given this, it seems more reasonable to take an argument on trust from someone if they are an *authority* in the relevant area than if they are not. So if you say, 'It must be true because Einstein said so', this carries more weight if we are discussing relativity theory than if we are discussing politics or religion – areas in which Einstein has no particular authority. In this context, it is worth bearing in mind Hans Eysenck's (1916–97) comment:

> Scientists, especially when they leave the particular field in which they have specialised, are just as ordinary, pig-headed and unreasonable as anybody else, and their unusually high intelligence only makes their prejudices all the more dangerous.

We might now ask whether we are ever justified in *rejecting* what someone says solely on the basis of who they are. If, for example, you were a juror in a criminal trial and discovered that one of the eye-witnesses had a history of telling lies, would you be committing the *ad hominem* fallacy if you rejected his evidence out of hand? Well, if someone has a history of lying, you should clearly not take what he says at face value. But since it is at least possible that *this time* he is telling the truth, you should at least listen to his testimony and see how consistent it is with the rest of the evidence.

Circular reasoning

Circular reasoning (also known as 'vicious circle' and 'begging the question') consists in assuming the truth of something that you are supposed to be proving. When someone commits this fallacy, what at first sight looks like an argument, turns out to be nothing more than a reassertion of their position. Imagine that someone says, 'I know that Jesus was the Son of God because he said he was, and the Son of God would not lie.' They are begging the question because they are *assuming* the very thing that they are supposed to be *proving* – namely that Jesus was the Son of God. The philosopher Anthony Flew gives another nice example of circular reasoning:

> Three thieves are arguing about how to divide up the seven pearls they have stolen. One of them picks up the pearls and gives two to each of the other two, keeping the remaining three for himself. One of the other men says 'How come you have kept three?' 'Because I am the leader.' 'Oh. But how come you are the leader?' 'Because I have more pearls.'

Special pleading

The fallacy of 'special pleading' involves the use of double standards – making an exception in your own case that you would not find acceptable if it came from someone else. For example, if your neighbour says 'I know there is a drought and we need to save water, but I am putting my prize flowers in a competition next week and I need to give them plenty of water', this is an example of special pleading. He is giving a justification for his behaviour that he would not accept if it were given by somebody else.

> **Activity 5.12**
>
> Imagine in the above example that you accuse your neighbour of special pleading, and he says 'No I'm not. Despite the drought, I think that everyone with prize flowers should be allowed to water them.' Is he still engaging in special pleading?

Human beings tend to be rather good at special pleading – perhaps because there are many situations in which it would be convenient if everyone followed the rules *except me*. We will look in more detail at our tendency to make exceptions in our own case when we consider ethics in Chapter 12.

Equivocation

Equivocation is a fallacy that occurs when a word is used in two different senses in an argument. Consider the following syllogism:

> A hamburger is better than nothing.
> Nothing is better than good health.
> Therefore a hamburger is better than good health.

Although this argument is formally valid in the sense that the conclusion follows from the premises, there is clearly something wrong with it. The problem lies with the word 'nothing' because it has a different meaning in each of the premises. In the first premise, it means 'not having anything'; in the second, it means 'there is not anything'. The second premise is clearly not intended to mean that 'not having anything' is better than having good health. In practice, it is not always easy to tell if someone is using a word consistently or not. This may be why so many arguments end up being about the meanings of words.

Argument *ad ignorantiam*

You commit the fallacy of argument *ad ignorantiam* if you claim that something is true on the grounds that there is no evidence to disprove it. We discussed this fallacy in Chapter 1, but here is an example to refresh your memory. During the 'witch hunt' against communists in the USA in the early 1950s, Senator Joe McCarthy's case against one alleged communist was that 'there is nothing in the files to disprove his communist connections'. The point is, of course, that to show that someone is a communist – which is, in any case, no crime – we need *positive* evidence of their political affiliation.

> **Activity 5.13**
>
> In most legal systems, someone who is accused of a crime is considered to be innocent until proved guilty. Is this an example of argument *ad ignorantiam*? If so, does this mean that we should abandon the assumption that someone is innocent until proved guilty?

The particular relevance of this fallacy to TOK is nicely expressed by the biologist Richard Dawkins (1941–): 'There is an infinity of possible things that one might believe – unicorns, fairies, millions of things – and just because you can't disprove them it doesn't mean there is anything plausible about them.'

Figure 5.5 Argument *ad ignorantiam*

False analogy

In trying to persuade people of something, you might use various analogies to support your argument, and this can be an effective rhetorical device. A false analogy arises when you assume that because two things are similar in some respects they must also be similar in some further respect. Consider the following syrupy example: 'Just as in time the gentle rain can wear down the tallest mountains, so, in human life, all problems can be solved by patience and quiet persistence.' Well, maybe and maybe not. The point is that there is not much of a similarity between the action of rain on mountains and that of patience on problems. For one thing, it takes millions of years for mountains to be worn down by the action of rain, and when it comes to solving problems we don't have that kind of time.

False dilemma

This is the fallacy of assuming that only two alternatives exist when there is in fact a wider range of options. If, for example, someone says 'Do those who advocate an increase in military expenditure really want to see our schools and hospitals close?' they are implying that we have only two choices: *either* we increase military expenditure *or* we keep our schools and hospitals open. Since you are probably in favour of keeping schools and hospitals open, you seem forced to conclude that we should not support an increase in military expenditure. But there may in fact be more than two choices. For example, if we raise taxes we might be able to increase military expenditure *and* keep our schools and hospitals open. (Of course, if there really are only two choices, then this kind of reasoning is perfectly valid. If John Smith is either alive or dead, and he is not dead, then it follows that he must be alive.)

One reason that false dilemma is a common fallacy is that we tend to see the world in black and white terms. (Someone once said that, 'The world is divided into those who divide things into two types and those who don't.') Such **binary thinking** may have served our ancestors well; for their survival must often have depended on making quick friend-or-foe, fight-or-flight type of decisions. However, it may not be as useful in the modern world where many issues are not black and white, but various shades of grey.

Loaded questions

A loaded question is one that contains a built-in assumption that has not been justified and may be false. For example, if someone says 'Do you always cheat in exams?', then if you answer 'yes', you are admitting that you always cheat, and if you answer 'no' you are implying that you *sometimes* cheat. What you have to do is challenge the assumption built into the question and say 'I *never* cheat in exams.'

When governments hold referenda, or social scientists or polling organisations seek to gather data of various kinds, they should try to avoid loaded questions. But in practice it may be difficult to decide whether a question is biased or not; for, as we saw in Chapter 3, it is difficult to express anything in a completely neutral way. We shall have more to say about the problem of loaded questions when we discuss the social sciences in Chapter 9.

Statements may also contain built-in assumptions. A sentence such as 'The headteacher was not drunk today' may in a narrow sense be true. But it carries with it the implication that this is unusual and that he or she is often drunk – and, in most schools at least, this is likely to be false.

Imagine that the Norwegian government has decided to hold a referendum about whether or not Norway should join the European Union. Your job is to phrase the referendum question in as neutral and unbiased a way as possible. What is your question? And why did you choose to phrase it the way you did?

Fallacies: a summary

We have now considered nine informal fallacies. If we add to these the fallacy of hasty generalisation from the previous section, we can speak of the 'ten deadly fallacies' of informal reasoning, which are summarised in the table below.

The ten deadly fallacies	
Ad ignorantiam	Claiming something is true because it cannot be proved to be false
Hasty generalisation	Generalising from insufficient evidence
Post hoc ergo propter hoc	Confusing a correlation with a causal connection
Ad hominem	Attacking/supporting the person rather than the argument
Circular reasoning	Assuming the truth of what you are supposed to be proving
Special pleading	Using double standards to excuse an individual or group
Equivocation	Using language ambiguously
False analogy	Assuming that because two things are alike in some respects they are alike in other respects
False dilemma	Assuming that only two black and white alternatives exist
Loaded question	A question that is biased because it contains a built-in assumption

As we have seen, it requires an element of judgement to determine whether or not one of the above fallacies has been committed; and it is worth noting that one of the most common fallacies is to falsely claim that someone has committed a fallacy!

In each of the twenty cases described below, state which of the following best applies to the argument:

A Valid

B Invalid syllogism

C Hasty generalisation

D *Post hoc ergo propter hoc*

E Circular reasoning

F *Ad hominem* fallacy

G Special pleading

H Argument *ad ignorantiam*

I False dilemma

J False analogy

K Equivocation

L Loaded question

1 Since strict gun control laws were introduced in Dodge City, the crime rate has risen. This shows that gun control does nothing to reduce crime.

2 Arisa said she trusted me, and she must be telling the truth because she wouldn't lie to someone that she trusted.

3 The ends justify the means. After all, if you want to make omelettes, you have to break eggs.

4 Since the English always talk about the weather, if you meet someone who talks about the weather you can be sure they are from England.

5 That can't be right. None of my friends would believe it.

6 Since many great scientists have believed in God, there must be some truth in religion.

7 We got on very well on both of our dates together. We are clearly well-suited. Let's get married!

8 Do you want to be part of the solution or part of the problem?

9 I agree that everyone should pay their taxes. But since I'm short of money this year and want to take my family on a much-needed holiday, it's OK if I don't declare my full income.

10 The average UK family has 2.5 children. The Smiths are very average people. Therefore they must have 2.5 children.

11 Since no one has been able to prove that we are alone in the universe, we must conclude that alien life-forms exist.

12 Are all your family stupid, or is it just you?

13 Many great artists were not recognised in their own lifetimes. Since my work has not been recognised, I must be a great artist.

14 Since there are two candidates for student president – Boris and Bertha – and I know he did not vote for Boris, he must have voted for Bertha.

15 As no one succeeds without hard work, the fact that you failed your exams shows how idle you have been.

16 No breath of scandal has ever touched the senator. So he must be an honest man.

17 Just as you are more likely to take care of a car that you own than one that you rent, so a slave owner is more likely to take care of his slave than an employer is of his worker.

18 To ignore the possibility that America was discovered by Africans simply because these explorers are unknown is irresponsible and arrogant. If we are unaware of an event, it does not mean it never happened.

19 In the fight against terrorism, you are either with us or against us.

20 The English can't cook. If he really is English, then obviously he won't be able to cook.

Causes of bad reasoning

If we ask ourselves why we sometimes reason poorly, and commit, or fail to recognise, the above kinds of fallacy, I think there are four main reasons: *ignorance, laziness, pride* and *prejudice*. In some cases, we do not realise that a particular form of reasoning is fallacious, and are taken in by it. In other cases, we have developed fixed habits of thinking and are too lazy to check the argument or see if it has supporting evidence. Perhaps it is psychologically easier to hold simple beliefs with confidence than get bogged-down with confusing details. Pride also plays a role in bad reasoning; for although we all like to think we are open-minded, once we get involved in an argument we can become more interested in winning than in establishing the truth. Unfortunately logic, the art of reasoning, can all too easily give way to rhetoric, the art of persuasion. And we may then be tempted to resort to any argument – valid or invalid – to defend our position. Indeed, on some occasions, we may simply begin with our prejudices, and then manufacture bad reasons in order to justify them. This is known as **rationalisation**, and we shall have more to say about it in Chapter 6.

> ### Activity 5.16
>
> Take any editorial or opinion article from a newspaper and see how many of the above fallacies you can find in it.

Reason and certainty

We have considered three different kinds of reasoning – deductive reasoning, inductive reasoning and informal reasoning. The fact that fallacies can arise with each of these suggests that we cannot always rely on reason to give us knowledge. Furthermore, we have seen that, when it comes to reasoning about the world, the conclusions of deductive arguments are no more certain than the premises they are based on. In practice, then, it would seem that, at best, reason is a means of preserving truth in the sense that if you begin with truth and reason validly then you will end with truth.

We might, however, say that, *as a way of thinking*, logical reasoning cannot really be doubted. Such reasoning is based on the following three **laws of thought**.

1   *The law of identity.* If *A*, then *A*. For example, 'If something is a banana, then it is a banana.'

2   *The law of non-contradiction.* Nothing can be both *A* and not-*A*. For example, 'Nothing can be both a banana and not-a-banana.'

3   *The law of the excluded middle.* Everything is either *A* or not *A*. For example, 'Everything is either a banana or not a banana.'

These three laws probably strike you as self-evident. If something is a banana, then it must be a banana. And given that it's a banana then it cannot *not* be a banana. Finally, if you put all the bananas in the universe on your left, and all the non-bananas on your right, there is nothing left in the middle hovering uncertainly between being and not being a banana. (A banana with an identity crisis, perhaps? A banana that has gone bananas?)

What, then, should we say to someone who asks 'Why should I be logical?' At one level, the question is self-defeating because in asking for reasons you are implicitly presupposing the value of logic. A statement such as 'Logic isn't useful' is equally self-defeating; for, in making it, you presumably wish to exclude the contrary idea that logic *is* useful, and you are therefore presupposing the usefulness of the principle of non-contradiction. The fact is that logic is presupposed in all meaningful communication, and any assertion *p* that you care to make must – if it is to say anything – exclude the contrary assertion *non-p*.

'But can't a man and a wife have a love–hate relationship?' you might ask. 'And, if so, doesn't that mean that you can both love and not-love someone?' Well, this is true in a sense, but not in a way that undermines logic. For you cannot love and not love the same person in the same way at the same time. What you really mean when you say you have a love–hate relationship with someone is that you love them in certain ways or at certain times, but not in other ways or at other times. And this, of course, does nothing to invalidate logic. (A man once explained his love–hate relationship with his wife as follows. 'It's quite simple', he said. 'I love her and she hates me!')

'You still haven't proved that the laws of logic are true', you might persist – 'you have just assumed that they are true'. This is admittedly true; but this follows from the fact that *all proof must end somewhere.* And since we cannot prove everything, where better to start than with principles that seem self-evident and are the basis for meaningful communication? In the end if someone ignores logic and keeps contradicting themselves, we are likely to get frustrated and will probably stop talking to them.

Activity 5.17

1   Find out what is meant by the phrase **infinite regress** and explain why all proof must end somewhere.

2   What is the difference between being irrational and being insane? How irrational must someone be before you classify them as insane?

Can deductive reasoning be doubted?

Despite what has been said above, some philosophers have in fact been willing to question the truth of the basic principles of logic. Here are three possible reasons for doubt:

1   We cannot be sure that the laws of logic do not simply describe the way we *think* rather than the way the universe *is*. G. K. Chesterton (1874–1936) claimed that 'It is an act of faith to assert that our thoughts have any relation to reality at all' and he concluded from this that 'Reason is itself a matter of faith.'

2   Logic depends on language in that it presupposes that we can organise the world into precise, clear-cut categories. But in reality this is never possible. For example, who can say where 'day' begins and 'night' ends? Even the concept of a banana is fuzzy round the edges; for if we genetically modified a banana one cell at a time, we can imagine a borderline case where it would be impossible to say whether it was still a banana. This point was well summarised by the philosopher Bertrand Russell (1872–1970):

> The law of excluded middle is true when precise symbols are employed, but it is not true when symbols are vague, as, in fact, all symbols are.

3   If we take seriously the idea that everything is constantly changing, then nothing stays the same long enough to be identical with itself, and there is nothing for logic to be true of. I think this is what the Greek philosopher Heraclitus (c. 540–470 BCE) was drawing attention to when he famously observed that 'You can never step in the same river twice.'

The above doubts are very abstract in nature, but they show that it is possible to doubt even the basic laws of logic. In practice, however, it is impossible to imagine abandoning logic; for if we did, the whole structure of knowledge would collapse.

Can inductive reasoning be doubted?

Let us now consider how far inductive reasoning can be doubted. We saw earlier that induction cannot give us certainty because it involves a jump from 'All observed X' to 'All X'. To illustrate the extent to which well-confirmed generalisations can sometimes let us down, consider the following story about some 'inductive turkeys' that arrive on a farm one January. They are well looked after, and every morning after breakfast the farmer comes and feeds them. After a few weeks, some of the more philosophical turkeys begin to notice that *whenever* the farmer appears they get fed. As good inductive turkeys they continue to observe patiently, and as January turns to February they become increasingly confident of the truth of the generalisation that 'Whenever the farmer comes, we get fed.' The months pass, and as spring turns to summer, and summer turns to autumn, this generalisation acquires the status of a law of nature. The connection between the farmer's appearance and the arrival of food is, the turkeys decide, a brute fact about reality, and to question it would be a clear sign of insanity. Things continue in much the same way until one cold December morning – 24 December to be precise – the farmer breaks the neck of the first turkey that comes up to him to be fed. (British people traditionally eat turkey for lunch on Christmas day.)

The story about the inductive turkeys may be a fairy tale, but it alerts us to the fact that even well-confirmed generalisations can fail us. For example, Newton's laws of motion were confirmed by observational evidence on countless occasions and were believed to be true for more than 200 years. Nevertheless, they eventually turned out to be false (or, at best, approximations to a deeper truth).

Despite the obvious survival value of inductive reasoning, we might ask how we can know that the future will be similar to the past *in any respect*. How can you be sure that the laws of physics, together with the countless everyday regularities that you take for granted, won't suddenly break down tomorrow? Imagine, for example, that you wake up tomorrow morning and discover that you have been transformed into an insect, like the character in Franz Kafka's (1883–1924) novel *Metamorphosis*. This is the stuff of nightmares, and you might reasonably insist that you *know* that this will not happen. After all, the world exhibits demonstrable regularities that prohibit you from turning into an insect. This has certainly been true up until now; but how can you be sure that the laws of nature won't suddenly break down tomorrow?

Most people do not lie awake at night worrying about whether or not the laws of physics will continue to hold in the future; but the question is whether we can *justify* our confidence in the comforting regularities of nature. You might argue that we know the future will be similar to the past on the basis of experience. For example, last Tuesday I predicted that on Wednesday – which was then in the future – the laws of physics would continue to hold true – and they did. And on Wednesday I predicted that they would continue to hold true on Thursday. And you know what? They did again! So it would seem that there is in fact a huge amount of evidence that the future will be like the past. The problem, however, is that, although the laws of nature held true in *past* futures, this does not prove that they will continue to hold true in *future* futures. From a logical point of view, it is possible that tomorrow, for the first time, they will break down.

Since inductive reasoning moves from the observed to the unobserved, there is in fact no way we can justify our belief in it on the basis of experience. And since it lacks the certainty of deduction, we cannot give a logical justification of it either. Therefore, it would seem that we cannot justify induction at all. So perhaps we should conclude that it is simply an *instinct* that we share with animals.

However, we might look at the situation in another way, and argue that *using inductive reasoning is simply part of what it means to be rational*. For, although we sometimes question the validity of a particular generalisation, it makes no real sense to question the general idea of using the past as a guide to the future. To see this, just imagine someone sticking their hand in a fire every day on the grounds that, although it has always hurt in the past, they have no reason to think that it will hurt them this time. You would surely say they are mad – and rightly so! For as the Scottish philosopher David Hume (1711–76) observed: 'None but a fool or madman will ever pretend to dispute the authority of experience.'

Lateral thinking

In the previous section, we saw that, although philosophical doubts can be raised about both deductive and inductive reasoning, it would be difficult if not impossible to survive without making use of them. Having said that, it is worth pointing out that we can sometimes become trapped in what has been called 'the **prison of consistency**'. The point is that once you have taken a position on something, you may find it difficult to change your mind without losing face. As the Russian novelist Leo Tolstoy (1828–1910) once observed:

> I know that most men, including those at ease with problems of the greatest complexity, can seldom accept even the simplest and most obvious truth if it is such as would oblige them to admit the falsity of conclusions which they have delighted in explaining to colleagues, which they have proudly taught to others, and which they have woven, thread by thread, into the fabric of their lives.

So perhaps it would be better if we all had a little more intellectual flexibility, and followed the example of the economist John Maynard Keynes (1883–1946). When a critic complained that he had changed his opinion about something, Keynes retorted 'When I discover I am wrong, I change my mind. What do you do?'

Activity 5.19

1 Which do you think is easier: having the courage of your convictions, or having the courage to question your convictions?
2 'The madman is not the man who has lost his reason. The madman is the man who has lost everything but his reason' (G. K. Chesterton, 1874–1936). Should you always try to be as rational as possible, or are there dangers in being too rational?

According to Edward de Bono (1933–) if we are to escape from the 'prison of consistency', then we must learn to 'think outside the box' and come up with more creative ways of looking at problems. To help us to do this, he has developed a way of reasoning called **lateral thinking** which complements traditional, 'vertical' logic. De Bono describes the difference between the two ways of thinking as follows:

> Vertical thinking [i.e. traditional logic] is digging the same hole deeper; lateral thinking is trying elsewhere.

His point is that, since we cannot rely on traditional logic to give us new ideas, we need to adopt a more creative way of thinking that encourages us to search actively for better solutions to problems.

"Never, ever, think outside the box."

Figure 5.6

Activity 5.20

1 Give a rational explanation for each of the following situations. In each case you will need to question your assumptions and try to 'think outside the box'.

  a A man walks into a bar and asks the barman for a glass of water. The barman pulls out a gun and points it at the man. The man says 'Thank you' and walks out.

  b A man is lying dead in a field. Next to him there is an unopened package. There is no other creature in the field. How did he die?

  c Anthony and Cleopatra are lying dead on the floor of a villa in Egypt. Nearby is a broken bowl. There is no mark on either of their bodies and they were not poisoned. How did they die?

  d A man rode into town on Friday. He stayed three nights and then left on Friday. How come?

2 Two boxers are in a boxing match (regular boxing, not kick boxing). The fight is scheduled for 12 rounds but ends after 6 rounds, after one boxer knocks out the other boxer. Yet no man throws a punch. How is this possible?

3 In your cellar there are three light switches in the OFF position. Each switch controls one of three light bulbs on the floor above. You may move any of the switches but you may only go upstairs to inspect the bulbs one time. How can you determine the switch for each bulb with one inspection?

4 A landscape gardener is given instructions to plant four special trees so that each one is exactly the same distance from each of the others. How would you arrange the trees?

5 Connect the nine crosses below using only four straight lines and without taking your pen off the paper.

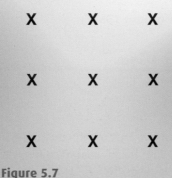

Figure 5.7

Conclusion

At the beginning of this chapter, we saw that rationalist philosophers such as René Descartes believed that reason is a way of knowing that can give us certainty. But we have seen that this belief is open to serious doubt. For reason is only as certain as the premises on which it is based, and it is always possible that we have reasoned badly in arguing from premises to conclusions. We also raised various philosophical doubts about deduction and induction, but in practice it is difficult to see how we could do without these two ways of reasoning.

What seems to come out of our discussion is that reason, like other ways of knowing, is a double-edged tool. We need reason to develop consistent beliefs about the world, but we can sometimes become trapped in the 'prison of logic' and this can stifle our creativity. Furthermore, reason is not appropriate in every situation, and if someone is *too* rational they may simply come across as a cold and unfeeling automaton. In private life, for example, the best way to resolve a dispute with a loved one may not be by proving their inconsistency to them but by showing them empathy and understanding. In other words, reason needs to be balanced by emotion. We must now look at emotion and see in what way, if any, it can contribute to our knowledge of the world.

Answers to selected questions

Uncritical inference test (pages 122–3)

All of the statements are uncertain except (3), which is false, and (6), which is true. If you answered differently, you might want to go back to the story and look more closely at it.

Lateral thinking questions (pages 136–7)

1a The man has hiccups.

1b The man's parachute failed to open.

1c Anthony and Cleopatra are goldfish.

1d Friday is the name of the man's horse.

2 The boxers are women.

3 Turn switch 1 on for about five minutes and then turn it off. Turn switch 2 on and then go upstairs. The hot unlit bulb is controlled by switch 1, the lit bulb by switch 2, and the cold unlit bulb by switch 3.

4 Plant 3 trees equidistant from each other in an equilateral triangle. Then build a mound of the right height in the middle of the triangle and plant the fourth tree on top of it.

5 As the diagram below shows, if you extend one of the lines outside the square formed by the dots, the solution is easy.

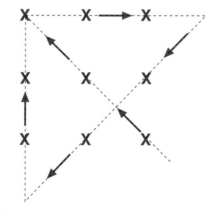

Figure 5.8

> **Key points**
>
> • Through reason we can acquire knowledge about the world that goes beyond the immediate evidence of our senses.
>
> • According to rationalism, reason is a more important source of knowledge than experience, and we can discover important truths about reality by using pure reason.
>
> • Deductive reasoning moves from the general to the particular, and inductive reasoning moves from the particular to the general.

- Pure logic is only concerned with the structure of arguments and the validity or invalidity of an argument is independent of the truth or falsity of its premises.
- When deductive reasoning is applied to the real world it is no more certain than the (inductively derived) premises on which it is based.
- Inductive reasoning sometimes leads to our making hasty generalisations which are then reinforced by our tendency to only notice things which confirm them.
- There are many other 'informal' fallacies that people sometimes commit when discussing things in everyday life.
- The main causes of bad reasoning are a combination of ignorance, laziness, pride and prejudice.
- Despite appearances, it is possible to doubt the certainty of even the basic laws of logic such as the law of identity.
- Although it is hard to see how we can justify our belief that the future will be relevantly similar to the past, this belief has obvious survival value.
- We sometimes get trapped in the prison of consistency and find it difficult to change our minds about things or look at them from a new perspective.

Terms to remember

ad hominem	fallacy	prison of consistency
argument *ad ignorantiam*	false analogy	quantifier
begging the question	false dilemma	rationalisation
belief bias	hasty generalisations	rationalism
binary thinking	induction/ inductive	rhetoric
circular reasoning	inference	special pleading
confirmation bias	infinite regress	syllogism
contradiction	lateral thinking	validity
deduction	laws of thought	Venn diagram
double standards	loaded questions	vested interest
enthymeme	*post hoc ergo propter hoc*	vicious circle
equivocation	premise	

Further reading

R. H. Thouless and C. R. Thouless, *Straight and Crooked Thinking* (Hodder and Stoughton, 1990). A useful and readable book which explores the most common reasoning errors and tricks that are used in argument to deceive people. The fallacies that are discussed are clearly explained and well-illustrated.

Stuart Sutherland, *Irrationality: Why We Don't Think Straight* (Rutgers University Press, 1992). Written by a psychologist, this book explores the many ways in which our thinking can go wrong. Among the topics covered are conformity, misplaced consistency, ignoring evidence and false inference.

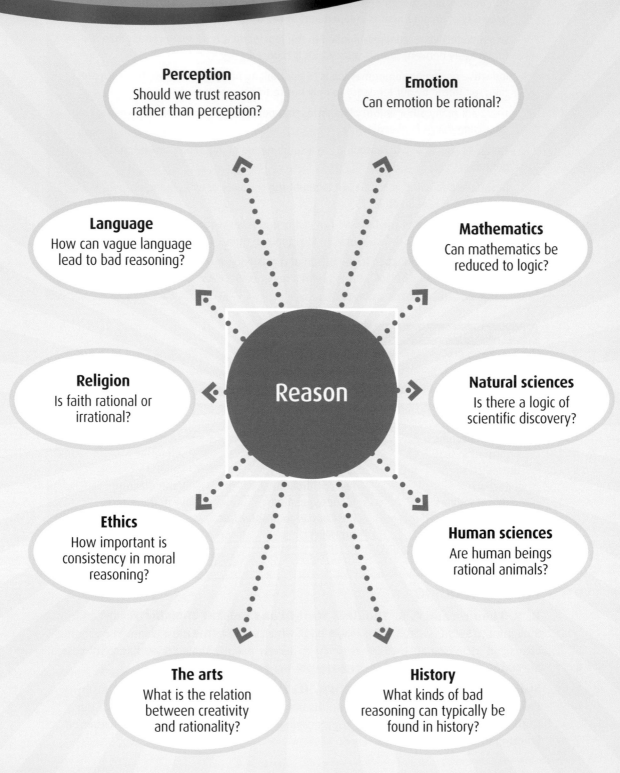

Perception
Should we trust reason rather than perception?

Emotion
Can emotion be rational?

Language
How can vague language lead to bad reasoning?

Mathematics
Can mathematics be reduced to logic?

Religion
Is faith rational or irrational?

Reason

Natural sciences
Is there a logic of scientific discovery?

Ethics
How important is consistency in moral reasoning?

Human sciences
Are human beings rational animals?

The arts
What is the relation between creativity and rationality?

History
What kinds of bad reasoning can typically be found in history?

THE TRIUMPH OF THE YELL

In this article, Deborah Tannen, a professor of linguistics, suggests that argument can sometimes result in polarised either–or thinking which does not bring us nearer to the truth, but takes us further away from it.

I put the question to a journalist who had written a vitriolic attack on a leading feminist researcher: 'Why do you need to make others wrong for you to be right?' Her response: 'It's an argument!'

That's the problem. More and more these days, journalists, politicians and academics treat public discourse as an argument – not in the sense of *making* an argument, but in the sense of *having* one, of having a fight.

When people have arguments in private life, they're not trying to understand what the other person is saying. They're listening for weaknesses in logic to leap on, points they can distort to make the other look bad. We all do this when we're angry, but is it the best model for public intellectual interchange? This breakdown of the boundary between public and private is contributing to what I have come to think of as a culture of critique.

Fights have winners and losers. If you're fighting to win, the temptation is great to deny facts that support your opponent's views and present only those facts that support your own.

At worst, there's the temptation to lie. We accept this style of arguing because we believe we can tell when someone is lying. But we can't. Paul Ekman, a psychologist at the University of California at San Francisco, has found that even when people are very sure they can tell whether or not someone is dissembling, their judgments are likely as not to be wrong.

If public discourse is a fight, every issue must have two sides – no more, no less. And it's crucial to show 'the other side', even if one has to scour the margins of science or the fringes of lunacy to find it.

The culture of critique is based on the belief that opposition leads to truth: that when both sides argue the truth will emerge. And because people are presumed to enjoy watching a fight, the most extreme views are presented, since they make the best show.

But it is a myth that opposition leads to truth when truth does not reside on one side or the other but is rather a crystal of many sides. Truth is more likely to be found in the complex middle than in the simplified extremes, but the spectacles that result when extremes clash are thought to get higher ratings or larger readership.

Because the culture of critique encourages people to attack and often misrepresent others, those others must waste their creativity and time correcting the misrepresentations and defending themselves. Serious scholars have to waste years of their lives writing books proving that the Holocaust happened, because a few fanatics who claim it didn't have been given a public forum. Those who provide the platform know that what these people say is, simply put, not true, but rationalize the dissemination of lies as showing 'the other side.' The determination to find another side can spread disinformation rather than lead to truth.

The culture of critique has given rise to the journalistic practice of confronting prominent people with criticism couched as others' views. Meanwhile, the interviewer has planted an accusation in readers' or viewers' minds. The theory seems to be that when provoked, people are spurred to eloquence and self-revelation. Perhaps some are. But others are unable to say what they know because they are hurt, and begin to sputter when their sense of fairness is outraged, in those cases, opposition is not the path to truth.

When people in power know that what they say will be scrutinized for weaknesses and probably distorted, they become guarded. As an acquaintance recently explained about himself, public figures who once gave long free-wheeling press-conferences now limit themselves to reading brief statements. When less information gets communicated, opposition does not lead to truth.

Opposition also limits information when only those who are adept at verbal sparring take part in public discourse, and those who cannot handle it, or do not like it, decline to participate. This winnowing process is evident in graduate schools, where many talented students drop out because what they expected to be a community of intellectual inquiry turned out to be a ritual game of attack and counter-attack...

In many university classrooms, 'critical thinking' means reading someone's life work, then ripping it to shreds. Though critique is surely one form of critical thinking, so are integrating ideas from disparate fields and examining the context out of which they grew. Opposition does not lead to truth when we ask only 'What's wrong with this argument?' and never 'What can we use from this in building a new theory, and a new understanding?'...

The most dangerous aspect of modelling intellectual interchange as a fight is that it contributes to an atmosphere of animosity that spreads like a fever. In a society where people express their anger by shooting, the result of demonizing those with whom we disagree can be truly demonic.

I am not suggesting that journalists stop asking tough questions necessary to get at the facts, even if those questions may appear challenging. And of course it is the responsibility of the media to represent serious opposition when it exists, and of intellectuals everywhere to explore potential weaknesses in others' arguments.

But when opposition becomes the overwhelming avenue of inquiry, when the lust for opposition exalts extreme views and obscures complexity, when our eagerness to find weaknesses blinds us to strengths, when the atmosphere of animosity precludes respect and poisons our relations with one another, then the culture of critique is stifling us. If we could move beyond it, we would move closer to the truth.

LOGIC AND CULTURAL RELATIVISM

In this extract from their textbook *Cultural Anthropology*, Emily Schultz and Robert H. Lavenda consider whether or not logical thinking is universal.

Syllogistic reasoning is enshrined in Western culture as the quintessence of rational thought. It has therefore been suggested that the rational capacities of non-Western peoples could be tested by presenting those people with logical problems in syllogistic form. Presumably their rationality would be confirmed if they could deduce correctly when the conclusion followed logically from the premises, and when it did not.

Cole and Scribner devised logical problems involving syllogistic reasoning and presented them to their Kpelle subjects [a West African tribe]. Typically, the logical problem was embedded in a folktale-like story. The experimenter read the story to the subjects and then asked them a series of follow-up questions designed to reveal whether the subjects could draw a correct conclusion from the premises given.

Here is one story that they prepared: 'At one time Spider went to a feast. He was told to answer this question before he could eat any of the food. The question is: Spider and Black Deer always eat together. Spider is eating. Is Black Deer eating?' The syllogism is contained in the question at the end of the story. Given the two premises, the conclusion should be that Black Deer is eating.

Now consider a typical Kpelle response to hearing this story:

Subject: *Were they in the bush?*

Experimenter: *Yes.*

Subject: *Were they eating together?*

Experimenter: *Spider and Black Deer always eat together. Spider is eating. Is Black Deer eating?*

Subject: *But I was not there. How can I answer such a question?*

Experimenter: *Can't you answer it? Even if you were not there, you can answer it. (Repeats the question.)*

Subject: *Oh, oh, Black Deer is eating.*

Experimenter: *What is your reason for saying that Black Deer was eating?*

Subject: *The reason is that Black Deer always walks about all day eating green leaves in the bush. Then he rests for a while and gets up again to eat.*

The subject's answer to the question and subsequent justification for that answer seem to have nothing whatever to do with the logical problem the subject is being asked to solve. One simplistic way to interpret this response would be to call it 'irrational', but reread the original story. The story itself contains an element of paradox: Spider will not be allowed to eat until he answers a question, yet the question he is to answer presumes that he is already eating! Of course, the paradox exists only if the subjects assume that the contextual material about the feast is relevant to the logical problem they are being asked to solve. Yet it is precisely this that we cannot assume... People have to be trained to exclude context from their judgments of truth or falsity, literality or figurativeness.

The experimenters devised this story the same way schoolteachers devise word problems for students of mathematics. That is, the contextual material is nothing more than a kind of window dressing. Smart students quickly learn to disregard the window dressing and seek out the mathematical problem it hides. In the same way, the Kpelle subjects hearing the story about Spider and Black Deer are supposed to demonstrate 'logic' by disregarding the contextual material about the feast, and seeking out the syllogism embedded within it. However, Kpelle subjects did not understand that they were being read this story in a testing situation for which considerations of context or meaningfulness were irrelevant. In the preceding example, the subject seemed to have difficulty separating the logical problem both from the introductory material about the feast and from the rest of his experiential knowledge.

Cole and Scribner interpreted their subject's response to this problem as being due not to irrationality but to a 'failure to accept the logical task'. In a follow-up study, Cole and Scribner discovered that Kpelle high school children responded 'correctly' to the logical problems 90 percent of the time. This suggests a strong correlation between Western-style schooling and willingness to accept context-free analytic tasks in testing situations.

But this is not all. David Lancy, one of Cole and Scribner's colleagues, discovered that Western-style syllogisms are very similar to certain forms of Kpelle riddles. Unlike syllogisms, however, those riddles have no single, 'logically correct' answer. 'Rather, as the riddle is posed to a group, the right answer is the one among many offered that seems most illuminating, resourceful, and convincing as determined by consensus and circumstance. This emphasis on edification as a criterion for "rightness" is found in Kpelle jurisprudence as well.'

Cole and Scribner conclude: 'We cannot draw conclusions about reasoning processes from the *answers* people give to logic problems. We have first to ask: "What is their understanding of the task? How do they encode the information presented to them? What transformations does the information undergo, and what factors control these?"'

6 Emotion

'We think and name in one world, we live and feel in another.'
Marcel Proust, 1871–1922

'Conquer your passions and you conquer the world.'
Hindu proverb

'The heart has its reasons of which reason knows nothing.'
Blaise Pascal, 1623–62

'Philosophy is the finding of bad reasons for what we believe on instinct.'
F. H. Bradley, 1846–1924

'Deep thinking is attainable only by a man of deep feeling.'
Samuel Taylor Coleridge, 1772–1834

'Axioms in philosophy are not axioms until they are proved upon our pulses.'
John Keats, 1795–1821

'If you can keep your head when all about you are losing theirs... you have probably misunderstood the situation.'
Anon

'Laws are only reached by non-logical methods. To make a law one has to have an intellectual love of the subject.'
Albert Einstein, 1879–1955

'Nothing great is accomplished in the world without passion.'
Georg Wilhelm Friedrich Hegel, 1770–1831

'All emotions were abhorrent to his cold, precise but admirably balanced mind.'
Sir Arthur Conan Doyle, 1859–1930 – about Sherlock Holmes

'The opinions that are held with passion are always those for which no good ground exists, indeed the passion is the measure of the holder's lack of rational conviction.'
Bertrand Russell, 1872–1970

'Man is a rational animal who always loses his temper when called upon to act in accordance with the dictates of reason.'
Oscar Wilde, 1854–1900

'Reason is always and everywhere the slave of the passions.'
David Hume, 1711–76

Introduction

In Theory of Knowledge the emotions are treated as one of the four ways of knowing, together with language, reason and perception. Since the emotions have traditionally been seen as more of an obstacle to knowledge than a source of it, this may initially seem surprising. There are some good reasons for the traditional suspicion of the emotions; for an angry, frightened or infatuated person is unlikely to see clearly or reason well. That is why we usually advise people to 'be reasonable' rather than 'be emotional'. When we have recovered from an emotional outburst, we typically say things like 'I don't know what came over me', and this suggests that we think reason *ought* to be in control.

At the same time, our feelings matter to us a great deal, and we naturally consult them when we make important decisions. Indeed, some people believe that feelings are a better guide to the truth than reason. This view was popularised by romantic writers and poets in the early nineteenth century and it is still common today.

> ### Activity 6.1
>
> 1 'You're being emotional' is usually taken as a criticism. Why? Could 'You're being rational' ever be seen as a criticism?
> 2 To what extent do you think we are able to control our emotions? Which emotion is the most difficult to control?
> 3 'What reason weaves, by passion is undone' (Alexander Pope, 1688–1744). Illustrate and analyse this quotation, by choosing a character from a novel, play or film whose reason is overcome by emotion.

Before looking in more detail at the relevance of the emotions to our search for knowledge, we should begin by saying something about their nature.

The nature of the emotions

The word 'emotion' is derived from the Latin verb *movere* meaning 'to move'. We shall be using it in a broad sense to include such things as feelings, passions and moods. An emotion usually consists of various internal feelings and external forms of behaviour, and it can vary in intensity from, say, mild irritation to blind anger. The word 'passion' is usually reserved for a strong emotion. You can, for example, be in a passionate rage, but you cannot be passionately irritated. A mood is an emotion which continues for a period of time. Thus you may be in a bad mood all day long and your behaviour may be punctuated by fits of anger. (Later in this chapter, we will also be looking at intuition – something which does not fit comfortably into the category of either reason or emotion.)

Primary emotions

According to psychologists, there are six basic emotions, or **primary emotions**, that are common to all cultures:

- happiness
- sadness
- fear
- anger
- surprise
- disgust.

When photographs of faces displaying these states of mind are shown to people they can readily identify the relevant emotion no matter what country they come from. Moreover, children who are born blind and deaf also show these emotions – which suggests that they are inborn rather than learnt.

The James–Lange theory

The fact that primary emotions have a typical facial expression associated with them suggests that there is a close connection between our emotions and our bodies. Indeed, according to the **James–Lange theory** (which is named after the psychologists who came up with it), the emotions are essentially *physical* in nature, and bodily changes come before, and cause, emotional changes.

Activity 6.4

Imagine the following situation. You are about to sit an exam and you are feeling very nervous. Your mouth is dry, you have a sinking feeling in the pit of your stomach, the palms of your hands are sweaty, and you want to go to the washroom. Now remove each of these physical symptoms one by one. What is left of your exam nerves?

If you went through the above thought experiment, you may have found that when you removed all the physical symptoms of nervousness, the nervousness itself disappeared. According to the James–Lange theory the same holds true for *all* of our emotions – if you remove the physical symptoms the corresponding emotion disappears.

Interestingly, the theory also suggests that if you mimic the appropriate physical symptoms you can generate the corresponding emotion. For example, if you smile you will feel happy, and if you scowl you will feel angry. You might like to test this idea out on yourself!

Figure 6.2

The James–Lange theory also suggests a mechanism through which we can come to know and **empathise** with other people's feelings. The idea is that when you talk to someone who is, say, feeling depressed, you unconsciously mimic some of the physical expressions of his mood. When he tells you his troubles, you might say something like 'Oh dear, I am sorry', and find yourself instinctively adopting his flat, depressed tone and hunched posture. As a result, you may pick up at least an echo of his depressed mood.

Activity 6.5

1 Have you ever noticed a class atmosphere or mood develop in a particular lesson at school? How helpful is the above mechanism in explaining how this comes about?
2 To what extent do you think that moods are generally infectious?

The role of beliefs

Despite the attractions of the James–Lange theory, it can be criticised because it ignores the fact that our emotions have a mental as well as a physical aspect. Although our emotions are closely connected with our bodies, they can also be affected by our beliefs. This, I think, is what distinguishes human emotions from the emotions of other animals. If you have a pet dog, you cannot seriously doubt that it has emotions, but dogs – and other animals – appear to lack the range and complexity of many distinctively human emotions.

Activity 6.6

1 How do you think human emotions differ from the kinds of emotions a dog can feel?

2 The picture below, called *The Scream*, is by the Norwegian expressionist painter Edvard Munch (1863–1944).

  a What is your response to the emotion being conveyed in this painting?

  b If the human figure was replaced by a dog in the same pose, would your response be different? Why?

Figure 6.3 Edvard Munch's *The Scream*

As well as the primary emotions mentioned above, we human beings can experience **social emotions** such as ambition, contempt, embarrassment, envy, gratitude, guilt, indignation, jealousy, pride, shame and sympathy. Our intelligence and imagination mean that we are also able to anticipate and picture more distant dangers. A dog may worry about threats in its immediate environment, but you can also be worried about your final exams, or the fact that you are going to die, or the eventual heat-death of the universe! One of the ways in which dogs have an easier time of it than we do is that they don't have to worry their heads about the meaning of life!

Since emotions have both a physical and a mental aspect, they can be affected not only by our bodies, but also by our beliefs. This suggests – in theory at least – that a change in our beliefs can lead to a change in the corresponding emotion. For example, if you enter a badly lit cellar and see a snake in the corner, you will probably be frightened. But if, when you look more closely, you discover that it is not a snake but a coiled rope, your fear will vanish. A change in your beliefs has led to a change in your emotions.

There is, then, a two-way relationship between emotions and beliefs: not only do our emotions affect our beliefs – as we saw when discussing perception in Chapter 4 – but our beliefs affect our emotions.

Emotional energy

One of the ways in which the emotions are relevant to our search for knowledge is that they provide us with the energy to engage in intellectual activity. The ability to come up with new ideas in any area of knowledge undoubtedly requires a certain amount of genius, but it also needs a long apprenticeship and a great deal of persistence. According to Thomas Edison's (1847–1931) famous estimate, 'Genius is one per cent inspiration and ninety-nine per cent perspiration.' A great deal of day-to-day academic work can be boring and repetitive. A mathematician sharpens her pencils, works on a proof, tries a few approaches, gets nowhere and finishes for the day. A biologist goes to the lab, gets the equipment out, does an experiment, it doesn't work, puts the equipment away again and goes home. A writer sits down at his desk, produces a few hundred words, decides they are no good, throws them in the bin and hopes for better inspiration tomorrow. To produce something worthwhile – if it ever happens – may require years of labour. The mathematician Andrew Wiles (1953–) spent eight years trying to prove Fermat's Last Theorem – one of the great unsolved problems in mathematics – before making his crucial breakthrough in 1994. The Nobel-prize-winning biologist, Peter Medawar (1915–87), estimated that four-fifths of his time in science was wasted, adding glumly that 'nearly all scientific research leads nowhere'. The Chilean writer Isabel Allende suffered from writer's block for more than three years. What sustained all of these people in their work, and motivated them when things were going badly, was a *passion* for their subject.

The fact that emotions provide energy for the pursuit of knowledge does not in itself mean that they are a source of knowledge. Food also gives us energy for the pursuit of knowledge, but that does not make it a way of knowing. In order to decide whether or not the emotions can be a source of knowledge we will need to take a closer look at the role that they play in our mental lives.

1 What do you think are the main qualities that make a person a good teacher? Would you include a word like 'passion' in your list? Give reasons.
2 What do you think is the relationship between liking a subject and being good at it? Do you like a subject if you are good at it, or are you good at a subject if you like it?
3 What are the pros and cons of holding a belief with passion?

Emotions as ways of knowing

If, as the traditional view claims, the emotions are more of an obstacle than a source of knowledge, we still need to look at them and consider how to guard against their disruptive influence. It could, however, be argued that the emotions play a more positive role in our mental lives and that without them we would be unable to make sense of the world. We also need to take a closer look at the nature of intuition. For some of our most fundamental beliefs seem to be more emotional matters of the heart than rational matters of the head.

This gives us an agenda for the rest of this chapter. In the next three sections, we shall look at:

1 emotions as an obstacle to knowledge
2 emotions as a source of knowledge
3 intuition.

Emotions as an obstacle to knowledge

Since emotions are an integral part of our mental lives, they are likely to influence the way we see and think about the world. Strong emotions can sometimes distort the three other ways of knowing.

- *Perception* Our perception of things can be coloured by strong emotions, and there is doubtless some truth in sayings like 'love is blind' and 'fear has many eyes'. Such **emotional colouring** can make us aware of some aspects of reality to the exclusion of others. If, for example, you are in love with someone you are likely to be blind to their faults; whereas if you loathe them you are likely to see only their faults.
- *Reason* Reason can also be negatively affected by our emotions, and if you hold your beliefs with too much passion, this can prevent you being open-minded and lead to a 'my theory right or wrong' kind of attitude.
- *Language* A person in the grip of a powerful emotion is likely to use slanted and emotive language.

You can find many examples in everyday life of the way in which emotions can undermine our ability to think clearly. At some time or other, you have probably been in a 'rational discussion' with someone which degenerated into a slanging match. When our emotions are aroused, it is all too easy to stop listening to the person we are arguing with and to start trading insults rather than reasons.

Rationalisations

When we are in the grip of strong emotions, we tend not to reason in an objective way but to *rationalise* our pre-existing prejudices. To clarify the difference between reasons and rationalisations, consider the following story by Aesop (sixth century BCE?), the legendary writer of Greek fables.

> A famished fox saw some clusters of ripe black grapes hanging from a trellised vine. She resorted to all her tricks to get at them, but wearied herself in vain, for she could not reach them. At last she turned away, hiding her disappointment and saying: 'The grapes are sour, and not ripe as I thought.'

This story suggests that if we have a particular emotional attitude about something we may manufacture bad reasons in order to justify it. According to psychologists, this kind of behaviour is quite common. We tend to rationalise when there is a conflict between two or more of our beliefs. For example, a cigarette smoker who is familiar with the evidence that smoking is bad for her health may try to explain away the evidence as follows:

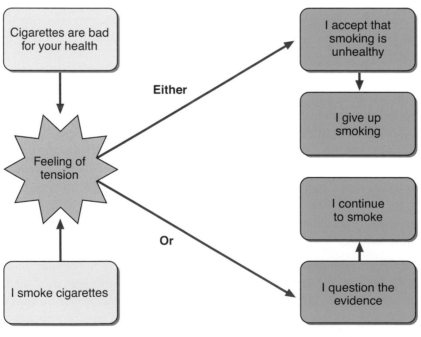

Figure 6.4

1 What is going on when someone who is losing badly at a game says that it is a 'stupid game'? Do you think they would say that if they were winning?
2 Are students who do badly on a test more or less likely to say that the test was unfair than students who do well on it? Give reasons.

At the limit, the tendency to rationalise can lead a person to develop an illusory but self-confirming belief system. The diagram below shows how this can happen.

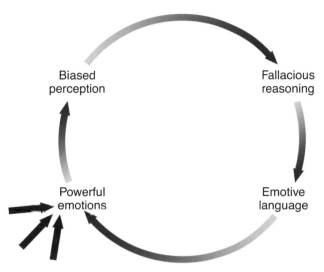

Figure 6.5 Rationalisation

To illustrate, imagine that Henry has an emotional prejudice against immigrants. His prejudice will probably lead to the following:

1 *Biased perception*   He notices only lazy immigrants and overlooks hard-working ones.
2 *Fallacious reasoning*   He makes hasty generalisations from his own limited experience.
3 *Emotive language*   He concludes that immigrants are 'bone idle' and 'don't know the meaning of hard work'.

The above factors will reinforce the original prejudice and make it difficult for Henry to be objective. He can escape from such a vicious circle only if he is willing to question his prejudiced assumptions and actively consider other ways of looking at things.

The trouble is that fanatics – by definition – refuse to question their assumptions or consider evidence that runs contrary to their own distorted way of looking at the world. As the psychologist Leon Festinger (1919–90) observed:

> A man with a conviction is a hard man to change. Tell him you disagree and he turns away. Show him facts or figures and he questions your sources. Appeal to logic and he fails to see your point. We have all experienced the futility of trying to change a strong conviction, especially if the convinced person has some investment in his belief. We are familiar with the variety of ingenious defenses with which people protect their convictions, managing to keep them unscathed through the most devastating attacks.

Irrational behaviour

Our emotions can not only distort our beliefs, but also lead us to make poor decisions. Some emotions are urgent and short sighted and they can easily blind us to the longer-term consequences of our actions. How often have you said something in a moment of anger that you immediately regretted? Or given in to temptation when it would have been better to exercise self-control? Aristotle defined man as a rational animal, and economics is based on the assumption that we are all – producers and consumers alike – rational people. But the underlying reality may be more in line with Thomas Schelling's (1921–) amusing description:

> How should we conceptualize this rational consumer whom all of us know and who some of us are, who in self-disgust grinds his cigarettes down the disposal swearing that this time he means never again to risk orphaning his children with lung cancer and is on the street three hours later looking for a store that's still open to buy cigarettes; who eats a high calorie lunch knowing that he will regret it, does regret it, cannot understand how he lost control, resolves to compensate with a low-calorie dinner, eats a high-calorie dinner knowing he will regret it, and does regret it; who sits glued to the TV knowing that again tomorrow he'll wake early in a cold sweat unprepared for that morning meeting on which so much of his career depends.

As this suggests, we are all masters of acting against our own best interests and making resolutions that we break at the first sign of temptation. ('I can resist everything except temptation', Oscar Wilde wryly observed.) We will have more to say about weakness of the will when we look at ethics in Chapter 12.

Since turbulent emotions can distort our ability to think clearly and behave intelligently, you might think that the ideal situation would be one in which we did not have any emotions at all and could look at the world in a balanced and objective way. In ancient times, such a belief was held by a group of philosophers known as the **Stoics**. The Stoics advocated a state of mind called **apathy** – literally 'without passion' – in which the mind could mirror reality in a calm and untroubled way.

Activity 6.10

1 What problems might there be in trying to be a good Stoic and striving to be apathetic?
2 Can you imagine a human life without emotions? If so, try to characterise what it might be like. If not, explain why not.
3 Under what emotional conditions do you think you are most likely to make an unbiased judgement about something: (a) a good mood; (b) a bad mood; (c) a neutral mood?

Emotions as a source of knowledge

Despite the Stoic ideal, it is difficult to imagine a meaningful human life without any emotions. If you describe someone as being 'cold and unemotional', you do not literally mean that they have no emotions, but that they have few emotions *compared with the average person*. You might think that Mr Spock, the half-human, half-Vulcan character in the original *Star Trek* series, comes close to having no emotions. But, as Steven Pinker has pointed out, Spock is not so much *lacking* in emotions as *in control* of his emotions.

> Spock's emotionlessness really just amounted to his being in control, not losing his head, coolly voicing unpleasant truths, and so on. He must have been driven by some motives or goals. Something must have kept Spock from spending his days calculating pi to a quadrillion digits or memorizing the Manhattan telephone directory. Something must have impelled him to explore strange new worlds, to seek out new civilizations, and to boldly go where no man had gone before. Presumably it was intellectual curiosity, a drive to set and solve problems, and solidarity with allies – emotions all. And what would Spock have done when faced with a predator or an invading Klingon? Do a headstand? Prove the four-color map theorem? Presumably a part of his brain quickly mobilized his faculties to scope out how to flee and to take steps to avoid the vulnerable predicament in the future. That is, he had fear. Spock may not have been impulsive or demonstrative, but he must have had drives that impelled him to deploy his intellect in pursuit of certain goals rather than others.

Some recent studies of brain-damaged patients in fact suggest that if you did not have any emotions then your life would quickly disintegrate. The psychologist Antonio Damasio cites the case of a patient called Elliot who suffered damage to the emotional centres in his brain. Elliot appeared normal in many respects and performed just as well on IQ tests as he did before his accident. Nevertheless, he became a 'rational fool' whose life fell apart because he had lost the ability to make decisions.

Damasio speculates that emotions help us to make rational decisions about things by narrowing down our options so that we can choose between a manageable number of them. Since patients such as Elliot do not have any emotions to guide them, they try to decide what to do on the basis of reason alone and end up experiencing a kind of mental paralysis.

Activity 6.11

1 Have you ever been in a situation where you had to choose between two equally attractive options? How did you come to a decision?
2 What role do you think is usually played by reason and emotion when people decide which universities to apply to? What role do you think each of these *should* play?
3 Peter has decided that he wants to marry Heloise. He came to his decision by weighing up all of Heloise's good points and bad points and comparing them with those of other potential life-partners. Heloise came out as the most rational choice. What can be said for and against this way of deciding whom you would like to marry? How would you feel if you were Heloise?

The relation between reason and emotion

The above discussion suggests that although we tend to think of reason and emotion as two different things, in practice they are closely related to one another and it is difficult to make a clear distinction between them.

Activity 6.12

1 Since you got out of bed this morning, how much time have you spent thinking and how much time feeling? What does this suggest about the relationship between thinking and feeling?

2 Can you ever feel literally nothing? Can you ever think literally nothing?

Rather than think of reason and emotion as completely different *either–or* things, it probably makes more sense to say that there is a *more-or-less* continuum of mental activity running from the very rational to the very emotional. When you are engrossed in a mathematics problem you are at one end of the continuum, and when you lose your temper you are at the other end. Most of the time you are probably somewhere in the middle and have a mixture of thoughts and feelings floating around in your mind.

Figure 6.6 Reason–emotion continuum

Furthermore, rather than think of reason and emotion as being opposed to one another, it may make more sense to say that our emotions can themselves be more or less rational. When we discussed the nature of the emotions, we saw that they have a mental as well as a physical aspect, and that a change in our beliefs can lead to a change in the corresponding emotion. While it might be reasonable to fear a snake in the cellar, if you later discover that it is in fact a coiled rope then your fear is no longer justified. Similarly, if you are angry with someone because they insulted you and you later find out that you misunderstood what they said, then your anger should disappear. With these examples in mind, we might say that in general *an emotion that is sensitive to the real nature of a situation is more rational than one that is not.*

The philosopher, Aristotle (384–322 BCE), was one of the first to suggest that emotions can be more rational or less rational. In speaking of anger, he observed that:

> Anyone can be angry – that is easy. But to be angry with the right person to the right degree, at the right time, for the right purpose and in the right way – that is not easy.

To get a sense of what Aristotle meant by this, compare the following two imaginary scenarios:

1 Paul has arranged to meet Tom at 3:00 p.m. Tom arrives at 3:02 p.m. and apologises for being late. Rather than accept Tom's apology, Paul starts screaming and shouting about Tom's lack of consideration and completely loses his self-control.

2 The hospital phones Judy with some terrible news. Her boyfriend has been assaulted by some hooligans and is lying unconscious in the intensive care unit. 'Oh dear', she says, 'that *is* annoying! I was hoping to play tennis this afternoon, but I suppose I had better come and visit him.'

The reactions of Paul and Judy in the above scenarios could both be described as irrational. Paul's problem is that he shows too much emotion, Judy's that she shows too little. If a friend arrives two minutes late for an appointment, you might reasonably show mild annoyance, but it is inappropriate to lose your temper. On the other hand, if you *only* show mild annoyance on learning that a loved one has been assaulted, then there is surely something wrong with your emotional responses; in this situation, you surely *ought* to feel shock, concern and anger. This suggests that showing too little emotion is as irrational as showing too much emotion. We need to find a balance between the two.

Activity 6.13

1 'If you are not horrified by genocide then you have not understood it.' Do you agree or disagree with this statement? Does it follow that the more horrified you are by genocide, the better you understand it? Could you be horrified by something and yet not really understand it at all?

2 What problems does the above raise for someone who is trying to write an 'objective' account of the genocide in Rwanda in 1994?

Allowing that our emotions may be more or less rational, there is still a problem that we may be able to see that a particular emotion is irrational and yet find it difficult to change it. This is particularly true with strong emotions such as fear and disgust. You may, for example, know that grass snakes are harmless, or that it is statistically safer to fly than to drive, but you may still be unable to contain your fear when you encounter a grass snake or are sitting in a plane. Many people also find it difficult to override unjustified feelings of disgust, as is shown by the following bizarre experiment. When subjects were invited to eat fudge that had been shaped to resemble dog poop, or drink apple juice poured out of a brand-new bed pan, the vast majority refused – even though such food and drink are usually desirable.

We all experience irrational emotions but, since it is difficult to switch them off, we may find it easier to adjust our beliefs to our emotions than bring our emotions into line with reason. We are back to the problem of rationalisation. When the object of our irrational fear and disgust is, say, an ethnic minority, the consequences can be serious.

Since you are much more likely to die in a car on the way to the airport than you are in a plane, would you agree that the fear of flying is an irrational fear? How would you explain it?

Intuition

For the rest of this chapter we will focus on a particular kind of feeling that is often given as a source of knowledge – namely intuition. Intuitions are, of course, very different from hot emotions, such as love and hate. But since they are usually seen as being more a matter of feeling than of thinking, it makes sense to discuss them here.

The word 'intuition' is typically associated with the aha moment of insight when you suddenly see the solution to a problem without going through any conscious process of reasoning. You are probably familiar with the story of Archimedes (*c.* 287–212 BCE) who hit upon his famous principle while lying in the bath. So excited was he by his insight that he leapt out of his bath and ran naked down the street shouting 'Eureka! Eureka!' ('I've found it! I've found it!'). You may not have run naked down the street, but you have probably had your own moments of insight when the solution to a problem suddenly dawned on you. The change from not being able to solve a problem to suddenly seeing the answer is quite mysterious and no one really understands how intuition works.

We use 'intuition' to describe not only flashes of creative insight but also our 'sixth sense' hunches about things. You may, for example, have an *intuition* that someone behind you is staring at you, and when you turn round you discover you are right! However, such intuitions do not seem to be very reliable. Sometimes when you turn round, no one is there!

Given their range and variety, we might distinguish between three different types of intuitions:

- *Core intuitions* – our most fundamental intuitions about life, the universe and everything
- *Subject-specific intuitions* – the intuitions we have in various areas of knowledge such as science and ethics
- *Social intuitions* – our intuitions about other people, what they are like, whether or not they can be trusted, etc.

Core intuitions

In an abstract sense, it could be argued that *all* of our knowledge is based on intuition. For although reason and perception are usually said to give us knowledge, they ultimately depend on intuition.

Reason   The laws of logic are the starting point for all our reasoning, but we cannot prove them in terms of any more fundamental laws. If asked to justify them, most people would say that they are *intuitively* obvious.

Perception Perception is an important source of knowledge, but we cannot be sure on the evidence of our senses alone that life is not a dream. (This is because any evidence we appeal to could itself be part of the dream.) Yet we have an overwhelmingly strong intuition that the dream hypothesis is false and that what we are experiencing is reality.

A good way of seeing that our knowledge claims are ultimately based on intuition is to play the *Why?* game. Ask a friend to tell you one thing she claims to know, and then ask her why she believes it. When she answers, ask her why she believes *that*, and so on. The game is usually quite short. Your friend may be able to explain *A* in terms of *B*, and *B* in terms of *C*, and *C* in terms of *D*..., but sooner or later she will run out of reasons and tell you that her final knowledge claim is self-evident or intuitively obvious. We cannot, of course, take such intuitions for granted, but nor can we deny the important role they play in our thinking.

Activity 6.15

If someone asked you why you believe each of the following statements, what evidence, if any, could you give in support of them?

a I exist.
b Life is not a dream.
c If something is a banana, then it is a banana.
d $1 + 1 = 2$.
e Parallel lines never meet.
f The laws of physics will not break down tomorrow.
g My friends are not androids.
h You should not torture innocent people for the fun of it.
i All human beings are created equal.
j Time has no beginning or end.
k Nothing comes from nothing.

There is a school of thought called **romanticism** that is associated with the emotions in much the same way that there are schools of thought associated with perception (empiricism) and reason (rationalism). Many people in the romantic movement were literary figures rather than philosophers, but what they had in common was an emphasis on the importance of the emotions for making sense of the world. Our discussion of core intuitions could be poetically summarised in Pascal's (1623–62) famous observation that, 'The heart has its reasons of which reason knows nothing', or John Keats' (1795–1821) claim that, 'Axioms in philosophy are not axioms until they are proved upon our pulses.' Since many – if not all – of our most fundamental beliefs seem to be based on intuition, romanticism may have something to be said for it.

But, before we get carried away singing the praises of hearts and pulses, we should take a reality check. A major objection to the claim that intuition is an important source of knowledge is that different people have conflicting intuitions. Wouldn't it be nice to think that decent, open-minded, well-educated people could all agree about what is intuitively obvious? But we only have to look around us to see that this is not the case. Does the existence of the universe require an explanation? Could a machine think? Could a mind exist without a body? Is abortion murder? Many people have strong intuitions about the answers to these kinds of questions, but as often as not they disagree with one another! What is obvious to you may not be obvious to me; and we can all too easily be blinded by our own sense of what is blindingly obvious!

Here are three general questions that might cast doubt on the value of taking intuition as a source of knowledge:

1 If something is intuitively obvious, must everyone agree about it? (Is there *anything* that everyone agrees about?)

2 Could you be wrong in thinking that something is intuitively obvious? (Might you one day come to see that what you now think is intuitively obvious is in fact a deeply rooted prejudice?)

3 Whose intuitions should you trust? Are some people's intuitions better than others?

Activity 6.16

Give some examples of things that once struck you as intuitively obvious which you no longer believe are true.

Subject-specific intuitions

We sometimes appeal to intuition to justify our knowledge claims in various areas of knowledge, but research suggests that such intuitions should be treated with caution. There is a wealth of evidence to suggest that our uneducated intuitions in subjects such as logic, mathematics, physics, biology, history, economics and ethics are at best confused and at worst false.

Activity 6.17

Test the reliability of your intuitions by trying the following questions.

1 Linda is thirty-one years old, single, outspoken, bright, and very much involved in social issues like disarmament and equal rights. Which of the following statements is more likely?

   a 'Linda is a bank teller.'

   b 'Linda is a bank teller and is active in the feminist movement.'

2 If an unbiased coin is tossed six times in a row, which of the following sequences is more likely?

   a H-T-H-T-H-T

   b H-H-H-H-H-H

3 Take a soccer match with eleven players on each side and a referee. What are the odds of two people on the field sharing the same birthday?

4   Briefly describe what will happen to the path of a ball after it is propelled through a spiral tube (see Figure 6.7) and shot out of the top of it.

5   Imagine that you are standing on a large flat plain holding a bullet in your left hand and a loaded gun in your right hand. If you fire the gun horizontally and at the same instant drop the bullet from your left hand, which of the two bullets will hit the ground first?

6   You and a friend have just spent $10 each to see a movie. After about half an hour you both realise that it is a really bad movie. List some good reasons for staying until the end of the movie, and then list some good reasons for leaving after half an hour.

[You will find the answers to the above questions at the end of this chapter.]

The fact that many people get the above questions wrong shows that our natural intuitions are poor guides to the truth. Perhaps this is because they evolved to cope with the stone-age environment rather than with the modern world. At one time, it was believed that knowledge is simply organised common sense. But most psychologists would now say that we need to 'debug' – rather than blindly follow – our intuitions. Indeed, it could be argued that the aim of education is to help us 'unlearn' our naive intuitions so that we can acquire a more sophisticated and reliable understanding of the world.

To show why we need to be cautious about trusting our natural intuitions, let us briefly consider three subject areas: physics, biology and ethics.

Physics   According to a common-sense belief that can be traced back to Aristotle (384–322 BCE), objects move only to the extent that they are given impetus or 'oomph', and if no force is applied to them they will grind to a halt. If something is going to move, you've got to push it, and if you stop pushing, it will stop moving. This reflects our everyday experience of the world, and for many centuries it struck people as intuitively obvious. However, this belief turns out to be false. For according to Newton's first law of motion, 'Every object continues in its state of rest or uniform motion unless acted upon by a force.' Since you learnt this at school, you probably have no difficulty in accepting this law as true, but it is worth noticing that it is far from obvious and is in many respects counter-intuitive. After all, when did you last see an object continuing endlessly in a state of uniform motion?

There are many other examples of the gap between the physicists' description of the world and our common-sense description of it. For example, as we saw in Chapter 4 (page 100), the desk I am sitting at strikes me as an obstinately solid object, but according to the physicists it consists mainly of empty space. And it gets worse. Many of the mainstream ideas of modern physics – such as quantum mechanics – are so contrary to our ordinary ways of thinking that even physicists struggle to make sense of them. At this level, our natural intuitions are not so much a guide as an obstacle to understanding. As one physics teacher ruefully observed, 'With each freshman class, I must again face the fact that the human mind was not designed to study physics.'

Biology   Two hundred years ago, it was intuitively obvious to biologists that everything in nature had a purpose, and that since each species had its own unique essence one species could not evolve into another. Since Darwin, however, there has been a consensus among biologists that nature works blindly with no goal in mind, and that species gradually evolve into other species.

Ethics   The problem with trusting our moral intuitions is that different people at different times have had different intuitions about what is right and wrong. For example, for many centuries it was 'obvious' that men were superior to women, and that some people were natural slaves; but I imagine that few people would accept such beliefs today.

Social intuitions

One of the problems with intuition as a source of knowledge is not only that it is fallible, but also that we tend to be over-confident about our own intuitions. This is particularly apparent in the case of social intuitions. We tend to put a lot of trust in our intuitions about other people and we pride ourselves on being good judges of character. (When did you last hear someone admit to being a *bad* judge of character?) However, the evidence suggests that our intuitions are not as good as we like to think. Can you, for example, tell if someone is lying to you? You probably think you can – that it is written all over the person's face (see Figure 6.8). But countless experiments have shown that when people try to distinguish true stories from false ones they do no better than they would if they simply guessed at random.

Figure 6.7

Test your social intuitions by studying the two faces below. One shows a genuine smile and one a false smile. Can you tell which is which?

Figure 6.8

Natural and educated intuitions

At the beginning of this section, we suggested that there is a sense in which all knowledge is based on intuition, but our subsequent discussion has raised doubts about its reliability. This raises the question of when, if ever, we should trust our intuitions.

At this point, I think it is worth making a distinction between *natural intuitions* on the one hand and *educated intuitions* on the other. We have seen that our natural intuitions do not always help us to understand the world. Expert intuition is another matter. Think of the way in which a chess grandmaster can survey a chessboard and intuitively see the right move to make. His intuition is the product not only of raw talent but also of a vast mental database of background knowledge. Top-level professionals in areas as varied as biology, brain surgery and baseball have similar intuitions.

Many of the great breakthroughs in the history of ideas have come about as a result of flashes of creative intuition. Typically, the person in question has been working doggedly on a problem without any success, only for the solution to hit them like a thunderbolt when they are idly daydreaming or taking a walk – or lying in the bath. (One eminent scientist even confessed to having his eureka moment of insight while sitting on the toilet!) The French mathematician Henri Poincaré (1854–1912) described how he came to one of his great intuitions as follows:

> For fifteen days I strove to prove that there could not be any functions like those that I have since called Fuchsian functions. I was then very ignorant; everyday I seated myself at my work table, stayed an hour or two, tried a great number of combinations and reached no results. One evening, contrary to my custom, I drank black coffee and could not sleep. Ideas rose in crowds; I felt them collide until pairs interlocked, so to speak, making a stable combination. By the next morning I had established the existence of a class of Fuchsian functions, those which come from the hypergeometric series; I only had to write out the results, which took but a few hours.

In reflecting on his experience, Poincaré came to the conclusion that mathematical creativity is not a matter of mechanically following rules to generate endless combinations of symbols, but of having the insight to see which combinations are worth exploring. 'It is', Poincaré concluded, 'by logic that we prove, but by intuition that we discover.'

Activity 6.19

1 Have you ever had the following experience: a really good idea comes to you in the middle of the night, but when you think about it again the following morning it seems much less impressive? Why do you think this is?
2 Do you think it is possible to have a valuable insight in an area in which you have little background? Has this ever happened to you?
3 From your own experience, what do you think is the relationship between intuition, background knowledge and intellectual effort?

In reflecting on the nature of these kinds of intuitions, we should keep in mind that despite appearances they are not a short-cut to knowledge. Some people might be tempted to celebrate intuition as an inexplicable and mysterious source of knowledge out of a kind of laziness. After all, wouldn't it be great if, from time to time, you effortlessly came up with brilliant new insights into the nature of things? Imagine that, like Newton, you are sitting under a tree one day when an apple falls on your head, and – 'pow!' – you suddenly come up with a revolutionary scientific theory! Sadly, it doesn't happen like that! For although the nature of intellectual creativity is still poorly understood, there seem to be at least two necessary conditions for having good ideas: (1) a thorough knowledge of the relevant field; and (2) unusually good powers of concentration. If your creative insights are to be of lasting value, you will have to sweat for them.

How reliable is intuition?

How reliable, then, is intuition as a source of knowledge? We can, I think, say that expert intuition is generally more reliable than natural intuition. But since most of us will never operate at the rarefied intellectual level of a Newton or a Poincaré, we might ask to what extent should we trust our own intuitions.

Since good intuitions are not God-given, we need to test them against other sources of knowledge. If your intuitions coincide with reason and experience and other people's intuitions, then it makes more sense to trust them than if they do not. What, then, should you do if your intuitions conflict with another source of knowledge? There is no easy answer to this question.

When we make decisions in the real world, such as which of two university offers to accept, reason and intuition may contradict one another. In the end, most people tend to go with their intuitions, but, as our discussion has suggested, we blindly trust them at our peril.

Conclusion

Our discussion of the emotions in this chapter has, I hope, convinced you of their relevance to the search for knowledge. For not only do they provide the energy that fuels intellectual endeavour, but they also play a central role in our mental lives. Some of our deepest beliefs about the world seem to be as much intuitive matters of the heart as rational matters of the head. So rather than think in terms of an either–or choice between reason and emotion, it might be better to say that a balanced intellectual outlook requires both reason *and* emotion.

At the same time, we need to be aware that the emotions can sometimes be an obstacle to knowledge. For, strong emotions can easily cloud our judgement and tempt us to find bad reasons to justify our pre-existing prejudices; and, despite their value, intuitions do not have any magical authority and cannot always be trusted. So it is worth keeping in mind that having strong convictions about something does not in itself guarantee that it is true.

In the last four chapters, we have seen that all of our knowledge tools are double-edged, and that they can both contribute to our knowledge of the world *and* be an obstacle to it. Rather than rely on any one way of knowing, we need to test them against one another when trying to establish the truth. The step beyond that is to compare our own opinions with those of other people to see how they stand up in the free market of ideas.

Answers to questions (pages 160–1)

1a It is more probable that Linda is a bank teller than that she is *both* a bank teller and an active feminist.

2 The probability of any two particular sequences of heads and tails is the same in each case – in this case $\frac{1}{2} \times \frac{1}{2} \times \frac{1}{2} \times \frac{1}{2} \times \frac{1}{2} \times \frac{1}{2} = \frac{1}{64}$

3 The simplest way to prove this surprising result is to begin by calculating, not the thing we are looking for, but its complement – i.e. the probability of no one sharing a birthday. Imagine people entering a room one-by-one. When the second person enters the room, there are 364 possible days for him to have a birthday that differs from the first person. So the probability that he will have a different birthday from the first person is $\frac{364}{365}$. When the third person enters, there are 363 possibilities of him having a birthday different from both of the first two, so the probability that all three will have different birthdays is $\frac{364}{365} \times \frac{363}{365}$. When the fourth person enters, the probability of all four having different birthdays is $\frac{364}{365} \times \frac{363}{365} \times \frac{362}{365}$. Continuing in this way, when 23 people are in the room, the probability of all of them having different birthdays is

$$\frac{364}{365} \times \frac{363}{365} \times \frac{362}{365} \times \ldots \times \frac{343}{365}$$

This works out to be 0.492. The above product first drops below 0.5 when you have 23 people. Thus, the probability that at least two of the 23 have the same birthday is $1 - 0.492 = 0.508$.

4   If no other force were acting on the ball, it would continue in a straight line at the angle from which it emerged from the tube, but the force of gravity will bring it down to the ground.

5   The two bullets will reach the ground at the same time because a bullet's rate of fall is independent of its horizontal motion.

6   As a reason for staying, you should *not* list the fact that you have already spent $10 on the ticket. If that were your only reason for staying, then you would end up wasting not only your money but also your time. All that matters now is how best to use your time.

Key points

- The emotions are relevant to the search for knowledge because they provide us with energy, affect our thinking and are sometimes used to justify our beliefs.
- The six primary emotions of happiness, sadness, fear, anger, surprise and disgust are found in all cultures.
- The James–Lange theory says that emotions are essentially physical in nature; but they also seem to be influenced by our beliefs.
- The emotions are sometimes an obstacle to knowledge, and strong emotions can colour our perception, distort our logic and inflame our language.
- Nevertheless, emotions give meaning and colour to our lives, and studies of brain-damaged patients suggest that without them we would become 'rational fools'.
- Rather than think of reason and emotion as opposites, it may make more sense to say that our emotions can themselves be more or less rational.
- Intuition is an immediate insight into something, and we can distinguish core intuitions, subject-specific intuitions and social intuitions.
- While there is a sense in which all knowledge is based on intuition, the problem is that people have conflicting intuitions.
- Our intuitive beliefs about many subjects are not very reliable and it could be argued that one of the aims of education is to debug human intuition.
- Many intellectual breakthroughs have come about in a flash of intuition; but you have to work hard for such intuitions.

Terms to remember

apathy	empathy	rational fool
debugging intuition	intuitions	romanticism
emotional colouring	James–Lange theory	social emotion
emotive language	primary emotions	stoicism

Further reading

Antonio Damasio, ***Descartes' Error*** (Grosset/Putnam, 1994). In this fascinating book, Damasio, a neuroscientist, goes beyond the traditional either–or approach of reason versus emotion, and argues that, in order to make intelligent decisions, logical thinking must be grounded in and supported by emotions and feelings.

David Myers, ***Intuition: Its Powers and Perils*** (Yale University Press, 2002). This book gives a balanced appraisal of the pros and cons of making judgements and decisions based on intuition. Myers, a psychologist, argues that while our intuitions are very good in some areas, they are very poor in others, and he advises smart thinkers 'to check their intuitions against available evidence'.

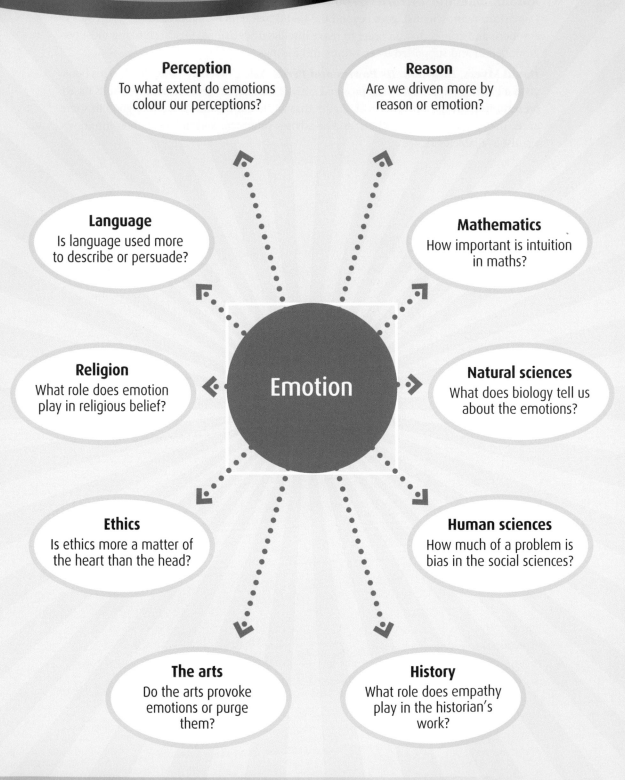

Perception
To what extent do emotions colour our perceptions?

Reason
Are we driven more by reason or emotion?

Language
Is language used more to describe or persuade?

Mathematics
How important is intuition in maths?

Emotion

Religion
What role does emotion play in religious belief?

Natural sciences
What does biology tell us about the emotions?

Ethics
Is ethics more a matter of the heart than the head?

Human sciences
How much of a problem is bias in the social sciences?

The arts
Do the arts provoke emotions or purge them?

History
What role does empathy play in the historian's work?

RETHINKING THINKING

The Economist, 16 December 1999
Traditional economics is based on the assumption that we are rational beings. This article from *The Economist* questions how accurate that assumption is.

Economists are starting to abandon their assumption that humans behave rationally, and instead are finally coming to grips with the crazy, mixed up creatures we really are.

'Are economists human?' is not a question that occurs to many practitioners of the dismal science, but it is one that springs to the minds of many non-economists exposed to conventional economic explanations. Economists have typically described the thought processes of homo sapiens as more like that of Star Trek's Mr Spock—strictly logical, centred on a clearly defined goal and free from the unsteady influences of emotion or irrationality—than the uncertain, error-prone groping with which most of us are familiar. Of course, some human behaviour does fit the rational pattern so beloved of economists. But remember, Mr Spock is a Vulcan, not a human.

Even economists are finally waking up to this fact. A wind of change is now blowing some human spirit back into the ivory towers where economic theory is made. It is becoming increasingly fashionable for economists, especially the younger, more ambitious ones, to borrow insights from psychologists (and sometimes even biologists) to try to explain drug addiction, the working habits of New York taxi-drivers, current sky-high American share prices and other types of behaviour which seem to defy rationality. Alan Greenspan, the chairman of the Federal Reserve, made a bow to this new trend when he wondered about the 'irrational exuberance' of American stockmarkets way back in December 1996 (after an initial flutter of concern, investors ignored him).

Many economic rationalists still hold true to their faith, and some have fought back by devising rational explanations for the apparent irrationalities studied by the growing school of 'behavioural economists'. Ironically, orthodox economists have been forced to fight this rearguard action against heretics in their own ranks just as their own approach has begun to be more widely applied in other social sciences such as the study of law and politics.

The golden age of rational economic man began in the 1940s. Famous earlier economists, such as Adam Smith, Irving Fisher and John Maynard Keynes, had made use of irrationality and other aspects of psychology in their theories. But in the post-war years these aspects were mostly brushed aside by the new wave of rationalists. The dominance of rationality went hand-in-glove with the growing use in economics of mathematics, which also happened to be much easier to apply if humans were assumed to be rational.

Rational behaviour was understood to

have several components. At a minimum – so-called 'narrow rationality' – homo economicus was assumed to be trying always to maximise his general 'happiness': what John Stuart Mill, a 19th-century philosopher, called 'utility'. In other words, given a choice he would take the option with the highest 'expected utility'. And he would be consistent in his choices: if he preferred apples to oranges, and oranges to pears, he also preferred apples to pears. In addition, there is a broader definition of rationality which includes the notion of a person's beliefs being based on logical, objective analysis of all the available evidence. Whether this is a meaningful definition continues to be the subject of much philosophical debate...

During the 1980s... the door of the ivory tower opened... to theories that included irrational behaviour. Today there is a growing school of economists who are drawing on a vast range of behavioural traits identified by experimental psychologists which amount to a frontal assault on the whole idea that people, individually or as a group, mostly act rationally.

A quick tour of the key observations made by these psychologists would make even Mr Spock's head spin. For example, people appear to be disproportionately influenced by the fear of feeling regret, and will often pass up even benefits within reach to avoid a small risk of feeling they have failed. They are also prone to cognitive dissonance: holding a belief plainly at odds with the evidence, usually because the belief has been held and cherished for a long time. Psychiatrists sometimes call this 'denial'.

And then there is anchoring: people are often overly influenced by outside suggestion. People can be influenced even when they know that the suggestion is not being made by someone who is better informed. In one experiment, volunteers were asked a series of questions whose answers were in percentages—such as what percentage of African countries is in the United Nations? A wheel with numbers from one to 100 was spun in front of them; they were then asked to say whether their answer was higher or lower than the number on the wheel, and then to give their answer. These answers were strongly influenced by the randomly selected, irrelevant number on the wheel. The average guess when the wheel showed 10 was 25%; when it showed 65 it was 45%.

Experiments show that most people apparently also suffer from status quo bias: they are willing to take bigger gambles to maintain the status quo than they would be to acquire it in the first place. In one common experiment, mugs are allocated randomly to some people in a group. Those who have them are asked to name a price to sell their mug; those without one are asked to name a price at which they will buy. Usually, the average sales price is considerably higher than the average offer price...

There is also a huge amount of evidence that people are persistently, and irrationally, over-confident. Asked to answer a factual question, then asked to give the probability that their answer was correct, people typically overestimate this probability. This may be due to a representativeness heuristic: a tendency to treat events as representative of some well-known class or pattern. This gives people a sense of familiarity with an event and thus confidence that they have accurately diagnosed it. This can lead people to 'see' patterns in data even where there are none...

Another delightfully human habit is

magical thinking: attributing to one's own actions something that had nothing to do with them, and thus assuming that one has a greater influence over events than is actually the case. For instance, an investor who luckily buys a share that goes on to beat the market may become convinced that he is a skilful investor rather than a merely fortunate one. He may also fall prey to quasi-magical thinking—behaving as if he believes his thoughts can influence events, even though he knows that they can't.

Most people, say psychologists, are also vulnerable to hindsight bias: once something happens, they overestimate the extent to which they could have predicted it. Closely related to this is memory bias: when something happens people often persuade themselves that they actually predicted it, even when they didn't.

Finally, who can deny that people often become emotional, cutting off their noses to spite their faces. One of the psychologists' favourite experiments is the 'ultimatum game' in which one player, the proposer, is given a sum of money, say $10, and offers some portion of it to the other player, the responder. The responder can either accept the offer, in which case he gets the sum offered and the proposer gets the rest, or reject the offer in which case both players get nothing. In experiments, very low offers (less than 20% of the total sum) are often rejected, even though it is rational for the responder to accept any offer (even one cent!) which the proposer makes. And yet responders seem to reject offers out of sheer indignation at being made to accept such a small proportion of the whole sum, and they seem to get more satisfaction from taking revenge on the proposer than in maximising their own financial gain. Mr Spock would be appalled if a Vulcan made this mistake.

FOOLS FOR LOVE

This extract from *How the Mind Works* by Steven Pinker casts an unsentimental eye on the nature of romantic love.

Why does romantic love leave us bewitched, bothered, and bewildered? Should we blame it on the moon, on the devil, on raging hormones?

Unsentimental social scientists and veterans of the singles scene agree that dating is a marketplace. Everyone agrees that Mr or Ms Right should be good-looking, smart, kind, stable, funny, and rich. People shop for the most desirable person who will accept them, and that is why most marriages pair a bride and a groom of approximately equal desirability. The 10s marry the 10s, the 9s marry the 9s, and so on. Mate-shopping, however, is only part of the psychology of romance; it explains the statistics of mate choice, but not the final pick.

Somewhere in this world of five billion people there lives the best-looking, richest, smartest, funniest, kindest person who would settle for you. But your dreamboat is a needle in a haystack, and you may die single if you insist on waiting for him or her to show up. Staying single has costs, such as loneliness, childlessness, and playing the dating game with all its awkward drinks and dinners (and sometimes breakfasts). At some point it pays to set up house with the best person you have found so far. But that calculation leaves your partner vulnerable. The law of averages says that someday you will meet a more desirable person, and if you are always going for the best you can get, on that day you will dump your partner.

But your partner has invested money, time, childrearing, and forgone opportunities in the relationship. If your partner was the most desirable person in the world, he or she would have nothing to worry about, because you would never want to desert. But failing that, the partner would have been foolish to enter the relationship.

Marriage laws offer some protection, but our ancestors had to find some way to commit themselves before the laws existed. How can you be sure that a prospective partner won't leave the minute it is rational to do so – say, when a newly single Tom Cruise or Cindy Crawford moves in next door? One answer is, don't accept a partner who wanted you for rational reasons to begin with; look for a partner who is committed to staying with you because you are you. Committed by what? Committed by an emotion. An emotion that the person did not decide to have, and so cannot decide not to have. An emotion that was not triggered by your objective mate-value and so will not be alienated by someone with greater mate-value. An emotion that is guaranteed not to be a sham because it has physiological costs like tachycardia, insomnia, and anorexia. An emotion like romantic love.

It is often said that people who are sensible about love are incapable of it. Even when courted by the perfect suitor, people are unable to will themselves to fall in love, often to the bewilderment of the matchmaker, the suitor, and the person himself or herself. Instead it is a glance, a laugh, a manner that steals the heart. Research on identical twins suggests that the spouse of one twin usually is not attracted to the other; we fall in love with the individual, not with the individual's qualities. The upside is that when Cupid does strike, the lovestruck one is all the more credible in the eyes of the object of desire. Murmuring that your lover's looks, earning power, and IQ meet your minimal standards would probably kill the romantic mood, even though the statement is statistically true. The way to a person's heart is to declare the opposite – that you're in love because you can't help it. Concerned parents and politicians notwithstanding, the sneering, body-pierced, guitar-smashing rock musician is typically not singing about drugs, sex, or Satan. He is singing about love. He is courting a woman by calling attention to the irrationality, uncontrollability, and physiological costs of his desire. I want you so bad, it's driving me mad, Can't eat, can't sleep, Heart beats like a big bass drum, You're the only one, Don't know why I love you like I do, You drive me crazy, Can't stop lovin' you, I like the way you walk, I like the way you talk, et cetera, et cetera.

Of course, one can well imagine a woman not being swept off her feet by these proclamations. (Or a man, if it is a woman doing the declaring.) They set off a warning light in the other component of courtship, smart shopping. Groucho Marx said that he would not belong to any club that would have him as a member. Usually people do not want any suitor who wants them too badly too early, because it shows that the suitor is desperate (so they should wait for someone better), and because it shows that the suitor's ardour is too easily triggered (hence too easily triggerable by someone else). The contradiction of courtship – flaunt your desire while playing hard to get – comes from the two parts of romantic love: setting a minimal standard for candidates in the mate market, and capriciously committing body and soul to one of them.

Appendices to Part 2

Appendix A: Propositions

Introduction

Since a great deal of our knowledge comes to us through language, we should say something about various kinds of proposition before looking at the different areas of knowledge in Part 3. The word 'proposition' is roughly synonymous with 'statement' and it can be defined as *anything that can be asserted or denied*. The following are all propositions:

'Snow is white.'
'John is a clever man.'
'Pigs have wings.'
'Janet loves spinach.'
'Life is a dream.'

As this list shows, something does not have to be true to qualify as a proposition. All that matters is that it can be asserted or denied – i.e. said to be true or false.

Four kinds of proposition

Four main kinds of proposition are commonly distinguished:

1   analytic statements
2   empirical statements
3   value-judgements
4   metaphysical statements.

1 An **analytic proposition** is one that is true by definition. We can know independent of experience that such propositions are true simply by *analysing* them. There are two main types of analytic proposition: definitional truths and truths of reason.

   a   *Definitional truths*   The standard example of this kind of proposition is 'All bachelors are unmarried men'. This statement is true but, to a native speaker, at least, it is not very informative. Rather than being an interesting fact about the world, it is a trivial fact about language. For example, if you want to know how many Bolivian bachelors are unmarried, you don't have to fly to Bolivia and conduct a survey. I have never been to Bolivia or met any Bolivian bachelors, but I already know that they are all unmarried.

   b   *Truths of reason*   The way to justify a proposition such as 'If a is bigger than b, and b is bigger than c, then a is bigger than c' is not by consulting a dictionary, but by reasoning it out. Propositions of this kind are typically found in mathematics and logic. The nature of mathematical propositions is something we shall discuss in more detail in Chapter 7.

Which of the following would you describe as a bachelor? What does this suggest to you about the nature of definitions?

a A divorced man

b Tarzan

c A 17-year-old living at home with his parents

d The pope

e A homosexual living with another man

2 An **empirical proposition** is one whose truth or falsity can be determined by appeal to evidence based on perception: for example, 'Pandas eat bamboo', 'Smoking can damage your health', 'Napoleon was defeated at the battle of Waterloo.' The vast majority of our knowledge in the natural sciences, social sciences and history is empirical in nature.

3 A **value-judgement** is one which contains a value word, such as 'good', 'bad', 'right', 'wrong', 'beautiful', 'ugly'. Value-judgements generally appeal to some kind of *standard* but, unlike empirical propositions, two people may agree on all the facts of the matter, and yet make different value-judgements. For this reason, it is generally more difficult to establish the truth or falsity of a value-judgement than that of an empirical statement.

4 A **metaphysical proposition** is one that is neither analytic, empirical nor a value-judgement. What this leaves are statements about the nature of ultimate reality. For example, 'God exists' is a metaphysical proposition because it is not true by definition, it cannot be verified or falsified by empirical evidence, and it is not a value-judgement. Here are some other examples:

Time has no beginning and no end.
Human free-will is an illusion.
The past does not exist.
We have all lived past lives.
Life is meaningless.

Importance

Since each of the four kinds of proposition is justified in a different way, it is important to know which kind you are dealing with when looking at a knowledge claim. While an analytic proposition can be justified on the basis of reason alone, an empirical proposition needs the support of perceptual evidence. When it comes to value-judgements and metaphysical propositions, you might appeal to a combination of reason, experience, intuition and authority to support them. There is, however, less general agreement about how these two kinds of proposition can be justified. Indeed, some people argue that the most they can give us is *belief* rather than *knowledge*.

1 Which of the following are propositions and which are not?

   a God created bananas.

   b Put that banana down!

   c Bananas are beautiful.

   d 2 bananas plus 2 bananas equals 4 bananas.

   e You shouldn't steal bananas.

   f Where are the bananas?

   g Yuri has gone bananas.

   h Bananas are blue.

2 State whether each of the following propositions is analytic, empirical, metaphysical or a value-judgement:

   a God is the creator of all things.

   b Mozart is a great composer.

   c Bananas are yellow.

   d Smith is a courageous man.

   e Napoleon was defeated at Waterloo in 1815.

   f You ought to eat more cabbage.

   g Every event has a cause.

   h A straight line is the shortest distance between two points.

   i John said that a cube has eight edges.

   j All mass murderers are insane.

3 How would you rank the four kinds of proposition we have discussed in this section in terms of their certainty?

Complications

The distinction between the above four types of proposition may seem straightforward, but in practice there are various grey areas and complications, some of which are considered below.

Factual disputes and verbal disputes

The dividing line between an analytic and an empirical proposition is not always clear-cut, and what looks like a factual dispute about evidence can sometimes collapse into a verbal dispute about the meanings of words. As we saw in Chapter 3, language is often ambiguous, and we can easily get into arguments about the meanings of words. For example, imagine two people arguing about whether or not Jones was driving too fast. The argument might take one of two forms:

   A 'Jones was driving too fast – he was doing at least 70 kilometres per hour.'
      'Actually, he was doing 40.'

   B 'Jones was driving too fast – he was doing at least 70 kilometres per hour.'
      'I don't consider 70 fast.'

In the first case, the argument is about the facts of the matter – whether or not Jones was driving at 70 kilometres per hour; in the second case it is about how the facts should be *described* and hinges on the meaning of the word 'fast'.

Here is another example: if two people are arguing about whether or not John Smith is bald, they may be arguing about how much hair he has on his head – a factual dispute; or they may simply be arguing about whether he should be *described* as bald. While you can settle a factual dispute by looking at the evidence, you can only resolve a verbal dispute by convincing the person with whom you are speaking to accept *your* definition of the disputed word.

Sometimes a dispute about the meaning of words can have important practical consequences. For example, if two people agree on all the facts, but one describes Bloggs' action as 'murder' and the other as 'manslaughter', this may be a verbal dispute, but it is not a *merely* verbal dispute – for it may determine how long Bloggs spends behind bars!

Activity 6A.3

To what extent are each of these disputes factual and to what extent verbal?

a Two people arguing about whether or not an embryo is a human being.

b Two people arguing about whether or not chimpanzees have language.

c Two people arguing about whether or not Russia and the USA are democracies.

d Two people arguing about whether a student who scored 45 in his IB exams is intelligent.

e Two people arguing about whether or not person X is a terrorist.

f Two people arguing about whether or not a table that belonged to their grandparents is an antique.

g Two people arguing about whether or not there is proof that the USA landed on the moon in 1969.

h Two people arguing about whether or not all human beings are selfish.

i Two people arguing about whether or not Hans, who was born in Germany but lives in Paris, is really German.

j Two people arguing about whether or not O'Leary, who attends church regularly, is a good Catholic.

k Two people arguing about whether or not human beings have free-will.

Another reason for being clear about the difference between analytic propositions and empirical propositions is that it can help us to distinguish genuine explanations from pseudo-explanations that look informative but actually explain nothing. In Chapter 5, we spoke of the ten deadly fallacies, and we might add the **nominal fallacy** to the list. This fallacy consists in assuming that we have explained something simply because we have put a name on it. For example, if you ask someone why a particular brand of pills puts people to sleep, and they tell you that it is because they have 'dormative powers', then you have learnt nothing. For 'dormative powers' simply means 'having the power to put people to sleep'. What may have initially looked like an explanation collapses into a trivial analytic truth: 'these pills put people to sleep because they have the power to put people to sleep'.

Which of the following are genuine explanations and which commit the nominal fallacy?

a 'What caused the baby's death?' 'Sudden infant death syndrome.'

b 'Why did the water pipes burst?' 'Because the temperature fell below freezing point, and water expands when it freezes.'

c 'What caused the earthquake?' 'A sudden movement of rocks beneath the earth's surface.'

d 'What caused the earthquake?' 'It was an act of God.'

e 'Why does sugar dissolve in water?' 'Because it is soluble.'

f 'Why did the apple fall to the ground?' 'Because of gravity.'

g 'Why did Peter Sutcliffe murder 13 people?' 'Because he is insane.'

h 'Why did the stock market fall yesterday?' 'Because of a technical adjustment and profit-taking by investors.'

i 'Why did he win the lottery?' 'Because he is a lucky person.'

Facts and values

Two points can be made about the relationship between empirical propositions and value-judgements.

1 *Many words have positive or negative connotations and this blurs the dividing line between facts and values.* As we saw in our discussion of language in Chapter 3, this means that it is sometimes difficult to describe things in a purely factual, value-neutral way. For example, the following statements about people have both a descriptive and an evaluative element:

> 'Gordon is a liar.'
> 'Sacha is a gossip.'
> 'Camille is quick-witted.'
> 'Jean-Claude is patient.'

2 *Some empirical facts may be relevant to the justification of value-judgements.* For example, the fact that Miller can swim 100 metres in a certain time is relevant to the judgement that he is a good swimmer; and the fact that Parker robbed an old lady is relevant to the judgement that he is a bad man. We will have more to say about the relationship between facts and values when we look at ethics in Chapter 12.

Empirical propositions and metaphysics

When we consider the relationship between empirical and metaphysical propositions, two points can again be made:

1 *Some empirical facts may be relevant to the justification of our metaphysical beliefs.* For example, you might argue that the order of the universe counts as preliminary evidence for the existence of God, and the suffering in the world counts as preliminary evidence against it.

2 *If you push an empirical proposition hard enough, it collapses into a metaphysical one.* To see this, consider the following exchanges:

'I know that my keys are on the table.'
'But how can you be sure you are not dreaming?'

'I know that all metals expand when heated.'
'But how can you be sure the laws of physics will hold tomorrow?'

'I know that Hitler invaded Poland in 1939.'
'But how can you be sure the past really exists?'

The responses to the above statements have a surreal quality because they bring to light background assumptions that we take for granted in everyday life. But it is at least *conceivable* that such assumptions are false. Perhaps one day you will wake up from the 'dream of life' and realise that the whole thing has been a fantasy. Perhaps the laws of physics will break down tomorrow and chaos will ensue. Perhaps God created the universe five seconds ago, together with apparent memories, copies of yesterday's newspapers and fossils in the rock strata.

These kinds of doubt are not very helpful in everyday life. If you ask a friend if she has seen your keys you expect a yes-or-no answer, not her reflections on whether life is a dream. If you take a flight from London to New York, you may worry about hijackers, but not about the reliability of the laws of physics. And if you are looking at a historical document, you might question its authenticity, but not the reality of the past.

Although such metaphysical doubts might be thought to cast a shadow of uncertainty over empirical propositions, it is still reasonable to say that I *know* my keys are on the table, all metals expand when heated, and Hitler invaded Poland in 1939. For, as we saw in Chapter 1, we do not need complete certainty in order to say that we know something.

What our discussion suggests is that at the most fundamental level our beliefs are underwritten by various metaphysical beliefs – or what in Chapter 6 we called *core intuitions*. This might be taken to mean that, at the deepest level, there is an element of faith built into all our knowledge claims. Most people don't have time to worry about the nature of ultimate reality in everyday life, but metaphysical speculation is taken more seriously in areas such as religion and philosophy.

Conclusion

The four kinds of proposition we have distinguished in this appendix can be found in almost all of the areas of knowledge we shall be looking at in Part 3. For example, a subject like physics includes not only empirical propositions, but also definitions, value-judgements and metaphysical assumptions. Thus, as well as making observations and conducting experiments, a physicist will also:

- be familiar with the meaning of key terms such as 'force', 'mass' and 'acceleration'
- exercise various *intellectual virtues* such as honesty and open-mindedness
- assume the truth of various metaphysical beliefs, such as that the universe is an orderly place and human beings are capable of discovering that order.

At various points in Part 3, we will have reason to refer to definitions, facts, values and metaphysical beliefs, and it is worth keeping in mind not only the differences but also the connections between them.

Appendix B: Paradigms

What is a paradigm?

In Chapter 2, we saw that knowledge differs from mere information in that it is organised into a meaningful whole. To know a subject consists of more than being able to reel off facts about it like a participant in a game show; it also requires a grasp of the subject's underlying principles and a sense of how its various parts are related to one another. As a preliminary to our exploration of areas of knowledge in Part 3, we should at this point introduce the concept of a *paradigm*. Although it is used in a variety of ways, we will define a paradigm as a *set of interrelated ideas for making sense of one or more aspects of reality*. The word comes from the Greek word *paradeigma* meaning 'pattern' and if you think of it as a model or framework for understanding something you are on the right track.

In its technical sense, the word 'paradigm' was first used to describe wide-ranging scientific theories. For example:

- the Newtonian *paradigm* in physics
- the atomic *paradigm* in chemistry
- the evolutionary *paradigm* in biology.

However, we can usefully speak of paradigms in other areas of knowledge as well. Here are some examples:

- **Mathematics**   The *Euclidean paradigm* is based on the axioms of the geometry which you study at school (see below).
- **Human sciences**   The *blank slate paradigm* holds that the mind starts out as a 'blank slate' and that heredity plays little role in determining human personality.
- **History**   The *Marxist paradigm* claims that history is driven by economic factors rather than by great individuals.
- **The arts**   The *realist paradigm* says that the purpose of art is to copy reality.
- **Ethics**   The *utilitarian paradigm* holds that ethics is about maximising happiness.

Typically, a paradigm will include each of the four kinds of proposition mentioned in Appendix A – facts, metaphysical assumptions, definitions and value-judgements. (For an example, see the brief discussion on physics at the end of Appendix A.)

We might group the paradigms that can be found in various subject areas into four **master paradigms**.

Type of paradigm	Typical areas of knowledge	Example
1 Deductive system	Logic and mathematics	Euclidean geometry
The geometry you learn at school is based on the work of Euclid, a famous mathematician who lived in Alexandria, Egypt around 300 BCE. Euclid's genius was to take various geometrical insights, many of which were known to other mathematicians, and show how they could be derived from five axioms which Euclid took to be self-evident. (We shall discuss Euclidean geometry in more detail in Chapter 7.)		

2 Scientific theory	Natural and human sciences	Newtonian physics
The system of physics developed by Sir Isaac Newton (1642–1727) is one of the great achievements in the history of science. Newton's laws enable us not only to make accurate predictions, but also to explain such diverse phenomena as the fall of an apple or the movement of the planets around the sun.		
3 Narrative	History and literature	A traditional novel
A narrative puts a story-like structure on experience by weaving individual episodes into a meaningful whole which has a beginning, a middle and an end. We use narrative paradigms not only in novels, but also in history, and when we tell 'the story of our lives'. With some justification human beings have been described as 'story-telling animals'.		
4 Style	The arts	Impressionism
Artists usually work within a style or tradition which influences how they see the world. Take, for example, the visual arts. While the Egyptians were concerned with the static, timeless quality of things, realists sought an 'exact likeness' and impressionists aimed to capture the changing play of light and shadow. Such background assumptions affected the way in which each of these groups approached their subject.		

As the above table suggests, different areas of knowledge have different general models for making sense of the world. Rather than say that only one of these master paradigms leads to the truth, it might be better to say that they are equally valid ways of making sense of the world. Why not think of knowledge as a symphony with many instruments rather than a monotonous solo?

Going beyond areas of knowledge, we could also describe **cultures** as paradigms; for cultures can be thought of as 'maps of meaning' which help us to make sense of reality. In Chapter 2 we saw that the culture you grow up in will influence your ideas about what is reasonable and unreasonable, right and wrong, etc. Thus a hunter–gatherer living in the Amazon will have a very different model of reality to a banker living in New York.

Paradigms as knowledge filters

Since it is impossible to see the world with 'clean eyes', we are always interpreting it through some paradigm or other. While paradigms help us to organise our beliefs into meaningful patterns, the danger is that they can also act as **knowledge filters** which trap us into a particular way of looking at things and close our minds to other possibilities.

We could liken a paradigm to a pair of tinted glasses which colour our perception of the world. If I am wearing red-tinted glasses and you are wearing blue-tinted ones, then we will see things in a different way. For example, if an evolutionary biologist and a 'creation scientist' – who believes that each species was uniquely created by God – look at the same facts, they will draw very different conclusions. And a believer in paranormal phenomena and a sceptic will have quite different perspectives on someone who claims to be able to communicate with the dead.

1 According to a well-known saying, 'To a person with a hammer, everything looks like a nail.' Using this model, suggest how the following might be completed:

  a To a person with a camera, ...

  b To a person with a computer, ...

  c To a person with paranoia, ...

2 What does the above have to do with our discussion of paradigms and knowledge filters?

3 Refer back to the relevant sections in Chapters 3–6 and explain how each of the following are related to what we have said about paradigms.

  a Language: the Sapir–Whorf hypothesis (Chapter 3, p. 68)

  b Perception: the role played by interpretation and expectation (Chapter 4, pp. 90–1)

  c Logic: the prison of consistency (Chapter 5, p. 135)

  d Emotion: emotional colouring (Chapter 6, p. 151)

We are often not aware of our assumptions because, like the glasses on the end of our nose, they are invisible to us and we look straight through them to make sense of the world. But if we are to think critically about our knowledge claims, then it is essential that we try – at least occasionally – to take a step back and question our own way of looking at things. Indeed, one of the aims of international education is surely to make us aware of our cultural paradigms so that we can then consider their strengths and weaknesses.

Paradigm shifts

Sometimes we *are* able to escape from our own assumptions and 'think outside the box'. Familiarity with lateral thinking, which we discussed in Chapter 5 (p. 135), may help us to achieve this. A paradigm shift occurs, not when we acquire more information about something, but when we change our perspective and come up with a new way of looking at it. Two examples of paradigm shifts in miniature can be found in ambiguous figures and jokes:

- *Ambiguous figures* are images that can be interpreted in two different ways. We saw several examples of such images in our discussion of perceptual illusions in Chapter 4 (p. 89). Here is another. The image in Figure 6A.1 may be seen as a woman's face, but if you change your perspective you can see it as a man playing the saxophone instead.

- *Jokes*, as we saw in Chapter 3, are based on ambiguity. If we are to 'get' the punch line, we usually have to change perspective.

Figure 6B.1

Take one of the cartoons in this book and explain how its humour hinges on a mini-paradigm shift.

"I'm afraid you've had a paradigm shift."

Figure 6B.2

When it comes to the big, informing ideas that shape our outlook, it takes a rare and subtle mind to escape from the tram lines of traditional thinking and strike out in a new direction. Among the great thinkers who helped to initiate paradigm shifts in their subjects are the following:

- Albert Einstein (1879–1955) in physics
- Dimitri Mendeleyev (1834–1907) in chemistry
- Charles Darwin (1809–82) in biology
- John Maynard Keynes (1883–1946) in economics
- Karl Marx (1818–83) in history
- Sigmund Freud (1856–1939) in psychology
- Noam Chomsky (1928–) in linguistics
- Pablo Picasso (1881–1963) in art.

Activity 6B.3

Do some research on one of the above individuals and then answer the following questions:
a How did the person in question revolutionise their subject?
b What intellectual and personal qualities did they have which helped them to do this?
c To what extent are their ideas still accepted today?

During periods of intellectual ferment, some people may question a dominant paradigm and suggest an alternative way of looking at things. At such times, disagreements will emerge on how to interpret the evidence, and some assumptions, definitions and values previously taken for granted may be thrown into doubt. For example, during the scientific revolution of the seventeenth century the medieval assumption that everything in nature has a purpose was replaced by the idea of the clockwork universe in which everything is explained in terms of mechanical causes and effects. While some people clung to the traditional belief that the seven 'planets' (the Moon, Mercury, Venus, Sun, Mars, Jupiter and Saturn) were carried around the earth on crystal spheres driven by angels, others, such as Copernicus (1473–1543) and

Figure 6B.3

Galileo (1564–1642), insisted that the planets travelled round the sun. To the traditionalists, the revolutionary idea that the earth is a planet which orbits the sun was one that simply made no sense; for up until then a *planet* had been defined as something which rotates round the earth. The Copernicans had to change the meaning of the word 'planet' to accommodate their ideas, and then convince people that defining a planet as something which goes round the sun was a more useful way of looking at things. Underlying these disagreements were different conceptions of knowledge and of what one *ought* to allow as evidence, with one side appealing to the authority of the Bible and the other to the empirical evidence.

Conclusion

The concept of a paradigm has been implicit in our discussion about knowledge since we introduced the idea of a mental map at the beginning of Chapter 1. Now that we have made it explicit, we need to consider how reliable the paradigms we currently use are. For it is always possible that there are better ways of looking at things. This complicates things. When we consider the various areas of knowledge in Part 3 we will need to examine some of the assumptions on which they are based and ask ourselves to what extent they can be justified.

Areas of knowledge

7 Mathematics

'Mathematics is neither physical nor mental, it's social.'

Reuben Hersh, 1927–

'The useful combinations [in mathematics] are precisely the most beautiful.'

Henri Poincaré, 1854–1912

'Mathematics is the abstract key which turns the lock of the physical universe.'

John Polkinghorne, 1930–

'Everything that can be counted does not count. Everything that counts cannot be counted.'

Albert Einstein, 1879–1955

'The mark of a civilized man is the ability to look at a column of numbers and weep.'

Bertrand Russell, 1872–1970

'The advancement and perfection of mathematics are intimately connected with the prosperity of the state.'

Napoleon Bonaparte, 1769–1821

'In the pure mathematics we contemplate absolute truths which existed in the divine mind before the morning stars sang together, and which will continue to exist there when the last of their radiant host shall have fallen from heaven.'

Edward Everett, 1794–1865

'A mathematician is a machine for turning coffee into theorems.'

Paul Erdos, 1913–96

'Mathematics began when it was discovered that a brace of pheasants and a couple of days have something in common: the number two.'

Bertrand Russell, 1872–1970

'Math – that most logical of sciences – shows us that the truth can be highly counterintuitive and that sense is hardly common.'

K. C. Cole

'To speak freely, I am convinced that it [mathematics] is a more powerful instrument of knowledge than any other...'

René Descartes, 1596–1650

'Instead of having "answers" on a math test, they should just call them "impressions", and if you got a different "impression", so what, can't we all be brothers?'

Jack Handey, 1949–

'If I could prove by logic that you would die in five minutes, I should be sorry you were going to die, but my sorrow would be very much mitigated by pleasure in the proof.'

G. H. Hardy, 1877–1947, to Bertrand Russell

'The enormous usefulness of mathematics in the natural sciences is something bordering on the mysterious, and there is no rational explanation for it.'

Eugene Wigner, 1902–95

Introduction

Mathematics is a subject that seems to charm and alarm people in equal measure. If someone asks you, 'What are you most certain of in the world?' you might reply '2 + 2 = 4'. Surely no one can doubt that! Mathematics seems to be an island of certainty in a vast ocean of doubt.

At the most general level, we might characterise mathematics as the search for abstract patterns. And such patterns turn up everywhere. When you think about it, there is something extraordinary about the fact that, for *anything* you care to name, if you take two of that thing and add two more of that thing you end up with four of that thing. Similarly, if you take any circle – no matter how big or small – and divide its circumference by its diameter, you *always* end up with the same number – π (roughly 3.14).

The fact that there seems to be an underlying order in things might explain why mathematics not only seems to give us certainty, but is also of enormous practical value. At the beginning of the scientific revolution, Galileo (1564–1642) said that the book of nature is written in the language of mathematics. If anything, mathematics is even more important than it was in the seventeenth century, and mathematical literacy is a prerequisite for a successful career in almost any branch of science.

The certainty and usefulness of mathematics may help to explain its enduring appeal. The mathematician and philosopher Bertrand Russell (1872–1970) recalled how he began studying geometry at the age of eleven: 'This was one of the great events of my life, as dazzling as first love. I had not imagined that there was anything so delicious in the world.' Russell's description would be greeted with blank incomprehension in some quarters. For many people, words such as 'love' and 'delicious' simply do not go with the word 'mathematics'. Mathematics may give some a reassuring feeling of certainty, but others find it threatening precisely because it leaves us with no place to hide. If you make a mistake in a maths problem you can be *shown* to be wrong. You can't say it's 'an interesting interpretation', or 'an original way of looking at it', or 'it all depends what you mean by...' You're just wrong!

Figure 7.1   *"Maybe it's not a wrong answer — maybe it's just a different answer."*

To what extent do you think people's beliefs about the value of mathematics are determined by their ability in the subject?

Mathematical thinking also requires a kind of selective attention to things; for you have to ignore context and operate at a purely abstract level. While some people find the resulting abstractions fascinating, others can find little meaning in them. The American novelist Philip Roth gives an amusing account of a father trying to sharpen the mind of his son, Nathan, by throwing maths problems at him:

> 'Marking Down', he [my father] would say, not unlike a... student announcing the title of a poem. 'A clothing dealer, trying to dispose of an overcoat cut in last year's style, marked it down from the original price of thirty dollars to twenty-four. Failing to make a sale, he reduced the price to nineteen dollars and twenty cents. Again he found no takers, so he tried another price reduction and this time sold it... All right, Nathan, what was the selling price if the last markdown was consistent with the others?' Or, 'Making a Chain.' A lumberjack has six sections of chain, each consisting of four links. If the cost of cutting open a link....' and so on.

> The next day... I would day dream in my bed about the clothing dealer and the lumberjack. To whom had the haberdasher finally sold the overcoat? Did the man who bought it realize it was cut in last year's style? If he wore it to a restaurant, would people laugh? And what did 'last year's style' look like anyway? 'Again he found no takers', I would say aloud, finding much to feel melancholy about in that idea. I still remember how charged for me was that word 'takers'. Could it have been the lumberjack with his six sections of chain who, in his rustic innocence, had bought the overcoat cut in last year's style? And why suddenly did he need an overcoat? Invited to a fancy ball? By whom?...

> My father... was disheartened to find me intrigued by fantasies and irrelevant details of geography and personality and intention, instead of the simple beauty of the arithmetic solution. He did not think that was intelligent of me and he was right.

The very success of mathematics has sometimes bred a kind of 'imperialism' which says that if you can't express something in mathematical symbols then it has no intellectual value. You might, however, feel that many important things in life escape the abstractions of a formal system.

The mathematical paradigm

A good definition of mathematics is 'the science of rigorous proof'. Although some earlier cultures developed a 'cookbook mathematics' of useful recipes for solving practical problems, the idea of mathematics as the science of proof dates back only as far as the Greeks. The most famous of the Greek mathematicians was Euclid who lived in Alexandria, Egypt, around 300 BCE. He was the first person to organise geometry into a rigorous body of knowledge, and his ideas have had an enduring influence on civilisation. The geometry you study in high school today is basically Euclidean geometry.

The model of reasoning developed by Euclid is known as a **formal system**, and it has three key elements:

- axioms
- deductive reasoning
- theorems.

When you reason formally, you begin with *axioms*, use *deductive reasoning*, and *derive theorems*. The latter can then be used as a basis for reasoning further and deriving more complex theorems.

Axioms

The axioms of a system are its starting points or basic assumptions. At least until the nineteenth century, the axioms of mathematics were considered to be self-evident truths which provided firm foundations for mathematical knowledge. You might want to be awkward and insist that we prove our axioms. But, as we saw in Chapter 5, you can't prove everything. If you tried to, you would get caught in an **infinite regress** – endless chain of reasoning – proving A in terms of B, and B in terms of C and so on for ever. We have to start somewhere, and there is surely no better place to start than with what seems to be obvious.

There are four traditional requirements for a set of axioms. They should be consistent, independent, simple and fruitful.

1   *Consistent*   If you can deduce both p and non-p from the same set of axioms they are not consistent. Inconsistency is bad news because, once you allow it into a system, you can prove literally anything.

2   *Independent*   For the sake of elegance, you should begin with the smallest possible number of axioms. You should not be able to deduce one of the axioms from the others – for then it is a theorem rather than an axiom.

3   *Simple*   Since axioms are accepted without further proof, they ought to be as clear and simple as possible.

4   *Fruitful*   A good formal system should enable you to prove as many theorems as possible using the fewest number of axioms.

Starting with a few basic definitions – such as a point is that which has no part, and a line has length but no breadth – Euclid postulated the following five axioms:

1   It shall be possible to draw a straight line joining any two points.

2   A finite straight line may be extended without limit in either direction.

3   It shall be possible to draw a circle with a given centre and through a given point.

4   All right angles are equal to one another.

5   There is just one straight line through a given point which is parallel to a given line.

Deductive reasoning

We discussed deductive reasoning in Chapter 5, and gave as one example of a syllogism:

All human beings are mortal (1)
Socrates is a human being   (2)
Therefore Socrates is mortal   (3)

(1) and (2), we said, are the **premises** and (3) the **conclusion** of the argument; and if (1) and (2) are true then (3) is *necessarily* true. In mathematics axioms are like premises and theorems are like conclusions.

Theorems

Using his five axioms and deductive reasoning, Euclid derived various simple theorems, such as:

1 Lines perpendicular to the same line are parallel.
2 Two straight lines do not enclose an area.
3 The sum of the angles of a triangle is 180 degrees.
4 The angles on a straight line sum to 180 degrees.

Such simple theorems can then be used to construct more complex proofs. Consider Figure 7.2. You are told that angle a plus angle c equals 180 degrees, and you are then asked to prove that angle b equals angle c.

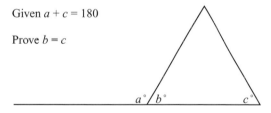

Given $a + c = 180$

Prove $b = c$

Figure 7.2

Here is a proof:

1		$a + c = 180$	given
2	and	$a + b = 180$	angles on a straight line (theorem 4 above)
3	therefore	$a + c = a + b$	by substitution
4	therefore	$b = c$	QED

One of the attractive things about this proof is its generality. Whatever the size of angle a – be it 102 degrees or 172 degrees – if we know that angle a plus angle c equals 180 degrees, then angle b *must* equal angle c.

"I think you should be more explicit here in step two."

Figure 7.3

Proofs and conjectures

We have seen that a formal system begins with axioms and uses deductive reasoning to prove theorems. To clarify what is meant by a 'proof' in the strict mathematical sense of the word, we can compare a proof with a conjecture. In a *proof* a theorem is shown to follow logically from the relevant axioms. A conjecture, by contrast, is a hypothesis that seems to work, but has not been shown to be *necessarily true*. To illustrate the difference between these two concepts consider the following proposition:

The sum of the first n odd numbers = n^2 (where n is any number).

If you are curious to know whether this is true, you might see what happens when you plug in the first odd number, then the first two odd numbers, then the first three odd numbers, and so on:

First	1	= 1	= 1^2	works
First two	1 + 3	= 4	= 2^2	works
First three	1 + 3 + 5	= 9	= 3^2	works
First four	1 + 3 + 5 + 7	= 16	= 4^2	works
First five	1 + 3 + 5 + 7 + 9	= 25	= 5^2	works

The proposition is true for every n we have tested. So can we say that we have *proved* that it is true – that it is true full stop? No! All we have done is reason **inductively**. You may remember that in Chapter 5 we said that induction involves reasoning from particular to general, and that although it is a useful way of reasoning it cannot give us certainty. No matter how many white swans you have seen, you cannot be sure that the next swan you see won't be black. Our claim about odd numbers works for the first five odd numbers; but that is no guarantee that it will work for the first twenty-four or hundred-and-four odd numbers. Relying on inductive reason we cannot be sure that at some point we won't encounter a metaphorical black swan.

To see the point, you might like to consider the following example. The question now is whether the following formula generates the sequence of square numbers (1, 4, 9, etc.) for any n.

$$n^2 + n \times (n-1) \times (n-2) \times (n-3) \times (n-4)$$

So let's test it:

When $n = 1$, we get: $1 + 1 \times (0) \times (-1) \times (-2) \times (-3) = 1$
When $n = 2$, we get: $4 + 2 \times (1) \times (0) \times (-1) \times (-2) = 4$
When $n = 3$, we get: $9 + 3 \times (2) \times (1) \times (0) \times (-1) = 9$
When $n = 4$, we get: $16 + 4 \times (3) \times (2) \times (1) \times (0) = 16$

Again, things seem to be working out. But now look at what happens, when $n = 5$:

When $n = 5$, we get: $25 + 5 \times (4) \times (3) \times (2) \times (1) = 145$

Shucks – a black swan! If you try it for 6, you get 756, and if you try it for 7, you get 2,569. In fact, beyond $n = 4$, the formula *never* generates the corresponding square number. (The example is in fact a contrived one. The formula was made in such a way that for numbers up to 4, one of the parts in brackets will sum to zero, thereby cancelling out everything to the right of the n^2. Beyond 4, this does not happen. Nevertheless, the example illustrates the danger of jumping to conclusions in mathematics.)

Now consider **Goldbach's conjecture** – a famous mathematical conjecture according to which every even number is the sum of two primes. If you try it out, it seems to work:

$2 = 1 + 1$	$12 = 7 + 5$
$4 = 2 + 2$	$14 = 7 + 7$
$6 = 3 + 3$	$16 = 13 + 3$
$8 = 5 + 3$	$18 = 13 + 5$
$10 = 5 + 5$	$20 = 17 + 3$

If you keep running through the even numbers into the hundreds, and the thousands and the tens of thousands, Goldbach's conjecture still works. So how far do you have to go before you can say you have *proved* it? Mathematicians have used computers to help test the conjecture for all the even numbers up to 100,000,000,000,000 and they have not found any counter-examples. You might think that is a good enough proof. But it is still abstractly possible that the next number – say, 100,000,000,000,002 – will not be the sum of two primes.

Furthermore, it is worth keeping in mind that although 100,000,000,000,000 may seem like a big number, compared with infinity, it's peanuts. For even a very large number is infinitely far away from infinity. The philosopher Ludwig Wittgenstein (1889–1951) put it well when he said 'Where the nonsense starts is with our habit of thinking of a large number as closer to infinity than a small one.' We may have tested Goldbach's conjecture up to 100,000,000,000,000, but the ratio of tested to untested cases is still incredibly small. (Imagine someone testing ten swans out of a total swan population of millions, and declaring on that basis that all swans are white.)

You want proof? I'll give you proof!

Figure 7.4

Most mathematicians believe that Goldbach's conjecture is in fact true, but since no one has yet shown that it is necessarily true for any randomly chosen even number, it remains one of the great unproven conjectures in number theory.

Before moving on, it is worth mentioning that the proposition on page 192, 'The sum of the first n odd numbers $= n^2$' has in fact been proved. We will not give a formal proof here but you can get a visual sense of it from Figure 7.5. If you begin from the top right square and then add successive odd numbers of small squares, first 3 squares, then 5 squares, then 7 squares, then 9 squares etc – you can see that each time they can be added to the previous square to make a larger one the side of which is equal to the number of odd numbers in the sequence.

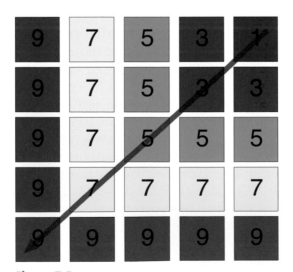

Figure 7.5

Beauty, elegance and intuition

Since any logical sequence of statements which leads to a theorem counts as a proof in mathematics, there may be many different proofs of a theorem. However, mathematicians generally seek proofs that are clear, economical and elegant. A particularly elegant proof might even be described as 'beautiful'. The great Hungarian mathematician, Paul Erdos (1913–96), used to speak of 'the BOOK' in which God keeps the most beautiful proofs for theorems; and he once joked that, even if God does not exist, you cannot doubt the existence of 'the book'.

Although the person in the street does not usually associate mathematics with beauty, we can get a sense of what mathematicians mean by a 'beautiful' or 'elegant' solution by considering a couple of simple examples.

Activity 7.2

1 There are 1,024 people in a knock-out tennis tournament. What is the total number of games that must be played before a champion can be declared?

2 What is the sum of the integers from 1 to 100?

The tennis tournament problem seems fairly straightforward, and to solve it you might reason as follows. In the first round, there will be 512 games, in the second round, 256, in the third round, 128, in the fourth 64, in the fifth 32, and then 16, 8, 4, 2, plus the final. Summing these figures, you get 1,023. But there is another simpler way of solving the problem. If 1,024 people enter the tournament, there will only be one person who wins all of their games, and that is the eventual winner. All of the other 1,023 players will lose one and only one game – for as soon as you have lost a game, you are out of the competition. Since every game results in one winner and one loser, there is a one-to-one correspondence between losers and games played. Therefore, there must have been 1,023 games. This explanation may sound a bit wordy when it is written out, but it is far more elegant and insightful than the standard way of solving the problem. While the first approach is, in effect, focusing on *winners* – there are 512 winners in the first round, 256 in the second round etc – the insight of the second approach is to change perspective and focus instead on *losers*.

Turning to the second problem, the standard approach of grinding through the arithmetic will – if you avoid careless errors – give you the right solution. $1 + 2 = 3$, $3 + 3 = 6$, $6 + 4 = 10$, etc. However, there is, again, a more elegant way of solving the problem. If you write the numbers from 1 to 50 out from left to right, and then underneath the numbers from 51 to 100, but this time from right to left, you get the following:

```
  1    2    3    4    5...     46  47  48  49  50
100   99   98   97   96     ...55  54  53  52  51
```

When you lay the numbers out like this, you can see that if you sum each pair of numbers vertically, $1 + 100$, $2 + 99$,..., $49 + 52$, $50 + 51$, each pair sums to 101. How many pairs of numbers are there? 50! So the sum of the first 100 integers is $50 \times 101 = 5,050$. This may again be clumsy to explain in words, but with this insight you can solve the problem in seconds rather than minutes.

The other interesting thing about the insightful solutions to the above two problems is that they can be *generalised*. We can say that in any knock-out tennis tournament of n entrants the total number of games played will be $n - 1$. And we can say that the sum of the first n integers is $\frac{1}{2}n(n + 1)$.

Activity 7.3

Give a proof that the sum of the first n integers is $\frac{1}{2}n(n + 1)$.

What comes out of this discussion is that creative imagination and intuition play a key role in mathematics. When the German mathematician, David Hilbert (1862–1943) was told that one of his students had given up mathematics to become a novelist, he is said to have replied: 'It's just as well – he had no imagination.'

Although some mathematicians, such as Henri Poincaré (1854–1912), stress the role played by intuition in creative mathematical work, it is important to keep in mind the distinction we made in Chapter 6 between *natural intuitions* and *educated intuitions*.

Activity 7.4

If you tie a string tightly around the 'equator' of a football, and you then want to add enough string to make it go all the way round the ball one inch from its surface – as in the diagram – it turns out that you will need to add about 6 inches to your original piece of string.

Imagine that you tie a string going round the equator of the earth. (Assume the earth is a smooth sphere.) Again you decide you want the string to go round the earth one inch from its surface. How much will you need to add to the original length of string?

a Make an intelligent guess about how much string you would need to add.

b *Calculate* how much string you would need to add. (Hint π = circumference/diameter.)

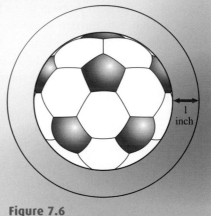

1 inch

Figure 7.6

I imagine you were surprised to discover that the answer for the earth is the same as the answer for the football – roughly 6 inches. This goes against most people's natural intuitions. But a mathematician with educated intuitions might not be surprised by the result. However, no matter how good a person's mathematical intuitions are, such intuitions will not be accepted by the mathematical community until they have been proved.

1 Do you think that mathematical insight can be taught, or would you say that it is something inborn and either you've got it or you haven't?
2 We sometimes use calculators and computers to help us solve mathematical problems. Does it follow that machines *understand* mathematics?

Figure 7.7

Mathematics and certainty

Having said something about the nature of formal systems, we must now look in more detail at the nature of mathematical certainty.

To do this, let us begin by making two distinctions. The first concerns the nature of propositions. As we saw in the appendix to Part 2, an **analytic** proposition is one that is true by definition. We now add that a **synthetic** proposition is any proposition that is not analytic. So we can say that every proposition is either analytic or synthetic.

The second distinction concerns how we come to *know* that a proposition is true. A proposition is said to be knowable *a priori* if it can be known to be true independent of experience; and it is said to be knowable *a posteriori* if it cannot be known to be true independent of experience. As with the analytic–synthetic distinction, we can say that every true proposition can be known either *a priori* or *a posteriori*.

Combining the two pairs of distinctions, we can generate the following matrix:

		Nature of proposition			
		Analytic		Synthetic	
How is it knowable?	A priori	1	✓	4	?
	A posteriori	2	✗	3	✓

Now let us try to explain what might fit into each of the four boxes:

Box 1 This concerns propositions that are true by definition and can be known independent of experience. Does anything go in this box? Yes! We can put all definitions in this box because they can all be known to be true independent of experience. You may recall the example on page 174 about Bolivian bachelors. I have never been to Bolivia and I know nothing about the profile of the average Bolivian bachelor, but I can say with complete confidence that every Bolivian bachelor is unmarried. Apart from a knowledge of the English language, I do not need any experience of the world to verify the truth of this proposition. It might, however, be described as a *trivial* truth. If you are told that all Bolivian bachelors are unmarried, you have learned nothing new about the world.

Box 2 For a proposition to go in box 2, it would have to be true by definition, but knowable only on the basis of experience. Now, if a proposition is true by definition, then we can know that it is true independent of experience. So the idea of an analytic *a posteriori* proposition is self-contradictory and box 2 is empty.

Box 3 This concerns propositions that are not true by definition and that cannot be known to be true independent of experience. Does anything go in this box? Yes – our **empirical** knowledge of the world! For example, the proposition 'There are elephants in Africa' is not true by definition, and its truth can be established only on the basis of experience – *a posteriori*. Someone actually has to go to Africa and see that there are some elephants there.

Box 4 What would something that goes in box 4 look like? Well, it must be a *non-trivial* proposition – i.e. one that is not true by definition – whose truth can be known independent of experience. Does anything go in this box? That is the million dollar question!

The question is: in which box should we put mathematics? Given that box 2 is empty, there seem to be three options.

Activity 7.6

Look over the above terminology and then try to decide which of the available boxes you would put mathematics in and why.

Option 1: Mathematics as empirical

Some people, such as the philosopher John Stuart Mill (1806–72), have claimed that mathematics goes in to box 3. According to Mill, mathematical truths are empirical generalisations based on a vast number of experiences that are no different in kind from scientific statements such as 'All metals expand when heated.' Mill said that the reason we feel more certain that $2 + 2 = 4$ than that all metals expand when heated is that we have seen so many more confirming instances of the former than of the latter, and this convinces us that $2 + 2 = 4$ must be true.

1 Imagine there are two hungry lions in a cage. You open the cage door and throw in two lambs. How many animals are in the cage when you return the next day? Does this do anything to convince you that 2 + 2 is not always equal to 4?

2 Can you imagine a world in which 2 + 2 = 5? For example, what if every time you brought two pairs of objects close to one another, a fifth one popped into existence?

3 Does the fact that we usually teach children arithmetic by beginning with concrete objects, such as two apples and two apples, mean that arithmetic is an empirical subject?

Looking over the above questions, I doubt that the example of the lions and the lambs shakes your confidence in arithmetic. The fact that when you put two lions and two lambs together in a cage you do not end up with four animals but with two somewhat fatter lions tells you something about zoology, not arithmetic. The relevant arithmetical description of the situation would be $(2 + 2) - 2 = 2$.

I think that most people would deal with the second question in a similar way. There is clearly something weird about the physics of a world where a fifth object magically appears every time you bring two pairs of objects close to one another. But I don't think we would allow this fact to stand against the truths of arithmetic. We would probably say that in this world $2 + 2 + 1 = 5$. (Admittedly, the inhabitants of such a strange world might never develop arithmetic – but that is another issue.) What comes out of this example is that, while we can imagine a world in which the laws of physics are different, it seems to be impossible to imagine a world in which the laws of arithmetic are different.

What, if anything, can we infer from the fact that when we teach children arithmetic we usually begin with concrete objects? Let's take a closer look at the process. You show a child 2 apples and another 2 apples and ask, 'How many apples are there altogether?' She says '4'. You then do the same with oranges and bananas, and she comes up with the right answer each time. Then, at a certain point – and this is the crucial step – you ask the child, 'So what is 2 + 2?', and you hope that she makes the *leap of abstraction* and says '4'. What the child has to grasp is that she is not simply learning interesting facts about fruit and vegetables. She has to catch on to the idea that $2n + 2n = 4n$ for any n – even if she is not yet capable of expressing it that way herself. Once the child has 'got it', she will know that if a person has 2 aardvarks and buys 2 more aardvarks, he will end up with 4 aardvarks – even if she has no idea what an aardvark is. So, while the child's knowledge undoubtedly begins with experience, it ends up going beyond experience.

Imagine that you try to teach a child arithmetic by beginning with concrete examples in the way described above. When you present them with various quantities of apples or oranges, they can do the relevant sums, but they never make the 'leap of abstraction'. They accept that 2 apples + 2 apples = 4 apples in this case, but they keep insisting that they cannot see why this should always be true. What, if anything, could you do to convince them of the general truth that 2 + 2 = 4?

Option 2: Mathematics as analytic

The above kind of discussion is enough to convince many people that mathematics is not empirical. We might conclude from this that it must therefore be analytic and fit in box 1 in the above diagram. According to this view, if you understand the meaning of the terms in the proposition 2 + 2 = 4, you will see that it is true by definition. To say that 2 + 2 = 4 is essentially the same as saying (1 + 1) + (1 + 1) = (1 + 1 + 1 + 1). So when you solve a maths problem, you are simply unpacking a truth that is, in some sense, already contained in the statement of the problem. What is 2 + 2? The answer is already there – you just need to take the wrapping off!

Despite its plausibility, there are some problems with the idea that the whole of mathematics simply consists of strings of definitional truths. To start with, if it is all just true by definition, you might wonder why mathematics is so hard. One response might be that it is difficult to keep in mind long chains of reasoning when you are trying to solve complex problems, and it is therefore easy to make an error. So perhaps a precondition for being good at mathematics is having a good short-term memory.

Another problem with the analytic claim is that mathematical truths do not seem to be trivially true in the way that 'All bachelors are unmarried men' is trivially true. Take, for example, the fact mentioned above that the sum of the first n odd numbers equals n^2. This seems more like an interesting *discovery* about numbers than something that is true by definition. The claim that mathematics is analytic seems even less plausible when we consider **Goldbach's conjecture** which has not yet been shown to be true or false. For if mathematics is analytic, we now find ourselves in the strange position of having to say that if it is true that every even number is the sum of two primes, then it is true by definition; and if it is false that every even number is the sum of two primes, then it is false by definition. This implies that we do not yet know the proper definition of terms such as 'even number' and 'prime number'. Against this, it would surely be better to say that we know what even numbers are, but have not yet discovered all of their properties, just as we might say that we know what gold is, but have not yet discovered all of its properties.

A final problem with the analytic claim is that, if we say that mathematical propositions are true by definition, we are left with the puzzling fact that they seem to fit the world so well.

Option 3: Mathematics as synthetic *a priori*

A third option is to say that mathematics is neither empirical nor analytic, but *synthetic a priori knowledge* and goes in box 4. The suggestion now is that mathematics gives us non-trivial, substantial knowledge about the most general features of reality, and that this knowledge can be known to be true independent of experience. If this is true, then it means that, on the basis of reason alone, human beings are able to discover truths about the nature of reality.

This is pretty much how people thought about mathematics from the time of Euclid until the nineteenth century. The system of geometry that Euclid devised seemed to combine two features that were greatly valued by those who sought the truth. First, it seemed to be absolutely certain that, if you begin with self-evident axioms and use deductive reason, you arrive at true theorems. Second, it seemed to give substantial knowledge about the nature of physical space. After all, we can use geometry to divide up areas of land, build pyramids and estimate the circumference of the earth.

Not surprisingly, Euclidean geometry was seen by many as a model for the whole of knowledge, and it became the dream of many philosophers to do for knowledge in general what Euclid had done for geometry in particular. Thus the French philosopher René Descartes (1596–1650) sought to establish a system of philosophy founded on the self-evident first principle, *Cogito, ergo sum* – 'I think, therefore I am.' (Another philosopher called Baruch Spinoza (1632–77) wrote a whole book on ethics in which he tried to prove various theorems from what he believed to be ethical axioms.) Descartes, who has been called the father of modern philosophy, famously observed:

> To speak freely, I am convinced that it [mathematics] is a more powerful instrument of knowledge than any other that has been bequeathed to us by human agency, as being the source of all others.

Activity 7.9

1 To what extent do you think the geometric paradigm can be applied to other areas of knowledge?
2 What are the dangers of trying to extend geometrical thinking to other areas of knowledge?

If we decide that mathematical knowledge is indeed *synthetic a priori*, we are faced with the question of how the human mind is able to discover truth about the world on the basis of reason alone. One answer is to say that God created a 'pre-established harmony' between the human mind and the universe. This may be fine if you believe in God, but it is less convincing if you do not. An alternative is to say natural selection ensured that we evolved in such a way that our minds are in harmony with the environment. However, it is hard to see why mathematical ability would have given our remote ancestors an evolutionary advantage. A caveman didn't need calculus, and nature had no way of knowing that this would *eventually* turn out to be useful to the species. Perhaps, then, mathematical ability is a *by-product* of other abilities which do have survival value.

We have now considered three different views about the status of mathematical knowledge, and it may be worth putting a label on each of them.

Empiricism (Option 1)	box 3	Mathematical truths are empirical generalisations
Formalism (Option 2)	box 1	Mathematical truths are true by definition
Platonism (Option 3)	box 4	Mathematical truths give us *a priori* insight into the structure of reality. (This view can be traced back to Plato – hence the name.)

The empiricist view of mathematics has probably been the least popular of the three options, but you can find plenty of formalists and Platonists hiding in mathematics departments!

Discovered or invented?

A good way of highlighting the difference between Platonism and formalism is to consider the question, *Is mathematics discovered or invented?* While Platonists believe that mathematical entities are discovered and exist 'out there', formalists argue that they are invented and exist only 'in the mind'.

Activity 7.10

1 What is the difference between saying that something has been 'discovered' and saying that it has been 'invented'? What sorts of things do we usually say are discovered, and what sorts of things invented?
2 Do you think that intelligent aliens would come up with the same mathematics as us, or might they develop a completely different kind of mathematics?

At first sight, neither the 'discovered' nor the 'invented' option looks very attractive. If mathematical entities exist out there, does that mean that if we travel far enough in a space ship, we will one day encounter pi? And if mathematics is all in the mind, does that mean that mathematicians are simply making it up as they go along?

If we think more deeply about this issue, we run into puzzling questions about the meaning of the word 'existence'. We want to say that mathematical objects exist because we are able to make objective discoveries about them. You can, for example, prove that a circle encloses the largest possible two-dimensional area for a given perimeter, and anyone who follows your proof will come to the same conclusion. However, it turns out that mathematical objects, such as circles, do not exist in the real world. Wait a minute! Aren't coins and car wheels circles, and can't you draw a circle on a piece of paper any time you feel like it? In a strict mathematical sense, the answer is 'no'.

To see this, we need to go back to the definition of a circle – 'the set of all points in a plane that are equidistant from a given point'. With that definition in mind, try drawing a circle. If you do it free-hand, your drawing will be far from perfect. You will get a better result if you use a pencil and compass; but if you look at it with a magnifying glass, you will see that the border is fuzzy and it is not a perfect circle. You cannot solve the problem by using a finer pencil because if you increase the power of your magnifying glass the same fuzziness will appear again. Extrapolating from this, you can see that it is in fact impossible to draw a mathematically perfect circle – or any other geometrical object. A line, for example, is defined as that which has length but no breadth – and that is clearly something you cannot draw on a piece of paper. In a similar way, it turns out that there are no exact measurements either. For example, there is no such thing as exactly 4 centimetres – only exactly 4 centimetres 'to a given number of significant places'. Such mathematical entities are **idealisations**; and, while you may get closer to the ideal, you will never be able to coincide with them.

The above discussion would seem to leave us with the following dilemma. On the one hand, since mathematical objects do not exist in the real world, they *must be mental fictions*. On the other hand, since we are capable of making discoveries about them, they *cannot be mental fictions*.

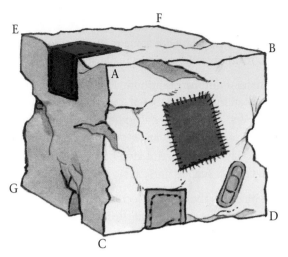

Figure 7.8 Platonism: physical reality is very different from mathematical perfection

Plato's solution to the above dilemma was to say that mathematical objects exist 'out there', but not in the we-might-one-day-encounter-them-in-a-space-ship sense in which physical objects exist. Rather, they have their own unique way of existing; and although they cannot be perceived, they are just as real as physical objects. Indeed, Plato believed that they are *more real* than physical objects. How could anyone believe *that*?

Here's an updated Platonic argument. Consider the physical world. A physicist will tell you that the underlying reality of an everyday object, such as a table, is quite different from its appearance. Despite its apparent sturdiness and immobility, a table consists mainly of empty space in which atoms are whizzing around at great speed. Furthermore, tables and chairs – and human beings – come into being, exist briefly, and then return to dust. By contrast, mathematical objects have a clarity and immutability which – for Plato at least – gives them a superior existence. When you study Pythagoras' theorem at school, you are studying the same eternal truth that Pythagoras discovered more than two and a half thousand years ago; and it will be as true in a million years' time as it is now.

Plato's argument for the superior reality of mathematical over physical objects can be reduced to two key claims:

1 Mathematics is more certain than perception.
2 Mathematics is timelessly true.

Activity 7.11

1 'In order for something to exist, it must be possible to observe it.' Do you agree or disagree with this statement? Give reasons.
2 Do you think that numbers have always existed? Did they exist at the time of the Big Bang? If they exist, where do you suppose they exist?
3 Do you think that the full expansion of pi, which goes on for ever, exists 'out there', and that we are gradually discovering more and more about it?

Criticisms of Platonism

While Platonism continues to be popular with some mathematicians, others dismiss it as 'pi in the sky' mysticism. Two main objections can be made against it:

1 Since the series of natural numbers is infinite, Platonism is committed to the view that there are literally an infinite number of abstract mathematical entities 'out there'. This seems hard to believe. If we abandon the idea that reality consists only of observable entities, we seem to be in danger of wandering off into mysticism.

2 If mathematical objects have some weird kind of ideal existence, then how can physically embodied beings such as ourselves get to know about them?

According to formalism, which sees the above objections as decisive, mathematics consists of nothing but man-made definitions, axioms and theorems. We might liken it to a game of chess. A certain position on a chessboard is like a theorem that follows from the 'axioms of chess'. Since no one would say that all possible chess moves exist 'out there' in a Platonic heaven, why should we be tempted to say this about mathematics?

Some philosophers have suggested that rather than think of mathematical entities as being either objective or subjective, we should think of them as having 'social existence'. Consider again the game of chess. In what sense does it exist? Does it still exist if no one is playing chess? What about if no one is thinking about chess? Would it still exist if we destroyed all the rule books on how to play chess? Most people would probably say that even if no one played chess for a year, there would still be certain statements about it that are true and others that are false. However, if the human race disappeared it wouldn't make much sense to say that the game of chess still existed.

Activity 7.12

Although Romeo and Juliet are fictional characters, it is true to say that Romeo loves Juliet and false to say that he hates Juliet. In what ways are mathematical objects similar to fictional characters and in what ways are they different?

Well, enough of these vexing questions about the meaning of existence. To develop our discussion about the nature of mathematics further, we must now look at the rise of alternative – 'non-Euclidean' – systems of geometry in the nineteenth century.

Non-Euclidean geometry and the problem of consistency

As we said earlier, Euclidean geometry was for many centuries seen as a model of knowledge because it seemed to be both certain and informative. There was, however, one small problem. The certainty of geometry was supposed to be guaranteed by the fact that one began with self-evident axioms and used deductive reason to derive theorems. However, one of Euclid's axioms, the axiom of parallels – which says that there is just one straight line through a given point which is parallel to a given line – struck people as being less self-evident than the other axioms. This doubt may have arisen from the fact that parallel lines are by definition lines that never meet even if you extend them to infinity – but who is to say what happens at infinity? Since mathematicians wished to get rid of all possible doubt, they expended a great deal of energy over the centuries in trying to demonstrate that the axiom of parallels was in fact a theorem. But no one succeeded in doing this!

Riemannian geometry

Then in the nineteenth century, a mathematician called Georg Friedrich Bernard Riemann (1822–66) came up with the clever idea of replacing some of Euclid's axioms with their contraries. Most people thought that if you based a system of geometry on non-Euclidean axioms, the system would lead to a contradiction and so collapse. This would then show that Euclid's axioms were in fact the only possible ones. However, to people's amazement, no contradictions turned up in Riemann's system.

Riemann's axioms differed from Euclid's as follows:

A Two points may determine more than one line (instead of axiom 1).
B All lines are finite in length but endless – i.e. circles (instead of axiom 2).
C There are no parallel lines (instead of axiom 5).

Among the theorems that can be deduced from these axioms are:

1 All perpendiculars to a straight line meet at one point.
2 Two straight lines enclose an area.
3 The sum of the angles of any triangle is greater than 180 degrees.

These theorems sound pretty strange. How can perpendiculars possibly meet at a point, or two straight lines enclose an area, or the angles of a triangle sum to more than 180 degrees? Fortunately, we can give intuitive sense to Riemannian geometry by imagining that space is like the surface of a sphere. Since we live on the surface of a sphere (more or less), this should not be too difficult to do!

The key to making sense of Riemann's system is to think about what a straight line will look like on the surface of a sphere. What is a straight line? The shortest distance between two points! Now, on the surface of a sphere, it can be shown that the shortest distance between two points is always an arc of a circle whose centre is the centre of the sphere. Such 'great circles' include not only all lines of longitude, but an endless number of other circles – as can be seen from the following diagram. (The only line of latitude that is a great circle is the equator.)

What this means is that, in Riemannian geometry, a straight line will appear curved when it is represented on a two-dimensional map. To illustrate this point, look at any airline flight map. Although the flight paths look curved, since airlines are in the business of making money, you can be sure that in reality they always take the shortest route to their destination.

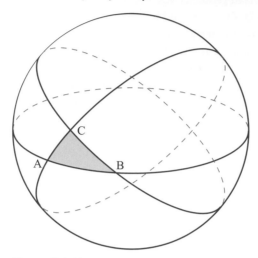

Figure 7.9 Riemannian geometry

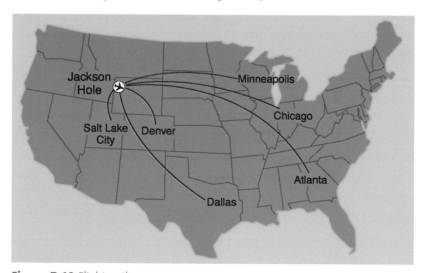

Figure 7.10 Flight paths

Once we have clarified the meaning of a straight line in Riemannian geometry, we can give a meaning to the three theorems mentioned above:

1 *All perpendiculars to a straight line meet at one point* Lines of longitude are perpendicular to the equator, but they meet at the north pole.
2 *Two straight lines enclose an area* Any two lines of longitude (straight lines) meet at both the north and south pole and so define an area (see Figure 7.9).
3 *The sum of the angles of any triangle is greater than 180 degrees* This can be seen in Figure 7.9.

With our discussion of Riemannian geometry in mind, try to solve the following puzzle. A hunter leaves his house one morning and walks one mile due south. He then walks one mile due west and shoots a bear, before walking a mile due north back to his house. What colour is the bear?

The problem of consistency

Although Riemann did not find any contradictions in his system of geometry, some of his contemporaries were convinced that sooner or later a contradiction would be found and Riemann's system would collapse. After all, he had not *proved* that his system was free from contradiction. As a result of this, mathematicians became increasingly interested in the problem of consistency, and the question of how we can be sure that any given formal system is free from contradiction.

You might think that if no contradictions have been found in a formal system that has been studied by the mathematical community then that is good enough. After all, people have been using Euclidean geometry for thousands of years, and not a single contradiction has turned up. While this would be enough to convince most people, it is not mathematically compelling. For it is still only a *conjecture* and it does not *prove* that the system in question is free from contradiction.

Another approach might be to appeal to intuition. Surely, if you begin with things that are intuitively obvious and reason consistently, you can be confident you will not run into contradictions. The problem with this is that, as we saw in Chapter 6, our intuitions can sometimes let us down.

To illustrate, consider the following story of a barber who had an affair with the king's daughter. When the king discovered what had happened, he was very angry and wanted to put the barber to death. But his daughter begged him to spare the barber's life. Wishing to appear merciful while ensuring that the barber eventually died, the king came up with a cunning plan. He told the barber that he would not execute him if he obeyed one simple instruction. He was to go back to his village the following day and *shave all and only those inhabitants who do not shave themselves.* 'Wow', thought the barber, 'that's easy!' Overjoyed, he headed back to his village and the next day he got to work shaving all and only those inhabitants who did not shave themselves. By dusk, he had completed his task, and tired but happy he returned home. Opening the front door, he happened to glance in the mirror in the hallway. 'Ah', he thought, 'I've missed someone. I, too, am an inhabitant of this village; so the king's instruction also applies to me.' As the barber turned this over in his mind, it slowly dawned on him that he had been trapped. For according to the king's instruction, if he shaved himself, then he shouldn't shave himself, and if he didn't, then he should! The instruction which had sounded simple enough turned out to be impossible to fulfil, and the barber was duly executed. Given our interests, the moral of the tale is not 'Don't mess with kings' daughters' but 'Apparently clear instructions can sometimes be impossible to fulfil.' What this means in terms of mathematics is that intuition alone is no guarantee that a system is free from contradiction.

Gödel's incompleteness theorem

The concern with consistency continued into the twentieth century. Finally in 1931, a young Austrian mathematician called Kurt Gödel (1906–78) came up with an extraordinary proof, known as ***Gödel's incompleteness theorem***, which shook the mathematical world to its foundations. What Gödel proved was that *it is impossible to prove that a formal mathematical system is free from contradiction*. We need to be a little careful here: Gödel did not prove that mathematics actually contains contradictions, but that we cannot be certain that it doesn't. What this means is that, at an abstract level, even mathematics is unable to give us certainty. For it is always possible that one day we will find a contradiction; and one small contradiction in a formal system would be enough to destroy the entire system. A mathematician friend of mine said that the first time he read Gödel's theorem it made him 'very sad'. Since as a matter of fact no contradictions have ever been discovered in the structure of mathematics, most mathematicians do not lose any sleep over Gödel's theorem, and they take a 'business as usual' approach to the subject. Nevertheless, there is a sense in which, after nearly two and a half thousand years, the last bastion of certainty has been breached by the turbulent waters of doubt.

Our story ends with not only the *certainty*, but also the *informative content* of Euclidean geometry coming under fire. For if there are alternative systems of geometry, the question now arises: 'Which one provides the best description of physical reality?' Although Euclidean geometry clearly works well enough at the 'local' level, according to Einstein's theory of relativity, it turns out that the universe obeys the rules not of Euclidean but of Riemannian geometry. According to our best scientific theories, space is curved!

Applied mathematics

To complete our discussion of mathematics, we now turn to applied mathematics – mathematics that is used to model and solve problems in the real world. Our discussion in the last section has shown that we can no longer unquestioningly assume that human reason gives us insight into the structure of reality. For the main alleged example of such rational insight – Euclidean geometry – turned out to be a false description of reality. At the same time, mathematics is still amazingly useful, and it is hard to avoid Galileo's conviction that the book of nature is written in the language of mathematics.

A particularly mysterious feature of the relationship between mathematics and the world is that mathematical ideas that are developed as a purely intellectual exercise sometimes turn out to be applicable to the real world. For example, in the third century BCE, the Greeks became interested in the geometry of **ellipses**, and a mathematician called Apollonius of Perga (*c.* 262–*c.* 190 BCE) wrote eight weighty volumes about them. As fascinating as the topic was – at least to Apollonius – the knowledge he acquired was completely useless. If someone had asked him what the point of studying ellipses was, he might have quoted Euclid's crushing response to a student who asked a similar question: 'Give him a penny – he wants to profit from his learning!' The pursuit of such knowledge was considered to be an end in itself that did not need a practical justification. The strange thing is that, when the seventeenth-century astronomer Johannes Kepler (1571–1630) was studying planetary motion, he discovered that, rather than being circular, as he had previously believed, the orbits of the planets round the sun are in fact elliptical. After being of merely academic interest for nearly two thousand years, Apollonius' work turned out to be of practical value!

Similarly, although Riemann developed non-Euclidean geometry as a purely intellectual exercise, thirty years later, Einstein concluded that space conforms to Riemannian rather than Euclidean geometry.

Activity 7.14

To what extent do you think governments should fund 'useless' research in pure mathematics?

So how can we explain what one physicist has described as 'the unreasonable effectiveness of mathematics'? Here is what Einstein had to say on the subject:

> How can it be that mathematics, being after all a product of human thought which is independent of experience, is so admirably appropriate to the objects of reality? Is human reason, then, without experience, merely by taking thought, able to fathom the properties of real things? In my opinion, the answer to the question is briefly this: – As far as the laws of mathematics refer to reality, they are not certain; and as far as they are certain, they do not refer to reality.

This is an interesting way of looking at the connection between mathematics and the world. What Einstein is saying is that mathematical systems are *invented*, but it is a matter of *discovery* which of the various systems apply to reality. You can invent any formal system you like and prove theorems from axioms with complete certainty. However, once you ask which system applies to the world, you are faced with an *empirical* question which can only be answered on the basis of observation. Thus Einstein discovered that Riemannian geometry is a better description of physical space than Euclidean geometry.

Now, you might ask why *any* purely invented system should have application to reality. A possible response is that some of the formal systems we invent are originally suggested to us by reality. For example, since geometry first arose in response to practical problems, and was then formalised by Euclid, it is perhaps not surprising that Euclidean geometry turned out to be a useful way of describing reality. The point, in other words, is that, even if mathematics is a game, the rules for the most interesting or useful games may be suggested to us by reality.

Nevertheless, there are many unexpected connections in mathematics that are difficult to explain. For example, π – which, as we saw earlier, is the circumference of a circle divided by its diameter – turns up in all kinds of quite unrelated places, such as the solution to **Buffon's needle problem**. This problem was posed by the French mathematician the Comte de Buffon (1707–78). Suppose you have a large sheet of paper ruled with parallel lines drawn at one unit intervals resting on a flat surface and you then throw a needle which is one unit long at random on to the paper. What is the probability that it will intersect one of the lines?

The answer to the problem turns out to be $2/\pi$. But why π should turn up in this context is a complete mystery.

At a deep level, then, there remains something mysterious about the 'unreasonable effectiveness of mathematics'. This is, I think, connected to the equally perplexing question of why there is order in the universe – in particular, order of the kind that can be uncovered by mathematical thinking. Perhaps all we can say is that if there wasn't any order we wouldn't be around to ask why not!

Figure 7.11 Buffon's needle problem

Conclusion

At the beginning of this chapter, we defined mathematics as 'the science of rigorous proof' and we spoke of the commonly held view that it is an island of certainty in an ocean of doubt. There is something immensely appealing about the idea of demonstrating something in such a way that any rational person will come to the same conclusion, and it is not surprising that mathematics has often served as a model for knowledge.

Nevertheless, we have seen that even in this most rigorous of subjects there are limits to certainty. At an abstract level, Gödel showed that we can never prove that mathematics is free from contradiction; and although this is unlikely to keep mathematicians awake at night, it means that the dream of absolute certainty will never be realised. At a more practical level, we have seen that when mathematics is applied to the real world we usually have a choice of axioms and we can only decide which are the most useful by testing them against reality.

Although mathematics cannot give us absolute certainty, it continues to play a key role in a wide variety of subjects ranging from physics to economics, and there is something surprising and mysterious about its extraordinary usefulness. Nevertheless, it is important to keep in mind that we cannot capture everything in the abstract map of mathematics and, despite its value, there is no reason to believe that it is the only, or always the best, tool for making sense of reality.

Key points

- Mathematics, which can be defined as 'the science of rigorous proof', begins with axioms and uses deductive reason to derive theorems.
- Although proof is the logical matter of deriving theorems from axioms, mathematicians consider some proofs to be more beautiful than others.
- According to three different views about the nature of mathematical truths they are either: (1) empirical, (2) true by definition, or (3) rational insights into universal truths.
- While some people believe that mathematics is *discovered*, others claim that it is *invented*; but neither view seems to be entirely satisfactory.
- The development of non-Euclidean geometries in the nineteenth century raised the question of how we can be sure that a formal system is free from contradiction.
- Kurt Gödel proved that it is impossible to prove that a formal mathematical system is free from contradiction.
- Mathematicians and philosophers are still perplexed by the extraordinary usefulness of mathematics.

Terms to remember

analytic	empiricism	Goldbach's conjecture
a posteriori	Euclidean geometry	idealisation
a priori	formal system	Platonism
axioms	formalism	synthetic
conjecture	Gödel's incompleteness	theorem
deduction	theorem	

Further reading

G. H. Hardy, *A Mathematician's Apology* (Cambridge University Press, 1994). In this short, readable book, G. H. Hardy seeks to justify his devotion to mathematics despite his insistence that '"real" mathematics is almost entirely "useless"'. The book contains many thought-provoking comments about the nature of mathematics and its relation to the arts and sciences. You don't have to be a mathematician to enjoy it.

John Allen Paulos, *Innumeracy: Mathematical Illiteracy and its Consequences* (Vintage, 1990). Paulos defines 'innumeracy' as 'an inability to deal comfortably with the fundamental notions of number and chance'. His book is full of entertaining examples of how we misinterpret data and misunderstand probability. The chapter on the relation between innumeracy and pseudo-science is particularly interesting.

Linking questions

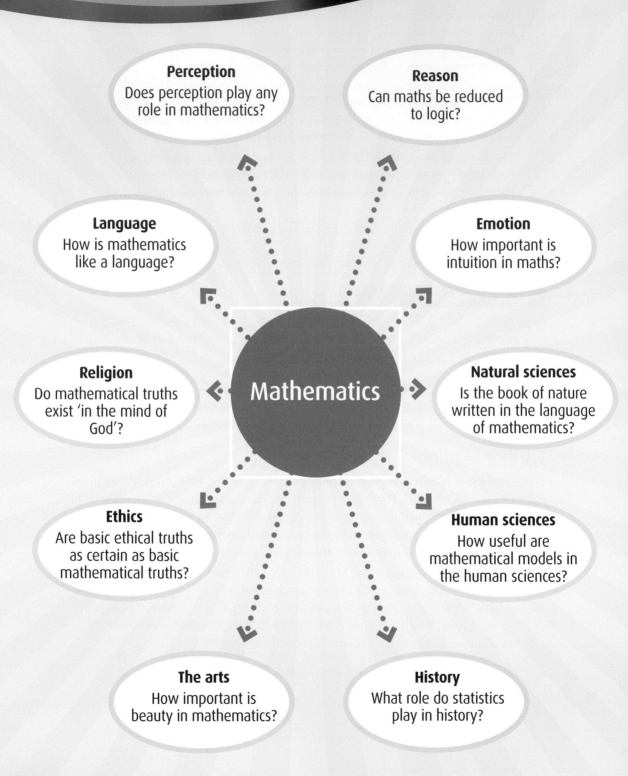

Perception
Does perception play any role in mathematics?

Reason
Can maths be reduced to logic?

Language
How is mathematics like a language?

Emotion
How important is intuition in maths?

Religion
Do mathematical truths exist 'in the mind of God'?

Mathematics

Natural sciences
Is the book of nature written in the language of mathematics?

Ethics
Are basic ethical truths as certain as basic mathematical truths?

Human sciences
How useful are mathematical models in the human sciences?

The arts
How important is beauty in mathematics?

History
What role do statistics play in history?

WHY IS MATH SO USEFUL?

The universe appears to speak the language of mathematics. In what follows, Michael Lemonick considers the mystery of why mathematics is so useful.

My father is a physicist, and I learned early on, sitting at the dinner table while he talked with his colleagues, that physicists speak a different language from the rest of us. They would fill the air with such phrases as 'angular momentum' and 'virtual particle' and 'photon,' while I sat awed by the thought of the mysterious ideas their conversations concealed.

I didn't realize at the time how deep the mystery went. As I grew old enough to ask questions, I found out that these exotic terms aren't part of the true language of physics at all, but only approximations. The universe works in a way so far removed from what common sense would dictate that words of any kind must necessarily be inadequate to explain it. The only way to describe what really goes on, I was told, is to speak in mathematics.

I learned about photons, the smallest conceivable bit of light. Sometimes a photon behaves like a particle, sometimes like a wave, depending on how you look at it. When it's a wave, it isn't a wave of anything. It's just a wave. If it ever came to rest, a photon would have no mass, but since it always travels at the speed of light, it does have mass. This didn't make sense to me; the reason, I was told, was that I didn't understand the math.

The speed of light itself turned out to be an equally baffling phenomenon. Imagine two photons, each rushing away from the same light bulb in exactly opposite directions. How fast are they moving away from each other? My answer: twice the speed of light. The correct answer: half that amount, as calculated with the equations of general relativity, which are yet to make an inaccurate prediction.

It always seemed curious to me that mathematics, so thoroughly a non-experimental science, should be so powerfully descriptive of the natural world. For example, Greek mathematicians invented ellipses purely as an intellectual exercise; they are, quite literally, figments of human imagination. It was centuries before anyone realized the planets move in elliptical paths.

It turns out that some physicists find this relationship curious too. In 1960, Eugene Wigner, a Hungarian emigre who would win a 1963 Nobel prize for his work on quantum mechanics, published an essay in the journal *Communications on Pure and Applied Mathematics*. Entitled 'The Unreasonable Effectiveness of Mathematics in the Natural Sciences,' it points out just how deep the mystery goes.

According to Wigner, some of the most important concepts in physics, including quantum theories and theories of gravitation, owe their success to mathematical systems devised without any idea they would someday be applied. 'It is difficult to avoid the impression that a miracle confronts us here,' he wrote.

Uncanny predictions

The first case he cites is Newton's law of gravitation, which states that the motion of a freely falling object – say, an apple – and the motions of planets, satellites and stars are special cases of the same phenomenon, describable by one set of equations. In this case, mathematician and physicist were the same person: He invented calculus, then applied it. (In the Greek tradition, Newton believed mathematics was too pure to be sullied by association with the real world. He wasn't entirely happy with his discovery.)

It happened again when physicists noticed similarities between the structure of quantum mechanics and a mathematical system called matrix theory. They made predictions based on the similarities, and the predictions were confirmed.

Other such serendipitous matchings have been noted as well. Writing in the October 1984 issue of the *American Journal of Physics*, William Pollard, of the Institute for Energy Analysis, in Oak Ridge, Tennessee, points out several: Einstein's equations of general relativity are based on the nineteenth-century, many-dimensional mathematics of Bernhard Riemann. The theory of quarks, the basic building blocks of matter, is based on a form of algebra concocted by a Norwegian mathematician, Sophus Lie, long before protons and neutrons were even postulated.

Can these all be coincidences? Neither Wigner nor Pollard thought so. Somehow the human mind seems to have a built-in capacity to deduce the structure of the universe without observing it first. It is nearly impossible to believe, and quite impossible to explain, but perhaps the physical laws governing the atoms in our brain tissues push our thinking in the direction of understanding those laws. As Wigner says, and Pollard repeats, 'The miracle of the appropriateness of the language of mathematics for the formulation of the laws of physics is a wonderful gift which we neither understand nor deserve.' The sense of mystery felt at those long-ago dinner-table discussions put me, it seems, in very good company.

THINK MATHS

Is mathematics the grand design for the Universe, or merely a figment of the human imagination, asks Ian Stewart.

Where does mathematics come from? Is it already out there, waiting for us to discover it, or do we make it all up as we go along? Plato held that mathematical concepts actually exist in some weird kind of ideal reality just off the edge of the Universe. A circle is not just an idea, it is an ideal. We imperfect creatures may aspire to that ideal, but we can never achieve it, if only because pencil points are too thick. But there are those who say that mathematics exists only in the mind of the beholder. It does not have any existence independent of human thought, any more than language, music or the rules of football do.

So who is right? Well, there is much that is attractive in the Platonist point of view. It's tempting to see our everyday world as a pale shadow of a more perfect, ordered, mathematically exact one. For one thing, mathematical patterns permeate all areas of science. Moreover, they have a universal feel to them, rather as though God thumbed His way through some kind of mathematical wallpaper catalogue when He was trying to work out how to decorate His Universe. Not only that: the deity's pattern catalogue is remarkably versatile, with the same patterns being used in many different guises. For example, the ripples on the surface of sand dunes are pretty much identical to the wave patterns in liquid crystals. Raindrops and planets are both spherical. Rainbows and ripples on a pond are circular. Honeycomb patterns are used by bees to store honey (and to pigeonhole grubs for safekeeping), and they can also be found in the geographical distribution of territorial fish, the frozen magma of the Giant's Causeway, and rock piles created by convection currents in shallow lakes. Spirals can be seen in water running out of a bath and in the Andromeda Galaxy. Frothy bubbles occur in a washing-up bowl and the arrangement of galaxies.

With this kind of ubiquitous occurrence of the same mathematical patterns, it is no wonder that physical scientists get carried away and declare them to lie at the very basis of space, time and matter. Eugene Wigner expressed surprise at the 'unreasonable effectiveness' of mathematics as a method for understanding the Universe. Many philosophers and scientists have seen mathematics as the basis of the Universe. Plato wrote that 'God ever geometrises'. The physicist James Jeans declared that God was a mathematician. Paul Dirac, one of the inventors of quantum mechanics, went further, opining that He was a pure mathematician. In the past few years Edward Fredkin has argued that the Universe is made from information, the raw material of mathematics.

This is powerful, heady stuff, and it is highly appealing to mathematicians. However, it is equally conceivable that all of this apparently fundamental mathematics is in the eye of the beholder, or more accurately, in the beholder's mind. We human beings do not experience the Universe raw, but through our senses, and we interpret the results using our minds. So to what extent are we mentally selecting particular kinds of experience and deeming them to be important, rather than picking up things that really are important in the workings of the Universe? Is mathematics invented or discovered?

If pushed, I would say that it is a bit of both because neither word adequately describes the process. Moreover, they are not alternatives, they are not opposites, and they do not exhaust the possibilities. They are not even particularly appropriate. We use 'discover' for finding things that already exist in the physical world. Columbus discovered America – it was already there, but neither he nor anyone else where he came from knew it was – and David Livingstone discovered the Victoria Falls. The word 'invention' means bringing into existence something that was not previously there. Edison invented electric light, Bell invented the telephone.

However, when Columbus landed in America he was actually trying to invent a new trade route to India. And Livingstone's discovery came as no great surprise to the local inhabitants, who saw the Victoria Falls every day. Edison would have felt as if he had invented the idea of electric lighting, but then spent many years trying to discover how to make it a reality. So invention and discovery both happen within a particular context – people becoming aware that there is something new in their world.

It is the same with mathematics. What to the outside world looks like invention often feels more like discovery to insiders. The distinction is made all the more tricky because mathematical objects lead a virtual existence, not a real one: they reside in minds, not embodied in any kind of hardware. But unlike, say, poetry, that virtual world obeys rigid rules, and those rules are pretty much the same in every mathematical mind.

In a way, the world of mathematical ideas is a kind of virtual collective comparable to Jung's famous 'collective unconscious' – the idea that all human minds have access to vast, evolutionarily ancient, subconscious structures and processes that govern much of our behaviour. But in what sense are they 'collective'? A crucial distinction has to be made here between a single unconscious entity, into which we all dip, and a large number of distinct but very similar unconsciousnesses, one for each of us. It is the difference between a community with a single municipal swimming pool, and one in which every back garden has its own pool.

From the point of view of specific action, the distinction is not terribly important: you can discuss the problems of keeping leaves out of 'the pool' with your neighbour without ever making it clear whether you think of it as a single common pool, or a typical representative of the individual pools that everybody has. But if you want to understand what's going on in general, then it does make a difference. The notion of a single unconscious mind for all of humanity is a mystical and rather silly concept that leads in the direction of telepathy. A collection of more or less identical individual subconsciousnesses, rendered similar by their common social context, is considerably more prosaic but a great deal more sensible.

The same point lies at the heart of how I think we should view mathematics. Because we have a single word for the virtual collective it is tempting to think of it as a single thing – like Jung's mystical telepathic unconscious–into which all mathematicians dip. This is a difficult concept to capture. Where is that thing? What is it made of? How does it grow? Instead, it is better to think of mathematics as being distributed throughout the minds of the world's mathematicians. Each has his or her own mathematics inside his or her head. Moreover, those individual systems are extremely similar to each other, much more so than Jungian subconsciousnesses. Not in the sense that each head contains the whole of mathematics. Mine contains dynamical systems, yours contains analysis, and hers algebra, say. But all three are logically consistent with each other, because of how mathematicians are trained, and how they communicate their ideas. If what is in my head is not consistent with what is in yours, then one of us has got it wrong and we will argue until it becomes clear to us both who it is.

Most areas of human activity are structured in this way. So the difficult questions of existence and discovery versus invention are not confined to mathematics. Take medicine, for example. What is medicine? Where does it live? Is it invented or discovered? Now replace medicine by plumbing, ballet, football, language or cycling, and it is clear just how widespread the structure is, and why the question doesn't make a great deal of sense in any area of human activity. What goes on is neither invention nor discovery, but a complex context-dependent mix of both.

When it comes to mathematics, sometimes it really does feel like discovery. When you are carrying out mathematical research in a previously defined area it feels like discovery because there is no choice about what the answer is. But when you are trying to formalise an elusive idea or find a new method, it feels more like invention: you are floundering around, trying all sorts of harebrained ideas, and you simply do not know where it will all lead. The more established an area of mathematics becomes, the more strongly it feels as if there is some kind of fixed logical landscape, which you merely explore. Once you've made a few assumptions (axioms), then everything that follows from them is predetermined. But this account misses out the most crucial features: significance, simplicity, elegance, how compelling the argument is, all things that give the landscape its character.

But if mathematics resides in mathematicians' heads, why is it so 'unreasonably effective'? (E. Wigner) The easy answer is that most mathematics starts in the real world. For instance, after observing on innumerable occasions that two sheep plus two more sheep make four sheep, ditto cows, wolves, warts and witches, it is a small step to introduce the idea that $2 + 2 = 4$ in a universal, abstract sense. Since the abstraction came out of reality, it's no surprise if it applies to reality.

However, that is too simple-minded a view. Mathematics has an internal structure of logical deduction that allows it to grow in unexpected ways. New ideas can be generated internally too, whenever anyone tries to fill obvious holes in the logical landscape. For example, having worked out how to solve quadratic equations, which arose from problems about baking bread, or whatever, it is obvious that you ought to try to solve cubic and quintic equations too. Before you can say 'Evariste Galois' you're doing Galois theory, which shows that you can't solve quintics, but is almost totally useless for anything practical. Then someone generalises Galois theory so that it applies to differential equations, and suddenly you find applications again, but to dynamics, not to bakery.

Yes, there is a flow of problems and concepts from the real world into mathematics, and a back-flow of solutions from mathematics to reality. Wigner's point is that the back-flow may not answer the problem that you set out to solve. Instead, it may answer something just as real, just as important, but physically unrelated. Why should this be? Well, mathematics is the art of drawing necessary conclusions, independently of interpretations. Two plus two has to be four, whether you are discussing sheep, cows or witches. In other words, the same abstract structure can have several interpretations. So you can get the ideas from one interpretation, and transfer the result to others. Mathematics is so powerful because it is an abstraction.

This is all very well, but why do the abstractions of mathematics match reality? Indeed, do they really match, or is it all an illusion? Enter cultural relativism – the idea that has lately become so fashionable in academic arts departments, which sees maths and science as social constructs no less and no more valid than any other social construct. Does this lead to the idea that science can be anything scientists want it to be?

True, science is a social construct. Scientists who claim that it is not are making the same mistake as those who think that we all dip into the same collective subconscious. But there is something special about science: it is a construct that has at every step been tested against external reality. If the world's scientists all got together and decided that elephants are weightless and rise into the air if they are not held down by ropes, it would still be foolish to stand under a cliff when a herd of elephants was leaping off the edge. In science, there has to be a reality check. Because it is done by beings who see reality through imperfect and biased senses, the reality check cannot be perfect, but science still has to survive some very stringent scrutiny.

So what's the reality check in maths? Well, the deeper we delve into the 'fundamental' nature of the Universe, the more mathematical it seems to get. The ghostly world of the quantum cannot be expressed without mathematics: if you try to describe it in everyday language, it makes no sense …

Human minds evolved in the real world, and they learnt to detect patterns to help us survive events outside ourselves. If none of the patterns detected by these minds bore any genuine relation to the real world outside, they wouldn't have helped their owners survive, and would eventually have died out. So our figments must correspond, to some extent, to real patterns. In the same way, mathematics is our way of understanding certain features of nature. It is a construct of the human mind, but we are part of nature, made from the same kind of matter, existing in the same kinds of space and time as the rest of the Universe. So the figments in our heads are not arbitrary inventions. There are definitely some mathematical things in the Universe, the most obvious being the mind of a mathematician. Mathematical minds cannot evolve in an unmathematical universe. Only a geometer God can create beings able to come up with geometry.

But that is not to say that only one kind of mathematics is possible: the mathematics of the Universe. That seems too parochial a view. Would aliens necessarily come up with the same kind of mathematics as us? I don't mean in fine detail. For example the six-clawed cat creatures of Apellobetnees Gamma would no doubt use base-24 notation, but they would still agree that twenty-five is a perfect square, even if they write it as 11. However, I'm thinking more of the kind of mathematics that might be developed by the plasma vortex wizards of Cygnus, for whom everything is in constant flux. Maybe they'd understand plasma dynamic a lot better than we do, though I suspect we wouldn't have any idea how they did it. But I doubt that they would have anything like Pythagoras's theorem. $[H^2 = \sqrt{(a^2 + b^2)}]$ There are few right angles in plasmas. In fact, I doubt they'd have the concept 'triangle'. By the time they had drawn the third vertex of a right triangle, the other two would be long gone, wafted away on the plasma winds.

8 The natural sciences

'Science may be described as the art of systematic oversimplification.'
Karl Popper, 1902–94

'When you cannot measure, your knowledge is meagre and unsatisfactory.'
Lord Kelvin, 1824–1907

'Science is a way of thinking more than it is a body of knowledge.'
Carl Sagan, 1934–96

'Don't believe the results of experiments until they're confirmed by theory.'
Sir Arthur Eddington, 1882–1944

'Science is a long history of learning how not to fool ourselves.'
Richard Feynman, 1918–88

'Science does not tell us how to live.'
Leo Tolstoy, 1828–1910

'Everything you've learned... as "obvious" becomes less and less obvious as you begin to study the universe.'
Buckminster Fuller, 1895–1983

'The arrogance of scientists is not nearly so dangerous as the arrogance that comes from ignorance.'
Lewis Wolpert, 1956–

'Science is a way of describing reality; it is therefore limited by the limits of observation, and it asserts nothing which is outside observation.'
Jacob Bronowski, 1908–74

'Science is the only genuine permanent revolution in human affairs, since it is committed to challenging the findings of its forebears.'
Daniel Bell, 1919–

'A new scientific truth does not triumph by convincing its opponents and making them see the light, but rather because its opponents eventually die out, and a new generation grows up that is familiar with it.'
Max Planck, 1858–1947

'The most incomprehensible thing about the world is that it is comprehensible.'
Albert Einstein, 1879–1955

'Science is built up of facts, as a house is built of stones; but an accumulation of facts is no more a science than a heap of stones is a house.'
Henri Poincaré, 1854–1912

'As a matter of historical fact, the history of science is, by and large, a history of progress.'
Karl Popper, 1902–94

Introduction

The story of the natural sciences is a story of remarkable achievements. The scientific revolution of the seventeenth century, which is associated with the names of such great scientists as Galileo Galilei (1564–1642), Isaac Newton (1642–1727) and Robert Boyle (1627–91), initiated a period of tremendous progress which shows no sign of coming to an end. In little more than three centuries, we have discovered the fundamental laws of physics, the 92 elements that make up the periodic table, and some of the secrets of life that are written into our DNA. Science has not only enabled us to split the atom, clone a sheep, and put men on the moon, it has also delivered all kinds of practical benefits such as cars, telephones and computers.

Perhaps not surprisingly, the extraordinary success of the natural sciences has led some people to see them as *the dominant cognitive paradigm* or model of knowledge. From time to time, there have been attempts to establish other areas of knowledge on a more scientific foundation that mimics the rigour and apparent certainty of subjects like physics. Some people have even argued that science is the *only* road to knowledge and that if you cannot prove something scientifically then you don't really know it at all.

Despite the success of the natural sciences, we should be cautious about some of the more extravagant claims that are made on its behalf. For science is not God and, like every other area of knowledge, it has its weaknesses and limitations. We often hear it said that *science has proved that* something or other is the case – as if scientific findings had the certainty of mathematical deductions. But, since science has a history and scientific beliefs change over time, we might wonder how far the natural sciences really do give us certainty. We also need to keep in mind that the natural sciences do not have a monopoly on the truth and that there may be other equally valid ways of making sense of the world.

Activity 8.1

Give some examples of things that were believed to be true by nineteenth-century scientists but which we now know to be false.

Recently some critics of science have drawn attention to the dangers as well as the benefits of scientific knowledge, and there has been something of a backlash against 'science worship'. In some quarters, there is a feeling that science is 'out of control', and that scientists are 'playing God' and meddling with things they do not fully understand. Alarming predictions about nuclear war or the harmful effects of cloning may lead us to question whether in the long-term the benefits of science outweigh the costs.

Activity 8.2

1 What connotations does the word 'science' have for you? Are they positive, negative or mixed?
2 How are scientists viewed in popular culture, such as novels and movies? Are they generally seen as heroes or as villains?

Our concern in this chapter is with the nature and status of scientific knowledge. We will begin by looking at why it is important to distinguish between science and non-science, and then go on to look at three different theories of how science works. Finally, we will come back to the question of science and values.

Science and pseudo-science

The natural sciences typically denote subjects like physics, chemistry and biology. Since the word 'science' is like a stamp of approval or guarantee of quality, advertisers sometimes appeal to the status of science to sell their products, and charlatans may describe dubious medicines and remedies as 'scientific' in order to deceive gullible people.

Activity 8.3

Find and analyse any two advertisements that use the language of science in order to market their products.

Among the huge number of things that have been described as 'scientific' by their proponents are the following.

- *Acupuncture* – the belief that by inserting needles into various parts of the body you can restore normal energy balance to relieve pain and cure various disorders.
- *Astrology* – the belief that our characters are determined by the celestial bodies (sun, moon, planets and stars) at the time of our birth.
- *Creationism* – the belief that the theory of evolution is false and that each species was uniquely created by God.
- *Crystology* – the belief that crystals have magical healing powers.
- *Feng shui* – the belief that the positioning and physical characteristics of your home can affect the balance and harmony of your life.
- *Graphology* – the belief that by analysing a person's handwriting you can learn about their character.
- *Homeopathy* – the belief that an extremely small quantity of a substance that can cause certain symptoms in a healthy person can cure similar symptoms in an unhealthy person.
- *Phrenology* – the belief that the structure of a person's skull determines their character and mental ability.

We should perhaps be open-minded about some of the above beliefs and find out more about them before deciding whether or not there is any truth in them. For it could be argued that if they 'work' for people and, for example, help to alleviate pain then, whether or not they are scientific, it would be foolish to condemn them. If millions of people claim to get relief from acupuncture, then even if we do not understand how it works, why not accept it as a useful tool in the medical armoury? Nevertheless, *if* acupuncture works then it surely makes sense to try to find out *why* it works, and this will inevitably involve doing such things as formulating hypotheses and conducting controlled experiments to test them. If we are to understand what is going on, there does not seem to be any other way to proceed.

Figure 8.1

While some people are willing to subject their beliefs to proper scientific tests, others are not. They simply *state* that their beliefs are scientific. But just because someone *says* that something is scientific does not mean that it *is* scientific. For example, a racist might claim that his theories are based on biological research, but we are not going to take *his* word for it. What we need are criteria for distinguishing genuine science from **pseudo-science** (fake science).

Of course, just because something is not a science does not mean that it is a pseudo-science. For example, literary criticism is not a science, but since it makes no claim to be scientific, it is not a pseudo-science either, and as a way of trying to make sense of a text it has its own validity. *What distinguishes a pseudo-science is that it claims the status of science while lacking its substance.*

Consider, for example, crystology, a set of beliefs about the magical power of crystals which claim to be scientific but have not been scientifically tested. Among the claims made by advocates of crystology is that quartz crystals generate 'a field of positive crystalline energy'. Something called a 'bioelectric shield' – a kind of magic pendant – is said to be 'medically proven' and 'based on Nobel Prize winning physics'. Among the alleged benefits of the shield are that it 'boosts your immune system and reduces stress while enhancing mental, emotional and physical performance'. You can buy such a shield for anything from $139 to over $1,000. Meanwhile, a 'certified Master of Crystology' advertises a comprehensive healing session in which 'your aura will be cleansed and balanced', and any weaknesses or areas of the body under stress will be addressed through the practitioner's 'intuitive use of crystals'. The cost of a half-hour session is $45. Perhaps there is something in all this, but you would be wise to investigate these claims more thoroughly before parting with your money.

1 What is the difference between astronomy and astrology? Why is the former classified as a science and the latter not? Do you agree with this classification?

2 As a scientist, how would you go about trying to test the claims of astrology?

3 Do some research on the *placebo effect* and give a short explanation of it. What is its relevance when we evaluate the claims of alternative medicine?

Figure 8.2

The difference between science and pseudo-science

The main difference between science and pseudo-science is that scientific hypotheses are *testable*, whereas pseudo-scientific ones are not. There are at least two ways in which pseudo-scientific hypotheses protect themselves from being testable:

1 ***Vagueness*** If a statement is sufficiently vague, it will be impossible to verify or falsify it. A claim such as 'quartz crystals can restore the balance and energy of your life' is, as it stands, virtually meaningless. To turn it into a genuinely scientific claim, we would need some kind of criteria – preferably measurable ones – to determine the meaning of words like 'balance' and 'energy'. We might also want to know the time period within which these improvements are supposed to take place.

2 **Ad hoc *exceptions*** A statement may be protected by various kinds of *ad hoc* exceptions. For example, if someone says 'All swans are white' and you show them a black one, they may qualify their statement by saying 'All swans are white except that mutation.' A good scientific hypothesis is one that is general in nature and does not keep making exceptions every time it meets counter-examples.

Given the above discussion, I think we can say that for a hypothesis to be a genuinely scientific statement it must be testable, and that it will be easier to test if the following are true:

1 It is clearly stated and makes precise rather than vague predictions.
2 It does not keep making *ad hoc* exceptions when it comes across counter-examples.

The scientific method

In trying to distinguish science from non-science, you might list all the subjects that count as science – such as physics, chemistry and biology – and then say that everything else is non-science. However, this does not seem very helpful because it does not explain *why* some things count as science and other things do not. A better approach might be to say that what distinguishes science from non-science is a distinctive *method*. On this view, science is not so much a fixed body of knowledge as a way of thinking about the world.

f   Speculating on the origins of the universe.

g   Studying human anatomy before making a sculpture.

h   Doing detective work to solve a murder.

i   Inventing the light bulb.

j   Predicting rain because the clouds look threatening.

k   Solving a crossword puzzle.

l   Noticing that you always need something just after you have thrown it away.

Inductivism

According to the traditional picture of the scientific method, which is known as **inductivism**, science consists of five key steps:

1   observation
2   hypothesis
3   experiment
4   law
5   theory

You begin by observing and classifying the relevant data. You then look for a pattern in the data and formulate a hypothesis. You then make a prediction, which you test by an experiment. A good experiment should have the following features:

- *Controllability*   You vary only one factor at a time so that you can determine its effect. For example, you might vary the temperature of a gas while keeping its volume constant. This helps you to isolate the cause of the phenomenon that you are investigating.

- *Measurability*   You can measure the relevant variables. This adds precision and objectivity to your experiment.

- *Repeatability*   Your experiment can be repeated by other people who will be able to confirm your results. This ensures that your results have some kind of objectivity.

If your experimental results confirm your hypothesis, then you may have discovered a *scientific law*. If your results disconfirm your hypothesis, then you will need to go back and think again.

Finally, you may develop a theory which explains and unifies various laws in terms of some underlying principles. A good theory explains why the laws are the way they are and provides a focus for further research.

An example: the Copernican revolution

To illustrate the scientific method, consider the way our views have changed about the place of the earth in the universe. Since it does not look or feel as if we are moving, it is natural to think that the earth is stationary. So it is not surprising that the Greek astronomer Claudius Ptolemy (85–165) developed a model of the universe with the earth at the centre of things and the sun and the planets going round it. Ptolemy's model not only reflected common sense, but also enabled people to make accurate predictions about the movements of the planets. The steps that led to the breakdown and eventual replacement of this model could be traced in the following simplified story:

Observation   As people made new and better observations, Ptolemy's model became increasingly complicated in order to accommodate them, so that, by the sixteenth century, it had become a 'disorderly monster'.

Hypothesis   This led Nicolaus Copernicus (1473–1543) to suggest a simpler and more elegant approach which put the sun at the centre of the solar system and had the planets revolve around it.

Prediction   In the Ptolemaic model, Venus orbits the earth and so always appears the same size; but Copernicus said that if Venus orbits the sun its apparent size should vary as its distance from the earth changes. To the naked eye Venus appears to be a constant size as predicted by the Ptolemaic model. But when Galileo (1564–1642) looked at it through a telescope in 1609, he discovered that its size does indeed vary as had been predicted by Copernicus.

Law   On the basis of the above observations and discoveries, Johannes Kepler (1571–1630), developed laws of planetary motion.

Theory   Finally, Isaac Newton (1642–1727) came up with the theory of gravity, which says that there is a force of attraction between objects whose strength is directly proportional to their masses and inversely proportional to the square of the distance between them. (Thus if you double the distance between two objects, the gravitational attraction between them will be 1/4 of its original strength.) This was part of a more general theory that enabled Newton to explain a wide variety of phenomena such as why an apple falls from a tree, why people have weight, the movement of the tides, and the orbit of the planets. Newtonian physics also enabled later astronomers to make accurate predictions that led to the discovery of new planets such as Uranus in 1781 and Neptune in 1846.

The following points are worth drawing out of this brief account:

- Scientific progress needs a background of careful observation. Kepler was able to develop his laws of planetary motion because another astronomer called Tycho Brahe (1546–1601) had made meticulous observations and discovered various **anomalies** in the orbits of the planets. (An anomaly is an observation that seems to contradict a generally accepted theory.)

- Technology can extend our powers of observation, thereby making it easier to test new ideas. Galileo was only able to detect the change in the apparent size of Venus by using the newly invented telescope.

- Imagination plays an important role in the development of new scientific ideas. Part of Copernicus' genius was that while he saw what everyone else saw when he looked up at the night sky, he came up with a different way of looking at it. (In fact, a Greek astronomer called Aristarchus had suggested that the earth goes round the sun as early as the third century BCE, but the idea didn't catch on.)

- Mathematics also plays a central role in the development of scientific ideas. Newton's law of gravity not only fitted the observational data, but could also be expressed in precise mathematical terms.
- Many scientific discoveries are *counter-intuitive* and go against untutored common sense. We now take it as obvious that the earth rotates on its axis and orbits the sun but, when you think about it, it is difficult to believe that the earth is spinning at 1,000 miles an hour and travelling round the sun at about 67,000 miles an hour.

Activity 8.7

Try explaining the following to someone who doesn't know much physics.
a If the earth is round, why don't people fall off the bottom?
b If the earth is moving round the sun and rotating on its axis, how come it doesn't feel like we are moving?
c Since birds fly far slower than the earth rotates, how come they don't get left behind when they fly in the direction of the rotation (west to east)?

Our discussion so far might suggest that there is a straightforward procedure for generating scientific truth from raw observations. All you have to do is follow the scientific method. But things are not that simple. If we go over the various stages of the scientific method again, we will see that each step is more complicated than it first appears.

Problems with observation

Science is based on observation but, as we saw in Chapter 4, observation is not as straightforward as it first seems. In what follows, we shall briefly consider problems of relevance, expectations, expert seeing and the observer effect.

Relevance

Activity 8.8

Imagine that you are interested in finding out why some students catch a cold in the winter term and other students do not. Which of the following factors might you look at in comparing the two groups, and which would you consider irrelevant?
a Diet   b Colour of underwear
c Exercise   d Middle name
e Domestic heating   f Movies watched
g Warmth of clothing

Quite reasonably, you probably said that (a), (c), (e) and (g) are relevant, and (b), (d) and (f) are irrelevant. How, after all, could the colour of your underwear, or your middle name, or the movies you have watched, affect whether or not you catch a cold?

The important point that comes out of this example is that we always begin with some idea of what is and what is not relevant to the problem. If we did not, we would drown in a flood of observations. However, the selective nature of perception means that it is always possible that we have overlooked a factor that later turns out to be relevant. For example, when you do an experiment in chemistry, you do not normally count how many people are in the room. However, this will affect the temperature of the room, and in a sensitive experiment that might affect the speed of the chemical reaction.

Expectations

Another problem with observation is that *our expectations can influence what we see*. When the planet Mercury was found to be deviating from the orbit predicted by Newton's laws, some nineteenth-century astronomers suggested that the anomaly was caused by an undiscovered planet called Vulcan. So confident were they in their belief that several astronomers then claimed that they had observed Vulcan. But it turned out that Vulcan does not exist. The correct explanation for the deviation of Mercury had to wait for Einstein's theory of relativity.

Expert seeing

The use of *scientific equipment* such as microscopes and telescopes to make observations further complicates things. We may laugh when we hear that some of Galileo's contemporaries refused to look through his telescope preferring to rely on the authority of the Church rather than the evidence of their senses. But it is worth pointing out that the telescope Galileo used to discover the phases of Venus and the moons of Jupiter was a fairly crude instrument. Some of Galileo's drawings of the moon are quite inaccurate and include some craters and mountains that do not in fact exist. From your own experience in the science lab, you are probably aware that it takes quite a lot of practice to learn how to see through a microscope.

The observer effect

A final problem with observation is that *the act of observation can sometimes affect what we observe*. To take a simple example, imagine that you want to know exactly how hot a cup of tea is. You put a thermometer in the tea and read off the temperature. The problem is that, instead of measuring the temperature of the tea, you are now measuring the temperature of the tea-with-the-thermometer-in-it. The very act of putting the thermometer in the tea has changed its temperature. Of course, for most practical purposes this does not make a significant difference. If you are in bed with a fever and the doctor comes and tells you that you have a temperature of 102 °F, it would be pedantic to point out that she has in fact taken the temperature of you *plus* the thermometer. However, the effect of the observer on the observed plays an important role in a branch of physics known as quantum physics. We shall also have more to say about the observer effect when we discuss the human sciences in the next chapter.

While our discussion has focused on the fallibility of perception, it is important not to exaggerate the problem. The great strength of science is that it is a communal and self-correcting enterprise. Sooner or later the errors of one individual are likely to be corrected by someone else.

'An uneducated child and a trained astronomer, both relying on the naked eye and twenty-twenty vision, will literally see a different sky.' What do you understand by this quotation?

Testing hypotheses

Testing hypotheses is also less straightforward than the naive account of the scientific method implies. Among the complications are: confirmation bias, background assumptions and the fact that many different hypotheses are consistent with a given set of data.

Confirmation bias

Confirmation bias refers to the fact that people tend to look for evidence that confirms their beliefs and overlook evidence that goes against them. If, for example, you believe that Virgos are particularly shy individuals, you will notice every time you come across a shy Virgo. But if you only observe confirming instances of your hypothesis this does not show that it is true. You also need to look for evidence that might falsify it.

In the above example, as well as looking at Virgos who are shy, what else might you look at that could falsify your hypothesis?

The two other key things you should look out for are: (a) Virgos who are not shy; and (b) people of other star signs who are also shy. When all the evidence is in, it may turn out that, despite your initial belief, there is no relationship between a person's star sign and whether or not they are shy.

A good scientist will be aware of the danger of confirmation bias and actively seek to combat it. In one of his notebooks Charles Darwin (1809–82) stated that 'I followed a golden rule, namely that whenever a new observation or thought came across me, which was opposed to my general results, I make a memorandum of it without fail and at once; for I had found by experience that such facts and thoughts were far more apt to escape from the memory than favourable ones.' This is a tribute to Darwin's intellectual integrity.

One common form of confirmation bias is for a scientist to dismiss results they don't expect as 'experimental error'. Imagine, for example, that you do an experiment and get the following results. You would probably be tempted to ignore observation X_4.

In Figure 8.3, to what extent do you think you would be justified in dismissing observation X_4 as experimental error?

In the case opposite, it might seem reasonable to assume that X_4 is a result of human error, but it would be wise to take more observations to be on the safe side. In practice, however, it is difficult to say where 'trimming' one's results to exclude experimental error ends and 'cooking the books' begins. Scientists naturally want to show their results in the best possible light, and they often have strong expectations about the way an experiment should turn out. When the notebooks of one famous physicist were examined, the following comments were found alongside his experimental observations:

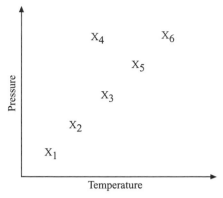

Figure 8.3 Pressure–temperature graph

> 'Very low. Something wrong.'
> 'This is almost exactly *right* and the best one I have ever had!!!'
> 'Agreement poor.'

To take another example, Gregor Mendel's (1822–84) work on the hereditary traits of peas laid the foundations for modern genetics. But according to some modern geneticists, his results are just too good to be believable, and he has been accused of only reporting results that favoured his case. The following is an amusing account of Mendel's method:

IN THE BEGINNING, there was Mendel, thinking his lonely thoughts alone. And he said: 'Let there be peas,' and there were peas, and it was good. And he put the peas in the garden, saying unto them, 'Increase and multiply, segregate and assort yourselves independently,' and they did, and it was good. And now it came to pass that when Mendel gathered up his peas, he divided them into round and wrinkled and called the round dominant and the wrinkled recessive, and it was good. But now Mendel saw that there were 450 round peas and 102 wrinkled ones; this was not good. For the law stateth that there should be only three round for every wrinkled. And Mendel said unto himself, 'Gott in Himmel, an enemy has done this; he has sown bad peas in my garden under the cover of night.' And Mendel smote the table in righteous wrath, saying, 'Depart from me, you cursed and evil peas, into the outer darkness where Thou shalt be devoured by the rats and mice,' and lo, it was done, and there remained 300 round peas and 100 wrinkled peas, and it was good. It was very, very good. And Mendel published.

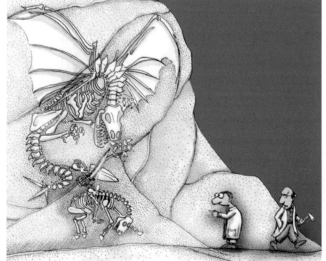

Figure 8.4   "No, ignore that one Davies. It's unscientific."

Background assumptions

Whenever we test a hypothesis, we make various background assumptions, any one of which could turn out to be false. For example, at the time of Copernicus, it was generally agreed that the fixed stars are relatively close to the earth. Given this, it follows that if the earth is orbiting the sun the position of nearby stars relative to more distant stars ought to change as the earth moves round the sun. Such a change of relative position is known as a *parallax*. (An analogy may help you to get the point here. Hold a pencil out in front of you so that it exactly covers a distant object, such as a tree. If you now close each of your eyes in turn, the position of the pencil relative to the tree will appear to change. In a similar way, the relative position of the stars should change if the earth is moving.) The problem was that no one was able to observe the required parallax; and neither Copernicus nor Galileo had an answer to this criticism. Finally it turned out that the assumption that the fixed stars are relatively close to the earth was wrong, and in the nineteenth century the stellar parallax was finally observed.

Many different hypotheses are consistent with a given set of data

Since it is possible to come up with many different hypotheses that are consistent with a given set of observations, it is in practice impossible to *prove* that any particular hypothesis is true. For example, in our discussion of astronomy above, I said that Galileo saw that the relative size of Venus changes as predicted by Copernicus' heliocentric theory. While this observation is inconsistent with Ptolemy's model, it is in fact consistent with another model according to which the sun orbits the earth and the other planets orbit the sun.

In fact, there are an endless number of different hypotheses consistent with a given set of observations. This can be easily shown by considering the graphs below. Imagine you are investigating the relationship between the temperature and pressure of a gas. You make some observations, X_1, X_2 and X_3. On the basis of your observations, you formulate a hypothesis H1, and make a prediction P. Your prediction is confirmed. Does this conclusively

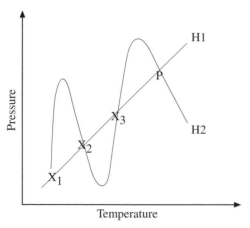

Figure 8.5 Temperature–pressure graph showing hypotheses H1 and H2

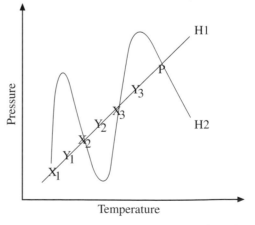

Figure 8.6 Temperature–pressure graph, with extra observations

confirm hypothesis H1? No! For your observations are also consistent with another hypothesis H2.

To decide between hypotheses H1 and H2 you might make some further observations, Y_1, Y_2 and Y_3 as in Figure 8.6. These new observations would seem to confirm H1 and eliminate H2.

But once again H1 is not conclusively confirmed. For we might now make another hypothesis H3 which is also consistent with our observations (Figure 8.7). Further observations might eliminate H3 and confirm H1, but you could then make another hypothesis H4 and so on.

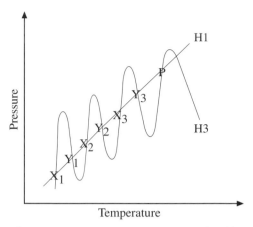

Figure 8.7 Temperature–pressure graph with new hypothesis H3

Extrapolating from this, you can see that, no matter how many observations you make confirming H1, there will always be other hypotheses that are also consistent with the data.

The principle of simplicity

Having said that, hypotheses such as H3 do seem absurd, and it is hard to avoid thinking that H1 is the more natural hypothesis. In fact, scientists usually appeal to a **principle of simplicity** which says that given two competing theories which make exactly the same predictions the simpler theory is to be preferred. This justifies our preference for H1 over H2 or H3. However, if you asked a scientist to justify their belief in the principle of simplicity, they would probably shrug their shoulders and say that's just what they believe. The principle reflects a deep belief in the orderliness and comprehensibility of nature, but no further justification can be given for it. Since simplicity is also related to concepts such as 'beauty' and 'elegance', we can say that in practice aesthetic considerations are likely to play a role in a scientist's choice of hypothesis.

But we must be careful. For our aesthetic prejudices can sometimes lead us astray. Copernicus was convinced that the planets must orbit the sun in circles because he thought that a circle is a perfect figure. However, it turned out that planetary orbits are elliptical rather than circular. The moral of the tale is that nature's aesthetic may not be the same as our own, and beautiful theories are sometimes slain by ugly facts!

The problem of induction

A final problem with the naive picture of the scientific method concerns induction. As we saw in Chapter 5, inductive reasoning goes from the particular to the general, and it plays a central role in the way that scientists think. Take, for example, our belief that all metals expand when heated. How did we come by this belief? Not by reason, or intuition, or divine revelation, but by observation. As far as we know, every time a piece of metal has been heated, it has expanded, and there are no recorded cases of metals not expanding when heated. So it seems reasonable to conclude that this is a law of nature. What's the problem?

Although it is unlikely to keep you awake at night, the problem is that when we reason inductively we are moving from the observed to the unobserved. For example, when we reason that since metal A and metal B and metal C etc. expand when heated, then *all* metals expand when heated, we are making a generalisation from things we have observed to things we have not observed.

Practical problems

At a practical level, the problem of induction raises the question of how many observations we should make before we are entitled to make a generalisation. We saw in Chapter 6 that we have a tendency to jump to conclusions on the basis of insufficient evidence, and we looked at various criteria for distinguishing reasonable generalisations from unreasonable ones. But there is no hard and fast rule about how many observations you should make before you are entitled to generalise. All we can say is the more observations you make that support your hypothesis the more confident you will feel about it.

The trouble is that even well-confirmed generalisations sometimes let us down. Up until the eighteenth century, it was commonly believed by Europeans that all swans are white. There were innumerable confirming instances of this belief and no disconfirming instances. Then some black swans were discovered in Australia. More dramatically, for two and a half centuries experiment after experiment seemed to confirm the truth of Newtonian physics. Nevertheless, Einstein showed that there is a deep sense in which Newton's laws are not the best description of physical reality. What this appears to show is that even very well-confirmed hypotheses can sometimes turn out to be wrong.

When you start to think about it, our confidence in scientific knowledge is quite breathtaking. On the basis of a few observations that we have made on planet Earth, we claim to have discovered laws of physics that apply to *all* times and *all* places – billions of years ago and billions of light-years away. Yet we have observed only a minute fraction of the universe. (As we mentioned in Chapter 1, astronomers estimate that there are ten times more stars in the night sky than grains of sand in the world's deserts and beaches!)

Given the above, you might argue that scientists should show greater humility and make less ambitious claims. For example, instead of saying 'all metals expand when heated', perhaps we should restrict ourselves to the more modest assertion that 'all *observed* metals expand when heated'. This may show admirable humility, but the fact is that deep down most physicists believe that they really are discovering the fundamental laws in accordance with which the universe operates.

Theoretical problems

The problem of induction bites not only at the practical level, but also at the theoretical level. For science is supposed to be an *empirical* discipline which makes no claims beyond what has been observed. Indeed, the claim that it is grounded in observation is supposed to be what distinguishes genuine science from pseudo-science. So we seem to be faced with a dilemma. On the one hand, we could take the alleged empiricism of science seriously, and refuse to make any claims that go beyond what has actually been observed. There would, however, be a very high price to pay for this. For it would mean that we would have to abandon any talk of discovering laws of nature that apply in all times and all places. On the other hand, we could defend the right of scientists to reason from the particular to the general, and abandon the claim that science is a strictly empirical discipline. Again, this seems to be a high price to pay. Another approach is to simply not worry about the problem too much and just get on with the business of doing science!

The scientific method: summary of problems		
Observation	1	Selectivity
	2	Expectations
	3	Expert seeing
	4	The observer effect
Hypothesis	5	Confirmation bias
	6	Background assumptions
	7	Under-determination
Law	8	Problem of induction

Activity 8.12

Write short paragraphs explaining each of the above problems in your own words.

Falsification

One person who took the problem of induction seriously and tried to resolve the dilemma was a philosopher called Karl Popper (1902–94). Popper's interest in the problem grew out of his concern to distinguish genuine science, such as Einstein's theory of relativity, from what he saw as pseudo-science, such as Marxism and psychoanalysis.

As a young man, Popper had been impressed by the ability of theories put forward by people such as Karl Marx (1818–83), Sigmund Freud (1856–1939) and Alfred Adler (1870–1937) to explain *everything*. Adler, for example, believed that human beings are dominated by feelings of inferiority. 'To be human', he said, 'means to feel inferior.' He then used this insight to explain more or less the entire range of human behaviour. As impressive as this seems, Popper came to the conclusion that what looked like a strength of the theory – its ability to explain everything – was in fact a weakness.

Imagine, for example, that a man is walking along the bank of a fast-flowing river when he sees a child fall in. He has two choices: either he jumps in and tries to rescue the child or he does not. Suppose that he jumps in and tries to rescue the child. 'Ah', says Adler, 'this is exactly what my theory predicted. The man was clearly trying to overcome his feeling of inferiority by demonstrating his bravery.' Now suppose that the man does not jump in to the river. 'Just as I thought', says Adler. 'This man is clearly suffering from an inferiority complex which he is unable to overcome.'

The above may be a caricature of Adler's beliefs, but the point I want to emphasise is that from a scientific point of view *a theory that explains everything explains nothing*. According to Popper, a genuinely scientific theory differs from the one considered above in that it puts itself at risk. For example, Einstein's general theory of relativity led to certain predictions being made which were famously tested and confirmed in 1919. Had the relevant observations not confirmed Einstein's theory, scientists would have rejected it.

Figure 8.8

Conjectures and refutations

The scientific method advocated by Popper is based on **conjectures and refutations**. A conjecture is basically an imaginative hypothesis and, in his discussion of conjectures, Popper emphasises the fact that there is no mechanical way of coming up with good hypotheses on the basis of the observational data. What is frequently required is a leap of imagination that enables you to look at the data in a different way. This is essentially what Copernicus did when he first put forward the idea that the earth goes round the sun rather than vice versa. As we saw when discussing intuition in Chapter 6, scientists often have their best ideas in a flash of intuition. For example, Newton is said to have come up with the idea of universal gravity when he saw an apple fall from a tree, and Mendeleyev's idea for the periodic table came to him in a dream. However, you are only likely to have such intuitions if you have the right background knowledge and have put in the necessary work. When Newton was asked how he had discovered the law of gravity, he replied 'By thinking on it continually'. And Mendeleyev made a set of cards with the names of the elements written on them, and played around with them endlessly before he finally made his great breakthrough.

The most important thing about genuinely *scientific* conjectures is that they are *testable*. This brings us to the concept of 'refutations' and Popper's attempt to solve the problem of induction. In thinking about this problem, Popper was struck by the asymmetry between confirmation and falsification. Consider again our standard example, 'All metals expand when heated.' We cannot be sure that the law is true no matter how many confirming observations we have made; for it is always possible that the next metal we test will *not* expand when heated. But we only need to find one metal which does *not* expand when heated to be sure that it is *false* that all metals expand when heated. In other words, while confirmation is tentative and cannot prove that a law is true, refutation is decisive: we need only one counter-example to prove that a law is false.

The conclusion Popper drew from this is that scientists should not waste their time trying to prove that their hypotheses are true; for the problem of induction shows that this is impossible. Rather, they should spend their time trying to prove that their hypotheses are *false*. Despite its strangeness, Popper's ingenious approach is in many ways attractive. He believed that a properly scientific approach to a subject should explore the shortcomings of currently accepted theories. What he disliked above all was any form of scientific dogmatism which blindly accepted the prevailing orthodoxy. For if science is to progress then people must question and criticise the current state of scientific knowledge.

There is, of course, no virtue in going around falsifying *absurd* hypotheses, such as 'an apple a day makes you good at calculus', or 'people who wear jeans are less likely to have car accidents'. The point is rather to look closely at apparently well-confirmed hypotheses in order to discover their shortcomings.

Take, for example, the scientific law that water boils at 100°C. If you mindlessly boil pan after pan of water, you will never conclusively prove that this law is true and you will not make any meaningful contribution to science. A better strategy would be to look for situations in which water does *not* boil at 100°C. If you adopt this approach, you might discover that, at high altitudes, water boils at less than 100°C. The challenge is then to find an explanation for why water boils at a lower temperature at a higher altitude. And you are then in a position to test new ideas and make real scientific progress.

According to Popper, any theory that resists our best efforts to falsify it should be *provisionally accepted* as the best we have for the time being. But he insists that it cannot be said to be true in any *absolute* sense; for it is always possible that in the future it will be replaced by a better theory. That, after all, is what happened to Newtonian physics!

Criticisms of Popper

Despite the attractions of Popper's philosophy of science, it is itself open to criticism.

Falsification is conclusive in theory but not in practice

Falsificationism turns on the idea that, although confirmation is provisional, falsification is decisive. While this is true in theory, it turns out that in practice falsification is no more conclusive than verification. Imagine, for example, that you do an experiment in the physics laboratory that contradicts one of Newton's laws of motion. Do you announce that you have just disproved Newton? I doubt it! The most reasonable conclusion is that you have messed up the experiment. What this example suggests is that, while in theory a single counter-example is enough to overturn a law of nature, in practice it is not. When there is a conflict between hypothesis and observation we have a choice: we can either reject the hypothesis, or we can reject the observation.

There are in fact many examples in the history of science of scientists refusing to abandon their theories in the face of observational evidence which appeared to contradict them. Here are three such examples.

- *Physics* Newton's theory of gravity implied that, given the attractive forces between the stars, the universe should collapse in a gigantic cosmic crunch. Newton saw that this was a serious problem, but rather than abandon his theory, he somewhat desperately concluded that God must be counteracting gravity and keeping the stars in their places.

- *Chemistry* When Dimitri Mendeleyev (1834–1907) came up with the periodic table by arranging elements according to their atomic weights, the weights of some elements did not quite fit his model. Mendeleyev did not abandon this theory but concluded that the anomalous weights must be due to experimental error.

- *Biology* Charles Darwin's (1809–82) theory of evolution required that the earth be hundreds of millions of years old to allow enough time for species to evolve. But according to the calculations of the leading physicist of the day, Lord Kelvin (1824–1907), the earth was no more than 100 million years old. Kelvin's figure was based on the best knowledge available at the time. Darwin found it 'preposterously inadequate', and he stuck with his theory.

With hindsight, we can say that Newton, Mendeleyev and Darwin were right to stick with their theories in the face of observations that seemed to contradict them. The universe does not collapse in on itself because the speed at which the stars are moving away from each other counteracts gravity. The anomalous weights of some of Mendeleyev's elements were due to the presence of various isotopes. And Kelvin's way of calculating the age of the earth was eventually shown to be wrong.

Auxiliary hypotheses can rescue a falsified theory

What these examples show is that we should not always reject a promising theory as soon as we come across counter-evidence. For the counter-evidence may turn out to be experimental error, or our background assumptions may turn out to be wrong. Of course, if the experimental evidence consistently goes against a theory, then we should eventually abandon it. But a well-established theory may survive a long time in the face of counter-evidence that no one is able to explain away. Consider, for example, the following story told by the philosopher of science Imre Lakatos (1922–74):

> The story is about an imaginary case of planetary misbehaviour. A physicist of the pre-Einsteinian era takes Newton's mechanics and his law of gravitation (N), the accepted initial conditions, I, and calculates, with their help, the path of a newly discovered small planet, p. But the planet deviates from the calculated path. Does our Newtonian physicist consider that the deviation was forbidden by Newton's theory and therefore that, once established, it refutes the theory N? No. He suggests that there must have been a hitherto unknown planet p1 which perturbs the path of p. He calculates the mass, orbit, etc. of this hypothetical planet and then asks an experimental astronomer to test his hypothesis. The planet p1 is so small that even the biggest available telescopes cannot possibly observe it: the experimental astronomer applies for a research grant to build a yet bigger one. In three years' time the new telescope is ready. Were the unknown planet p1 to be discovered, it would be hailed as a new victory for Newtonian science. But it is not. Does our scientist abandon Newton's theory and his idea of the perturbing planet? No. He suggests that a cloud of cosmic dust hides the planet from us. He calculates the location and properties of this cloud and asks for a research grant to send up a satellite to test his calculations. Were the satellite's instruments (possibly

new ones, based on a little-tested theory) to record the existence of the conjectural cloud, the result would be hailed as an outstanding victory for Newtonian science. But the cloud is not found. Does our scientist abandon Newton's theory, together with the idea of the perturbing planet and the idea of the cloud which hides it? No. He suggests that there is some magnetic field in that region of the universe which disturbed the instruments of the satellite. A new satellite is sent up. Were the magnetic field to be found, Newtonians would celebrate a sensational victory. But it is not. Is this regarded as a refutation of Newtonian science? No. Either yet another ingenious auxiliary hypothesis is proposed or... the whole story is buried in the dusty volumes of periodicals and the story never mentioned again.

As this story suggests, there is in fact no such thing as a perfect theory, and you will find anomalies and unresolved problems in every area of science. If a theory is well-established and generally successful, then practitioners in the field tend to assume that, with time, outstanding problems will be resolved. For example, when it was discovered that the planet Uranus was not behaving as predicted by Newton's laws, scientists did not abandon Newtonian physics but argued that there must be some unknown planet affecting it. In this case, they rejected neither the observation nor the theory, but made an **auxiliary hypothesis** – the existence of an unknown planet – to explain their observations. This led to the discovery of Neptune in 1846. However, when they tried to explain the misbehaviour of Mercury in the same way by postulating the existence of a planet called Vulcan, they turned out to be wrong. This time Mercury's behaviour could not be explained within the Newtonian paradigm, and this eventually led to a scientific revolution and the replacement of Newtonian physics by the theory of relativity.

The rationalist strand in scientific thinking

When there is a conflict between observation and hypothesis, there are in fact three options:

- reject the hypothesis
- reject the observation
- accept both the hypothesis and the observation and make an auxiliary hypothesis.

What our discussion shows is that there is both a **rationalist** and an **empiricist** strand in scientific thinking. You may remember that a rationalist is someone who sees reason as the main source of knowledge and an empiricist is someone who sees experience as the main source of knowledge. When prediction and observation conflict with one another, a rationalist is more likely to stick with a beautiful theory, and an empiricist is more likely to stick with the observational evidence. Many great scientists have had rationalist sympathies in the sense that they have been unwilling to abandon a promising theory in the light of contrary evidence. Einstein was once asked how he would have reacted if his general theory had not been confirmed by experiment. He replied, 'Then I would have felt sorry for the good Lord. The theory is correct anyway.'

The power of science derives from the fact that it combines reason in the form of mathematics with experience in the form of observational data. The rationalist part of science is the belief that there is order 'out there', and that this order can be captured in scientific theories. The empiricist part is that if a theory is to survive and flourish then it must be consistent with the observational facts.

What comes out of our discussion of Popper is that scientific theories cannot be conclusively verified or falsified. They cannot be conclusively verified because of the problem of induction; and they cannot be conclusively falsified because, when an observation contradicts a theory, it is always open to you to reject the observation rather than the theory. Strictly speaking then, the concept of *proof* is only relevant to mathematics and logic and we cannot speak of science *proving* things in any absolute sense. In science, as in every other area of knowledge that applies to the world, we have to make do with something less than certainty.

Science and society

We have seen that neither inductivism nor falsificationism can give us an adequate account of the nature of science. A third perspective is provided by the historian and philosopher of science Thomas Kuhn (1922–96) who is best known for having introduced the concept of a **paradigm** to the philosophy of science. As we saw in the appendix to Part 2, a paradigm is an overarching theory shared by a community of scientists, such as physicists, chemists or biologists, which is used to make sense of some aspect of reality. Three important paradigms you are likely to have come across at school are Newtonian mechanics in physics, atomic theory in chemistry, and evolutionary theory in biology.

Normal science

While Popper argued that scientists should constantly be questioning their assumptions, Kuhn drew attention to the fact that during periods of what he calls 'normal science' the vast majority of scientists are busy solving problems within a paradigm while taking the paradigm itself for granted. To take an example mentioned earlier, the irregularity in the orbit of Uranus did not lead scientists to seriously question Newtonian mechanics; rather they tried to solve the problem within the framework of Newtonian mechanics. Popper might condemn such an uncritical approach, but the fact is that, if you are going to get anything done, you cannot endlessly question your assumptions. While great scientists such as Newton, Dalton and Darwin were architects who established new paradigms, most scientists are bricklayers patiently filling in the details and extending the body of scientific knowledge.

Scientific revolutions

Despite his emphasis on the stability of normal science, Kuhn argued that, far from progressing smoothly over time, the history of science is punctuated by revolutions. A **scientific revolution** takes place when scientists become dissatisfied with the prevailing paradigm, and put forward a completely new way of looking at things. If their ideas triumph, the new paradigm will replace the old one and inaugurate another period of normal science. The shift from the geocentric to the heliocentric model of the universe is the classic example of a scientific revolution. Other examples are the replacement of Aristotelian physics by Newtonian mechanics in the seventeenth century, and the replacement of Newtonian mechanics by Einstein's theory of relativity in the early twentieth century.

While we tend to think of science progressing along the lines of Figure 8.9, according to Kuhn the reality is more like Figure 8.10.

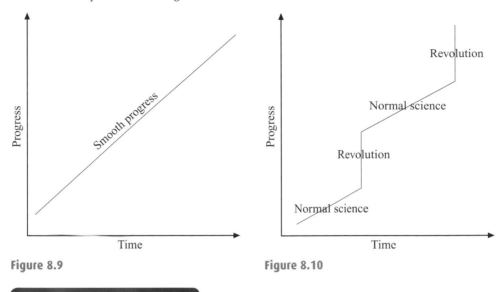

Figure 8.9

Figure 8.10

Activity 8.13

Do you think Figure 8.9 or Figure 8.10 more accurately reflects the way in which a subject with which you are familiar progresses over time?

We said earlier that there is no such thing as a perfect theory in science and that at any given time there are all kinds of problems and puzzles that have not yet been solved. During periods of normal science, there is widespread confidence that such problems can be solved by the existing paradigm. However, if over time the number of unresolved problems reaches a critical mass, some people may begin to question the paradigm itself. If a new paradigm provides a better explanation of things a scientific revolution is likely to occur. But not everyone will be converted to the new way of thinking, and during periods of scientific crisis there are likely to be violent arguments between those who adhere to the old paradigm and those who advocate the new one. Often, the new ideas triumph only after older, more conservative, scientists have died and a new generation has grown up that is familiar with the new way of thinking.

Activity 8.14

1 What truth, if any, do you think there is in the idea that older people are more conservative and suspicious of new ideas than younger people?
2 Find out how old some of the key figures in the history of science were when they came up with the ideas for which they later became famous. What conclusions, if any, can you draw from your enquiry?

How rational is science?

According to Kuhn, the progress of science is not as rational as is sometimes thought. During periods of scientific crisis there may be no definite point at which we can say it is irrational or unscientific to adhere to an old paradigm rather than convert to a new one. This follows from the point made earlier that in practice a theory can never be conclusively verified or falsified. For we can always dismiss observations that seem to falsify the old paradigm as experimental error or explain them away by making various auxiliary hypotheses. (Recall Lakatos' story of planetary misbehaviour.) Since there may be no purely rational way of choosing between competing theories, Kuhn likened switching from one paradigm to another to a religious conversion which may be influenced by a range of non-scientific factors such as personal ambition and social pressure.

There is doubtless an element of truth in Kuhn's view. We may like to think that scientists are motivated purely by love of truth, but that only tells part of the story. A brief glance at the history of science suggests that other more questionable motives, such as ambition, vanity and envy, also play a role. The vicious **priority disputes** that punctuate the history of science would seem to bear out the wry observation of the French biologist Charles Nicolle (1866–1936) that 'Without ambition and without vanity no one would enter a profession so contrary to our natural appetites.' (A priority dispute is a dispute about who was the first to discover a particular law or come up with a particular theory.) The fact is that scientists are as concerned as the next person with their social status and public recognition. The astronomer Edwin Hubble (1889–1953) was so anxious to get the Nobel Prize that he even employed a public relations expert to help him secure it. Sadly for Hubble, there is no Nobel Prize for astronomy and his efforts were in vain.

The social context also plays a role in the development of science and it may determine a scientist's choice of problems and the questions he or she is willing to investigate. A great deal of scientific research is connected with the military's desire for power and big business's desire for profit, and this has undoubtedly influenced the direction it has taken in recent decades. Ambitious scientists may be attracted to areas in which there is a plentiful supply of money to fund research; and they may shy away from politically sensitive areas, preferring to work in less controversial ones. Moreover, if they seek promotion, they will also be under pressure to conform to the beliefs and values of the scientific community.

Assessment of Kuhn's position

We have now looked at three key elements in Kuhn's theory of science, which can be summarised as follows:

1   During periods of normal science, most scientists do not question the paradigm in which they are operating and focus instead on solving problems.
2   The history of science suggests that, rather than progressing smoothly, science goes through a series of revolutionary jumps.
3   During periods of scientific crisis, there is no purely rational way of deciding between rival paradigms.

To determine how convincing Kuhn's ideas are, let us look more closely at each of the above points.

Normal science

There is probably some truth in Kuhn's claim that during periods of normal science most scientists work within the dominant paradigm without seriously questioning it. The question, however, is whether or not it is a good thing. Admittedly, if scientists are to make any progress they cannot be endlessly questioning their assumptions, but if they *never* do this, their beliefs may end up freezing into dogmatism. That, at least, was Popper's view:

> In my view the 'normal' scientist, as Kuhn describes him, is a person one ought to be sorry for... The 'normal' scientist... has been taught badly. I believe... that all teaching on the University level (and if possible below) should be training and encouragement in critical thinking. The 'normal' scientist, as described by Kuhn,... has been taught in a dogmatic spirit: he is a victim of indoctrination. He has learned a technique which can be applied without asking for the reason why... He is, as Kuhn puts it, content to solve 'puzzles'. The choice of this term seems to indicate that Kuhn wishes to stress that it is not a really fundamental problem which the 'normal' scientist is prepared to tackle: it is rather, a routine problem, a problem of applying what one has learned... The success of the 'normal' scientist consists, entirely, in showing that the ruling theory can be properly and satisfactorily applied in order to reach a solution of the puzzle in question.

Activity 8.15

To what extent are you encouraged to question your assumptions in your science classes at school? Can questioning your assumptions sometimes be counter-productive?

Scientific revolutions

We also need to be careful with Kuhn's account of the history of science in terms of revolutions. For it is sometimes taken to imply that *all* of our current scientific beliefs will one day be swept away in a new revolution. However, the fact that science is punctuated by periods of intellectual upheaval does not necessarily mean that when one paradigm replaces another the old one vanishes without trace. In fact, the history of science suggests that scientific knowledge is broadly cumulative and that, over time, scientific knowledge is getting closer to the truth.

Take, for example, physics. Despite the fact that Newtonian mechanics was replaced by Einstein's theory of relativity, the former is still valid across a vast range of phenomena, and is in fact a special case of the latter. This suggests that, rather than being straightforwardly right or wrong, we would do better to think of theories as being more or less inclusive. Despite its limitations, Aristotle's physics provided a reasonable description of many everyday phenomena. It was replaced by Newtonian physics, which is more rigorous and can account for a far wider range of phenomena. But if we wish to explain the motion of electrons inside an atom or the nature of a gravitational field near a black hole then we must turn to the theory of relativity.

We can illustrate the idea of inclusiveness with the following analogy. If you are laying the foundations of a house, you can treat the earth as if it were flat and make your calculations in accordance with plane geometry. However, if you are dealing with a much larger area, then you will need to take into account the curvature of the earth. Here, plane geometry turns out to be a special case of the geometry that is appropriate to the surface of a sphere. In much the same way, physicists see Newtonian mechanics as a useful approximation that can be incorporated into the more general theory of relativity.

Given what we have said, it seems reasonable to suppose that science will continue to progress in a cumulative way in the future. Admittedly, some of our well-tested theories may eventually turn out to be false; but it is difficult to imagine future scientists rejecting our belief that the earth goes round the sun or that water consists of two atoms of hydrogen and one of oxygen. They may, however, discover that such beliefs are approximations to richer and more inclusive theories the details of which we cannot at present imagine.

Choosing between rival paradigms

Kuhn claims that during periods of scientific crisis there is no purely rational way of deciding between rival paradigms, and that a scientist's beliefs will be influenced by the society in which she lives.

As we saw earlier, there is doubtless some truth in this claim. At this point, however, we should distinguish between the *origin* of a belief and its *justification*. For the origin of a belief is not of any great relevance to science. All that matters is that the belief should be *testable*. If it is confirmed by experiment, then we provisionally accept it; if it fails then we reject it.

Since different paradigms interpret the world in fundamentally different ways and we can never conclusively prove which one is true, some have taken Kuhn's ideas to be a form of relativism. However, the fact that there are no conclusive proofs does not mean that scientific knowledge is relative, but simply that – as in every area of knowledge – it depends on *judgement*. We need judgement to decide such things as which factors should be observed and which can be safely ignored, which hypotheses make good sense of the data and which are too outlandish to be useful, which anomalies to take seriously and which to dismiss as experimental error. Such judgements are of course fallible, and they may turn out to be wrong, but this does not make them any less rational. When astronomers speculated that the irregular orbit of Mercury was due to an undiscovered planet, Vulcan, they were wrong; but given the previous successes of Newtonian mechanics, it was a perfectly rational hypothesis. The point, in short, is that just because reason is fallible, it does not follow that it has no value.

One of the great strengths of science is that in the long run it tends to be self-correcting. The fact that scientists work in communities may put pressure on them to conform to the prevailing orthodoxy; but their natural competitiveness will ensure that they check up on one another's results. Moreover, the history of science suggests that good ideas are eventually accepted; and it appears that the time it takes for such ideas to win acceptance is getting shorter. While Copernicus' theory took more than a hundred years to win general acceptance, Einstein's theory was accepted by physicists in less than fifteen years.

Just as good ideas win acceptance, so crackpot theories are weeded out. Despite the support of an oppressive dictatorship, the Soviet biologist Trofim Lysenko (1898–1976), who denounced genetics as 'reactionary and decadent', could not make his wheat grow. Similarly, when in 1989 two scientists, Stanley Pons and Martin Fleischmann, claimed they had produced a nuclear reaction called 'cold fusion' – thereby raising the prospect of a source of energy that would be 'too cheap to meter' – no one else was able to replicate their results and they were quickly discredited.

What comes out of our discussion is that, although there is no straightforward criterion for choosing between rival paradigms, some theories begin to look increasingly plausible and others increasingly implausible as evidence accumulates over time. Beyond a certain point, we are probably justified in dismissing a discredited theory as irrational. Almost no one now takes seriously the claims of the Flat Earth Society. Some ideas have had their day!

Science and truth

We have come a long way in our discussion of scientific knowledge and it is time to take stock. Despite the high regard in which science is held, we have seen that there can be no absolute proof in science and that we can neither conclusively verify nor falsify a hypothesis. But this does not mean that we should embrace relativism. If a scientific theory accounts for the known evidence, is internally consistent, and works in practice, then we should – for the time being at least – accept it as true. Admittedly, it may be replaced by a better theory in the future; but it seems reasonable to think that as one theory follows another we can at least get closer to the truth.

At the same time we should maintain a critical attitude to our scientific beliefs and be willing to question our assumptions. Given our tendency to notice only things that confirm our beliefs, there is, at the psychological level, something to be said for actively seeking evidence that falsifies them. This, I think, is one of the advantages of Popper's approach to science.

A theory of everything?

Some people believe that the ultimate goal of science is to discover a theory that is so general that we have a complete understanding of nature. Yet it seems unlikely that the map of science will ever be able to reproduce the territory of reality. The American physicist Richard Feynman (1918–88) once observed that understanding nature is like understanding chess. In both cases, to understand means to know 'the rules of the game'. Now, to learn the rules of chess is a relatively straightforward matter but, even if you know them all, it is impossible to predict the course of any particular game. (It has been estimated that there are 10^{120} possible moves in chess – an unimaginably large number!) When it comes to nature, we are dealing with a game that is a great deal more complicated than chess. Not only is it very difficult to discover the rules of the scientific game, but – as with chess – even if we succeed in doing this, our understanding remains general rather than specific. You may be armed with all the rules, but you will never get anywhere near knowing all of the ways in which atoms can combine with one another. So a 'complete' understanding of the rules of nature will still leave plenty of room for surprises!

My own hunch is that in the case of nature we will never even know all the rules of the game. Science operates on the assumption that by isolating key variables we can discover the truth. When we do experiments we assume that some factors are relevant and that others can safely be ignored. Up until now this has been a successful strategy. Yet the history of science suggests that as science advances we have to take more and more factors into account that were previously dismissed as irrelevant. Perhaps, as we delve into the complexities of nature, we will eventually find that at the deepest level *everything* is connected to everything else. Since we are finite creatures, we will never be able to grasp the totality of connections, and at that point we will have reached the limits of science.

Activity 8.16

If you drop a stone into a pond, ripples spread out from the point of impact. The ripples gradually diminish in size, but at what point do the effects of your action end? What has this got to do with the above discussion?

Science and scientism

The success of science and technology has sometimes led people to make extravagant claims about the scope of scientific knowledge. According to the view known as **scientism**, science is the only way we can make sense of reality and discover the truth. A typical representative of this view was the philosopher Rudolf Carnap (1891–1970): 'When we say that scientific knowledge is unlimited, we mean that there is no answer in principle unattainable by science.' What Carnap is, in effect, saying is that science is capable of finding all the answers to all the questions, and if something is non-science then it is little different from nonsense.

There is a big difference between such dogmatic scientism and the more modest conception of science we have looked at in this chapter. We can be proud of what science has achieved; but it is important to keep in mind that it is a fallible human enterprise which may get us closer to the truth but can never give us certainty. Whatever Carnap may have thought, it seems clear that science does not have all the answers, and there are many perplexing questions that lie beyond its scope.

Conclusion

The scientific spirit which is opposed to the uncritical acceptance of dogma has, in large part, been responsible for the enormous growth of knowledge over the last three centuries, and science is widely seen as one of humanity's great success stories. Our pride in science should, however, be tempered by a degree of humility, and it is worth keeping in mind Bertrand Russell's comment that 'Science tells us what we can know, but what we can know is little, and if we forget how much we cannot know we become insensitive to many things of great importance.' It is striking that some of the world's greatest scientists have been aware of the limited nature of their achievements and the extent of their ignorance. Towards the end of his life, Albert Einstein observed that 'All science, measured against reality, is primitive and childlike.' And yet he still believed that it is 'the most precious thing we have'.

Key points

- The success of the natural sciences has led some people to see them as the most important form of knowledge.
- The main difference between science and pseudo-science is that scientific hypotheses can be tested and pseudo-scientific ones cannot.
- According to the traditional picture of the scientific method, science consists of five key steps: observation, hypothesis, experiment, law, theory.
- Among the problems that arise in applying the scientific method are that observation is selective, and that you are more likely to notice things that confirm your hypothesis than those that contradict it.
- Since scientific laws are based on a limited number of observations, we can never be sure that they are true.
- According to Karl Popper, science should be based on the method of conjectures and refutations, and scientists should try to falsify hypotheses rather than verify them.
- In practice, a hypothesis can no more be conclusively falsified than it can be conclusively verified.
- Thomas Kuhn drew attention to the role played by paradigms in science and argued that the history of science is punctuated by revolutionary jumps or 'paradigm shifts'.
- Although scientific beliefs change over time, it could be argued that each new theory is closer to the truth than the previous one.
- Despite the success of the natural sciences, they cannot give us absolute certainty and there are many perplexing questions that lie beyond their scope.

Terms to remember

anomaly	hypothesis	pseudo-science
conjectures and refutations	law	rationalist
controlled experiment	logical positivism	relativism
empirical	paradigm	science worship
empiricist	physics envy	scientism
falsification	principle of simplicity	

Further reading

A. C. Chalmers, ***What Is This Thing Called Science?*** (Open University Press, 1982). This book gives a good overview of the main ideas about the nature of science. You might not want to read it from cover to cover, but there are useful chapters on traditional inductivism, Popper's falsificationism and Kuhn's paradigms.

Richard P. Feynman, ***'Surely You're Joking Mr. Feynman!'*** (W. W. Norton, 1997), pp. 338–46, 'Cargo Cult Science'. Richard Feynman was one of the great physicists of the twentieth century. In this chapter he considers the difference between science and pseudo-science in his own inimitable and entertaining style.

Linking questions

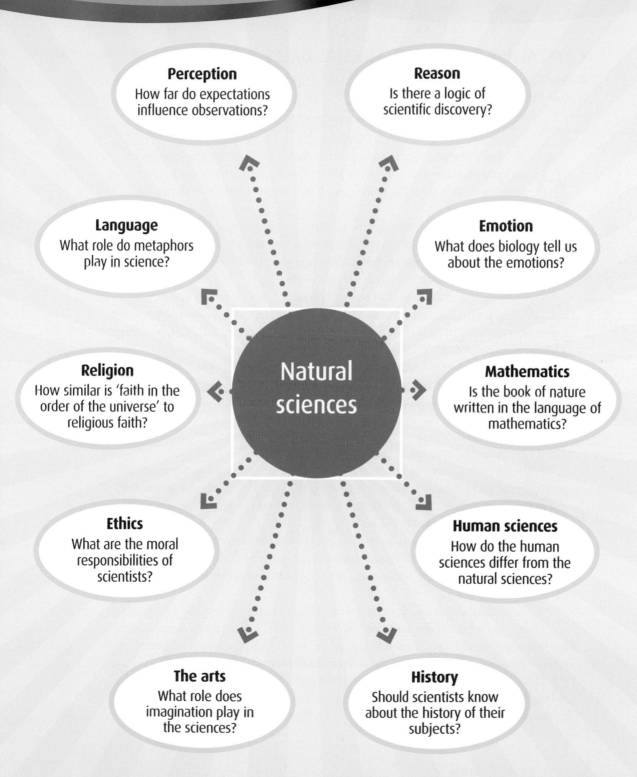

Perception
How far do expectations influence observations?

Reason
Is there a logic of scientific discovery?

Language
What role do metaphors play in science?

Emotion
What does biology tell us about the emotions?

Natural sciences

Religion
How similar is 'faith in the order of the universe' to religious faith?

Mathematics
Is the book of nature written in the language of mathematics?

Ethics
What are the moral responsibilities of scientists?

Human sciences
How do the human sciences differ from the natural sciences?

The arts
What role does imagination play in the sciences?

History
Should scientists know about the history of their subjects?

CRYSTALLINE TRUTH AND CRYSTAL BALLS

Richard Dawkins does not pull his punches in this trenchant defence of scientific thinking against the siren voices of pseudo-science.

A celebrated film star 'places four quartz crystal clusters in the four corners of her bathtub every time she takes a bath'. This doubtless has some mystic connection with the following recipe, found on the World Wide Web, for meditation:

'Each of the four quartz crystals in the meditation room should be "programmed" to project gentle, loving, relaxing, crystalline energy towards all those present within the Meditation group. The quartz crystals will then generate a field of positive crystalline energy surrounding everyone in the room.'

Language like this is a con trick. It sounds 'scientific' enough to bamboozle the innocent. 'Programming' is what you do to computers. The word means nothing when applied to crystals. 'Energy' and 'field' are carefully defined notions in physics. There is no such thing as 'loving' or 'crystalline' energy, whether positive or no.

New Age lore advises placing a quartz crystal in your water jug. Another Web site states: *'You will soon appreciate the sparkling purity of your crystal water'*.

See how the trick works? Somebody with no understanding of the real world could make a kind of poetic association with 'crystal clear' water. But that is no more sensible than trying to read by the light of a ('bright as a') button. Or putting ('hard as') nails under your pillow to assist an erection.

'Try the following experiment when you next suffer from flu: hold your personal quartz crystal and visualise yellow light radiating through it, then place your crystal in a jug of water and drink this water the next day; one cup of water at two-hourly intervals. You will be amazed at the result!'

Drinking water at two-hourly intervals is a good idea, anyway, when you have flu. Putting a quartz crystal in it will have no additional effect. In particular, no amount of 'visualising' of coloured light will change the composition of either the crystal or the water.

Pseudoscientific drivel like this is a disturbingly prominent part of the culture of our age. I have limited my examples to crystals because I had to draw a line somewhere. But 'star signs' would have done just as well. Or 'angels', 'channelling', 'telepathy', 'quantum healing', 'homeopathy', 'map dowsing'. There is no obvious limit to human gullibility. We are docile credulity-cows, eager victims of quacks and charlatans who milk us and grow fat. There is a rich living to be made by anyone prepared to prostitute the language – and the wonder – of science.

But isn't it all – crystal ball-gazing, star signs, birth stones, ley-lines and the rest – just a bit of harmless fun? If people want to believe in garbage such as astrology or crystal healing, why not let them? But it is so sad to think about all that they are missing. There is so much wonder in real science. The universe is mysterious enough to need no help from warlocks, shamans and 'psychic' tricksters. These are, at best, a soul-sapping distraction. At worst, they are dangerous profiteers.

The real world, properly understood in the scientific way, is deeply beautiful and unfailingly interesting. It is worth putting in some honest effort to understand it properly, undistracted by false wonder and prostituted pseudo-science. For illustration, we need look no farther than crystals themselves.

In a crystal like quartz or diamond the atoms are arranged in a precisely repeating pattern. The atoms in a diamond – all identical carbon atoms – are arrayed like soldiers on parade, except that the precision of their dressing far outsmarts the best-drilled guards regiment, and the atomic soldiers outnumber all the people that have ever lived, or ever will. Imagine yourself shrunk to become one of the carbon atoms in the heart of a diamond crystal. You are one of the soldiers in a gigantic parade, but it will seem a little odd because the files are arrayed in three dimensions. Perhaps a prodigious school of fish is a better image.

Each fish in the school is one carbon atom. Think of them moving in space, keeping their distance from each other, and holding precise angles, by means of forces that you can't see, but which scientists fully understand. But if this is a fish school, it is one that, to scale, would fill the Pacific Ocean. In any decent-sized diamond, you are likely to be looking along arrays of atoms numbering hundreds of millions in any one straight line.

Carbon atoms can take up other crystal-lattice formations. To revert to the military analogy, they can adopt alternative drill conventions. Graphite (the lead in pencils) is also carbon, but is obviously nothing like diamond. In graphite, the atoms form sheets of hexagons like chicken wire. Each sheet is loosely bonded to those above and below it, and when impurities are present, the sheets slide easily against each other, which is why graphite is a good lubricant. Diamond is very much not a lubricant. Its legendary hardness abrades the toughest materials. But the atoms in soft graphite and hard diamond are identical; if you could persuade the atoms in graphite crystals to adopt the drill rules of diamond crystals, you would be rich. It can be done, but you need colossal pressures and high temperatures – presumably the conditions that produce diamonds naturally, deep in the earth...

Go into any museum and look at the collection of minerals. Even go into a New Age shop and look at the crystals on display, along with all the other apparatus of mumbo-jumbo and kitsch con trickery. The crystals won't respond to your attempts to 'program' them for meditation, or 'dedicate' them with warm, loving thoughts. They won't cure you of anything, or fill the room with 'inner peace' or 'psychic energy'. But many of them are very beautiful, and it surely adds to the beauty when we understand that the shapes of the crystals, the angles of their facets, the rainbow colours that flash from inside them, all have a precise explanation that lies deep in the patterns of atomic lattice work.

Crystals don't vibrate with mystical, loving energy. But they do, in a much stricter and more interesting sense, vibrate. Some crystals have an electric charge across them which changes when you physically deform the crystal. This 'piezoelectric' effect, discovered in 1880 by the Curie brothers (Marie's husband and his brother), is used in the styluses of record-players (the deforming is done by the groove of the turning record), and in some microphones (the deforming is done by sound waves in the air). The piezo effect works in reverse. When a suitable crystal is placed in an electric field, it deforms itself rhythmically. Often the timing of this oscillation is extremely accurate. It serves as the equivalent of the pendulum or balance wheel in a quartz watch.

Let me tell you one last thing about crystals, and it may be the most fascinating of all. The military metaphor makes us think of each soldier as a yard or two from his neighbours. But actually almost all the interior of a crystal is empty space. My head is 18 centimetres in diameter. To keep to scale, my nearest in the crystalline parade would have to be standing more than a kilometre away. No wonder the tiny particles called neutrinos (even smaller than electrons) pass right through the earth and come out the other side as if it wasn't there (on average, one passes through you every second).

But if solid things are mostly empty space, why don't we see them as empty space? Why does a diamond feel hard and solid instead of crumbly and full of holes? The answer lies in our own evolution. Our sense organs, like all our bits, have been shaped by Darwinian natural selection over countless generations. You might think that our sense organs would be shaped to give us a 'true' picture of the world as it 'really' is. It is safer to assume, however, that they have been shaped to give us a useful picture of the world, to help us to survive. In a way, what sense organs do is assist our brains to construct a useful model of the world, and it is this model that we move around in. It is a kind of 'virtual reality' simulation of the real world. Neutrinos can pass straight through a rock; but we can't. If we try to, we hurt ourselves. When constructing its simulation of rock, the brain therefore represents it as hard and solid. It is almost as though our sense organs are telling us: 'You can't get through objects of this kind'. That is what 'solid' means. That is why we perceive them as 'solid'.

In the same way, we find much of the universe, as science discovers it, difficult to understand. Einstein's relativity, quantum uncertainty, black holes, the Big Bang, the expanding universe, the vast slow movement of geological time – all these are hard to grasp. No wonder science frightens some people. But science can even explain why these things are hard to understand, and why the effort frightens us. We are jumped-up apes and our brains were only designed to understand the mundane details of how to survive the Stone Age African savannah.

These are deep matters, and a short article is not the place to go into them. I shall have succeeded if I have persuaded you that a scientific approach to crystals is more illuminating, more uplifting and also stranger than anything imagined in the wildest dreams of New Age gurus or paranormal preachers. The blunt truth is that the dreams and visions of gurus and preachers are not nearly wild enough. By scientific standards, that is.

THE FALLACY OF SCIENTIFIC OBJECTIVITY

In this article, Hilary Lawson argues that scientific thinking is less objective than is commonly thought and that we don't really understand why it works.

We are ruled by science. It is our religion. Not because of its technological prowess but because it provides the framework of our thinking. Just as, centuries ago, we were ruled by the Church. For, if once we lived in a world of heaven and hell, of the living and the after-life, now we live in a world of atoms and molecules, of planets and galaxies, of laws and forces. Moreover, we think that our account of the world, this scientific account, is true.

But perhaps a time will come when our scientific arguments about subatomic particles or black holes will be seen to be as absurd as theological arguments about the number of angels that can dance on a pin-head: a time when our present theories are regarded as superstitious myths and the institutions of science and the Church are spoken of in the same breath as the means of maintaining orthodox belief. For if the world of the Church was a fiction that in medieval times was regarded as the truth, is not the world of science the fiction that is our truth?

Science appears indisputable because it is based on observation and fact. But observation and facts turn out to be dependent on the theory we choose to believe. We are all familiar with drawings that can be interpreted in two ways.

What we see depends on how we choose to look at it. As a result, it is not possible to imagine that we can in some pure and unhindered way examine reality. We can only do so in the light of a theory or hypothesis. We see the things that we do, the everyday objects that surround us, because of the way we structure the data we receive.

It is because seeing is such an active process that attempts to get computers to see have been so disappointing. It is not sufficient to provide a computer with the data from a television camera, for without a way of dividing this data into groups, the computer is unable to 'see' anything. Seeing is a two-way process. We do not simply see what is there. We have to impose a form on what is there in order to see anything at all. Some of the more successful computer programs work on precisely that basis. In order to 'see', the computer hallucinates its ideal form of an object and searches for something similar in the data it is receiving.

Without the ability to structure what we see, we would be unable to make sense of the world at all. This becomes apparent in cases of visual Agnosia. Until a few years ago, John Collins was in charge of a British subsidiary of an American company, but after an operation he suffered minor brain damage and lost the ability to structure his perception in the way we take for granted. Now John does not recognise himself in the mirror; he does not recognise his wife, his children or grandchildren. Fifty yards from his home he is hopelessly lost; yet he is highly intelligent and can see detail as well as you or I. John is as lost in his world as we might be lost in the depths of a rain-forest. Although we would be able to see the leaves and the branches, we would have no idea what to make of it. And so it is with John, all the time.

As we imagine John's world, we catch sight of what we have to do to give meaning and order to our experience. Without that order we would be unable to survive. But if seeing relies on our concepts and context, so the facts, observations and theories which make up our currently agreed account of the world – science – depend on context, too.

What we take to be the facts on which scientific theories are based turn out to be products of our own making. Professor David Bohm worked with Einstein in the late Forties and early Fifties and subsequently developed his own account of quantum theory. 'Facts depend on theories, they depend on concepts, they depend on schemata of thought. The very word "fact" comes from a Latin root meaning "to make", as in manufacture; and the fact is what is made or done.' The seeing that is done in science is an active process, more like seeing a picture in a fire, or seeing images in a cloud, than it is like a mirror reflecting nature.

We imagine that the great scientists from Galileo to Einstein proved their results conclusively with the help of repeatable experiments. Historians like Simon Schaffer, however, now argue that scientists did not, and do not, prove their results at all. 'We now all believe the simple fact that the Earth moves round the Sun. And we have a hero – Galileo, who at the start of the 17th century, with a series of very simple experiments, allegedly proved that the Earth does indeed move around the Sun. The Church, who opposed Galileo's views, are treated as if they were charlatans and idiots because they opposed something which seems to us to be absolutely obvious. But in fact the Church had many good arguments on its side and there was no reason for the Church to accept a single word that Galileo was saying.' From the point of view of the Church, truth was not to be found by observing the world (after all, God might have arranged it so as to be deliberately confusing), but by access to the authority of God's own word. Furthermore, even if one were to consider Galileo's work as evidence, there was no reason to believe that what one saw through the telescope was an accurate version of what was actually there. 'None of the evidence which Galileo offered carried conviction, none of it actually proved then that the Earth was moving round the Sun. We believe Galileo's experiments because we believe that the Earth moves round the Sun.'

But if there was no reason to take Galileo seriously, why do we now see the universe as he did? According to Simon Schaffer, it has more to do with practice than with truth. 'By the end of the 17th century, telescopic astronomy had become a very useful resource for the new maritime and commercial powers of northern Europe. Galileo triumphed not because he was right but because his theories were extremely useful. And because they were useful, his observations came to be believed to be true.'

The great heroes of science, from Galileo to Einstein, only made sense of the information available to them by inventing a new order. The same is just as true of all scientists today. Scientific debates are not decided by simply looking at reality, by looking at the facts. The theories and laws of science which we now take for granted are the result of imposing a view on the world. A view that is then backed by the institutions of science.

It appears that science has climbed a grand staircase that leads us from error to truth. But science is full of moments when scientists had chosen one path and discarded another. The paths we did not follow get covered up and forgotten and it seems that there is only one path to truth. It turns out that the path we have taken is the result of a series of accidents. But if science has not discovered the secret key to the truths of the universe, how has it achieved its successes? David Bohm has no straightforward answers: 'Science is a kind of magic that is not recognised to be magical. Fundamentally, we don't understand in any simple terms how it works. If we take physics, for example, we now have a set of equations, both for quantum mechanics and for relativity. But one has no way of picturing just how these mathematical relationships are able to correspond with reality. Theory is a kind of theatre of the mind which gives you insight. This is the major point, to see theory as a creative activity, to see all perception as a creative activity. If you don't have theoretical insight, your facts don't mean anything.'

The gradual recognition of these arguments may affect the practice, the funding and the institutions of science, but its greatest impact is perhaps a personal one. For, if once we believed in the world of the Church, today we believe in the world of science. Our belief in the objectivity of science is now, however, beginning to collapse, although on this occasion there is no alternative world to replace it. Science may remain powerful, but the nature of our belief will have to alter. Science is there to be used – it is not there to tell us how things are. Science is not powerful because it is true: it is true because it is powerful.

The account given here, this story about science, this 'fiction' about science, does not pretend to provide a final picture. It can perhaps try to achieve objectivity but it can't succeed. We can play with the concepts and the categories of our time, but we cannot escape them. To say this is not to say that we can make up any old story, for there are always constraints, but it does mean that we cannot arrive at the final account. For, if once we had faith and then we had science, now we have our necessary fictions.

9 The human sciences

'I am more interested in how a man lives than how a star dies.'
Sherwin Nuland, 1930–

'In every science man speaks only of himself.'
Oswald Spengler, 1880–1936

'We make our surroundings and then they make us.'
Winston Churchill, 1874–1965

'Life is heredity plus environment.'
Luther Burbank, 1849–1926

'If the brain were simple enough to understand, we would be too simple to understand it.'
Anon

'The only possible conclusion the social sciences can draw is: some do, some don't.'
Ernest Rutherford, 1871–1937

'An economist is an expert who will know tomorrow why the things he predicted yesterday did happen today.'
Laurence J. Peter, 1919–88

'It is quite possible – overwhelmingly probable, one might guess – that we will always learn more about human life and human personality from novels than from scientific psychology.'
Noam Chomsky, 1928–

'Maybe in order to understand mankind we have to look at the word itself. MANKIND. Basically, it's made up of two separate words – "mank" and "ind". What do these words mean? It's a mystery, and that's why so is mankind.'
Jack Handey, 1949–

'Human behaviour makes most sense when it is explained in terms of beliefs and desires, not in terms of volts and grams.'
Steven Pinker, 1954–

'In carefully controlled laboratory conditions animals do what they damned well please.'
The Harvard law of animal behaviour

'Know then thyself, presume not God to scan / The proper study of mankind is man.'
Alexander Pope, 1688–1744

'We need more understanding of human nature, because the only real danger that exists is man himself.'
Carl Jung, 1875–1961

'I can calculate the motions of heavenly bodies, but not the madness of crowds.'
Sir Isaac Newton, 1642–1727

Introduction

Since human beings have been able to reflect about themselves and their place in the scheme of things, they have been struck by their own complex and mysterious nature. The human sciences are an attempt to reduce the mystery by studying human behaviour in a systematic way. Under the heading 'human science' (or social science) are subjects such as psychology, economics, anthropology and sociology. Despite the obvious differences between these subjects, they are all based on observation and seek to discover laws and theories about human nature.

We may, however, wonder to what extent human beings can be studied in a purely scientific way. At one level we are simply animals composed of atoms and molecules. According to the theory of evolution, we have descended from the apes, with whom we share 99% of our genes. And we are made up of the same basic ingredients as all other living things – 63% hydrogen, 25.5% oxygen, 9.5% carbon, 1.5% nitrogen, and 0.5% of a few other elements.

Figure 9.1

But most people would reject the idea that we are 'just animals', or 'nothing but a bunch of chemicals', and would draw attention to the differences between us and the rest of the natural world. One of our most important distinguishing characteristics – from which all others could be said to flow – is that we are *self-conscious* animals. Many other animals are conscious, but unlike us it seems that they are not aware of themselves. Some evidence for this is provided by the so-called **mirror test**. Although you recognise yourself in a mirror, a dog will bark at its own image without ever realising that it is barking at itself. (Some chimpanzees have passed the mirror test, and this suggests that they may have the glimmerings of self-consciousness.)

Among the other features associated with self-consciousness that seem to be unique to us are **language**, **reason**, **free-will** and **creativity**. Some people also believe that we have an animating spirit or soul which cannot be explained in terms of material processes. Whatever your opinion about this, there are likely to be special challenges in studying human beings in a scientific way.

In this chapter, we will look at four key aspects of the scientific method – observation, measurement, experiments and laws – and consider what special problems arise when these steps are applied to the study of human beings. This will lead on to a more general discussion of the similarities and differences between the natural and human sciences.

Activity 9.1

1 List as many features as you can that distinguish human beings from other animals.
2 To what extent do these features make it difficult to study human beings in a scientific way?

Observation

Perhaps the most important characteristic of science is that it is based on observation. One problem in the human sciences is that, although you can observe other people's behaviour, you cannot directly observe their minds. You may be able to make an educated guess about what they are thinking, but you can never be entirely sure that you are right.

One way to find out what people think is, of course, to ask them. Since most people are reasonably honest, we can learn a lot from questionnaires, opinion polls and interviews. At the same time, since people generally want to see themselves in a good light, you cannot always take what they say at face value. There is evidence from psychology to suggest that we tend to overestimate our strengths and underestimate our weaknesses. For example, in one well-known survey of a million US high-school seniors, *all of them* ranked themselves as above average in terms of their ability to get on with other people! Since people care about what others think of them, they may also be unwilling to admit holding unpopular opinions. This may explain why extreme political parties often do better in general elections than in opinion polls.

1 Complete the following short questionnaire as honestly as possible. Then collate the results for the class as a whole. How would you interpret the results and what conclusions would you draw from them?

	Below average	Average	Above average
a How much do you worry about what other people think of you?			
b To what extent do you see yourself a considerate person?			
c Do you have a good sense of humour?			
d How open are you to new ideas?			
e How worried are you about environmental problems?			

2 In some countries it is forbidden to publish opinion polls in the week running up to a general election. Do you think that this is a good policy, or a denial of free speech?

Loaded questions

Another problem with asking people what they think is that it is not easy to frame questions in an unbiased way. A **loaded question**, which contains a hidden assumption, may encourage people to answer one way rather than another. Consider, for example, the following 1980 US poll in which a similar question was worded in two different ways:

	In favour	Opposed
1 Do you think there should be an amendment to the Constitution prohibiting abortions, or shouldn't there be such an amendment?	29%	67%
2 Do you believe there should be an amendment to the Constitution protecting the life of the unborn child, or shouldn't there be such an amendment?	50%	34%

1 Which of the above questions do you think is loaded? Give reasons.
2 Take a controversial topic – such as abortion, or capital punishment – and try to design an unbiased questionnaire to discover people's opinions about it.

This example suggests that if you ask questions with sufficient skill and cunning, you may be able to get people to give you the answer you want. An amusing example of this can be found in an episode of the British comedy series *Yes, Prime Minister*. Two bureaucrats, Sir Humphrey Appleby and Bernard Woolley, are discussing an opinion poll which shows that 67 per cent of people are in favour of reintroducing National Service (compulsory military service). Sir Humphrey asks Bernard to commission another opinion poll which will give them the opposite result. When Bernard asks how this can be done, Sir Humphrey demonstrates how two different lines of questioning can lead a person to give a different answer to the same question.

Line One

'Mr Woolley, are you worried about the rise in crime among teenagers?'

'Yes'

'Do you think there is lack of discipline and vigorous training in our Comprehensive Schools?'

'Yes'

'Do you think young people welcome some structure and leadership in their lives?'

'Yes'

'Do they respond to a challenge?'

'Yes'

'Might you be in favour of reintroducing National Service?'

'Yes'

Line Two

'Mr Woolley, are you worried about the danger of war?'

'Yes'

'Are you unhappy about the growth of armaments?'

'Yes'

'Do you think there's a danger in giving young people guns and teaching them how to kill?'

'Yes'

'Do you think it's wrong to force people to take up arms against their will?'

'Yes'

'Would you oppose the reintroduction of National Service?'

'Yes'

A final point we can make about questionnaires is that there is often a difference between what people say they would do in a hypothetical situation and what they actually do in reality. You might, for example, say that you would be willing to buy a product at a certain price, but have second thoughts about it when you actually have to part with your money. More dramatically, you might fondly imagine that if you were trapped in a burning building, you would selflessly help other people to escape before leaving yourself. We are all heroes in our dreams, but if this happened in reality, you might be the first to run for safety!

"How would you like me to answer that question?
As a member of my ethnic group, educational class,
income group, or religious category?"

Figure 9.2

The observer effect

Another problem with observation in the human sciences is the so-called **observer effect**. If a geologist is studying rocks they are indifferent to his presence; but if a psychologist is observing people they may become nervous or embarrassed by his attention and this may lead them to change their behaviour.

Imagine, for example, learning that national TV are coming to your school tomorrow to film a typical Theory of Knowledge class. How would this affect your behaviour? You might dress differently, try to look interested in class, and speak with unusual eloquence. Or you might be so anxious not to make a fool of yourself that you are not able to contribute at all. Either way, the presence of the TV cameras will ensure that the class is not a typical one.

> **Activity 9.4**
>
> 1 What ways, if any, are there of getting round the 'observer effect'?
> 2 Reality TV has become popular in many countries, with series like *Big Brother*, *Survivor* and *Star Academy*. What, if anything, do we learn about human nature from such programmes?

Figure 9.3

There are at least two ways in which a human scientist can try to get round the observer effect. The first is *habituation*. If national TV came and filmed your TOK class for a whole term, you would probably get used to the presence of the cameras and eventually ignore them. Anthropologists use a similar strategy when they **go native** and live with a tribe for an extended period of time. The hope is that the people they are studying will eventually get used to them and behave normally in their presence.

Another solution to the observer effect is to use hidden cameras. If you don't know that you are being observed, then it won't affect your behaviour. But this raises ethical questions about whether or not it is acceptable to film people without their knowledge.

A variant of the observer effect concerns the way in which a prediction can affect what is predicted. A classical example of this can be found in the Greek tragedy *Oedipus Rex*. When Oedipus was born, a prophecy was made that he would kill his father and marry his mother. When his father, the king of Thebes, learned of this he was horrified and abandoned the new-born child in the mountains, hoping that he would die so that the prophecy would not come true. But Oedipus was rescued by a shepherd and eventually adopted by the king and queen of Corinth. He grew up believing that they were his real parents. Then, as a young man, he learned of the prophecy about himself and fled home in terror. On the road, he got into an argument with a stranger and killed him. He then turned up in Thebes where he eventually married the recently widowed queen. Without realising it, Oedipus had killed his father and married his mother. When at the end of the play, he discovered the truth, he was not a happy man. Sophocles' tragedy derives its power from the fact that in the very act of trying to escape the prophecy Oedipus brought it down on himself. If only he had stayed in Corinth, everything would have been fine!

The effects of predictions on human behaviour are not usually as dramatic as in *Oedipus Rex*, but they can still have serious consequences. Here are three examples taken from different human sciences.

1 Psychology

In a well-known psychology experiment, school children were randomly allocated to one of two groups labelled 'bright' and 'less bright'. Although there was no initial difference between the two groups, the children labelled 'bright' made greater academic progress in the following year than the students labelled 'less bright'. This suggests that teachers' expectations affected how well the students did and helped to produce the differences between the two groups.

Activity 9.5

1 To what extent do you think your teachers' expectations about your abilities affect how well you do at school?
2 Would it be better if teachers had no expectations about you? To what extent is that possible?
3 Do you think that primary-school teachers should divide up children into good readers and not-so-good readers? What would be the pros and cons of doing this?
4 To what extent can your own expectations about yourself affect your academic performance?

2 Economics

If you follow the stock market, you are probably aware that people's expectations can affect share prices. In a **bull market**, when most people expect prices to rise, a rational investor will buy stocks now, hoping to sell them later at a higher price thereby making a profit. If everyone behaves like that, the demand for stocks will increase and cause prices to rise. Conversely, in a **bear market** when most people expect prices to fall, a rational investor will sell stocks now, hoping to buy them back later at a lower price. But if everyone does that, the increased supply of stocks will push prices down. So if everyone expects prices to rise they will rise, and if everyone expects prices to fall they will fall.

Activity 9.6

1 Do you think the behaviour of stock markets is governed more by reason or more by emotion?
2 Do you think that it is possible to predict with accuracy where the stock market will be in twelve months' time? Give reasons.

3 Anthropology

According to anthropologist Wade Davis, when a sorcerer in an aborigine tribe points at an individual and casts a death spell over him, 'the individual invariably sickens and almost always dies'. One explanation for such cases of 'voodoo death' is that the individual has been conditioned since childhood to believe in the power of the sorcerer's spell. So when the sorcerer curses him, he in effect loses the will to live. He may, for example, retire to his shelter and refuse to eat until he wastes away and dies. The individual's belief that he is going to die seems to be an important factor in his eventual death.

Activity 9.7

1 Have you ever been caught breaking a **taboo** and said something like 'I feel so ashamed I could die'?

2 Do you think that mental states, such as happiness or depression, can affect our physical well-being?

3 Try to find some information about alleged cases of 'voodoo death'. Do you believe they really happen? If so, how would you account for them?

A final point to notice about predictions is that they can be self-negating as well as self-fulfilling. For example, if I predict that you are going to break your leg playing soccer this afternoon, you will have a strong incentive not to play, thereby falsifying my prediction. In this case, the very act of making the prediction helps to ensure that it does *not* come true.

Activity 9.8

According to a phenomenon known as **psychological reactance**, if a person is inclined to do X, and you then tell him to do X, he becomes more likely not to do X. This may explain why some teenage anti-smoking campaigns have the perverse effect of *encouraging* teenagers to smoke. With this in mind, how would you try to organise an effective anti-smoking campaign?

Measurement

While measurement plays an important role in the sciences by adding precision to our knowledge, it is generally more difficult to measure things in the human sciences than in the natural sciences. Consider, for example, consciousness. If I were to ask you *how many* thoughts you have had today, I doubt that you could answer this question. Part of the problem is that we have no units for measuring thoughts and determining where one ends and another begins, for they simply melt into one another. Furthermore, if you try to count your thoughts, the very process of counting will interfere with what you are trying to count. So, rather than think of consciousness as a series of discrete thoughts, it may make more sense to follow the American psychologist William James (1842–1910) and think of it as a continuous **stream of consciousness**.

While consciousness played a key role in William James' conception of psychology, some twentieth-century psychologists dismissed it as unscientific on the grounds that it can be neither objectively observed nor precisely measured. This gave rise to a school of psychology known as **behaviourism**, which redefined the subject as the scientific study, not of consciousness, but of *behaviour*. Despite the difficulties involved in trying to pin consciousness down, there are many variables in the human sciences that *can* be measured with relative ease: for example, population, income and the rate of inflation. Furthermore, as the Jared Diamond reading at the end of this chapter makes clear, human scientists have developed a variety of sophisticated techniques for translating what look like qualitative concepts into measurable ones.

1   When you try to make sense of other people, do you pay more attention to what they say or to what they do?
2   Do you agree that since consciousness cannot be objectively observed, it should not be part of psychology?
3   Would you be willing to reject talk of electrons in physics and genes in biology on the grounds that they cannot be directly observed?

Who really won the Centennial Olympics?

When we put numbers on things it sometimes creates a spurious sense of objectivity. After the 1996 Olympic Games in Atlanta, an article appeared in a Canadian newspaper headed 'Who really won the Centennial Olympics?' You might think that we can find the answer simply by consulting the official rankings.

Rank	Country	Medals total
1	USA	101
2	Germany	65
3	Russia	63
4	China	50
11	Canada	22

The above table shows some of the results, ranking the countries in terms of the total number of medals won. The USA came first with 101 medals, and Canada eleventh with 22. However, you might point out that simply knowing the *number* of medals each country got does not give us enough information to decide who really won the Olympics. We also need to know the *colour* of the medals. If the USA had 101 bronze and Germany 65 gold, there would be a strong case for saying that Germany, not the USA, had won the Olympics. Here, then, is the breakdown of medals won:

Country	Gold	Silver	Bronze	Medals total
USA	44	32	25	101
Germany	20	18	27	65
Russia	26	21	16	63
China	16	22	12	50
Canada	3	11	8	22

We now have to decide how to *interpret* these figures. Consider Germany and Russia: Germany won two more medals in *total* than Russia, but Russia won six more *gold* medals than Germany. So who did the best? Well, the standard Olympic convention is to award 3 points for a gold, 2 for a silver and 1 for a bronze. Following that convention we get the following results:

Rank	Country	Gold	Silver	Bronze	Points
1	USA	44	32	25	221
2	Russia	26	21	16	136
3	Germany	20	18	27	123
4	China	16	22	12	104
11	Canada	3	11	8	39

The only change at the top is that Russia and Germany change places. Canada stays in eleventh place.

But what if we now take into account the *population* of each country? After all, the USA has a much larger population base than Canada from which to choose its athletes. (At the time of the Atlanta Olympics, the figures were 255 million as against 28 million.) This dramatically changes the picture. If we now look at points per million we get the following result:

Rank	Country	Points per million
1	Tonga	20
2	Bahamas	6.6
3	Cuba	4.6
25	Canada	1.3
37	USA	0.9

If we look at the results in this way, some island nations rise to the top of the table. Cuba's results are now more than five times better than those of the USA, and Canada's results are 1.5 times better.

But we don't have to stop there. We might think of more ways of refining the ranking.

- Since children and seniors do not form part of the pool of potential athletes, we should perhaps take into account age distribution, and look not at points per million, but points per million of eligible age – say between 16 and 60.
- We might consider comparative wealth on the grounds that athletes from wealthy countries have better training facilities than their poorer counterparts.
- We might want to compensate for the fact that the USA had 'home advantage' – for it is well known that a team playing at home tends to do better than one playing away from home.

We now risk getting lost in a welter of rankings established in accordance with different criteria. It is beginning to look as if there is no clear answer to the question, 'Who won the Centennial Olympics?' Perhaps we should simply abandon the obsession with ranking countries. That, however, is easier said than done!

Activity 9.10

1 Do you think it is possible to answer the question 'Which country won the Centennial Olympics?' Does it matter?
2 'You can no more say that a gold medal is worth three bronzes than that an apple is worth two oranges.' What do you think of this criticism of Olympic rankings?
3 What effect do you think doing well in the Olympics, or winning the World Cup, might have on a country's economy?
4 What value, in general, is there in ranking things? Have you ever looked at university rankings? How seriously do you take them? How seriously should you take them?

One thing that seems to come out of the above discussion is that we run into problems when we try to measure different things – such as gold, silver and bronze medals – on a common scale. People are often accused of 'comparing apples and oranges' when they try to do this. However, an economist might argue that we can in fact compare different things on a common scale by looking at how much people are willing to pay for them. Whether or not it is in practice possible to put a price on everything, I leave for you to decide!

Activity 9.11

1 How would you go about trying to put a monetary value on a human life?
2 Can you think of situations in which society does the above? How do you feel about trying to weigh a life in terms of dollars and cents?
3 Which of the following is easy to measure and which is not? How would you go about trying to measure it?

a Weight   b Brand loyalty
c Temperature   d Social class
e Inflation   f Intelligence
g Happiness   h Reading ability
i Progress   j Age

4 What truth do you think there is in the following poem?
Economists have come to feel
What can't be measured isn't real.
The truth is always an amount
Count numbers only numbers count.
[Robert Chambers]

Experiments

We typically associate the word 'science' with a person in a white coat doing experiments in a laboratory. Ideally, experiments should play as big a role in the human sciences as they do in the natural sciences; but in practice this is not usually the case. There are at least three reasons for this.

1. Human scientists are often trying to make sense of complex real-world situations in which it is simply impossible to run controlled experiments.
2. The artificiality of some of the experiments that can be conducted may distort the behaviour of the participants.
3. There are ethical reasons for not conducting experiments that have a negative effect on the people who participate in them.

Faced with the above difficulties, what are human scientists to do? One solution is to wait for nature to provide the appropriate experimental conditions. We can, for example, learn something about how a normal brain functions by looking at people who have suffered brain damage; and we can gain some insight into the roles played by genes and the environment by studying identical twins who have been separated at birth and brought up in different families. In the case of economics, economic history can provide us with a bank of – admittedly not very well-controlled – experimental data.

However, human scientists do not just sit around waiting for natural experiments to arise. They also devise ingenious experiments of their own. Suppose you want to know how a baby sees the world. Does it see it as a 'blooming, banging confusion' as the psychologist William James (1842–1910) thought, or is there more of a structure to its experience? We cannot, of course, ask the baby since it has not yet learnt to speak. So it might seem that all we can do is *speculate*. That is what people thought until two psychologists, Elizabeth Spelke and Renée Baillargeon, pointed out that babies tend to stare at surprising things longer than at unsurprising ones. This key insight was like opening a window on to the developing mind. There was now a way of testing babies' expectations and getting some idea of how they see the world. The resulting experimental evidence suggests that, before they are six months old, babies have figured out that objects consist of parts that move together, are aware of the difference between living and non-living things, and can even do simple arithmetic!

Activity 9.12

1. How accurate do you think 'stare time' is as a way of measuring a baby's expectations? What if a baby looks at something for two seconds, looks away for three, and then looks back again for another two?
2. Do you think there is any danger in psychologists seeing what they want to see in these kinds of experiment?

The Milgram experiment

One of the best-known experiments in the history of psychology took place at Yale (USA) in 1963. Stanley Milgram was interested in the extent to which people are willing to obey orders. He advertised for volunteers to participate in an experiment allegedly to 'test the effects of punishment on learning'. When a volunteer arrived he was told that he was to play the role of 'teacher', and another 'volunteer' – in reality an actor – was to play the role of 'learner'. The learner was strapped to a chair and electrodes were put on his wrists. The teacher was then taken to an adjoining room and asked to give the learner a simple memory test. Every time the learner answered incorrectly, the teacher was to give the learner a successively higher electric shock by flicking a switch on a generator. Each switch was clearly labelled with voltage levels ranging from 15 to 450 volts, and verbal descriptions such as 'slight shock', 'strong shock', 'intense shock', 'danger', and finally 'XXX'. Although the teacher could not see the learner, he was able to hear his responses. Once the voltage reached 120V, the learner began to complain; at 150 volts he demanded that the experiment be stopped; at 270V he started screaming; and after 330V there was an ominous silence. Whenever the teacher hesitated to administer a shock, a scientist standing behind him insisted that it was very important that he continue with the experiment. In reality, of course, the learner did not receive any shocks, but the 'teacher' was not aware of this at the time.

Activity 9.13

1 Given your knowledge of human nature, what percentage of 100 volunteers do you think would continue administering electric shocks up to 450 volts?
2 If you had been a volunteer in this experiment, what do you think you would have done?

The result of the experiment was that almost two-thirds of the volunteers continued to give electric shocks up to 450 volts. Many expressed concern about what they were doing, and had to be reassured that they would not be held responsible for the fate of the learner; but it did not seem to occur to them to refuse to comply. Only one-third of the volunteers refused to continue to the end.

The Milgram experiment raises some disturbing questions about human nature. Why were so many of the volunteers willing to obey white-coated authority figures and give what they thought were lethal shocks to complete strangers? One crumb of comfort was that if, instead of working alone, the volunteer was paired with two other teachers (who were again actors), and the other teachers rebelled, then only 10% of the volunteers were willing to continue giving shocks up to 450 volts.

Changing perspective, we might question the ethics, not of the participants, but of the experiment. After all, the volunteers were misled about what they were getting involved in, were made to feel uncomfortable during the experiment, and may have suffered a permanent loss of self-esteem once the experiment was over. You are probably not going to feel great about yourself if you discover that you are the kind of person willing to administer a lethal electric shock to a stranger! On the other hand, it could be argued that the knowledge gained from the experiment outweighs any moral qualms we might have about the way it was carried out.

1. What difference do you think it would have made if the original advertisement asking for volunteers had mentioned electric shocks? What conclusion would you draw from this?
2. Design your own ethical code of conduct for the running of experiments in the human sciences. What three or four key points would you include and why?

Laws

While observation, measurement and experimentation are important parts of the scientific method, the main goal of science is to develop laws and theories to explain the phenomena that it studies. When it comes to the human sciences, however, our belief in **human free-will** would seem to conflict with the idea that there are law-like regularities in human behaviour. How, after all, could we ever reduce the behaviour of inconsistent, wilful and unpredictable human beings to a neat set of laws? Isaac Newton (1642–1727), for one, was doubtful, and famously observed: 'I can calculate the motions of heavenly bodies, but not the madness of crowds.'

Despite Newton's comment, a great deal of human behaviour does in fact seem to be fairly predictable. If people lack food, they are unhappy; if the price of lemons goes up, people buy fewer lemons; and – at least in the last school I worked in – if someone drops their tray in the dining hall, everyone cheers! We make literally thousands of generalisations about human beings every day, and if they were completely unpredictable no one would ever get in to a car and venture onto the road.

Activity 9.15

1. To what extent do you find the behaviour of your friends and family predictable? Do you ever find that when your parents are giving you advice you are able to finish many of their sentences for them?
2. What makes a person an interesting person? Would you prefer to have predictable friends, or unpredictable friends, or some combination of the two?
3. State three generalisations about human behaviour that you think are true of all human beings.

The law of large numbers

Although individual behaviour may be unpredictable, we can make surprisingly accurate short-term predictions about such things as the number of births, marriages and deaths in a country. The explanation for this derives from the **law of large numbers**, which says that in a large population *random variations tend to cancel out*. For example, there are all kinds of social customs and expectations which affect the number of people who get married in a particular time period. In general we can say that confirmed bachelors are unlikely to get married and engaged couples are likely to get married. However, random factors are also at work and occasionally confirmed bachelors fall in love and marry, and engaged couples fall out of love and do not. If we are dealing with a large enough population, then the number of unexpected marriages is likely to be cancelled out by the number of unexpected non-marriages.

Since the law of large numbers enables us to predict group rather than individual behaviour, many laws in the human sciences are probabilistic in nature. Although I cannot predict with any certainty whether or not John Smith will get married this year, I may be able to predict the probability of this happening.

You might think that such probabilistic laws are inferior to the universal laws that are typically associated with the natural sciences. But in fact the laws governing the behaviour of atoms and genes are also of a probabilistic kind, and a physicist can no more predict the behaviour of an individual gas molecule than a human scientist can predict the behaviour of a man in a crowd.

Trends and laws

Despite the law of large numbers, the human sciences do not have a very good record of prediction. There is, for example, no consensus among demographers about the size of world population in fifty years' time; economic forecasters seem to get it wrong as often as they get it right; and almost no one predicted the collapse of communism in the 1980s. A well-known example of a prediction that turned out to be way off the mark was the one made by the population economist Paul Ehrlich in 1973. Ehrlich was very pessimistic about the state of the planet and he predicted that, by 1990, 65 million Americans would be starving to death. Ironically, that turned out to be the number of Americans who were overweight in 1990!

To understand why the predictions of human scientists sometimes turn out to be wrong, we need to explain the difference between a *trend* and a *law*. Critics argue that too often human scientists have simply uncovered trends rather than genuine laws. A trend shows the direction in which a variable is moving, but since it gives no explanation for the movement it is not very reliable. That is why 'betting on a trend' is a dangerous game. A horse may have won its last three races, and a company may have made profits for the last three years, but this alone does not mean that the horse will win its next race or the company will make a profit next year. If we know something about the horse's breeding and physical condition, or the company's financial background and investment strategy, we are likely to make better predictions than if we simply bet on a trend.

A good example of the danger of betting on a trend is the **Phillips curve** in economics. In the 1960s, an economist called A. W. Phillips gathered data on the relationship between inflation and unemployment in the UK from 1861 until 1967. The data appeared to suggest a stable relationship between the two, as illustrated in Figure 9.4.

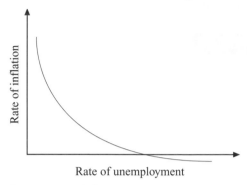

Figure 9.4 A Phillips curve

Many governments understood the curve to show that there was a trade-off between inflation and unemployment, and that lower unemployment could be bought at the cost of higher inflation, and vice versa. Unfortunately, when they tried to reduce unemployment by allowing inflation to rise, the Phillips curve broke down, and for much of the 1970s many countries experienced both rising inflation *and* rising unemployment.

What this example shows is that just because two things are *correlated* it does not follow that the first is the cause of the second. To think that it does is to commit the **fallacy of post hoc ergo propter hoc** (see Chapter 5). A correlation between two variables, A and B, could mean either that A causes B, or that B causes A, or that A and B are both caused by some other factor, C.

Activity 9.17

How might you explain each of the following correlations?
a Children with low self-esteem tend to do badly at school.
b People who watch violent movies tend to be violent in real life.
c As a country develops economically, birth rates tend to go down.
d Children brought up by talkative parents tend to be talkative themselves.
e Married people tend to be happier than unmarried people.

The complexity of real-world situations

Another reason why it might be difficult to uncover laws in the human sciences is the complexity of the situations they deal with. In the real world, it is often difficult to untangle a complicated web of causal relationships to determine which one is decisive.

Imagine, for example, that one night a man is driving along a country lane and crashes into a wall. He is lucky to escape unhurt, but his car is a write-off. What caused the crash? Here is some background information.

- The accident happened on a sharp bend on an unlit road.
- There was ice on the road.
- The man was speeding.
- He had drunk two pints of beer earlier in the evening.
- He was known to enjoy driving fast.
- He had just broken up with his girlfriend.

Given this information, it may be impossible to determine the *one* thing that caused the crash. Rather than search for a single cause, it might make more sense to say that it resulted from a *combination* of things. Perhaps if any one of the above facts had been different, the accident would never have happened. What this suggests is that it may be impossible to come up with a simple law of car accidents of the form 'If *X*, then there will be a car accident.'

If it is difficult to determine the cause of a small-scale event like a car accident, then it is a great deal more difficult to determine that of such complex phenomena as teenage depression, crime or inflation. And if we cannot say what the cause of an event was, then it will be hard to predict what will happen when similar events happen in the future. So it is perhaps not surprising that economists sometimes get their forecasts wrong!

Summary: the role of laws in the human sciences

We have seen that, although individuals may be unpredictable, the law of large numbers means that we can sometimes make accurate predictions about the behaviour of a large population. However, some of these predictions are based on trends rather than laws, and we should be careful not to confuse a correlation with a causal connection. In practice, the complexity of real-world situations means that it is difficult to unearth simple laws of the 'If..., then...' variety. Nevertheless, subjects such as economics still have many tried and tested laws, such as the law of demand and the law of diminishing returns.

The relationship between natural and human sciences

When we consider the relationship between the various sciences, it is commonly thought that there is a continuum of subjects running from the 'hard' natural sciences to the 'soft' human sciences. This reflects the fact that the human sciences have generally been held in lower esteem than their natural science cousins. For they seem to lack the explanatory power of Newtonian mechanics, or the atomic theory of gases, or molecular biology. Human scientists themselves have sometimes envied the mathematical rigour, immutable laws and cumulative nature of the natural sciences; and some people might even agree with Ernest Rutherford's (1871–1937) dismissive observation that, 'The only possible conclusion the social sciences can draw is: some do, some don't.'

> Do you think there is a hierarchy of sciences? If so, try to order the various sciences according to any criteria of your choice. If not, explain why not.

Doubtless, subjects such as psychology, economics and anthropology are a great deal more valuable than uninformed common sense in helping us to make sense of the human condition. Nevertheless, there is a suspicion in some quarters that they still lack the well-established paradigms that characterise the natural sciences. Consider, for example, the following comparison between biology and psychology by the neuroscientists V. S. Ramachandran and J. J. Smythies:

> Anyone interested in the history of ideas would be puzzled by the following striking differences between advances in biology and advances in psychology. The progress of biology has been characterized by landmark discoveries, each of which resulted in a breakthrough in understanding – the discoveries of cells, Mendel's law of heredity, chromosomes, mutations, DNA and the genetic code. Psychology, on the other hand, has been characterized by an embarrassingly long sequence of 'theories,' each really nothing more than a passing fad that rarely outlived the person who proposed it.

Reductionism

Some thinkers hold out the hope that, as our knowledge in areas such as neuroscience and genetics grows, it will eventually be possible to establish the human sciences on firmer foundations. Since it seeks to explain some subjects in terms of other, more fundamental, ones, such a position is known as **reductionism**. A reductionist might, for example, argue that one day we will be able to understand economics in terms of psychology, and psychology in terms of neuroscience. At the limit, a reductionist might argue that everything is ultimately a matter of atoms whizzing around in space in accordance with the laws of physics (see Figure 9.5).

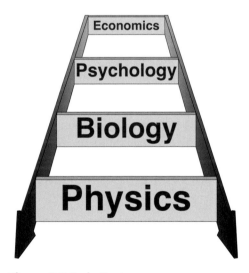

Figure 9.5 Reductionism

Since science is supposed to explain complex phenomena in terms of simpler underlying principles, reductionism might seem to be an attractive position. A subject such as physics has, after all, been amazingly successful in explaining a wide variety of phenomena in terms of a small number of underlying laws. A good example of the success of this approach was the reduction of thermodynamics to mechanics, which enabled scientists to explain heat in terms of the motion of molecules. Perhaps in a similar way we will one day be able to explain mental phenomena in terms of underlying physical ones.

The reductive fallacy

When we try to explain complex things in terms of simpler underlying ones, there is, however, a danger that we commit the **reductive fallacy**. This is the fallacy of saying that just because *A* is composed of *B* it follows that *A* is *nothing but B*. Here are some examples of such 'nothing-butism':

A cathedral is nothing but a heap of stones.
A violin sonata is nothing but a sequence of vibrating strings.
A human being is nothing but a bunch of chemicals.

At one level, it is true that we are 'just a bunch of chemicals'; and it is humbling to discover that there is no secret ingredient in the recipe for a human being, and that we are made of the same basic stuff as cats, cucumbers and chrysanthemums. Nevertheless, there is all the difference in the world between so much hydrogen, oxygen and carbon measured out in a chemistry laboratory and a living human being. We may know the ingredients that make up a human being, but we are still very far from understanding the recipe!

There are, in fact, good reasons for doubting that the reductionist programme can succeed. For it has been pointed out that when simple things are combined together the resulting properties cannot always be predicted in advance from their constituent elements. This is as true in the physical world as in the human world. For example, if you combine hydrogen with oxygen, the property of wetness emerges from two non-wet elements. Similarly, when you combine sodium, one of the most unstable elements, with chlorine, one of the most toxic, you end up with salt – a stable compound which tastes good on food!

Since we cannot even reduce chemistry to physics, it seems unlikely that we will ever be able to explain the human sciences in terms of physics. In any case, the resulting knowledge would probably not be very useful. Trying to understand the laws of supply and demand at the level of atoms and molecules would be like trying to learn a computer program by analysing the flow of electrons through the electrical circuits. If you want to know what determines the price of fish, you would do better to read a book on economics than one on atomic physics!

Holism

The reductionist idea that the best way to understand something is to break it up into parts seems particularly inappropriate when it comes to the study of living things. For, as the writer Douglas Adams (1952–2001) observed, 'If you try to take a cat apart to see how it works, the first thing you have on your hands is a non-working cat.' This might suggest that we can only make sense of some things by looking at them as a whole. Such a view is known as **holism**, and its central claim is that *the whole is greater than the sum of the parts* – that the whole contains properties that cannot in principle be discovered through an analysis of the parts.

When applied to the human sciences, holism means that you cannot understand a group only in terms of the individuals that make it up, or an action independent of the context in which it takes place. Thus economists distinguish between macro-economics – which studies the economy as a whole – and micro-economics – which studies the behaviour of individual economic agents – on the grounds that you cannot understand a complex economy simply by analysing the behaviour of individual economic agents. And anthropologists insist that you should immerse yourself in a culture before trying to make sense of its individual practices. At a more mundane level, you may have noticed that a class at school can have an atmosphere which cannot always be explained in terms of the people in it.

> ## Activity 9.19
>
> 1 Do you think that a group can have a 'character' that is distinct from the individuals that make it up?
> 2 A football team may consist of eleven great players and yet do badly in the league. How would you explain this?
> 3 What do you understand by 'team spirit'? Is 'team spirit' the sum of the 'spirit' of each individual on the team? If not, where does it come from?

At the heart of the argument between holism and reductionism is the question of the relation between wholes and parts. Rather than make an *either–or* choice between these two positions and say that you must understand the whole in terms of its parts, or the parts in terms of the whole, perhaps it would be better to think in terms of there being two-way traffic between parts and wholes. Take, for example, the relation between individuals and society. Although society is influenced by the individuals that make it up, it is also true that individuals are affected by the society they live in. To ask which comes first may make no more sense than asking whether the chicken comes before the egg or the egg before the chicken.

The *Verstehen* position

One reason for doubting that we will ever be able to reduce the human sciences to the natural sciences is that they typically explain things in terms of *meanings* and *purposes* rather than mechanical causes and effects. To illustrate the difference between these kinds of explanation, imagine that a group of Martian scientists land on planet Earth on a busy road near some traffic lights. They notice that when the lights turn red the traffic stops and when the lights turn green it moves again. After observing the traffic for several hours, they conclude that red light causes a temporary malfunction in car engines. Unfortunately, they have come up with the wrong *kind* of explanation. What causes the traffic to behave as it does is the existence of a social *rule* which says that a red light *means* stop and a green light *means* go. If the Martians analyse the situation in terms of physics they will never figure out what is happening – for you cannot conjure social rules out of atoms and molecules.

According to what is known as the **Verstehen position** – *Verstehen* is German for 'understanding' – the main aim of the human sciences is to understand the meaning of various social practices *from the inside* as they are understood by the agents themselves. The common sense of this is that, if you want to figure out what a group of people are up to, you cannot simply observe their physical movements, but must try to get 'inside their heads' and understand how *they* see the situation. If you are unable to do this, then you are likely to misunderstand what is happening. For example, a Martian anthropologist who knows nothing about sports might misinterpret a cricket match as a religious ritual in which a bowler tries to kill a batsman with a speeding projectile.

Imagine that you are such a Martian anthropologist with no understanding of human practices. Try to think up bizarre explanations for some of the following rituals:

a Eating at McDonalds

b Taking an IB exam

c Attending a birthday party

d Checking in at an airport

e Shopping at a supermarket

f Working out in a gym

g Going to the hairdressers

Since many explanations in the human sciences are in terms of meaning rather than mechanism, it is perhaps not surprising that the human sciences have few universal laws to their credit. For the meaning of an action depends on the *context* in which it takes place, and it is therefore difficult to generalise. For example, if a man is writing his name on a piece of paper, he could be writing a cheque, giving an autograph, or signing a death warrant. Since the consequences of the same physical action are completely different in each case, you cannot make a universal law of the form, 'If a person writes his name, then...'

Think of as many different explanations as you can for each of the following actions:

a A woman picks up a glass of wine.

b A man goes out with an umbrella.

c A woman walks into a room, walks round, and walks out again.

d A man gets a gun out.

e A woman waves her hand.

While the *Verstehen* approach to making sense of human behaviour is illuminating, we should not get carried away with it. Just because a lot of human behaviour can only be understood in context, we should not, for example, conclude that there are *no* universals in the human sciences. On the contrary, anthropologists have found many traits that seem to be common to all cultures – including gossiping, joking, and taking an interest in sex!

We should also be cautious about taking people's self-descriptions at face value, for the consequences of their actions sometimes bear little relation to their intentions. In the case of economics, Adam Smith (1723–90) famously argued that although individuals tend to seek their own gain, they are led by an 'invisible hand' to promote the general good. For example, an entrepreneur's desire for profit may result in our ending up with cheap high-quality goods and services. This suggests that as well as trying to understand people's behaviour from the inside, social scientists should also look at the *unintended consequences* of their actions. When it comes to studying something as complicated as a human being, there is no reason why we should limit ourselves to a single approach. Truth has many eyes!

The problem of bias

One common accusation against the human sciences is that they are more prone to bias – and therefore less scientific – than their natural science cousins. We are, after all, more likely to begin with prejudices about the nature of individuals and societies than we are about the nature of atoms and molecules. This means that we may find it difficult to be genuinely open-minded about controversial topics such as gender differences or taxation policy. In this situation, the danger is that we simply look for evidence that confirms our pre-existing prejudices while overlooking evidence that contradicts them.

Since we naturally form emotional attachments with other people, a related problem is that a human scientist may over-identify with the people she is studying. When, for example, an anthropologist 'goes native' and lives with a tribe, her insider's understanding of the culture may be bought at the expense of her ability to be objective.

At this point, it is worth recalling that bias can also be a serious problem in the natural as well as the social sciences (see our discussion of **confirmation bias** on pages 230–1). A physicist, for example, may be so committed to his own pet theory that he obstinately refuses to abandon it in the light of contrary evidence. Since natural scientists are only human, they will sometimes be swayed by emotion as well as reason, and there are plenty of controversies in physics, chemistry and biology that are as vicious and partisan as anything that can be found in the human sciences.

Whatever the subject matter, a good antidote to bias is to make it a matter of principle to actively look for evidence that would count *against* your hypothesis. For example, if you think that younger siblings are more rebellious than older ones, you should not only trawl for evidence that confirms your hypothesis, but also look for examples of rebellious older siblings and conformist younger ones. Fortunately, scientists routinely check up on and criticise one another's results, and this helps to ensure that poor and obviously biased research is discredited. Indeed, it could be argued that one of the great strengths of science is that in the long run it tends to be self-correcting – and there is no reason to think that this is any less true of the human sciences than of the natural sciences.

Activity 9.22

1 Who do you think would be the best judge of a child's character?
   a their parents
   b their teachers
   c a professional psychologist
   Give reasons.
2 Give some specific examples of bias that you have come across in the natural sciences and human sciences that you have studied.
3 Explain what is meant by 'falsificationism', and how it can help to reduce the danger of bias in scientific research. (You may wish to refer back to Chapter 8 to remind yourself about falsificationism.)

Predictions

We saw in our discussion of laws and trends that the human sciences have been less successful than the natural sciences in making accurate predictions. In seeking to explain this fact, three points can be made in their defence:

1   The human sciences usually deal with extremely complex situations in which it is not possible to run controlled experiments. Indeed, it could be argued that when critics contrast the success of the natural sciences with the lack of success of the human sciences they are not comparing like with like. For it is a great deal more difficult to make accurate predictions in the real world than in the controlled conditions of the physics laboratory. You may, for example, know a lot of physics, but still be unable to predict where a leaf blown off a tree on a windy autumn day will land. Changing the analogy, we might say that trying to predict human behaviour is a bit like trying to predict the course of a water molecule going over Niagara Falls. While there is nothing difficult about it in theory, in practice there are simply too many variables for us to be able to make accurate predictions.

> **Activity 9.23**
>
> Do you think that weather forecasting is generally more or less reliable than economic forecasting?

2   Some of the predictions made by social scientists are valuable, not because they accurately describe the future, but because they give us an incentive to change it. If, for example, economists in Ruritania predict that unemployment is likely to rise by 20 per cent in the next two years unless something is done, then the Ruritanian government will have a strong incentive to change its policies and try to ensure that the prediction is falsified.

3   Advocates of the *Verstehen* position might argue that the purpose of the human sciences is not so much to explain and predict as to describe and understand.

The above points might help to explain the human sciences' poor record of prediction. But a critic might give a less flattering explanation and argue that the human sciences' lack of success shows that they are at a pre-paradigm stage in their development and await a Newton to establish them on a proper scientific foundation.

Look at the table below. In seeking to defend the human sciences, how would you respond to each of the problems mentioned?

Human sciences: summary of problems

Observation	1	We cannot directly observe other people's minds.
	2	Questionnaires may be misleading or biased.
	3	Observing people may affect the way they behave.
Measurement	4	Social phenomena are difficult to measure.
Hypothesis	5	The act of prediction may affect the behaviour predicted.
Experiments	6	Human sciences study complex social situations in which it is difficult to run controlled experiments.
	7	Various moral considerations limit our willingness to experiment.
Laws	8	Human sciences are not very good at predicting things.
	9	Human sciences usually uncover trends rather than laws.
	10	Science laws are probabilistic in nature.

Conclusion

We might conclude our discussion of the human sciences by saying that they are neither as flawed as their critics believe nor as successful as their defenders hope. Since they deal with complex phenomena, it is perhaps not surprising that they seem to lack the explanatory power of the natural sciences. Nevertheless, we can learn a great deal more about human beings by studying subjects such as psychology, economics and anthropology than we can by relying on uninformed common sense.

Any discussion about the human sciences inevitably raises some big questions about our place in the scheme of things. How, for example, are minds related to bodies? Could a machine think? Do we have free-will? Could a mind exist without a body? Perhaps scientific research will cast light on these questions, but it may be that in this area there are mysteries that will always lie beyond our understanding.

- Since human beings seem to be different from other natural phenomena, we may wonder to what extent they can be studied in a purely scientific way.

- Among the problems that arise in trying to get information about other people are that it is difficult to frame questions in a neutral way and that observing people may affect the way they behave.

- Some important phenomena in the human sciences are difficult to measure, and this can make it difficult to study them scientifically.

- Social scientists have devised many ingenious experiments, but ethical considerations limit our ability to conduct experiments on human beings.

- Although a great deal of human behaviour is predictable, it is unclear how far it can be reduced to law-like regularities.

- Since we typically explain human behaviour in terms of its meaning and purpose, we may never be able to reduce the human sciences to the natural sciences.

- Since they deal with controversial topics, the human sciences are more prone to bias than the natural sciences, but the extent of the problem should not be exaggerated.

- A question that continues to perplex both scientists and philosophers is how the mental is related to the physical.

Terms to remember

bear market	law of large numbers	reactance
behaviourism	loaded question	reductionism
bias	mirror test	reductive fallacy
bull market	nature–nurture debate	stream of consciousness
free-will	observer effect	trends and laws
going native	Phillips curve	*Verstehen* position
holism	*post hoc ergo propter hoc*	
human free-will	fallacy	

Further reading

Reuben Abel, *Man is the Measure* (Macmillan, 1976), Chapter 11: 'The social sciences'. This chapter is a good introductory account of the social sciences. A large part of it is taken up with an excellent discussion of the *Verstehen* position.

Steven Pinker, *The Blank Slate* (Penguin, 2002), Chapter 17: 'Violence'. Pinker argues that many human traits, such as violence, are more the result of genetic inheritance than environmental conditioning. He writes with such verve and style that, whatever your own beliefs, this chapter should engage your interest.

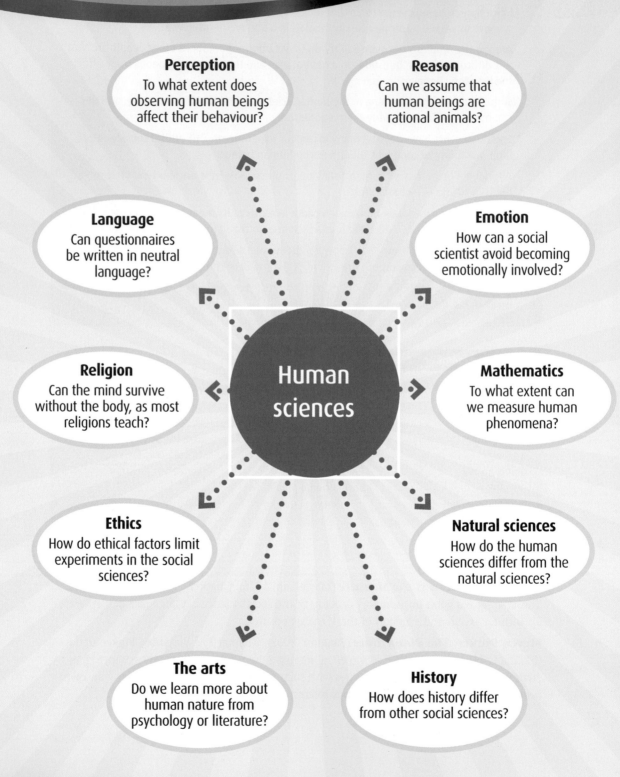

Perception
To what extent does observing human beings affect their behaviour?

Reason
Can we assume that human beings are rational animals?

Language
Can questionnaires be written in neutral language?

Emotion
How can a social scientist avoid becoming emotionally involved?

Human sciences

Religion
Can the mind survive without the body, as most religions teach?

Mathematics
To what extent can we measure human phenomena?

Ethics
How do ethical factors limit experiments in the social sciences?

Natural sciences
How do the human sciences differ from the natural sciences?

The arts
Do we learn more about human nature from psychology or literature?

History
How does history differ from other social sciences?

SOFT SCIENCES ARE OFTEN HARDER THAN HARD SCIENCES

In this extract, Jared Diamond questions the commonly held prejudice that the human sciences are somehow easier or less rigorous than their natural science cousins.

We often view hard science [physics, chemistry, molecular biology] as the only type of science. But science (from the Latin *scientia* – knowledge) is something much more general, which isn't defined by decimal places and controlled experiments. It means the enterprise of explaining and predicting – gaining knowledge of – natural phenomena, by continually testing one's theories against empirical evidence. The world is full of phenomena that are intellectually challenging and important to understand, but that can't be measured to several decimal places in labs. They constitute much of ecology, evolution, and animal behaviour; much of psychology and human behaviour; and all the phenomena of human societies, including cultural anthropology, economics, history, and government.

The soft sciences, as they are pejoratively termed, are more difficult to study for obvious reasons. A lion hunt or revolution in the Third World doesn't fit inside a test tube. You can't start it and stop it whenever you choose. You can't control all the variables; perhaps you can't control *any* variable. You may even find it hard to decide what a variable is. You can still use empirical tests to gain knowledge, but the types of tests used in the hard sciences must be modified. Such differences between the hard and soft sciences are regularly misunderstood by hard scientists, who tend to scorn soft sciences and reserve special contempt for the social sciences...

The issue that... is central to any science, hard or soft... may be termed the problem of how to 'operationalize' a concept... To compare evidence with theory requires that you measure the ingredients of your theory. For ingredients like weight or speed it's clear what to measure, but what would you measure if you wanted to understand political instability? Somehow, you would have to design a series of actual operations that yield a suitable measurement – ie, you must operationalize the ingredients of theory.

Scientists do this all the time, whether or not they think about it. I shall illustrate operationalizing with four examples from... research, progressing from hard science to softer science.

Let's start with mathematics, often described as the queen of the sciences. I'd guess that mathematics arose long ago when two cave women couldn't operationalize the intuitive concept of 'many'. One cave woman said, 'Let's pick this tree over here, because it has many bananas.' The other cave woman argued, 'No, let's pick that tree over there, because it has more bananas.' Without a number system to operationalize their concept of 'many', the two cave women could never prove to each other which tree offered better pickings.

There are still tribes today with number systems too rudimentary to settle the argument. For example, some Gimi villagers with whom I worked in New Guinea have only two root numbers, *iya* = 1 and *rarido* = 2, which they combine to operationalize somewhat larger numbers: 4 = *rarido-rarido*, 7 = *rarido-rarido-rarido-iya* etc. You can imagine what it would be like to hear two Gimi women arguing about whether to climb a tree with 27 bananas or one with 18 bananas.

Now let's move to chemistry, less queenly and more difficult to operationalize than mathematics but still a hard science. Ancient philosophers speculated about the ingredients of matter, but not until the eighteenth century did the first modern chemists figure out how to measure these ingredients. Analytic chemistry now proceeds by identifying some property of a substance of interest, or of a related substance into which the first can be converted. The property must be one that can be measured, like weight, or the light the substance absorbs, or the amount of neutralizing agent it consumes.

For example, when my colleagues and I were studying the physiology of hummingbirds, we knew that the little guys liked to drink sweet nectar, but we would have argued indefinitely about how sweet sweet was if we hadn't operationalized the concept by measuring sugar concentrations. The method we used was to treat the glucose solution with an enzyme that liberates hydrogen peroxide, which reacts (with the help of another enzyme) with another substance called dianisidine to make it turn brown, whereupon we measured the brown colour's intensity with an instrument called a spectrophotometer. A pointer's deflection on the spectrophotometer dial let us read off a number that provided an operational definition of sweet. Chemists use that sort of indirect reasoning all the time, without anyone considering it absurd.

My next-to-last example is from ecology, one of the softer of the biological sciences, and certainly more difficult to operationalize than chemistry. As a bird-watcher, I'm accustomed to finding more species of birds in a rain forest than in a marsh. I suspect intuitively that this has something to do with a marsh being a simply structured habitat, while a rain forest has a complex structure that includes shrubs, lianas, trees of all heights, and crowns of big trees. More complexity means more niches for different types of birds. But how do I operationalize the idea of habitat complexity, so that I can measure it and test my intuition?

Obviously, nothing I do will yield as exact an answer as in the case where I read sugar concentrations off a spectrophotometer dial. However, a pretty good approximation was devised by one of my teachers, the ecologist, Robert MacArthur, who measured how far a board at a certain height above the ground had to be moved in a random direction away from an observer standing in the forest (or marsh) before it became half obscured by the foliage. That distance is inversely proportional to the density of the foliage at that height. By repeating the measurement at different heights, MacArthur could calculate how the foliage was distributed over various heights.

In a marsh all the foliage is concentrated within a few feet of the ground, whereas in a rain forest it's spread fairly equally from the ground to the canopy. Thus the intuitive idea of habitat complexity is operationalized as what's called a foliage height diversity index, a single number. MacArthur's simple operationalization of these foliage differences among habitats, which at first seemed to resist having a number put on them, proved to explain a big part of the habitat's differences in numbers of bird species. It was a significant advance in ecology.

For the last example let's take one of the softest sciences, one that physicists love to deride: clinical psychology. Marie works with cancer patients and their families. Anyone with personal experience of cancer knows the terror that a diagnosis of cancer brings. Some doctors are more frank with their patients than others, and doctors appear to withhold more information from some patients than from others. Why?

Marie guessed that these differences might be related to differences in doctors' attitudes towards things like death, cancer, and medical treatment. But how on earth was she to operationalize and measure such attitudes, convert them to numbers, and test her guesses?...

Part of Marie's solution was to use a questionnaire that other scientists had developed by extracting statements from sources like tape-recorded doctors' meetings and then asking other doctors to express their degree of agreement with each statement. It turned out that each doctor's responses tended to cluster in several groups, in such a way that his responses to one statement in a cluster were correlated with his responses to other statements in the same cluster. One cluster proved to consist of expressions of attitude towards death, a second cluster consisted of expressions of attitudes toward treatment and diagnosis, and a third cluster consisted of statements about patients' ability to cope with cancer. The responses were then employed to define attitude scales, which were further validated in other ways, like testing the scales on doctors at different stages in their careers (hence likely to have different attitudes). By thus operationalizing doctors' attitudes, Marie discovered (among other things) that doctors most convinced about the value of early diagnosis and aggressive treatment of cancer are the ones most likely to be frank with their patients.

In short, all scientists, from mathematicians to social scientists, have to solve the task of operationalizing their intuitive concepts... Physicists have to resort to very indirect (albeit accurate) operationalizing in order to 'measure' electrons. But the task of operationalizing is inevitably more difficult and less exact in the soft sciences, because there are so many uncontrolled variables. In the four examples I've given, number of bananas and concentration of sugar can be measured to more decimal places than can habitat complexity and attitudes towards cancer.

Unfortunately, operationalizing lends itself to ridicule in the social sciences, because the concepts being studied tend to be familiar ones that all of us fancy we're experts on. Anybody, scientist or no, feels entitled to spout forth on politics or psychology, and to heap scorn on what scholars in those fields write. In contrast, consider the opening sentences of [the mathematician] Lang's paper *Diophantine Approximation on Abelian Varieties with Complex Multiplication*: 'Let A be an abelian variety defined over a number field K. We suppose that A is embedded in projective space. Let Ak be the group of points on A rational over K.' How many people feel entitled to ridicule these statements while touting their own opinions about abelian varieties?

IS ECONOMICS A SCIENCE?

In the two articles below, Arthur Williamson and Seamus Hogan debate whether or not economics is a genuine science.

An unbiased account from a physical-chemist's point of view

Arthur Williamson, First Vice President New Zealand Institute of Chemistry

Recently I have noticed that economists have begun to draw on some of the jargon and concepts of physical chemistry and are using the ideas of thermodynamics to support their assertions about the possibility of continued economic growth. I guess this gives a thermodynamicist some reciprocal right to expound on the methods of economics.

An aspect of economics that interests me is the relationship between theory and real behaviour. In both fields it appears that one can devise theories about the behaviour of a system and then use them to make predictions about the future behaviour of the system, which can then be compared with actual behaviour. At this point physical science and economics seem to diverge. When actual and predicted behaviour differ, the physical scientist generally concludes that either the observations or the theory are in error. If the observations are trustworthy, then the theory has to be wrong. In economics there seems to be a third possibility which is illustrated by the current 'free market' approach. In this case disagreement between prediction and actuality is often ascribed to 'market failure'. I imagine that the equivalent in physical science would be to say that a disagreement between theory and experiment is due to 'reality failure'. Perhaps even more mystifying to the physical scientist is the fact that the economist will then sometimes go one step further and propose a measure to 'correct' this failure. This is equivalent to the physical scientist attempting to bring reality more into line with the existing theory.

One must conclude that the relationship between theory and reality is indeed different in these two fields. Physical science aims at elucidating characteristics assumed to be inherent in the system and expressed in its behaviour, while economics seems to be about the construction of models and attempts to impose these models on the system. To my mind the ability that the economist has to 'interfere' with the object of his theory adds a dimension of subjectivity that is not present in physical science and suggests that there can be no inherent rightness in any particular economic theory.

A reply

By Seamus Hogan, Department of Economics, McGill University, Montreal

There are a number of similarities in the methodologies of physical science and economics. Unfortunately, the similarities in substance are not as great as the similarities in the language used to express the substance. A lot of our technical language is borrowed from the physical sciences (principally physics, since many of the economists who first brought mathematical rigour to the subject earlier this century had received their original training in physics). Naturally, the borrowed language has taken on its own meaning in economics, adapting to the differences in the disciplines. This can lead to misunderstanding if professionals from one area try to read material from the other.

One similarity between the physical sciences and economics is that both involve the systematic investigation of complex phenomena. The human brain has only a limited capacity to comprehend complex systems of interacting forces without an organizing framework. One way of providing such a framework is to invent ideal worlds that contain many of the interactions that we wish to comprehend but are still relatively simple and can be used as benchmarks against which the real world is analysed.

For instance, a physicist might consider the dynamics of a body on a frictionless surface attached to an ideal spring (i.e. a spring that has no mass and gives rise to a restoring force that is proportional to the distance the body is displaced from rest). Obviously, ideal springs or frictionless surfaces do not exist, but it is easier to comprehend the observed behaviour of a spring by considering how the presence of friction or spring mass distort the dynamics that it is trying to model. Similarly, modern economic theory is built on a mathematical structure that can analyse the simultaneous interaction of all decision-making agents in an economy (consumers, firms, governments, etc). This structure makes a number of simplifying assumptions that are palpably false, but, as with the ideal spring,

it provides a benchmark, exceptions from which generate our comprehension of the real economic world.

One reason for calling the simplified worlds 'ideal' is that they often contain a number of desirable properties that one would like to approximate in practice (e.g. minimizing friction can reduce the amount of energy that one needs to supply in order to achieve a particular amount of work). Since the economic benchmark also has some desirable properties, one set of real-world deviations from this benchmark are termed 'market failures'. To continue with the analogy, an economist's recommendation that economic policy be used to remove a market failure would be equivalent to a physicist's recommendation that a lubricant be used to reduce friction.

Professor Williamson's final point is that 'the ability of an economist to "interfere" with the object of his theory adds a dimension of subjectivity which is not present in physical science'. There is an important difference between physical sciences and economics in the methodology of connecting theory (in the physical science use of the term) and reality. The most important of these is that economists can almost never use controlled experiments. One can think of a controlled experiment as being an attempt to create the conditions of an imagined 'ideal' world in order to isolate a small number of phenomena from the distractions of real-world interactions. Economics certainly does have a 'dimension of subjectivity which is not present in physical science', but this is precisely because the economist cannot 'interfere' with the object of his theory in the way that a physical scientist can through the use of controlled experiments.

The free-will problem

Introduction

One of the issues that we touched on in our discussion of the human sciences was the problem of free-will. This concerns the question of how we can reconcile the belief that human beings have free-will with our scientific picture of the world. Since it raises questions about both our place in the universe and the nature of knowledge, it is worth looking at this problem in more detail.

At first sight, the existence of free-will seems to be a self-evident and unproblematic fact. In our everyday negotiations with the world, we constantly experience ourselves making choices about our actions. To take a trivial example, suppose at lunch-time you are faced with a choice between a pizza and a hamburger – both of which you like – and that you choose the pizza. There is nothing that *compelled* you to choose the pizza, and you could just as easily have taken the hamburger if you had wanted to. So in making your choice you surely exercised free-will. There seem to be countless equally simple and compelling demonstrations of free-will. Right now, you can, for example, either raise your hand or not raise it, and nothing is forcing you to choose one way or the other.

Our belief in free-will is not only based on our own experience, but is also deeply embedded in the way we think about other people; and it is hard to imagine how social life could function without it. Every time you praise or criticise someone's actions, you are implicitly assuming that they are free and that they could have done otherwise. Indeed, the whole of ethics is based on the assumption that we have free-will. It would, after all, be unreasonable to pass judgement on someone for doing something that they couldn't help doing and about which they had no choice. That is why we do not hold insane people criminally responsible for their actions. The existence of free-will, then, is central to our conception of what it is to be a responsible human being, and to deny its existence would seem to rob us of our dignity and reduce us to the status of biological machines.

Figure 9A.1

"I told my parents that if grades were so important they should have paid for a smarter egg donor."

Determinism

Despite such troubling consequences, some scientists and philosophers have nevertheless denied that human beings have free-will and have adopted a position known as **determinism**. According to this, the universe operates in accordance with the causal principle that every event has a cause. Since this principle is said to apply to human actions as well as the natural world, determinists believe that our actions can ultimately be traced back to factors beyond our control, thereby robbing us of our free-will.

The determinist position would seem to be supported by scientific developments in areas such as genetics which confirm the common-sense observation that we inherit many of our personality traits from our parents. Admittedly social scientists may argue about whether our characters are determined more by 'nature' in the form of our genetic inheritance, or 'nurture' in the form of the environment in which we grow up; but, whatever the proportions, neither of these alternatives seems to leave much room for free-will. After all, you chose neither your genes nor the family in which you grew up.

Activity 9A.1

1 How different do you think your personality would have been if you had been adopted at birth and brought up in a different culture?

2 Some controversial research has been done which suggests that there are striking similarities between identical twins who were separated at birth and brought up by different families.

  a Find out something about this research and some of the criticisms that have been made of it.

  b What would you conclude about the roles played by nature and nurture in determining our characters?

3 How far do you think our behaviour is determined by unconscious motives? How might one go about testing such a hypothesis?

4 To what extent do you think the behaviour of the following individuals is predictable?

  a Your parents   b Your friends   c You

Further support for determinism would seem to come from our knowledge of the brain. A determinist might point to the fact that our mental activities are correlated with various brain states, and that our brains are subject to the laws of physics and chemistry. As far as neuroscience is concerned, when you do something, such as raise your arm, the cause of your action is the various neurons firing in your brain. This pattern of neuronal activity is in turn caused by the previous material state of your brain, which is in turn caused by an earlier state, and so on in a backward chain. Looked at in this way, it seems that the real causes of our actions are to be found at the level of physics and chemistry, and the feeling that they flow from our freely made decisions is merely a beguiling illusion.

Perhaps the most comprehensive case for determinism can be made at the level of atoms moving around in space in accordance with the laws of physics. As the French mathematician Pierre Laplace (1749–1827) famously expressed it:

> We ought to regard the present state of the universe as the effect of its antecedent state and as the cause of the state that is to follow. An intelligence knowing all the forces acting in nature at a given instant, as well as the momentary positions of all things in the universe, would be able to comprehend in one single formula the motions of the largest bodies as well as of the lightest atoms in the world, provided that its intellect were sufficiently powerful to subject all data to analysis; to it nothing would be uncertain, the future as well as the past would be present to its eyes.

According to Laplace, then, every event in the universe has been rigorously determined by the preceding one, and it is – in principle at least – possible to predict the entire future history of the universe. In this bleak and uncompromising picture of things, there seems to be no room for human free-will.

How does determinism threaten free-will?

To respond to the threat that determinism poses to our belief in free-will, we should begin by clearing up two common misconceptions which may help to reduce the gap between the two positions.

On the one hand, a believer in free-will is not saying that we are free to do anything we like, and would readily admit that we are limited in various ways by our nature and environment. Indeed, one of life's great frustrations is to bump up against our own limitations. You may desperately want to be a concert pianist, but if you have a tin ear and a poor sense of timing, then, sadly, you are never going to make it. Since we are not endlessly talented, it is clear that we all have a restricted menu of options in the banquet of life. Nevertheless, a believer in free-will insists that we do *still* have options, and that, at least sometimes, we are capable of exercising them and making genuinely free decisions.

On the other hand, a determinist is not saying that the future is determined irrespective of what you do. For that would be to adopt fatalism, and determinism is not the same as fatalism. According to fatalism, your destiny is written in the stars and there is nothing that *you* can do to change the future. This belief is, I think, straightforwardly false. For it is clear that what you do *does* affect the future. If, for example, you work hard, then you are more likely to pass your exams than if you do nothing. Admittedly, there are no guarantees, but what you do will certainly change the balance of probabilities. So much for fatalism. Coming back to determinism, a good way to think of it is as steering between fatalism and free-will. Against fatalism, it says that the choices you make do affect the future; but, against free-will, it says that you have no control over your choices.

To summarise, we can say that a believer in free-will will accept that much of our behaviour is determined by factors beyond our control; and a determinist will accept that the choices we make do affect our future. Yet a seemingly unbridgeable gap remains between these two positions. For a believer in free-will will continue to insist that there is some space for genuinely free decisions: something which a determinist will continue to deny.

Faced with the free-will problem, I think there are at least three possible responses we could make. We could:

1   reject the claim that every event has a cause and argue that this leaves room for free-will

2   accept determinism, but insist that free-will and determinism are compatible with each other

3   accept determinism and conclude that, no matter how unpalatable it might be, human free-will is an illusion.

Does every event have a cause?

With the first of the above options in mind, let us begin by asking what evidence there is for the claim that every event has a cause. You might say that it is an *empirical* claim which is supported by the fact that, as science has developed, we have discovered the causes of more and more events. Extrapolating from this, it seems reasonable to suppose that if we look hard enough we can always find the cause of an event. We may not know the exact cause of AIDS, but nobody doubts that there is a cause, and most people believe that we will eventually discover it.

Thinking about it, I rather doubt that we would allow anything – in the physical world, at least – to count against our belief that every event has a cause. Imagine, for example, that your table lamp suddenly stops working. You check the bulb, and the fuse and the electricity supply, but are unable to find the cause of the problem. You call an electrician, but he is no more successful than you. Do you conclude that you have discovered an uncaused event and that there was no reason why your lamp stopped working? No, you conclude that you hired an incompetent electrician! I suspect that, even if you never solve the problem, you will still insist that *something* must have caused your lamp to stop working.

Activity 9A.2

If you were unable to find the cause of an event, would you ever be willing to conclude that it did not have a cause?

This suggests that the belief that every event has a cause is not so much an empirical one that can be verified or falsified by evidence as a metaphysical one about the nature of ultimate reality. What makes it attractive is the underlying belief that the universe is an orderly place in which things don't happen randomly or for no reason. Indeed, without some such belief, science – which is essentially a search for causes – would be impossible.

Subatomic randomness

Now, it might be pointed out that there is an area of science where the causal principle that every event has a cause does not seem to hold. For, the world of subatomic particles is governed by **Heisenberg's uncertainty principle** which says that it is impossible to know both the position and velocity of subatomic particles with complete certainty. It would seem to follow that – at this level, at least – events are governed by pure chance.

The indeterminacy that can be found at the subatomic level might seem to loosen the vice-like grip of the causal principle, and provide a physical basis for our belief in free-will. There is, however, reason to think that what is happening at the subatomic level is irrelevant to the free-will problem. For even if random events sometimes occur, mere randomness is not what the believer in free-will is looking for. Imagine, for example, that you are holding a gun and that a random event in your brain causes various neurons to fire which results in your finger squeezing the trigger. You would be as surprised as anyone else by what had happened and could hardly be held responsible for it. *So free-will is not the same as random will;* and in rejecting determinism we do not want to say that our actions are uncaused, but rather that they are caused by our wills. In any case, Heisenberg's uncertainty principle applies only to the subatomic level, and when it comes to anything bigger – which is everything that is of interest to us – physicists are agreed that the law of cause and effect still holds sway.

Capturing a free action

Despite the above discussion, a believer in free-will might say that, no matter what physics says, we should not be bullied into denying the plain facts of experience. For our immediate experience of freedom surely *proves* that the causal principle is false.

There may be something in this; but to find and describe a moment of free choice turns out to be harder than you might think. For a start, we seem to spend quite a lot of each day on 'automatic pilot', going through well-rehearsed routines that do not involve much conscious thought. When, for example, the alarm goes off in the morning, I doubt if you consciously decide on each step of your morning routine – getting out of bed, getting in the shower, brushing your teeth, putting your clothes on, and so on. For it would simply be too exhausting if you had to agonise over each of these micro-decisions every day. I think a more accurate picture of what happens is that you simply get out of bed and initiate 'plan A' – your tried and tested routine for getting ready for school.

Nevertheless, our days are punctuated by various mundane decisions, such as what to wear or what to have for lunch. Let's go back to an earlier example, and take a closer look at your lunch-time choice between pizza and hamburger. How exactly does the choice get made? Well, if you are someone who loves pizzas and hates hamburgers, you do not really have a choice and you will take the pizza. So let us assume that you love pizzas and hamburgers and haven't had either of them for a long time. How do you decide which one to take? The strange thing is that there seems to be a kind of emptiness at the moment of decision. Do you make some kind of mental grunt and choose the pizza, or do you dither for a moment and then simply find yourself taking it? It is very difficult to say exactly what does happen. Things do not get any easier to describe when it comes to important decisions.

Activity 9A.3

1 Describe as accurately as you can what happens when you make a free decision, such as getting out of bed when the alarm goes off rather than snoozing for another twenty minutes.

2 How much of what you do every day would you say is determined by routine and habit, and how much by your conscious decisions?

3 When do you feel most free?

   a When you fulfil your desires

   b When you overcome your desires

   c When, on a whim, you suddenly decide to do something

   d When you do something creative

   e Some other situation

Suppose you have a choice between two university offers and must decide which one to take. If university A ranks much higher than university B in terms of all your preferences, then there is again a sense in which you have no choice: you are bound to choose A. But what if it is finely balanced and you prefer A in some ways and B in others? If you still can't make up your mind after agonising over it and discussing it with your friends and family, you will probably 'sleep on it' and hope that the decision comes to you. So, once again, it seems that either the odds are stacked in favour of one particular option, in which case you are not really making a choice; or the two options are finely balanced, in which case it is very difficult to say just how you do make a choice.

Despite the difficulties involved in capturing and describing a freely chosen action, we do generally experience ourselves as active beings who are the authors of their actions. So, even if it is impossible to explain how free-will works, we surely cannot doubt that it exists.

Is the feeling of freedom an illusion?

However, a determinist is unlikely to be satisfied with this admission of ignorance. He may want to know exactly how a free decision affects what is going on in our brains. Does it somehow cause an atom or subatomic particle to swerve from its original course? If so, how can this be made consistent with the laws of physics? You might, once again, want to appeal to the uncertainty principle, but it is far from clear how this can help us to solve the problem.

Furthermore, it might be pointed out that just because you *feel* free doesn't mean that you *are* free – for the feeling could simply be an illusion. That, at least, is what the philosopher Baruch Spinoza (1632–77) thought: 'Men think themselves free because they are conscious of their actions, but ignorant of their causes.' If falling stones were conscious, said Spinoza, they would probably believe that they were falling of their own free-will. So perhaps we are simply puppets that are unaware of the strings of physical causation that are pulling us.

1 If every morning someone delivered in a sealed envelope some precise predictions about what you would do during the day, and every evening you opened the envelope and found that they were all true, would this convince you that you did not have any free-will?
2 If the future is determined for the kinds of reasons that Laplace gave, but we are never in practice able to predict it, why, if at all, should we be worried?

At this point in our discussion, we seem to reach an impasse. If you are more convinced that the universe is orderly than that human beings have free-will, you are likely to insist that every event has a cause; and if you are more convinced that human beings have free-will than that the universe is orderly, you are likely to deny that every event has a cause.

Is free-will compatible with determinism?

One way of trying to get beyond the above impasse is to take the second of the options mentioned above and argue that free-will and determinism are compatible with one another. This view is known as **compatibilism** and it has proved popular with some philosophers.

Is freedom simply a matter of doing what you want?

While compatibilists believe that every event has a cause, they insist that this still leaves room for free-will. To be free, they say, is simply to be able to do what you want. And so long as you are not compelled or hindered by someone else, you are surely free. Such a common-sense view of freedom is quite consistent with determinism. Indeed, compatibilists argue that free-will is possible only to the extent that determinism is true. For, as we saw above, if your actions were uncaused they could not be said to be yours at all. This looks like a neat solution to the free-will problem which allows us to have our cake and eat it. For it seems to give us human free-will *and* an orderly and rule-governed universe.

1 If a dog does what it likes, can it be called free? How does its freedom differ from that of a human being?
2 To what extent do you think the free-will debate is simply an argument about the meaning of the word 'freedom'?

Can we control our desires?

The trouble with the compatibilist solution to the free-will problem is that it depends on a superficial analysis of the word 'freedom'. To see this, consider a smoker who feels like a cigarette and smokes one. Since he is doing what he wants without any external hindrance, a compatibilist would say that he is acting freely. But suppose our smoker is trying to quit smoking, and that when he desires a cigarette he has at the same time a higher-order desire *not* to desire a cigarette. Although at one level he is doing what he wants, at another level it is tempting to say that he is a *victim* of his desires. This description becomes more and more appropriate as we move up the scale of addictive habits. At the limit, I doubt that anyone would describe a heroin addict as free; and it might therefore be better to think of an addict as sick rather than criminal.

1 At what point on the road from non-addiction to addiction would you say that free-will ends and compulsion begins?
2 To what extent do you think we should hold drug addicts responsible for their behaviour?

In response to the above, you might point out that most of our desires are not in fact addictive, and that there is a clear difference between being in the grip of an addiction and making ordinary choices. While there may be some truth in this, the smoker example is not so easily dismissed. For it raises not only the question of where ordinary behaviour ends and addiction begins, but also the deeper question of the extent to which we are able to control or change our desires. Compatibilism says that you are free when you can do what you desire; but if your desires are themselves beyond your control, there would seem to be a deeper sense in which you are not free even when you are doing what you want.

1 What distinguishes addictive behaviour from ordinary behaviour?
2 Which of the following might be described as addictive?
   a Coffee   b Hamburgers
   c Marijuana   d Work
   e Shopping   f Love
   g Crime   h Extreme sports
3 To what extent do you think we are able to change our desires? Could you, for example, decide to:
   a like cheese, if you have always loathed it
   b find someone interesting, if you have always found them boring
   c work hard, if you have always been lazy
   d show more concern for others, if you have always been selfish

To common sense, this talk of victimhood is at best misleading and at worst false. Such language may be appropriate to a smoker who is unable to quit, but the fact is that we are quite happy with many of our desires and have no wish to change them. If I enjoy listening to music and eating cheese and pickle sandwiches, why should I think of myself as a *victim* of these desires? 'Because' you are unable to change them, comes the response. The fact that you are happy with your desires does not mean you are free. A prisoner may be happy if he does not want to leave his cell, but he is still a prisoner.

But surely this talk of our being imprisoned by our desires is again misleading. For while a prisoner cannot decide to leave prison, we can – in some cases at least – change our desires. After all, some people quit smoking. This suggests that if you really want to give up smoking – or change yourself in some other way – then you can. Perhaps it is simply a matter of positive thinking, about which we hear so much in self-help manuals.

Could you have done otherwise?

This brings us to the heart of the matter. Any freedom worth having surely requires not simply that you can do what you want, but more radically that *you could do otherwise*. Let us go back to our smoker who wants to give up smoking and zoom in on a moment of temptation. He feels like a cigarette, briefly tries to resist, and then gives in and reaches for the packet. Could he have resisted the temptation to have a cigarette? One response is to say that he could *if he had chosen to*. But that simply transforms the question into, 'Could he have chosen otherwise?' You might be tempted to say 'yes' on the grounds that if he had shown more will power then he could have chosen to resist. However, I think that determinism is committed to saying that if you replayed the videotape it would come out the same way every time. Admittedly, our smoker could have resisted temptation if he had shown more will power; but the point is that, being the kind of person that he was, in the situation that he was in, he just did not have the necessary self-control.

For a determinist, then, although your decisions may be determined by your character, your character itself has been determined by factors beyond your control. The upshot is that, given the kind of person that you are, you cannot help making the kinds of decisions that you do. Indeed, we sometimes excuse our behaviour by saying 'I can't help it – that's just the way I am.' And we are all aware how difficult it is to change aspects of ourselves that we dislike. Just think of those broken New Year resolutions!

Activity 9A.8

To what extent do you think you can change your character, and to what extent do you think you just have to live with it?

The upshot of our discussion would seem to be that determinism is incompatible with free-will in the sense that, although you can do what you want, you can never do otherwise than you do, and your wants and your will power are ultimately determined by factors beyond your control. This does not mean that determinism is true, but it does suggest that compatibilism is false. So in trying to solve the free-will problem, we seem to be back at square one.

Is free-will an illusion?

As a final approach to the free-will problem, we might take the bull by the horns and say that determinism is true and human free-will is an illusion. But this implies that there is no such thing as moral responsibility or rationality, and many people would say that this is too high a price to pay for accepting determinism.

Does determinism undermine ethics?

Some philosophers have argued that the implications of determinism for ethics are not in fact as serious as they look. Admittedly, we will have to abandon the idea that people deserve to be praised and blamed, or rewarded and punished for their actions. For, in a deterministic world, good people cannot help being good, and bad people cannot help being bad. Given this, you might think that we should close the courts and empty the prisons. After all, criminals are not responsible for the rotten genes and bad neighbourhoods that shaped their behaviour. However, a determinist would say that we are still justified in locking up criminals in order to: (1) protect society; and (2) modify their future behaviour. Without wishing to offend human dignity, we might make an analogy with the way we treat dogs. We do not hold dogs responsible for their actions, but we still lock up mad dogs in order to protect people, and punish bad ones in order to reform them.

"So I blame you for everything—whose fault is that?"

Figure 9A.2

Here we have touched on two different theories of punishment: the **retribution theory**, which justifies punishing criminals on the grounds that they deserve it; and the **reform theory**, which justifies punishing them only if it will change their behaviour. While the former is retrospective and looks to the past, the latter is prospective and looks to the future. And while the former is inconsistent with determinism, the latter is perfectly consistent with it.

A determinist might argue that, even if we have free-will, the only civilised reason for punishing people – apart from protecting society – is to reform them. To punish someone if it is not going to improve their behaviour – merely 'because they deserve it' – smacks of vindictiveness. As critics of capital punishment say, executing someone for murder 'won't bring the victim back'. On this view, then, punishment is best seen as a form of education. And to punish for any reason other than reform (or protection) is itself a crime.

*"Great news, Phil! The governor has determined that you
don't have a high enough I.Q. to merit execution."*

Figure 9A.3

Activity 9A.9

1   Imagine a criminal contemplating a crime and thinking to himself: 'If I am caught, they will say that it's not my fault, that I couldn't help it. As a result, I will probably get off lightly. So I might as well do it.' Is this a good argument against the reform theory of punishment?

2   Do you think that punishment should be based more on reason, or emotion, or a combination of the two?

3   At what age would you say that a person becomes criminally responsible? Justify your view.

4   Do you think we should punish someone for a crime they committed fifty years ago? Does it depend on the nature of the crime? Give reasons for and against.

5   What is the difference between evil and insanity? Are mass murderers necessarily insane?

6   What difference do you think it would make if we thought of criminals as ill rather than bad, and spoke in terms of cure rather than punishment? Is this a better or worse way of looking at things?

7   To what extent do you think it is true that 'to know all is to forgive all'?

Despite its attractions, the reform theory of punishment is not without its critics. Two common objections to it are that it weakens the deterrence effect of punishment, and that it is hard to know where reform ends and brainwashing begins. More could be said about both of these points, and there are doubtless responses that could be made to them. However, we will not pursue this discussion further here. For, even if we allow that determinism is consistent with some forms of punishment, there is another, more serious, problem facing the theory.

Does determinism undermine rationality?

The problem I have in mind is that determinism does not seem to leave any room for the possibility of rationality. For reasoning implies that we are free to believe something or not to believe it; and it typically involves such things as weighing up evidence, considering implications, and making judgements. But if determinism is true, none of these factors plays any role in shaping our beliefs, which – like everything else – are determined by our characters and the surrounding environment. I, being the kind of person that I am, simply cannot help believing the kinds of things that I do; and you, being the kind of person that you are, cannot help believing the kinds of things that you do. It follows that trying rationally to prove that determinism is true is self-defeating in the same way that trying rationally to prove that you don't exist is self-defeating. In both cases, if the argument is convincing, then it undermines itself. What comes out of this is not that determinism is false, but that if it is true then you cannot rationally believe that it is true (or false) because in a deterministic world you cannot rationally believe anything.

More radically, one might argue that if determinism is true, then there is not even any room for language. For if we are not free to think about what we are saying and reflect on what we are hearing, then there would seem to be no difference between the talking of human beings and the singing of birds or the barking of dogs.

Activity 9A.10

1 To what extent do you think that people's beliefs are shaped by:
   a their characters
   b their environment?
2 Where do your thoughts come from? Does it make more sense to say that you think your thoughts or that your thoughts think you?

Conclusion

We have explored three ways of trying to resolve the conflict between our everyday belief that human beings have free-will and the scientific belief that we live in a law-governed and deterministic universe. But we have not been able to solve the problem. While there are some good arguments in favour of determinism, I think that in practice it would be almost impossible for us to abandon our belief in free-will. Some people take human free-will to show that we are fundamentally different from the rest of the natural world and have some kind of spiritual dimension. However, the free-will problem is as much of a problem for someone who believes in God as it is for an atheist. For, as we shall see in Chapter 13, if God is all-knowing, then He presumably knows our future as well as our past. And this, again, suggests that our future is in some sense already determined.

So there is, it seems, no easy way of avoiding the free-will problem. Perhaps the only conclusion we can draw from our discussion is that there are limits to knowledge and that some things lie beyond human understanding.

10 History

'The past is never dead.
It's not even past.'
William Faulkner, 1897–1962

'The past is another country. They do
things differently there.'
L. P. Hartley, 1895–1972

'Who controls the past controls the
future, who controls the present
controls the past.'
George Orwell, 1903–50

'What is history but a fable
agreed upon?'
Napoleon Bonaparte, 1769–1821

'History will be kind to me, for I intend
to write it.'
Winston Churchill, 1874–1965

'No man ever yet tried to write down
the entire truth of any action in which
he was engaged.'
T. E. Lawrence, 1888–1935

'History abhors determinism, but
cannot tolerate chance.'
Bernard de Voto, 1897–1955

'History is but the register of human
crimes and misfortunes.'
Voltaire, 1694–1778

'History is a kind of experiment, albeit
an imperfectly controlled one.'
Steven Pinker, 1954–

'The history of the world is but the
biography of great men.'
Thomas Carlyle, 1795–1881

'A page of history is worth a volume
of logic.'
Oliver Wendell Holmes, 1841–1935

'Anybody can make history. Only a
great man can write it.'
Oscar Wilde, 1854–1900

'The only thing we learn from history is
that we learn nothing from history.'
G. W. F. Hegel, 1770–1831

'History An account, mostly false, of
events mostly unimportant, which are
brought about by rulers, mostly knaves,
and soldiers, mostly fools.'
Ambrose Bierce, 1842–1914

'The aim of the historian, like that of
the artist, is to enlarge our picture
of the world, to give us a new way of
looking at things.'
James Joll, 1918–94

'Those who don't study the past are
condemned to repeat it.'
George Santayana, 1863–1952

Introduction

Imagine waking up one morning to discover that you have lost your memory. After a few minutes of blind panic, you begin to examine the room you find yourself in. You discover a scribbled note which says 'Meet George, Piccadilly Circus, 9:30.' You glance at the clock. It is 8:00 a.m. Since you don't want to tell anyone about your predicament, you give yourself an hour and a half to work out who you are from the contents of what is clearly *your* bedroom and make it to Piccadilly Circus to meet George – whoever he is...

Activity 10.1

If you found yourself in the above situation, to what extent do you think you would be able to reconstruct your identity by examining the objects in your room? What problems would you experience in trying to do this, and how similar are they to those facing a historian?

The thought of losing your memory is a frightening one not only because memories are precious in themselves, but also because your sense of who you are and where you are going is bound up with what you have done. Without the compass of memory to guide you, you would be adrift in a meaningless ocean of time with no sense of identity or direction.

One interesting approach to thinking about history is to begin with our own micro-histories. To a greater or lesser extent, we all try to make sense of the past by weaving the various episodes of our lives into a meaningful narrative. This raises a number of interesting questions.

Activity 10.2

1 Why should you care about your past? What dangers are there in being obsessed with your past, and what dangers are there in ignoring it?
2 How good is your memory, and how reliable do you think it is as a guide to the past?
3 If you keep a diary, what determines what you choose to include and what you choose to omit?
4 Would you be more inclined to trust an autobiography, or a biography about the same person written by a historian?
5 To what extent do you think that people learn from their mistakes, and to what extent do you think they keep making the same mistakes?

There are some interesting parallels between the above questions and those that arise when we consider history as an academic subject. In thinking about the latter, a good place to start is with the question of what we mean by history. Why, after all, do we normally think of history as the catalogue of 'great events' and assume that the details of our own micro-histories have nothing to do with it?

What is history?

In answering the question 'What is history?', we might begin by saying that it is the study of the past. This may be a reasonable first approximation, but the answer is in fact more complicated than that.

Evidence

To start with, since we can know the past only to the extent that we have *evidence* for it, it would be more accurate to say that history is not so much the study of the past as of the *present traces* of the past.

In trying to reconstruct the past on the basis of the evidence, one of two problems may arise: *too little* evidence, or *too much* evidence. When we study the distant past, the problem is usually that of too little evidence. A real danger in such a situation is that we misinterpret the evidence that exists, and jump to conclusions that are not justified by it. Imagine, for example, that after our civilisation has vanished, a Martian archaeologist unearths exhibit A in Figure 10.1. If he knows nothing about our culture and its practices, he might interpret his find as a 'ceremonial collar' and reconstruct it as in Figure 10.2.

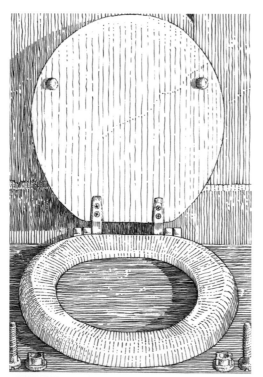

Figure 10.1

Figure 10.2

The problem of lack of evidence is a real one, and it is sometimes surprising to discover that our knowledge claims about the past are less well justified than we might have imagined. For example, our knowledge of the wars between Persia and Greece in the fifth century BCE is based on a single, quite unreliable, source – the Greek historian Herodotus (*c.* 485–420 BCE).

When it comes to modern history, we are usually faced with the opposite problem: that there is too much evidence. If you tried to write a definitive history of the world for a single year – say, 2000 – you would be overwhelmed by a tidal wave of evidence from newspapers, TV and the Internet.

Significance

This brings us to a second qualification we need to make about the nature of history. History is not a record of *everything* that happened in the past, but is concerned with only the *significant* events in the past. For example, while the assassination of John F. Kennedy on 22 November 1963 is a historically significant event, the fact that I had porridge for breakfast on 9 February 1998 is probably not.

Activity 10.3

Using any criteria of your choice, rate the historical significance of the following events.
a The publication of Charles Darwin's *The Origin of Species* in 1859.
b Your last TOK class.
c The assassination of Mahatma Gandhi in 1948.
d The 1930 soccer World Cup Final – which was won by Uruguay.
e The birth of Bill Gates in 1955.
f Former US president Bill Clinton's affair with Monica Lewinsky.
g The terrorist attacks on the World Trade Center and the Pentagon in 2001.

Once we start talking about 'significant events' we run in to the problem of how to decide whether or not an event is significant. While you might think that significance – like beauty – is in the eye of the beholder, there are various *criteria* we might appeal to in order to decide whether or not an event is historically significant. For example, you can look at how many people are affected by the event, and the extent to which they are affected. While a dramatic event, such as political assassination, is likely to affect many people in a significant way, the same cannot be said of a TOK class.

So is there any way in which a TOK class might become at least a footnote in history? Here are a couple of possibilities:

- Your teacher makes a chance remark in a TOK class that inspires you to enter politics, and you eventually become world president. Years later when you write your memoirs, you observe: 'During that fateful TOK class in February 2011, I first felt the hand of destiny on me and knew that I must enter politics.'

- A series of nuclear wars at the end of the twenty-first century devastates the planet. Many centuries pass before civilisation re-establishes itself. As luck has it, one of the few things that survive from the early twenty-first century are your TOK notes. Future historians pore over them and try to get an idea of what life was like at the beginning of the twenty-first century.

Explaining the past

In going beyond our preliminary characterisation of history as the study of the past, we have mentioned *evidence* and *significance*. A third important feature of history is that it is concerned not simply with describing the past, but also with *explaining and understanding* it. After all, history is more than just a catalogue of important dates and events; and although a historian may need to devote considerable energy to establishing *what* happened, this is usually a prelude to trying to understand *why* it happened. Historians might typically be trying to understand such things as the collapse of the Roman Empire, or the causes of the First World War, or the rise of Fascism.

Why study history?

Since history does not seem to have the immediate practical value of science, you might wonder why we should bother studying it. The car maker Henry Ford (1863–1947) dismissed history as 'more or less bunk', and in an age obsessed with progress, it is sometimes seen as 'yesterday's news' with no relevance to the present. There are, however, some good reasons for studying the past.

We can justify history on the grounds that it: (1) gives us a sense of identity; (2) is a defence against propaganda; and (3) enriches our understanding of human nature.

Activity 10.4

'The study of history is so important that it should be a compulsory IB subject.' Think of as many arguments as you can for and against this claim.

History gives us a sense of identity

According to a well-known saying, a country without a history is like a person without a memory. At the beginning of this chapter, I asked you to imagine waking up one morning to discover that you had lost your memory. As we saw, if that were to happen, you would lose not only your sense of who you are but also your sense of direction. What is true of an individual is also true of a country. If as a community you don't know where you have come from, it will be impossible for you to make any sense of the present or what you should do in the future.

To extend the analogy between a person and a country, it could be said that just as you can know a person only if you know something about their history, so you can know a country only if you know something about *its* history. If you are to have informed opinions about current affairs, and your judgements about other countries are to go beyond mere prejudice, then a knowledge of history is indispensable. Anyone trying to make sense of the Middle East situation needs to have a good knowledge of the history of the region.

1 How important do you think it is for our political leaders to have a good knowledge of history?
2 Do you think that some countries are more obsessed with their history than others? What dangers, if any, are there in:
   a ignoring the past
   b being obsessed with the past?

History is a defence against propaganda

Since most governments take a great interest in the way history is taught in schools, it is easy for national pride to dictate a one-sided interpretation of the past which highlights a country's achievements and overlooks its mistakes. At worst, history can be exploited by a corrupt regime to legitimise its rule, justify territorial expansion, and whitewash past crimes. One of the best-known examples of the abuse of history is from the Stalinist era in the former Soviet Union. Not content with liquidating his political opponents, Stalin (1879–1953) also sought to erase them from the historical record.

Figure 10.3

Figure 10.4

In the first of these photographs, which was taken on the second anniversary of the October Revolution in 1919, Trotsky (1879–1940) can be seen centre-stage, standing to Lenin's left. After Trotsky fell from grace and fled into exile, he and other 'undesirables' were erased from the photograph to leave a rather lonely-looking Lenin in the middle of the picture.

Such blatant abuses of history are rare, but governments may try to 'spin' the historical record to serve their interests in more subtle ways. A politician standing for re-election might trumpet the achievements of her first term in office while showing a remarkable blindness to her policy failures and errors of judgement. And when in later life politicians come to write their memoirs, they are generally keen to paint themselves in as good a light as possible. (There is doubtless some truth in the observation that people are at their most creative when they write their autobiographies!)

History can also be used to puncture some of the myths we have about the past. Consider the following words allegedly spoken by American Indian Chief Seattle (1786–1866) in 1854 when the US government sought to buy some of his land:

> How can you buy or sell the sky? The land? The idea is strange to us... Every part of this earth is sacred to my people. Every shining pine needle, every sandy shore, every mist in the dark woods, every meadow, every humming insect. All are holy in the memory and experience of my people... Will you teach your children what we have taught our children? That the earth is our mother? What befalls the earth befalls all the sons of earth. This we know: the earth does not belong to man, man belongs to the earth. All things are connected like the blood that unites us all. Man does not weave the web of life, he is merely a strand in it. Whatever he does to the web, he does to himself.

These fine words have sometimes been used to support the idea that before the arrival of the Europeans native Americans were living in peace and harmony with nature. However, historical research reveals that no one knows what Chief Seattle said on the day in question, and that the above speech was in fact written for an *ABC* television drama in 1971 by someone called Ted Perry!

Activity 10.6

What do you understand by George Orwell's observation, 'Who controls the past controls the future, who controls the present controls the past'? To what extent do you think it is true?

History enriches our understanding of human nature

History enriches our understanding of human nature by showing us what human beings have thought and done in a wide variety of circumstances. While subjects such as psychology, sociology and economics seek to explain things in terms of general principles, history focuses on the concrete and particular and reminds us that human behaviour can never be fully explained in terms of neat and tidy models.

Read the following quotation from the German philosopher Immanuel Kant (1724–1804):
'One cannot avoid a certain feeling of disgust, when one observes the actions of man displayed on the great stage of the world. Wisdom is manifested by individuals here and there; but the web of human history as a whole appears to be woven from folly and childish vanity, often, too, from puerile wickedness and love of destruction: with the result that at the end one is puzzled to know what idea to form of our species which prides itself so much on its advantages.'
From your own study of history, to what extent do you think that Kant's pessimistic assessment of human beings is justified? Are there any grounds for taking a more optimistic view?

Whether the historical record should make us feel optimistic or pessimistic about human nature is open to question. We should, however, be careful with the phrase 'History shows...' when it is used by someone who is trying to prove that something or other is an enduring feature of the human condition. It has, for example, been said that history shows that war is inevitable, or that different races are unable to live together in harmony. The problem with such beliefs is that they can easily become **self-realising expectations**; for if you think that something cannot be changed, you won't even bother *trying* to change it. However, the historical record can sometimes be a source of hope rather than despair; for it suggests that the future does not have to be like the past, and that it is possible to change things. The last 200 years have seen many historically unprecedented changes, such as the abolition of slavery, the emancipation of women, and the birth of the United Nations. Such changes would never have come about if people had seen themselves as the victims of history. Perhaps if we focused our energies on putting an end to war we really could bring about a more peaceful world!

How can the past be known?

History is concerned with the past, and one obvious problem with trying to know the past is that it no longer exists. Like fleeting shadows, things that happened long ago sometimes have an air of unreality about them, and we may find it hard to believe they really happened. At a sceptical extreme, it is abstractly possible that God created the universe five seconds ago together with apparent memories, fossils and copies of yesterday's newspapers. Since any evidence you give to the contrary – such as Stonehenge, the Rosetta stone, or the Elgin marbles – might itself have been created five seconds ago, it is impossible to falsify this belief. However, it is difficult to see why God should engage in such an elaborate deception. When it comes to it, no sane person seriously doubts the existence of the past any more than they seriously doubt the existence of the external world.

At the opposite extreme from scepticism, it could be argued that, since the past no longer exists, it cannot be changed and is therefore completely objective. In this vein, the historian G. R. Elton (1921–94) provocatively argued that:

> In a very real sense the study of history is concerned with a subject matter more objective and independent than that of the natural sciences. Just because historical matter is in the past, is gone... its objective reality is guaranteed; it is beyond being altered for any purpose whatsoever.

Activity 10.8

Compare Elton's claim that history is objective with Samuel Butler's (1835–1902) wry comment: 'Though God cannot alter the past, historians can.' Which of these views do you think is closer to the truth?

While you would probably agree that the past cannot be changed, when it comes to the question of whether or not history is objective, we should make a distinction between the past and our *knowledge* of the past. Elton's argument may show that the past is objective, but it says nothing about our knowledge of the past. Such knowledge is problematic because we can know the past only by reconstructing it on the basis of evidence that exists in the present. Since memory is fallible, evidence ambiguous, and prejudice common, we might have serious doubts about the claim that historical knowledge is more objective than scientific knowledge.

Despite these doubts, objectivity surely remains an important ideal in history. For if we abandon it, we have no way of distinguishing between history on the one hand, and propaganda and fiction on the other. The real question is to what extent a trained historian can approach the ideal of objectivity, and this requires that we look in more detail at the nature of historical evidence.

Primary sources

Historians commonly distinguish between **primary sources** and **secondary sources**. Roughly speaking, a primary source is one that is written by someone who was there at the time, while a secondary source is a later, second-hand account of what happened. For example, Julius Caesar's (100–44 BCE) *The Conquest of Gaul* is a primary source because it is Caesar's own account of the wars he fought. By contrast Edward Gibbon's (1737–94) *The Decline and Fall of the Roman Empire* is a secondary source because it is a much later reconstruction of the fate of the Roman Empire.

Some accounts of what happened in the past are based only on secondary sources. For example, if you write an essay about the causes of the French Revolution, your bibliography may list a range of history books but no original documents. But it is obvious that if such sources are to have any authority they must ultimately be grounded in primary sources – the first-hand accounts of individuals who witnessed the events in question. For this reason, primary sources are often described as the 'bedrock of history'.

Given our discussion of ways of knowing in Part 2, you might wonder how firm this bedrock is. For there are reasons for thinking that primary sources cannot be taken at face value and that they are, in a sense, already contaminated.

How can the four knowledge tools of perception, language, reason and emotion distort the production of a primary source such as a diary?

Fallible eye-witness

Imagine that several diarists are witness to the same historical events. We would probably end up with as many different accounts as there are writers. Since no two individuals see things in the same way, their perceptions are likely to be shaped by such things as their interests, expectations and cultural background. The role played by emotion and prejudice in perception may explain why rival soccer fans and warring countries often give such different accounts of the same events. Further biases may creep in when pen is put to paper. For a diarist must decide not only what to write down, but also how to describe what he has seen, and how to shape the stream of events into a coherent narrative. While some events may be exaggerated or described in emotional language, others may be played down or completely ignored.

Social bias

Another problem with primary sources is that they sometimes reflect the interests of one particular social group rather than society as a whole, and this may give us a distorted picture of things. For example, we tend to think that medieval Europe was a very religious place; but this may simply reflect the fact that the chroniclers of the time were mainly religious people who considered it important to record everything related to religion. If, as is usually the case, the people with the power control the pens and the printing presses, it is not surprising that primary sources have often reflected their interests and activities at the expense of other social groups. Since the illiterate usually pass through history without a trace, we will probably never know much about how Greek slaves, or feudal peasants, or Aztec warriors saw the world. Although their stories may be irredeemably lost, it is at least worth being aware of the blank pages in history.

Activity 10.10

If you were to make a time capsule to be opened in five thousand years' time, what things would you put in it to give future historians as objective a picture as possible of life in the early twenty-first century?

Deliberate manipulation

A more disturbing problem arises when primary sources are deliberately manipulated by governments and other interest groups to change the 'facts' of history. (Recall the photo on page 305 in which Trotsky has been airbrushed out.) Writing in 1944, the English writer George Orwell (1903–50) made the following observation:

Up to a fairly recent date, the major events recorded in the history books probably happened. It is probably true that the battle of Hastings was fought in 1066, that Columbus discovered America, that Henry VIII had six wives, and so on. A certain degree of truthfulness was possible so long as it was admitted that a fact may be true even if you don't like it. Even as late as the last war it was possible for the Encyclopedia Britannica, for instance, to compile its articles on the various campaigns partly from German sources. Some of the facts – the casualty figures, for instance – were regarded as neutral and in substance accepted by everybody. No such thing would be possible now. A Nazi and a non-Nazi version of the present war would have no resemblance to one another, and which of them finally gets into the history books will be decided not by evidential methods but on the battlefield....

   During part of 1941 and 1942, when the Luftwaffe was busy in Russia, the German radio regaled its home audiences with stories of devastating air raids on London. Now, we are aware that those raids did not happen. But what use would our knowledge be if the Germans conquered Britain? For the purposes of a future historian, did those raids happen, or didn't they? The answer is: If Hitler survives, they happened, and if he falls they didn't happen.

Orwell's point is that if the Nazis had won the war then the basic 'facts' would have been what the propaganda ministry said they were, and all kinds of lies would have made their way into the history books and so become 'truths'. Fortunately, the Nazis did not win; and in an open society freedom of speech helps to ensure that there are some limits on a government's ability to manipulate the truth. Doubtless, we are still the victims of a great deal of 'spin' and misinformation; but behind the propaganda fog one hopes that it is still possible to discern at least an outline of the truth.

Activity 10.11

According to a well-known adage, 'history is written by the victors'. How different do you think it would be if it were written by the losers instead?

So what are we to say about the worth of primary sources? Despite their limitations, I think that, if they are properly used, we should not be overly sceptical about their value. There are, after all, ways of distinguishing a more reliable from a less reliable source. To start with, we can ask questions such as: Who wrote it? What was their motive in writing? How long after the event was it written? In addition, we can compare different primary sources to see how far they agree with one another. For example, if Israeli and Palestinian eye-witnesses agree about something, then it is likely to be true. Finally, we can look at documents of a legal and administrative nature which are less likely to be biased than such things as letters and diaries. So although it would be naive to accept primary sources at face value, some of them are reliable, and in the end they are all that we have to distinguish truth from fiction.

   The fact that historians frequently disagree with one another should not blind us to the truth that there are a vast number of basic historical facts that everyone agrees about. No one seriously doubts that Julius Caesar crossed the Rubicon in 49 BCE, or that the atomic bomb was dropped on Hiroshima in 1945, or that Nelson Mandela was released from prison in 1990. There is, however, far less agreement about the meaning and significance of such facts.

Writing history

As we said earlier, history is more than a catalogue of past events, and the main job of the historian is to explain and interpret the past. The starting point of historical investigation is often a question or problem which reflects contemporary preoccupations. Such preoccupations may give the historian an interest in the causes of war, or the growth of democracy, or the status of women. Our current worries about the environment have led to a growing interest in the role played by environmental factors in the rise and fall of civilisations.

History is a selection of a selection

When it comes to writing history, the historian will usually have to make a selection from the available evidence – for, as we saw earlier, it is usually impossible to deal with in its entirety. Since primary sources are themselves a selective interpretation of events, this effectively means that history is a selection of a selection, and so is twice removed from what actually happened.

    The fact that our knowledge of the past is filtered first through the eyes of those who witnessed it, and then through the eyes of the historian who wrote about it can make it difficult to establish the truth, but, as we saw above, it is by no means a hopeless task. For if a historian is aware of the bias in her primary sources, she may be able to compensate for it. Moreover, when it comes to secondary sources, an exhaustive survey of all the available evidence would be as undesirable as it is impossible. Imagine trying to read a history of the cultural revolution in China which included literally all of the evidence. Not only would the book be absurdly large, but you would end up drowning in a sea of detail and be unable to see the wood for the trees. This may explain Lytton Strachey's (1880–1932) paradoxical observation that 'Ignorance is the first requisite of the historian, ignorance which simplifies and clarifies, which selects and omits.'

The advantages of hindsight

One of the advantages a historian has over the people whose behaviour he describes is *hindsight*. Unlike them, *he* knows how things turned out. An event which seemed insignificant at the time might later turn out to be of great importance, and vice versa. At the end of the day on which the Bastille fell, Louis XVI is said to have written in his diary the single word '*Rien*' – 'Nothing'; but we now see this event as heralding the beginning of the French Revolution.

    Furthermore, certain ways of describing events may not be available to people at the time, but only retrospectively. For example, we can say 'The author of *War and Peace* was born in 1828', but that was not a description available to Tolstoy's mother at the time of his birth. Similarly, we can talk about the First World War, but since people in the 1920s did not know there would be another one they called it the Great War. (Sadly, their description of the First World War as 'the war to end all wars' now sounds very hollow.)

The division of history into various periods is similarly influenced by hindsight. In European history, we commonly speak of eras such as 'the Dark Ages', 'the Renaissance', and 'the Enlightenment'. But, of course, no one drew the curtains one morning in fourteen-hundred-and-something and said 'Hey people, it's the Renaissance!' Such terms are retrospective ways of trying to capture the spirit of a particular historical era.

Activity 10.12

1 What description do you think future historians will use to sum up the age in which we are living?
2 According to the historian G. M. Trevelyan (1876–1962), 'Unlike dates, periods are not facts. They are retrospective conceptions that we form about past events, useful to focus discussion, but very often leading historical thought astray.' How can dividing history into periods be useful and how can it be misleading?

The writing of history is also influenced by the era in which it is written. The passage of time is constantly adding new pages to the book of history, and this means that what has gone before will be reassessed by each new generation in the light of subsequent experience. Since we judge events partly in the light of their consequences, this suggests that we may be too close to recent events to understand their significance. We can, for example, only speculate about how future historians will look back on the invasion of Iraq in 2003. As an event recedes into the past, it is usually easier to see it in its historical context, but we may never be able to come to a definitive interpretation. When the Chinese premier Chou En Lai (1898–1976) was asked what he thought the impact of the French Revolution was, he famously replied: 'It is too soon to tell.' This may have been said in jest, but it reminds us of the fact that, until the story of humanity comes to an end, there can be no last word in history.

Since each generation interprets the past in the light of its own experience, we might agree with E. H. Carr's characterisation of history as 'an unending dialogue between the present and the past'. This suggests that when you read Gibbon's *The Decline and Fall of the Roman Empire* you may learn as much about the values and prejudices of eighteenth-century England as about the events Gibbon purports to describe.

Activity 10.13

Do you think you should study current events in history – say, things that have happened in the last five years – on the grounds that they are relevant to your experience, or do you think they should be excluded on the grounds that they are too close for you to see them objectively?

The disadvantages of hindsight

Despite the advantages of hindsight in helping us to determine the significance of things, it can also distort our understanding of the past. When you are living through events they seem genuinely open and you are not sure how they will turn out; but when you look back on them, it is hard to avoid the feeling that they were inevitable and could not have happened any other way. This can easily lead to **hindsight bias**. After a catastrophe, it is easy to believe that any fool could have seen what would happen, and that if you had been in the situation in question you would never have made the same mistake.

To give an example, in March 1980, US president Jimmy Carter sought to rescue seventy Americans who were being held hostage in Tehran, Iran. The mission was aborted when a sandstorm disabled half the helicopters being used in the operation. Afterwards, many journalists said that the rescue attempt had been 'doomed from the start', but they said this only after they knew that it had failed. If there had been no sandstorm and the hostages had been successfully rescued, the same journalists might have been praising Carter for his vision, courage and daring.

The fact is that we are all good at being wise after the event. When we look back at the Second World War, it is hard to avoid thinking that Hitler was bound to lose; but that was hardly a foregone conclusion in 1940 when Britain was on the verge of collapse and the United States had not yet entered the war. Similarly, many commentators now see the collapse of communism in Eastern Europe as inevitable, but almost no one was predicting its fall in the 1970s. If we are to get into the minds of historical actors and see situations as they themselves saw them, then we must try to avoid such hindsight bias.

Our discussion suggests that hindsight can be both a benefit and a drawback to the historian. On the plus side, it enables us to see the significance of events in the light of their consequences; on the minus side, it may lead to our being wise after the event and failing to appreciate how open and uncertain the past was to the people living through it.

The problem of bias

We should now go back to the problem of **bias** – which we mentioned in our discussion of primary sources – and address the widespread perception that history is more prone to bias than the natural sciences. There are at least three reasons why someone might think that this is the case:

1   *Topic choice bias*   A historian's choice of topic may be influenced by current preoccupations; and the questions that he asks – or fails to ask – are likely to influence the answers that he finds.

2   *Confirmation bias*   A historian might be tempted to appeal only to evidence that supports his own case and to ignore any counter-evidence. (As we have seen in Chapters 8 and 9, this is also a problem in the natural and human sciences: see pages 230–1 and 278.)

3   *National bias*   Since people come to history with a range of pre-existing cultural and political prejudices, they may find it difficult to deal objectively with sensitive issues that touch on things like national pride. Questions such as 'To what extent were ordinary Germans aware of the Holocaust?', or 'Was the British bombing of Dresden a war crime?', or 'Why did the United States drop the atomic bomb on Hiroshima?' may be hard to answer without strong emotions colouring our interpretation of the facts. Faced with such questions, the danger is that we begin with our prejudices and then search for the evidence to support them. At worst, history may then become little more than the finding of bad reasons for what we believe on prejudice.

Although we should not underestimate the danger of bias in history, something can be said in response to these points.

Topic choice bias   Although a historian's choice of topic may be influenced by the society he grows up in, this does not necessarily mean that the topic, once chosen, cannot be studied objectively. This is not so different from the situation in the natural sciences. For example, during the Second World War, some US physicists were doing atomic research as part of the Manhattan Project to develop the atomic bomb. The direction of research was clearly determined by social priorities, but the research itself was objective in the sense that it was conducted in accordance with the scientific method. With respect to both science and history, it could therefore be said that, while there may be an element of bias in one's *choice* of topic, this will not necessarily affect one's *treatment* of it.

Confirmation bias   Although history is selective and a bad historian may be tempted to simply find the facts he is looking for, a good historian is likely to do the opposite and actively seek out evidence that goes against his hypothesis. As a matter of fact, as the historian Keith Windschuttle (1942–) has observed, it is a common experience among historians to find that the evidence 'forces them, often reluctantly, to change the position they originally intended to take'.

National bias   When it comes to the third point, it must be admitted that there is a serious danger of national bias infecting history. However, if rival historians of different nationalities and with different background assumptions and prejudices are able to critique one another's work, then at least the more obvious errors and biases should be rooted out.

Activity 10.14

Do you think that it will ever be possible to write a history of the world that can be agreed on by all countries?

A pluralistic approach

There is, of course, no easy solution to the problem of bias, for we can never entirely escape from our own prejudices and achieve a god's-eye view of history. Since history has often been used to promote the interests of dominant nations and powerful elites it is not surprising that some people are suspicious of the official version of the truth. And in an increasingly multi-cultural world, one might argue that textbooks should reflect the experiences not only of elites, but also of groups such as women, the poor, and ethnic minorities. Indeed, rather than speak of *history* in the singular, it might be better to think in terms of *histories*. The ideal might then be a kind of **cubist history** which, like a painting by Picasso, explores the past from a variety of perspectives.

Such a pluralistic approach to history does not mean that we have to abandon the ideal of historical truth, or say that there are as many truths as there are people writing history. For within each approach to history there are likely to be better and worse reconstructions of the past. For example, while some women's histories may be more propagandist and emotional, others are likely to be more accurate and objective. Thus we can embrace a pluralistic approach to history without succumbing to relativism.

While there are many different perspectives in history, I think that we still need to keep hold of some notion of historical truth. For at a brute level, it is surely the case that event X either did or did not happen. And although it is often difficult to discover the truth, this does not mean that there is no truth to discover. We surely owe it to the victims of the genocides that have punctuated world history to bear witness to the fact that these things really happened.

Theories of history

In discussing the nature of history earlier in this chapter, I said that it is not simply concerned with *describing* the past, but also with *explaining* it. We usually explain something in terms of the causes that brought it about; but since history deals with complex situations, it is often difficult to isolate *the* unique cause of an event.

Activity 10.15

1 At the battle of Waterloo in 1815 Napoleon Bonaparte was defeated by the British commander, the Duke of Wellington. Which of the following factors do you think a historian might take into account in explaining Napoleon's defeat?

   a There was a communications breakdown between Napoleon's generals.

   b Napoleon's parents did not die in infancy.

   c At Waterloo, Napoleon was suffering from chronic haemorrhoids which made it difficult for him to mount a horse.

   d The wet weather led Napoleon to postpone his attack on Wellington.

   e Napoleon underestimated Wellington's abilities as a general.

   f Newton's laws of motion determined the flight of the artillery shells.

   g The French troops didn't have any nails to put Wellington's captured artillery pieces out of action.

   h During the battle Marshall Ney had five horses shot from underneath him and this caused him to make errors of judgement.

2 Do you think it would be possible to isolate one of the above factors and see it as decisive in explaining Napoleon's defeat?

In considering the above factors, you probably dismissed **b** and **f** as irrelevant to the historian. Admittedly, if Napoleon's parents had died in infancy, Napoleon would not have been around to lose at Waterloo; and if the laws of motion had been different, the artillery would not have worked as expected. But neither of these factors explains Napoleon's defeat because the existence of Napoleon and Newton's laws of motion were as necessary to victory as to defeat.

What we are looking for when we seek to explain Napoleon's defeat is *the factor that made the difference*. At this point, however, it is worth pointing out that there is rarely one single cause of an event – especially a complex event such as a battle. Indeed, we might agree with the historian H. A. L. Fisher (1856–1940) when he observed: 'The human universe is so enormously complicated that to speak of *the* cause of any event is an absurdity.' Rather than there being a unique cause of Napoleon's defeat, it is more likely that it resulted from a combination of factors, such as bad communications, the weather and (possibly) haemorrhoids!

In considering the engine of historical change, we might think in terms of a range of causal factors from the more general to the more specific. Such factors might include:

- geographical conditions   individual motives
- social and economic conditions   chance occurrences.

Some historians who are interested in the broad sweep of history have argued that the history of civilisations ultimately depends on such geographical factors as situation, climate and soil. For example, a country with access to the sea and good natural harbours is likely to develop in a quite different way to a land-locked mountainous country. In a fascinating book called *Guns, Germs and Steel*, the American academic Jared Diamond has argued that the main reason why some cultures have been historically more successful than others has more to do with differences in geography than with differences in the natural abilities of different races. This is an attractive thesis for anyone interested in promoting international understanding (although we should keep in mind that the attractiveness of a thesis does not in itself make it true).

Activity 10.16

To what extent do you think that your country's history has been influenced by its geography?

The 'great person' theory of history

As the name suggests, the 'great person' theory of history holds that the course of history is mainly determined by great individuals. For example, the historian A. J. P. Taylor (1906–90) claimed that 'The history of modern Europe can be written in terms of three titans: Napoleon, Bismarck and Lenin.' What this theory implies is that if one or other great individual had not existed, then the course of history would have been different. Winston Churchill (1874–1965), who wrote history as well as making it, was sympathetic to this view. His grandson Nicholas Soames tells the story of how, when he was six years old, he once crept in to Churchill's study and asked in awe 'Grandpapa, is it true you are the greatest man in the world?' 'Yes,' replied Churchill, 'and now bugger off!'

Collingwood on empathy

If the focus of historical research is on individuals, then we need to get beyond the outside of events, and think ourselves into the minds of the agents. According to the historian R. G. Collingwood (1889–1943), with whom this idea is particularly associated:

> When a historian asks 'Why did Brutus stab Caesar?' he means 'What did Brutus think which made him decide to stab Caesar?' The cause of the event, for him, means the thought in the mind of the person by whose agency the event came about: and this is not something other than the event, it is the inside of the event itself... All history is the history of thought.

What Collingwood meant by his observation that 'all history is the history of thought' is that we can understand people's actions only by delving in to their minds and trying to make sense of their motives. Collingwood drew particular attention to the importance of **empathy** in trying to understand a situation in the same way that a historical agent would have understood it. Some people have gone further and used ideas from psychoanalysis to shed light on the motivations of historical characters.

Despite its merits, a number of criticisms can be made of Collingwood's approach to history. To start with, although the ability to empathise may be a useful tool of the historian's trade, it clearly has its limits. For most people would find it difficult to empathise with some of the monsters of history, such as Genghis Khan, Ivan the Terrible, or Adolf Hitler. Furthermore, in trying to explain historical events, it is not clear why we should limit ourselves to the agent's perception of the situation. As we saw earlier, one of the advantages that a historian has over the people he studies is hindsight, and his retrospective vantage point may enable him to find a significance in events that was not apparent to people at the time.

How important are individuals?

A more fundamental criticism of the 'great person' approach is that it exaggerates the role played by individuals in the process of historical change. In his novel *War and Peace*, the Russian writer Leo Tolstoy (1828–1910) speculates on the nature of history and argues that, far from being in control of events, Napoleon was the passive instrument of much deeper historical currents:

> Although in that year, 1812, Napoleon believed more than ever that to shed or not to shed the blood of his peoples depended entirely on his will (as Alexander said in his last letter to him), yet then, and more than at any time, he was in bondage to those laws which forced him, while to himself he seemed to be acting freely, to do what was bound to be his share in the common edifice of humanity, in history.

Economic determinism

At the other extreme from the 'great person' view of history is a theory known as **economic determinism**. This theory claims that history is determined by economic factors, and its most famous exponent was Karl Marx (1818–83). Marx claimed to have discovered the laws of historical change which operate with 'iron necessity', and from which the future course of history can be predicted; and he claimed to have done for history what Isaac Newton (1642–1727) did for physics almost two centuries earlier. According to Marx, it is not great individuals but rather technological and economic factors that are the engines of historical change. For changes in technology determine how society is organised, and this in turn determines how individuals think. An industrial economy, for example, will need to be organised in a very different way from a peasant economy, and this will affect how people think about such things as time, work and money. So rather than focusing on the actions of great men, we might do better to study the effects of key inventions such as the printing press, the steam engine and the computer.

Activity 10.19

1 Which invention do you think has had the most decisive impact on history in the last two thousand years, and why?

2 Do you agree or disagree with Marx's claim that technology plays a bigger role in shaping the future than the actions of individuals?

3 We can predict the behaviour of a gas with a great deal of accuracy even though the behaviour of an individual molecule is unpredictable. Do you think that, in a similar way, we can make accurate predictions about society even though individual behaviour is unpredictable?

Marx's emphasis on economics as the engine of historical change has been very influential, but most people now reject his deterministic approach to history. The idea that one can predict the future from a study of history seems intuitively implausible, and Marx's own predictions about where revolutions would occur have not in fact come true.

The philosopher Karl Popper (1902–94) went further in his criticism of Marx, saying that the belief in the predictability of the future is not merely implausible, but *incoherent*. The essence of Popper's argument is that if you could perfectly predict the future then you would be able to predict such things as future scientific discoveries; but if you could predict the details of such discoveries, you would then have discovered them now and not in the future – and that contradicts the original supposition.

The role of chance

Some people have concluded that there is no meaning in history and that it is governed by chance. This idea was dramatised by the French philosopher Blaise Pascal (1623–62) when he observed: 'Had Cleopatra's nose been shorter, the whole history of the world would have been different.' For if Cleopatra's nose had been shorter Mark Antony might have found her less attractive and not fallen in love with her. If Mark Antony had not fallen in love with Cleopatra, he might not have fallen out with Octavian (the future emperor Augustus). If Mark Antony and Octavian had not fallen out, Rome might have remained a republic rather than becoming an empire. If Rome had remained a republic it might have been able to resist the barbarian invasions of the fourth and fifth centuries. And if Rome had resisted the barbarian invasions it might never have fallen, and Europeans and North Africans might still be living under the Roman dispensation!

Most people would agree that unpredictable events do play an important role in history. For example, if Hitler had died in a car accident in 1930, the subsequent history of Europe – and, indeed, the world – would probably have been quite different. Nevertheless, it seems too extreme to say that history is an entirely random process. So perhaps we should adopt a compromise position and say that history is driven by a mixture of great people, technological factors and chance events. We may not be able to find any fixed patterns, but a good historian can still help us to make sense of the past by distinguishing its main strands and weaving them into a meaningful narrative.

Conclusion

Despite the fact that the past no longer exists, history seeks to reconstruct it on the basis of evidence that can be found in the present. In this chapter we have seen that scepticism about the past is no more justified than any other form of scepticism and that it is possible to establish a bedrock of generally agreed historical facts. There is, however, much less agreement about the meaning and significance of these facts. For there are many different interpretations of the past, and trying to determine which one is the best is a matter of judgement rather than proof. But if history is not to collapse into fiction, we must take seriously the idea that there is some kind of truth about the past and that a good historian can at least help us to get closer to this truth.

Why study history? To understand the present! Do we learn from history? The jury is still out! You have doubtless heard it said that we should study the past to learn from our mistakes. But, since history never repeats itself, there are no simple lessons that we can take from the past and mechanically apply to the present. What the study of history can perhaps give us is something altogether more elusive: good judgement about human affairs. If that is the case, then we might agree with the historian Jacob Burckhardt (1818–97) that it does not 'make us more clever the next time, but wiser for all time'.

- History seeks to study and explain the significant events of the past on the basis of currently existing evidence.
- The study of history can be justified on the grounds that it contributes to our sense of identity, is a defence against propaganda, and enriches our understanding of human nature.
- History is based on primary sources, but since they are a selective interpretation of events, they cannot always be taken at face value.
- Since historians usually make a selection from the available evidence, there is a sense in which history books are twice removed from what actually happened.
- In seeking to explain the past, a historian has the advantage of hindsight, but this can sometimes result in hindsight bias.
- Although it is impossible to achieve a completely objective, God's-eye view of history, we can perhaps get closer to the truth by exploring the past from a variety of perspectives.
- Since history deals with complex situations, historical events rarely have a single cause but are usually the result of a combination of factors.
- Two contrasting theories of history are the great person theory, which says that history is determined by great individuals, and economic determinism, which says that it is determined by economic factors.
- We can understand both the past and ourselves better if we study history than if we choose to ignore it.

Terms to remember

bias	hindsight bias
cubist history	primary source
economic determinism	secondary source
empathy	self-realising expectations
great person theory of history	

Further reading

Barbara Tuchman, *Practising History* (Papermac, 1983). This book consists of a series of insightful essays on the nature and value of history. Try 'When does history happen?' or 'The historian as artist'.

Niall Ferguson (ed.), *Virtual History* (Picador, 1997). This book consists of nine speculative essays on what might have happened if historical episodes had turned out differently, such as 'What if Germany had invaded Britain in May 1940?' and 'What if Communism had not collapsed?' Read any one of these essays and it will soon have you thinking about the nature of historical explanations.

Linking questions

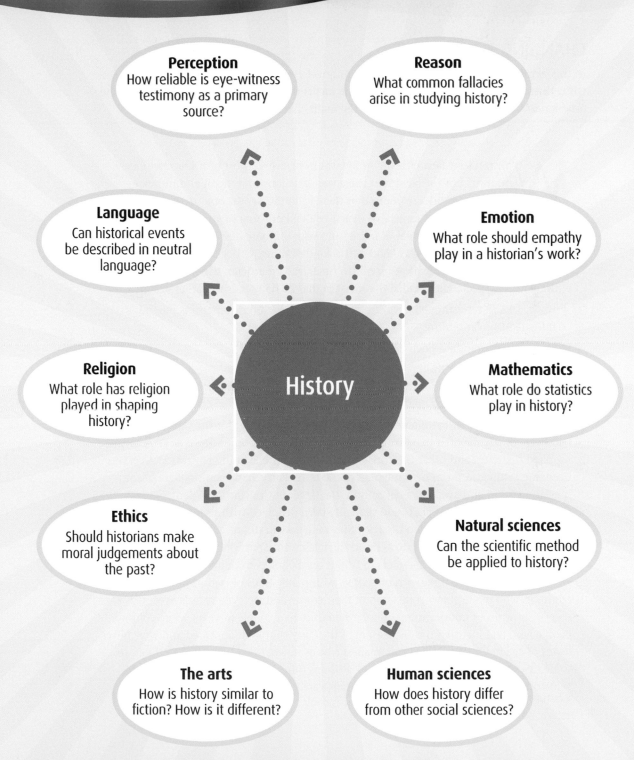

Perception
How reliable is eye-witness testimony as a primary source?

Reason
What common fallacies arise in studying history?

Language
Can historical events be described in neutral language?

Emotion
What role should empathy play in a historian's work?

Religion
What role has religion played in shaping history?

History

Mathematics
What role do statistics play in history?

Ethics
Should historians make moral judgements about the past?

Natural sciences
Can the scientific method be applied to history?

The arts
How is history similar to fiction? How is it different?

Human sciences
How does history differ from other social sciences?

CHANGING THE PAST

In this extract from George Orwell's dystopian novel *1984*, we glimpse a chilling world in which history is rewritten every time someone incurs the displeasure of Big Brother and the totalitarian state in which Winston Smith, the main character of the book, lives.

Winston's greatest pleasure in life was in his work. Most of it was a tedious routine, but included in it there were also jobs so difficult and intricate that you could lose yourself in them as in the depths of a mathematical problem – delicate pieces of forgery in which you had nothing to guide you except your knowledge of the principles of Ingsoc and your estimate of what the Party wanted you to say. Winston was good at this kind of thing. On occasion he had even been entrusted with the rectification of the *Times* leading articles, which were written entirely in Newspeak. He unrolled the message that he had set aside earlier. It ran:

> times 3.12.83 reporting bb dayorder doubleplus-ungood refs unpersons rewrite fullwise upsub antefiling.

In Oldspeak (or standard English) this might be rendered:

> The reporting of Big Brother's Order for the Day in the *Times* of December 3rd 1983 is extremely unsatisfactory and makes references to nonexistent persons. Rewrite it in full and submit your draft to higher authority before filing.

Winston read through the offending article. Big Brother's Order for the Day, it seemed, had been chiefly devoted to praising the work of an organization known as FFCC, which supplied cigarettes and other comforts to the sailors in the Floating Fortresses. A certain Comrade Withers, a prominent member of the Inner Party, had been singled out for special mention and awarded a decoration, the Order of Conspicuous Merit, Second Class. Three months later FFCC had suddenly been dissolved with no reasons given. One could assume that Withers and his associates were now in disgrace, but there had been no report of the matter in the press or on the telescreen. That was to be expected, since it was unusual for political offenders to be put on trial or even publicly denounced. The great purges involving thousands of people, with public trials of traitors and thought-criminals who made abject confession of their crimes and were afterwards executed, were special showpieces not occurring oftener than once in a couple of years. More commonly, people who had incurred the displeasure of the Party simply disappeared and were never heard of again. One never had the smallest clue as to what had happened to them. In some cases they might not even be dead. Perhaps thirty people personally known to Winston, not counting his parents, had disappeared at one time or another.

Winston stroked his nose gently with a paper clip. In the cubicle across the way Comrade Tillotson was still crouching secretively over his speakwrite. He raised his head for a moment: again the hostile spectacle-flash. Winston wondered whether Comrade Tillotson was engaged on the same job as himself. It was perfectly possible. So tricky a piece of work would never be entrusted to a single person; on the other hand, to turn it over to a committee would be to admit openly that an act of fabrication was taking place. Very likely as many as a dozen people were now working away on rival versions of what Big Brother had actually said. And presently some master brain in the Inner Party would select this version or that, would re-edit it and set in motion the complex processes of cross-referencing that would be required, and then the chosen lie would pass into the permanent records and become truth.

Winston did not know why Withers had been disgraced. Perhaps it was for corruption or incompetence. Perhaps Big Brother was merely getting rid of a too-popular subordinate. Perhaps Withers or someone close to him had been suspected of heretical tendencies. Or perhaps – what was likeliest of all – the thing had simply happened because purges and vaporizations were a necessary part of the mechanics of government. The only real clue lay in the words 'refs unpersons,' which indicated that Withers was already dead. You could not invariably assume this to be the case when people were arrested. Sometimes they were released and allowed to remain at liberty for as much as a year or two years before being executed. Very occasionally some persons whom you had believed dead long since would make a ghostly reappearance at some public trial where he would implicate hundreds of others by his testimony before vanishing, this time forever. Withers, however, was already an unperson. He did not exist; he had never existed. Winston decided that it would not be enough simply to reverse the tendency of Big Brother's speech. It was better to make it deal with something totally unconnected with its original subject.

He might turn the speech into the usual denunciation of traitors and thought-criminals, but that was a little too obvious, while to invent a victory at the front, or some triumph of over-production in the Ninth Three-Year Plan, might complicate the records too much. What was needed was a piece of pure fantasy. Suddenly there sprang into his mind, ready-made as it were, the image of a certain Comrade Ogilvy, who had recently died in battle, in heroic circumstances. There were occasions when Big Brother devoted his Order for the Day to commemorating some humble, rank-and-file Party member whose life and death he held up as an example worthy to be followed. Today he should commemorate Comrade Ogilvy. It was true that there was no such person as Comrade Ogilvy, but a few lines of print and a couple of faked photographs would soon bring him into existence.

Winston thought for a moment, then pulled the speakwrite toward him and began dictating in Big Brother's familiar style: a style at once military and pedantic, and, because of a trick of asking questions and then promptly answering them ('What lessons do we learn from this fact, comrades? The lessons – which is also one of the fundamental principles of Ingsoc – that,' etc., etc.), easy to imitate.

At the age of three Comrade Ogilvy had refused all toys except a drum, a submachine gun, and a model helicopter. At six – a year early, by a special relaxation of the rules – he had joined the Spies; at nine he had been a troop leader. At eleven he had denounced his uncle to the Thought Police after overhearing a conversation which appeared to him to have criminal tendencies. At seventeen he had been a district organizer of the Junior Anti-Sex League. At nineteen he had designed a hand grenade which had been adopted by the Ministry of Peace and which, at its first trial, had killed thirty-one Eurasian prisoners in one burst. At twenty-three he had perished in action. Pursued by enemy jet planes while flying over the Indian Ocean with important despatches, he had weighted his body with his machine gun and leapt out of the helicopter into deep water, despatches and all – an end, said Big Brother, which it was impossible to contemplate without feelings of envy. Big Brother added a few remarks on the purity and singlemindedness of Comrade Ogilvy's life. He was a total abstainer and a nonsmoker, had no recreations except a daily hour in the gymnasium, and had taken a vow of celibacy, believing marriage and the care of family to be incompatible with a twenty-four-hour-a-day devotion to duty. He had no subjects of conversation except the principles of Ingsoc, and no aim in life except the defeat of the Eurasian enemy and the hunting-down of spies, saboteurs, thought-criminals, and traitors generally.

Winston debated with himself whether to award Comrade Ogilvy the Order of Conspicuous Merit; and in the end he decided against it because of the unnecessary crossreferencing that it would entail.

Once again he glanced at his rival in the opposite cubicle. Something seemed to tell him with certainty that Tillotson was busy on the same job as himself. There was no way of knowing whose version would finally be adopted, but he felt a profound conviction that it would be his own. Comrade Ogilvy, unimagined an hour ago, was now a fact. It struck him as curious that you could create dead men but not living ones. Comrade Ogilvy, who had never existed in the present, now existed in the past, and when once the act of forgery was forgotten, he would exist just as authentically, and upon the same evidence as Charlemagne or Julius Caesar.

HISTORY AS 'SOME KIND OF A NOVEL'

In this article, the diplomat and historian George F. Kennan (1904–2005) explores the similarities and differences between history and fiction.

The historian is not a mere purveyor. He does not stand entirely outside the historical evidence he brings to your attention. He stands in many ways inside of it. True, he describes historical events. And if he is a true historian he describes them as accurately as they can be described on the strength of the available record. But he was not there. He did not see these events with his own eyes; or if he was there, and did see them, then what we are talking about is journalism or autobiography but not history. And not having been there and not having seen them, what does he have to start with when he envisages them and portrays them for us? He has as a rule only the hieroglyphics of the written word, as preserved in the crumbling old documents, and sometimes a few artifacts that have survived the ravages of time and neglect – perhaps even a portrait, or a drawing, or, if he works in recent history, a photograph or two. But these evidences only hint at the real story – they don't tell it. It is up to the historian to examine them critically and imaginatively, to select among them (for they are often multitudinous in number), to try to penetrate the reality behind them and to try to depict them in a way that reveals their meaning. And to accomplish this task what does he have to draw upon? Only what he already has within him: his knowledge, of course, of the historical background, his level of cultural sensitivity, his ability to put the isolated bit of evidence into the larger context and, above all, his capacity for insight and empathy, his ability to identify with the historical figures he describes, his educated instinct for what is significant and what is not – in other words, his creative imagination.

What emerges from this scrutiny is something that is, of necessity, highly subjective. It is not, and cannot be, the absolute and total truth. It is, if the writer is a conscientious historian, as close to the truth as he can possibly make it. But it remains a vision of the past – not the past in its pure form (no one could ever recreate that), but the past as one man is capable of seeing it, of envisaging it, of depicting it. It is perceived reality – reality in the eyes of the beholder – the only kind of reality that can have meaning for other human beings and be useful to them. This is why every work of history – at least of narrative or explanatory history – is at least as revealing of the person who wrote it, and of the period in which it was written, as it is of the people it portrays, and of the epoch in which they lived.

I can recall experiencing upon the completion of my first work of history (a work on the initial months of the Soviet–American relationship in 1917–18) a moment of panic when the question presented itself to me: What is it that I have done here? Perhaps what I have written is not really history but rather some sort of a novel, the product of my imagination – an imagination stimulated, inspired and informed, let us hope, by the documents I have been reading, but imagination nevertheless.

In retrospect, I think the panic was exaggerated and unnecessary. I had, after all, obeyed to the best of my ability the rules of my trade as a historian – the first of which was to respect the evidence and not to go beyond it. And this, the question of the restrictions and limitations one accepts, is the point at which historical writing does indeed differ from other forms of literature. The historian may not give his imagination free rein. He is bound to respect the chronology of events as the documents reveal it, even when that chronology is contradictory and confusing. He cannot arrange the facts for dramatic or aesthetic effect, as can the novelist. He has to take his characters as he finds them; he may not invent them, or make them up as an amalgam of people he has known. The historical truth he pursues (even though he never fully achieves it) is not the same sort of truth as that pursued by the novelist or the poet. These latter also pursue truth – sometimes even historical truth – and they also have restraints and limitations they have to respect, but what they are after is truth of a deeper and more intimate nature. It is primarily truth sensed, felt and moulded for effect, only secondarily truth observed; whereas in the case of the historian it is just the other way around.

Sometimes the historian... is carried away with the obvious elements of drama or tragedy in what he is describing, and is tempted to reach beyond his prescribed field and to encroach upon the liberties of the novelist in order to make his point more emphatically. In the last work of history I published, I had occasion to describe a rather pathetic funeral – the funeral of a Russian statesman, Nicholas Giers, foreign minister under Czar Alexander III, a modest man for whose strivings I had much

sympathy but one who had outlived his time and become forgotten almost before he was dead. I described the funeral in these words:

'Giers' body was laid to rest, with a few family members and officials in attendance, at the so-called Sergiyevskaya Pustyn – a monastery retreat on the shores of the Gulf of Finland, along the road to Peterhof, on January 31, 1895. It was a clear, bleak wintry day. It had snowed during the night. A chill wind swept in from across the partially frozen waters of the gulf. The little band of mourners were no doubt glad to get home, after the ceremony, and to inaugurate, with a warming glass of vodka, the process of oblivion that so soon overtakes the memory of statesmen who have labored too modestly and lived too long.'

Now I confess that I cannot swear that a cold wind was sweeping in across the waters of the Gulf of Finland on that wintry day. I was not totally without reason for supposing that this was the case. I had once lived for six months on the shores of that same gulf. I had memories of the winds that could blow across it. I had taken the trouble to consult the weather reports in the St. Petersburg papers of that time. The day was indeed a cold one. It had indeed snowed. But I have no binding evidence that the wind was actually blowing; and I must admit that in suggesting it was, I exceeded my true competence as a historian.

This was, however, a small transgression, a rare and isolated lapse, I hope, from the rules of the trade. I cite it only as an example of the temptations to which the historian is sometimes subject. Generally speaking, I was supported, as all historians must be, by the discipline of my profession – the stricture, that is, against going against what the evidence reveals. And if there were odd moments when this discipline hampered me, in general I found it a source of strength. It is not everyone who can safely and effectively give full rein to his feelings and his imagination, as does the poet, the playwright or the writer of fiction. That is heady stuff, and not for everyone. Some of us need the protection of an external discipline – in this case the commitment to demonstrable historical fact – to keep us in touch with reality. And this is not a bad thing. It was, after all, a poet, Goethe, who observed that it was precisely in the restraints the artist consents to accept that the true artistic mastery reveals itself.

Let us go on then, hand in hand – the poet, the novelist or the dramaturgist in his own stratosphere of the inspired imagination and the commitment to sheer beauty; the historian crawling, earthbound, among his dusty records, like a bird without wings, but also a searcher for the truth, and sometimes the discoverer of it.

Both are committed to the task of helping contemporary man to see himself: the one through the searching prism of personal experience, the other through the revealing footprints that his ancestors – men, after all, like himself – can be shown to have left on the sands of time.

Each of these literary efforts serves, in its own way, the cause of self-knowledge. And in this bewildering and dangerous age, when the very preservation of civilization has been placed, as though by some angry and impatient deity, in the weak and trembling human hands that have so long abused it, what greater cause, what nobler commitment, could there be than to help people to see themselves as they really are? And what generation could ever have been more in need of that self-scrutiny, that self-awareness and that self-judgment than the one to which we, poor denizens of this 20th century, have the fortune, and the misfortune, to belong.

11 The arts

'Art is what you can get away with.'
Andy Warhol, 1928–87

'Life imitates art more than art imitates life.'
Oscar Wilde, 1854–1900

'Art is meant to disturb, science reassures.'
Georges Braque, 1882–1963

'The essential function of art is moral.'
D. H. Lawrence, 1885–1930

'Art is not a copy of the real world; one of the damn things is quite enough.'
Virginia Woolf, 1882–1941

'Lying, the telling of beautiful untrue things, is the proper aim of art.'
Oscar Wilde, 1854–1900

'An artist is always out of step with the time. He has to be.'
Orson Welles, 1915–85

'Art is a human activity, whose purpose is the transmission of the highest and best feelings to which men have attained.'
Leo Tolstoy, 1828–1910

'God is really only another artist. He invented the giraffe, the elephant and the cat. He has no real style. He just goes on trying other things.'
Pablo Picasso, 1881–1973

'The art of seeing nature is a thing almost as much to be acquired as the art of reading the Egyptian hieroglyphs.'
John Constable, 1776–1837

'Art is a lie that makes us realize the truth – at least the truth that is given us to understand.'
Pablo Picasso, 1881–1973

'[In poetry] new things are made familiar and familiar things are made new.'
Ben Jonson, 1572–1637

'The only end of writing is to enable the readers better to enjoy life or better to endure it.'
Samuel Johnson, 1709–84

'Good writers define reality; bad ones merely restate it.'
Edward Albee, 1928–

'The great artist is a simplifier.'
Henri Frédéric Amiel, 1821–81

Introduction

Imagine waking up one day to discover that the Martians have landed on Earth. Fortunately, they are benign, curious and highly intelligent – and they are keen to learn about human civilisation. You begin by telling them something about our mathematical and scientific theories, and they quickly grasp what you are talking about. You then show them some of our technological and engineering achievements – skyscrapers, planes and computers – and they are quite impressed. Your brief account of human history also interests them. You then take them to an art gallery. They are completely baffled. 'But what is this stuff for?', they ask. You mumble something about art illuminating the human condition. 'This stuff illuminates the human condition?', they ask in genuine surprise as you stroll through the modern art section. You then take them to a concert to listen to Bach's *St Matthew Passion*, but for all the pleasure it gives them you might as well take them to listen to the roar of traffic on a busy intersection. They simply cannot see the difference between music and noise. Finally, you get them to read a selection of plays, novels and poems. When they ask if *War and Peace* is true, you explain to them that literature is concerned not with fact but with fiction. The Martians quickly lose interest in this stuff called literature, and cannot see why anyone is interested in heaps of words that contain nothing but falsehoods. 'If you want to understand human beings', they say, 'why not simply study history, psychology and anthropology?'

Activity 11.1

How would you go about trying to explain to the Martians the difference between art and non-art? And how would you try to convince them of the value of art?

Figure 11.1 Lascaux bull and horses

The desire to create objects which are aesthetically pleasing rather than of practical value seems to exist in all cultures. More than twenty thousand years ago, our ancestors were daubing the walls of caves in Lascaux, France, with images of animals; and the irrepressible urge to paint, sing, dance, act and beautify one's surroundings has continued up to the present time. The Martians might be mystified about why we engage in such apparently useless activities, but the aesthetic urge is deeply rooted in the human psyche, and – along with language, tool-making and self-awareness – seems to distinguish human beings from other animals. Indeed, many people think that being a creative artist is the highest and most satisfying form of human life.

We will consider four main questions in this chapter, all of which are connected with the relationship between art and knowledge.

1   What is art?
2   Are aesthetic judgements objective or subjective?
3   How do the arts contribute to our knowledge of the world?
4   What are the similarities and differences between the arts and the sciences?

Although many of the examples in this chapter come from the visual arts, you should keep in mind that the arts include not only painting and sculpture, but also such things as dance, film, literature, music and theatre. You will therefore need to decide whether the points we make about a particular art-form apply to the arts in general.

What is art?

Since the arts have traditionally claimed a right to our thoughtful attention, we need to spend some time exploring their nature and value. Hence the question 'What is art?' In thinking about this question, the real focus of our interest is on what distinguishes worthwhile art from junk. At a practical level, this is an important question because we have limited amounts of time and money and we have to decide what to spend them on. We don't want to waste our time on junk and we don't want governments to waste our tax dollars buying junk for the national gallery, or supporting its production.

Most people would agree that for something to be a work of art, it must be man-made. A sunset may be beautiful and the Grand Canyon awe-inspiring, but neither would be called a work of art. Beyond this, opinions differ about what makes something art. We will explore three possible criteria:

1   the intentions of the artist
2   the quality of the work
3   the response of spectators.

Activity 11.2

Which of the following would you classify as art? Give reasons for your choice.
1 Pottery
2 Manufactured pots and pans
3 Ballet
4 Gymnastics
5 Soccer
6 The Grand Canyon

7 A holiday snap-shot of the Grand Canyon

8 A painting of the Grand Canyon

9 A beautiful face

10 A rock that happens to resemble a face

11 A child's drawing of a face

12 An artist's drawing of a face done in the naive style of a child

13 A caricature

14 Opera

15 Rap music

16 A piece of music generated by a computer

17 Bird song

18 The *Mona Lisa*

19 A copy of the *Mona Lisa* with a moustache and beard added

20 *Hamlet*

21 A TV soap opera

22 A nursery rhyme

23 A joke

24 A man dripping paint randomly on a canvas

25 A monkey dripping paint randomly on a canvas

26 Flower arranging

27 Flowers growing in a field

28 A bucket and mop left in an art gallery by a cleaner

29 A bucket and mop exhibited in an art gallery by an artist

30 A meal made by a famous chef

Intentions of the artist

According to the intention criterion, something is a work of art if it is made by someone with the intention of evoking an aesthetic response in the audience. (**Aesthetics** is a branch of philosophy which studies beauty and the arts.) We naturally think of an artist as wanting to communicate something to us, and communication is a deliberate, intentional activity. A sunset may evoke various emotions in us, but it is not a work of art because it does not *intend* to have any effect on us. Similarly, if some ants crawling around on a patch of sand happen to trace out what looks like a portrait of Barack Obama, we would not say they had produced a work of art. This is because the portrait is the result of random activity rather than conscious design.

If something is to count as a work of art, then it should not be made with a practical end in mind, but simply with the intention of pleasing or provoking people. You would not describe a manufacturer of pots and pans as an artist because his intention is to produce kitchen utensils rather than works of art. Admittedly, many functional objects also have an aesthetic element built into them, and I prefer attractive and elegant pots and pans to ugly and awkward ones. Nevertheless, there exists a special class of objects that are made with a specifically aesthetic intention, and these are the ones that we properly call works of art.

We can say, then, that works of art differ from natural objects in that they are made with an intention, and they differ from everyday objects in that they are made with the specific intention to please or provoke rather than for some practical end.

Criticisms of the intention criterion

Despite the appeal of the intention criterion, some critics have doubted that simply intending something to be art is enough to magically transform it into art. For example, if I take my desk with papers and a half-drunk cup of coffee on it, put it in an art gallery with a glass case around it, and call it *Teacher's Work Desk – VIII*, is it magically transformed into a work of art simply because I intend it to be so?

The artist Tracey Emin did something not so different with a work called *My Bed*, which was exhibited at the Turner Prize exhibition in London in 1999, and which consists of an unmade bed with packets of condoms and a bottle of vodka next to it. (When Emin's work was first exhibited, two art students caused a stir by staging a semi-naked pillow fight on it with the intention, they said, of making it 'more interesting'. They claimed that what they did was itself a work of art, which they called *Two Naked Men Jump Into Tracey's Bed*. Some years ago, a canny Scotsman called Fife Robertson came up with a name for this kind of thing: he called it PHony ART, or 'phart' for short. Emin's work was eventually bought by the collector Charles Saatchi for £150,000.)

Figure 11.2 Tracey Emin: *My Bed*

Imagine that Tracey Emin's work *My Bed* comes up for sale again. Would you be happy for your tax dollars to be used to buy the work for your local art gallery?

In his book *The Culture of Complaint*, the art critic Robert Hughes gives the following amusing example of what happens when art is judged merely by the intentions of the creator with no regard to its quality:

> In Holland... the government set up a fund to buy work by artists almost irrespective of how good it was. All that mattered was that they should be alive and Dutch. About 8000 Dutch artists are represented in that collection. None of it is shown and as everyone in Holland except the artists involved now admits, about 98 per cent of it is rubbish. The artists think it's all junk except their own work. The storage, air-conditioning and maintenance expenses are now so high that they have to get rid of the stuff. But they can't. Nobody wants it. You can't give it away. They tried giving it to public institutions, like lunatic asylums and hospitals. But even the lunatic asylums insisted on standards – they wanted to pick and choose. So there it all sits, democratic, non-hierarchical, non-elitist, non-sexist, unsalable and, to the great regret of the Dutch government, only partially bio-degradable.

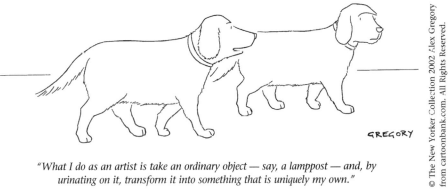

"What I do as an artist is take an ordinary object — say, a lamppost — and, by urinating on it, transform it into something that is uniquely my own."

Figure 11.3

Taken together, our two criticisms of the intentions criterion suggest that the intentions of the creator are neither a necessary nor a sufficient condition for something to be a work of art. They are not necessary because something that was not originally intended as art may now be treated as such; and they are not sufficient because something that is intended as art might simply be junk.

Quality of the work

The second criterion for distinguishing art from non-art is the intrinsic quality of the work. This criterion is closely connected with the idea of *skill*. We generally expect an artist to have a high level of technical competence, and feel that an artist should be able to make a good likeness, a musician a pleasing melody, and a poet a well-crafted rhyme. In short, we feel that a work of art should not be something that a person with no talent or training in the arts could have made.

The belief that a work of art should have some kind of intrinsic quality has often been associated with the idea of beauty. Traditionally, it was believed that beautiful art is produced by painting beautiful objects, or by *revealing* the beauty in everyday objects. But, since we can speak of beauty with respect to the *form* of a work of art as well as its *content*, perhaps we should say that a great work of art is a perfect marriage of form and content.

- The *content* of a work of art is what it depicts – such as a face, a landscape, or a bowl of fruit.
- The *form* of a work of art concerns the way it is put together, and such things as unity, order, rhythm, balance, proportion, harmony and symmetry are relevant to it.

In fact, a great deal of modern art seems less concerned to produce beautiful things which please the senses than to shock or challenge the viewer. However, you might still feel that if a work of art is to be worthy of our interest it should have some kind of quality which reflects the skill of its creator.

Activity 11.5

1 According to one definition, 'beauty is the proper conformity of the parts to one another and to the whole'. Do you agree with this definition, or can you suggest a better one?
2 Do you think there are universal standards of beauty, or do you think they vary from country to country?
3 Do you think art can reveal the beauty in something that has not previously been seen as beautiful?
4 Compare the following two dictionary definitions of music, the first from 1911, the second from 1974. What do these suggest to you about the changing role of beauty in the arts?
   a 'Art of combining sounds with a view to beauty of form and expression of emotion.'
   b 'The science or art of ordering tones or sounds in succession, in combination, and in temporal relationship.'
5 Can something be a great work of art and be disturbing or ugly or disgusting?

Criticisms of the quality criterion

Despite the appeal of the quality criterion, it is open to criticism. A work of art may, for example, have a great deal of technical competence but lack originality. There are plenty of competent but unoriginal artists churning out impressionist pictures for calendars and greeting cards. Such art is known as **kitsch** – from the German *verkitschen etwas* meaning to 'knock something off'. Kitsch is basically any form of clichéd art. The USA's 'most popular painting' – see page 342 – is an example of kitsch, as is the music you hear in shopping malls, or the soap operas you see on TV.

The problem of **forgeries** is also relevant here. Perhaps the most famous forger of paintings was the Dutch artist Han Van Meegeren (1889–1947) who painted some fake Vermeers in the 1930s that fooled the art world and were widely accepted as genuine. (Vermeer was a seventeenth-century Dutch painter.) Even after Van Meegeren's hoax was exposed, some art critics continued to insist that the paintings were genuine! The best-known of Van Meegeren's 'Vermeers', called *The Disciples at Emmaus*, is shown opposite:

Figure 11.4 Van Meegeren: *The Disciples at Emmaus*

Activity 11.6

1 What do you think of the above painting? If it is any good, why should its value depend on who painted it?

2 Why is an exact copy of a painting worth far less than the original? Can this difference be justified, or is it simply an irrational prejudice?

The other side of the above point is that a work of art can sometimes show originality, and yet require little technical skill. Consider the bull's head by Pablo Picasso (1881–1973). The head is made of an old bicycle saddle and a rusty pair of handlebars, and a small child probably *could* have put it together. Yet for Picasso to see beyond the everyday function of these objects was an astonishing insight and is, in a way, similar to a great writer making a strikingly original metaphor.

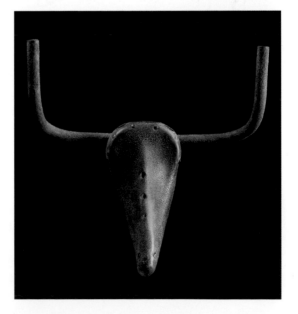

Figure 11.5 Picasso: *Bull's Head*

To summarise, we can say that quality and skill seem to be neither a necessary nor a sufficient condition for something to be a work of art. It is not necessary because works such as Picasso's *Bull's Head* are original but do not require much skill; and it is not sufficient because kitsch and forgeries may require skill but are hardly interesting works of art.

Response of spectators

The third criterion for distinguishing between art and non-art is the response of spectators. It might be said that, just as a joke requires someone to laugh at it, so a work of art requires an appreciative spectator in order to complete it. Writers want to be read, painters want exhibitions, and choirs crave an audience.

One of the key questions in thinking about this criterion is *which* spectators we should appeal to. Since 'the general public' usually prefer the familiar to the strange and content to form, they have often been hostile to new artistic movements, and many artists have had little time for their opinions. The poet Percy Bysshe Shelley (1792–1822) once observed that 'Time reverses the judgement of the foolish crowd', and there seems to be some truth in this. The 1913 world premiere of Stravinsky's *Rite of Spring* in Paris was booed off stage by the audience, and Picasso's *Les Demoiselles d'Avignon* (1907) met with shock and outrage from his contemporaries. Both works are now considered to be part of the canon of great works of art.

"I like his earlier work better, particularly the ones I said I didn't like at the time."

Figure 11.6

At the same time, we must keep in mind that some artists may have a vested interest in dismissing the opinions of the 'uninformed' public – for the public have the annoying habit of pointing out the absurdities of the more extreme fringes of modern art. An artist may comfort himself with the thought that many new works of art now accepted as great art were originally dismissed as 'rubbish' by the public; but perhaps some of the things the public dismiss as rubbish really are rubbish!

At this point, we might appeal to expert opinion to help us to decide which works of art are genuinely worthwhile. Some people think it makes no sense to speak about 'expert opinion' in the arts on the grounds that you cannot argue about matters of taste. But good critics can help you to decide which of the millions of art works available are worth your time and attention; and they can also help you to see things in a work of art that you might otherwise have overlooked. Indeed, just as a psychoanalyst may reveal things about a person that they are not consciously aware of, so a good critic may understand the meaning of a work of art better than the artist who made the work. Admittedly, experts sometimes disagree in their judgements, but their arguments are usually much more sophisticated than the 'I like it' / 'I don't like it' disagreements of those who do not have any background knowledge.

Activity 11.7

Do you think that the idea of expert opinion is more problematic in the arts than in the sciences? Give reasons.

Other ideas about the nature of art

Given the difficulties with the above criteria, a simple answer to the question 'what is art?' might be 'art is what is found in an art gallery or treated by experts as a work of art'.

Is everything art?

In the early twentieth century, the French artist Marcel Duchamp (1887–1968) began exhibiting what he called 'readymades'. As the name suggests, these were simply objects taken out of their everyday context, renamed, and put in an art gallery. Perhaps the most famous of Duchamp's readymades was his work called *The Fountain*, which was a white porcelain urinal with the pseudonym 'R Mutt' daubed on it.

By suggesting that everyday objects might have aesthetic value, Duchamp can be seen as raising the question of where art ends and non-art begins. Taking our cue from Duchamp, we might be tempted to say that if we just opened our eyes we would see that *everything* is

"I know more about art than you do, so I'll tell you what to like."

Figure 11.7

art. But if we say that *everything* is art, then the word 'art' is in danger of losing its meaning because it no longer distinguishes some things from other things. Just as 'high' only means something relative to 'not-high', so 'art' only means something relative to 'not-art'.

Instead of saying that everything is art we could perhaps rescue the above idea by saying that *everything can be looked at from an aesthetic point of view*. When something is put in an art gallery, that is precisely the way we are invited to look at it. Thus, while an unmade bed in a hotel room is unlikely to engage your aesthetic interest, if you put a glass case round it and put it in an art gallery, you will stop looking at it as a purely functional object, and this might set in motion the wheels of thought and feeling... But then again it might not! After all, just because something is in an art gallery does not necessarily mean that it is worthy of our interest.

Figure 11.8 Marcel Duchamp: *The Fountain*

Inexhaustibility

Perhaps the distinguishing feature of a great work of art is that it is *inexhaustible* in the sense that every time you come back to it you discover new things in it. A related idea is that great works of art stand the test of time and speak across generations and cultures. There is, for example, something extraordinary about the fact that Sophocles' play *Oedipus Rex* can move us with the same power and intensity that it moved Athenian audiences two and a half thousand years ago. Indeed, it could be argued that the winnowing effects of time act as a kind of *ideal spectator* helping us to distinguish enduring art from art which is merely fashionable.

Activity 11.8

Which of the music produced in the last ten years do you think will still be admired and listened to in a hundred years' time? Give reasons.

Judging art

Sophocles' play *Oedipus Rex* is generally considered to be part of the **canon** of great works of world literature, and it is widely studied in schools and colleges. You are doubtless familiar with other canonical works of art such as pieces by Mozart and Beethoven in music, Shakespeare and Goethe in literature, and Leonardo and Picasso in the visual arts. The question I now want to consider is how far our judgements about what distinguishes good art from bad are objective and how far they are influenced by the culture we grow up in and our personal tastes.

The paradox of aesthetic judgement

We might begin by observing that there is something paradoxical about aesthetic judgement. On the one hand, we take seriously the idea that there are *standards* of aesthetic judgement and that some judgements are better than others; on the other hand, we say that beauty is in the eye of the beholder and there is no accounting for tastes.

The first half of the paradox – that there are standards of judgement – is what justifies a teacher grading a piece of creative writing, or a composition, or a painting, and it suggests that there are criteria for distinguishing good art from bad art. But the second half seems to be equally compelling; for it would appear that you cannot *argue* about tastes in the arts any more than you can argue about tastes in food. Either you like something or you don't like it. If I hate oysters and love burgers, you cannot tell me I am wrong, so why should you do this if I say that I hate Shakespeare and love J. K. Rowling (the author of the Harry Potter books)?

Activity 11.9

1 With reference to food and drink, does it make sense to speak of someone educating their palate, and learning to appreciate, say, good French wine?
2 'Tiger Woods is one of the best golfers in the world.' Is this a fact or an opinion? How is it similar to and how is it different from the kinds of judgements we make in the arts?
3 'It's a great work of art, but I don't like it.' How, if at all, can someone say this with consistency?

With reference to culinary tastes, it is worth pointing out that although we have some basic likes and dislikes that are permanent features of our make-up – I cannot imagine *ever* liking oysters – it may still make sense to speak of educating our culinary tastes. You may, for example, learn to appreciate the 'vocabulary' of Thai cuisine, such as the subtle blend of peppers, coconut and lemon grass in a green curry. If we can learn to educate our culinary tastes, then perhaps we can also learn to educate our artistic tastes.

Should aesthetic judgements be disinterested?

According to the philosopher Immanuel Kant (1724–1804), there is a big difference between judgements of taste and aesthetic judgements. For, unlike judgements of taste, aesthetic judgements make a universal claim and have a sense of 'ought' built in to them. You can see this if you compare the following two statements:

1 'I like this painting.'
2 'This painting is beautiful.'

If I say I like the painting and you say you *don't* like it, these two statements can happily coexist with one another. But if I say that the painting is beautiful and you say that it is *not* beautiful, then we are contradicting one another. To say that something is beautiful implies that other people *ought* to find it beautiful. Kant put it well when he said that in our aesthetic judgements we are 'suitors for agreement'.

According to Kant, what distinguishes aesthetic judgements from personal tastes is that they are **disinterested**. If you see a picture of a Banana Split on a dessert menu, you are *interested* in the sense that it is likely to fuel your desire for ice-cream rather than evoke an aesthetic response. Similarly, if you like a play because you are in love with the actress, or a piece of music because it reminds you of 'a happy time in your life', or Cézanne's *Still Life with Apples* because you are hungry, you are in each case *interested*. There is nothing wrong with such responses, but they are not *aesthetic* responses.

The point is that if you are going to judge a work of art on its merits you should not bring your biography with you. I imagine that Mary Todd Lincoln hated the play *Our American Cousin* because her husband, Abraham Lincoln, was assassinated during a performance of it. But the tragedy of Lincoln's assassination has no bearing on the literary merits or demerits of the play. When Kant says that we should look at a work of art disinterestedly, he does not mean that we should be *uninterested* in it, but rather that we should try to go beyond our individual tastes and preferences so that we can appreciate it from a more universal standpoint.

There is an interesting parallel here between aesthetic judgements and judgements about sports. A soccer fan, for example, is *interested* if he refuses in principle to recognise the beauty of a rival team's playing style. He is *disinterested* if he is able to rise above his own prejudices and appreciate their style – even though he does not like them. We also take seriously the idea that there are standards in sports. For example, if you say 'Pele was one of the best footballers of all time', it could be argued that it is more of a *fact* than an opinion. You may not be interested in Pele, or in soccer; but the fact is that he is considered a great player by people who know about these kinds of thing.

Since we take seriously the idea of standards in sports, then perhaps we should also do so in the case of the arts. Admittedly, the arts differ from sports in that they do not have any clear rules for determining winners and losers. But if someone thinks that Shakespeare is a useless writer they are surely at least as wrong as if they think that Pele was a bad footballer. This is not to say that everyone should *like* Shakespeare; but you can acknowledge that he is a great writer even if you find that he is not to your taste.

Are there universal standards in art?

Psychological factors

Since all human beings share the same basic perceptual equipment, you might expect to find some similarities in our aesthetic judgements. Consider, for example, the two paintings on page 341 – the first by J. M. Turner (1775–1851) and the second by David Bomberg (1900–1957).

Activity 11.10

Write down five to ten adjectives that come to mind when you look at the first painting. Now do the same for the second painting. Compare your list with someone else's. How similar are your lists? What, if anything, does this suggest to you about the nature of aesthetic judgement?

Figure 11.9 Turner: *The Lake, Petworth: Sunset, a Stag Drinking*

Figure 11.10 Bomberg: *The Mud Bath*

I wonder what adjectives you came up with to describe these paintings. My guess is that you used words like 'peaceful' and 'serene' for the first, and 'disturbing' and 'aggressive' for the second. I would be very surprised if any of you described the first painting as 'disturbing' and the second as 'peaceful'. Why do most people find the Turner peaceful and the Bomberg disturbing? The fact that the former consists mainly of horizontals and the latter mainly of diagonals is surely relevant; and it could be argued that since we are subject to the pull of gravity, we naturally tend to find the former peaceful and the latter disturbing. There is, of course, a great deal more to paintings than the juxtaposition of lines, but this is a significant element we can analyse in considering the effect they have on us.

Find some more examples of paintings in which either horizontals or diagonals predominate and consider the extent to which the former are generally peaceful and the latter generally disturbing.

Komar and Melamid

Further evidence for the idea that some aesthetic judgements are universal comes from two Russian artists, Vitaly Komar and Alexander Melamid, who set out to discover what kinds of painting people find most attractive. To their surprise, they found a striking similarity in the most popular paintings across a wide range of cultures. What these paintings had in common was that they depicted landscapes in which one can see without being seen. Some people have argued that our preference for such landscapes is rooted in our biological past, and it is not hard to see why they might appeal to a human animal struggling to survive in a hostile world.

Courtesy Ronald Feldman Fine Arts, New York

Figure 11.11 Komar and Melamid: *America's Most Wanted*

Other research by Komar and Melamid indicates that there is a similar universality in people's musical tastes. We might speculate that the metronome of the human pulse is the biological basis for our sense of rhythm in music.

Rather than attribute the similarity of people's aesthetic tastes to biology, some people argue that it derives from the fact that we live in a world that is dominated by American culture. Since we are increasingly exposed to the same kind of image on posters, the same kind of music in shopping malls, and the same kind of movie in cinemas, it is perhaps not surprising that, despite our cultural differences, we end up with broadly similar tastes.

Cultural differences

At this point we might ask how similar the artistic tastes of different cultures really are. To some extent, it is simply a matter of perspective: for some people are more inclined to see the similarities between things, and others are more inclined to see the differences between them. Given our discussion, we may decide that there are universal elements running through all cultures; but this should not blind us to the differences between them. You can get an idea of such differences by looking at two paintings below of Derwent Water in England, the top done by an English painter, the bottom by a Chinese painter. Although they show the same scene, they are strikingly different in style.

Figure 11.12 Two paintings of Derwent Water

The difference between Chinese opera and European opera is even more striking, and those accustomed to one tradition may – initially at least – find it very difficult to make sense of what is going on in the other. In the same way, someone raised on baseball may find it difficult to make sense of cricket. However, in the case of both sports and the arts, we may be able to learn a new vocabulary and gradually come to appreciate the subtleties of a sporting or artistic tradition that is different from our own.

Activity 11.13

How much can we learn about the way a culture sees the world by studying the art that it produces?

Art and knowledge

Since works of art do not have any practical function like other man-made objects, you might think that their only purpose is to give pleasure. Doubtless, works of art *do* frequently give us pleasure, but many people would say that they also contribute to our knowledge of the world. To explore this idea further, let us consider three popular theories about the nature of art:

1   art as imitation
2   art as communication
3   art as education.

Art as imitation

Perhaps the best-known theory of art is the imitation or copy theory which says that the purpose of art is to copy reality. (This is also known as the mimetic theory of art. **Mimesis** is Greek for 'imitation'.) Many great artists, such as Michelangelo (1475–1564) and Auguste Rodin (1840–1917), have subscribed to some version of this theory, which derives its plausibility from the fact that we naturally expect a portrait to be a good likeness of its sitter, or a novel to be true to life. Since it requires great skill to paint well or to describe something accurately in words, the arts have for much of their history been driven by the desire to achieve a perfect likeness.

The development of perspective in the fifteenth century was a major step forward in the pursuit of this goal in the visual arts. But the invention of the camera in the nineteenth put the whole project in question. Why try to copy the world by daubing paint on a canvas when a perfect image can be produced at the click of a button? This led to revolutionary changes in the visual arts which spilled over into the other arts and led people to start questioning traditional assumptions in other areas such as music and literature. The copy theory had, in any case, never seemed satisfactory when applied to music. What, after all, could a Mozart piano concerto, or a Beethoven symphony, be a copy of?

You might even have doubts about the copy theory when applied to photography. For although photos are in a sense copies of reality, some capture a landscape or a person's likeness better than others. A good likeness, we might say, is one that, out of the thousands of possible images, captures 'the essential you'. While holiday snapshots are simply meant to remind us of 'happy times' and do not have much to do with art, a skilled photographer with a good eye is clearly doing a great deal more than pressing a button and taking a copy of the world.

Activity 11.14

1 According to a well-known saying, 'The camera never lies.' Do you agree or disagree with this?
2 Do you think that some photos of you capture your likeness better than others? How is this possible?
3 Does a colour photograph capture nature more accurately than a black and white one?
4 Give some arguments for and against the claim that photography is an art.

Before rejecting the copy theory, we should perhaps analyse in more detail what it means to copy something. You might think that to copy something is simply to reproduce what you see and that there is no more to be said. But in reality things are not as simple as that; for as we saw in Chapter 4, seeing does not passively mirror reality, but has an element of interpretation built into it. This point opens the way to a more sophisticated version of the copy theory in which we think of art not as a slavish reproduction, but as a *creative reinterpretation* of reality.

According to this more sophisticated view, great art helps us to see the world with new eyes by drawing attention to previously unnoticed features of reality. This, I think, is what the Swiss painter Paul Klee (1878–1940) meant when he observed, 'Art does not reproduce the visible; rather, it makes visible'. For example, an artist may reveal the beauty of an everyday object, or the play of light on a lily pond, or the geometric forms underlying the human body, which we have never noticed before, but which we *now recognise for the first time*. When reading a novel, you may have had the experience of reading a passage and thinking to yourself, 'That is exactly what I have always felt' – and yet you were never previously aware of it!

The idea here, then, is that the arts can subtly influence the way in which we experience the world. Some people have suggested that we see faces differently after Rembrandt's self-portraits, think about love differently after *Romeo and Juliet*, and feel differently about the seasons after Vivaldi's *Four Seasons*. Although these may not be your aesthetic points of reference, you might ask yourself how much the images you see, and the films you watch, and the music you listen to affect the way you see things.

Activity 11.15

1 Oscar Wilde (1854–1900) once said that 'Life imitates art far more than art imitates life.' What do you think he meant by this?
2 When Picasso (1881–1973) was told that his portrait of Gertrude Stein didn't look like her, he said, 'Never mind, it will!' What do you think he meant by this?
3 The poet Wallace Stevens (1879–1955) once said 'Reality is a cliché from which we escape by metaphor.' What do you think he meant by this?

While new movements in the arts *challenge* our understanding of reality, they can in time lose their shock value and simply become part of the way in which a culture sees the world. Thus what is **avant-garde** art to one generation may be normal to the next and kitsch to the third. Rather than challenge and provoke, kitsch is designed to soothe and reassure people. Against kitsch, it could be argued that the real job of art is to question traditional ways of looking at things and give us new ways of experiencing the world. Since many people prefer the comfortable to the challenging, it is perhaps not surprising that many great artists who struck out in new directions were not recognised by their contemporaries.

Figure 11.13 Picasso: *Gertrude Stein*

Activity 11.16

1 To what extent can Thomas Kuhn's talk of **paradigms** be applied to the arts?
2 Do you think that people turn to the arts more to be challenged or more to be comforted?
3 Give some examples of great artists who were not recognised by their contemporaries. Give some examples of great artists who *were* recognised by their contemporaries. What conclusions would you draw from this?

Art as communication

A second way of thinking about art is as a means of communication. It seems natural to think of an artist as trying to communicate a message to a spectator. Indeed, we sometimes speak of 'the language of art'; but it is, of course, quite different from ordinary language. If you try to explain a poem in prose, the real meaning of the poem will escape you. Similarly, the sense of triumphant joy in the last movement of Beethoven's Ninth Symphony goes beyond anything that can be expressed in words.

The analogy between art and language suggests that, just as you need to understand the grammar and vocabulary of a language to know what a native speaker means, so you may need to understand the grammar and vocabulary of art in order to know what an artist means. So perhaps before dismissing, say, classical music or modern art, we need to make an effort to learn the language. We are then in a better position to decide whether what is being communicated is worthwhile or not.

We might think of the art-as-communication theory as having two dimensions to it: a horizontal one which enables us to explore the breadth of human experience, and a vertical one which enables us to explore its depth.

With respect to breadth, literature, in particular, can be a remarkably effective way of imaginatively projecting ourselves into situations that lie beyond the frontiers of our own lives, and in this way it enables us vicariously to broaden the scope of our experience. As the Russian novelist Alexander Solzhenitsyn (1918–2008) put it:

> Art can amplify man's short time on this earth by enabling him to receive from another the whole range of someone else's lifelong experiences with all their problems, colours and flavours. Art recreates in flesh experiences that have been lived by other men, and enables people to absorb them as if they were their own.

With respect to depth, the arts seem to be particularly concerned with communicating emotions. According to philosopher R. G. Collingwood (1889–1943), 'The artist proper is a person who, grappling with the problem of expressing a certain emotion, says, "I want to get this clear".' Many people instinctively turn to the arts if they feel something deeply enough. Part of the reason for this may be that ordinary language seems to be unable to capture the uniqueness and complexity of our deepest emotions. When you are in love with someone, the words 'I love you' somehow fail to do justice to your feelings – for that is what everyone says. So you may reach for a poem or a piece of music to try to make sense of the depth and intensity and uniqueness of your feelings.

1 How is music similar to a language and how is it different from a language?
2 Are there things that can be expressed in music, but not in language? Are there things that can be expressed in language but not in music?
3 Why do you think so much pop music has love as its theme? To what extent does such music help you to understand your own emotions?

Art as education

According to a third theory of the arts, the arts have a moral and educative role. The connection between the arts and ethics is said to derive from the fact that they provoke emotions that influence our behaviour. They also shape our attitudes by offering us a range of role-models. For the ancient Greeks, Homer's *Iliad* played a key role in a young man's moral education. We now have Hollywood, and we might speculate about the extent to which the movies we watch influence our attitudes about good and bad, and right and wrong. At a more general level, it could be said that great art challenges us to question our assumptions by giving us a different perspective on things. Almost all works of art raise some kind of question about how we ought to see things, or think about things, or live our lives. So, in this broad sense, we might describe art as a moral provocation.

Thinking more about the relationship between art and ethics, we might say that the arts broaden our awareness, develop our empathy, and sharpen our intuitions. In discussing art as communication, we saw that literature can be said to give us a sense of the variety of possible lives that can be lived, and so help to give us a broader conception of what it means to be human. The awareness that there are other equally valid perspectives on the world may make us more willing to question and reflect on our own values and move beyond the inevitable limitations of our own culture towards a more universal perspective on things.

Literature can also develop our ability to empathise with other people by enabling us to imaginatively project ourselves into situations that lie beyond the frontiers of our own experience. By communicating the inside of another person's experience to us, a great novel or play can move and inspire us in a way that a purely factual description or an abstract book on ethics cannot. We may, for example, get a sense of what it is like to be a woman in a conformist society struggling to break out of an oppressive marriage, or a prisoner coping with the numbing harshness of life in a Soviet labour camp, or a young black man trying to maintain his integrity in the face of a racist apartheid regime, or a victim of the Pinochet regime in Chile coming to terms with the disappearance of her children.

Activity 11.19

What can a war poem tell you about the First World War that a purely factual account cannot?

We might also think of works of literature as thought experiments which give us a space in which to test and sharpen our moral intuitions. Since good literature presents us with moral problems in all their real-life messiness and ambiguity, it encourages us to go beyond simplistic black-and-white ways of thinking about ethics. This may explain why in recent years some universities have introduced compulsory literature courses for their law students.

Despite the above points, some people insist that a work of art should be judged purely on its aesthetic rather than its ethical merits. When an artist starts to preach and tries to teach moral lessons through her art, there is a danger that she will end up being both a bad artist and a bad preacher.

Plato versus Aristotle

While the arts are sometimes described as 'the language of the emotions', some people are suspicious of them precisely because they appeal to emotion rather than reason. This view can be traced back to Plato (428–348 BCE) who held that, by inflaming the emotions, art weakens our ability to lead rational lives. He therefore banished artists from the ideal society which he described in his famous work, *The Republic*.

Plato's younger contemporary, Aristotle (384–322 BCE), had a different view of the relation between art and emotion. According to him, art does not *incite* emotion as much as *purge*, or *cleanse* us of it. This cleansing effect is known as **catharsis**. A good example would be someone who goes to watch a 'tear jerker' at the movies, and feels better after 'a good cry'. Given the number of violent and pornographic movies that are readily available, the dispute between Plato and Aristotle is of great contemporary relevance.

Whatever your view of the effect of the arts on our emotions, there are reasons for doubting that they have a civilising influence on people. Some people have argued that even morally uplifting art stimulates sentimentality rather than action. You may weep at scenes of injustice in a movie, thereby convincing yourself that you are a caring individual, and yet be blind to injustice in the real world. The great thing about imaginary – as opposed to real – injustice is that it requires only an imaginary response. At worst, literature can make us feel good about ourselves in a way which costs us nothing and becomes a substitute for rather than provocation to action.

More disturbingly, the historical record suggests that the arts have done little to inoculate people against barbarism. The twentieth century has thrown up plenty of literate tyrants, such as Hitler, Lenin, Stalin and Mao; but their interest in the arts did nothing to stop them organising the slaughter of human beings on an industrial scale. Perhaps the problem with such tyrants was, as the Russian poet Joseph Brodsky (1940–96) noted with chilling understatement, that their hit lists were longer than their reading lists.

In the absence of clear evidence one way or the other, the belief that the arts can civilise us may come down to a matter of faith. I, for one, would like to believe that it is true!

Science, art and truth

Whatever the relationship between the arts and knowledge, there seems to be a big difference between the contribution made by the arts to our understanding of the world and that made by the sciences. Indeed, these two areas of knowledge have often been separated by a gulf of mutual incomprehension. On the one hand, some artists accuse the sciences of robbing the world of its mystery. 'Knowledge', said the English writer D. H. Lawrence (1885–1930), 'has killed the sun making it a ball of gas with spots.' On the other hand, the arts have sometimes been dismissed by people of a scientific bent as little more than a frivolous diversion.

Reason, imagination and beauty

Despite the obvious differences between the arts and the sciences, there are also some interesting similarities between them. At the deepest level, we might say that both are trying to make sense of the world by looking for patterns in things. The difference is that in science the patterns are expressed in mathematics and logic, and in the arts they are expressed in more allusive and intuitive forms.

Furthermore, although science appeals more to reason, and art more to imagination, reason and imagination play an important role in both areas of knowledge. On the one hand, an artist needs to impose some kind of rational control on her creative insights if they are to be of lasting value. If, for example, you are writing a love poem, you can't simply write down your feelings – you need to impose some kind of form on them. On the other hand, a scientist needs to have a good imagination if he is to come up with new ways of looking at things.

Interestingly, many great scientists have appealed to the beauty of some of their ideas to justify them. For example, Albert Einstein (1879–1955) once observed that the theory of relativity was too beautiful to be false. After the theory was confirmed by astronomers during a solar eclipse in 1919, Einstein was asked what he would have done if the results had contradicted rather than confirmed his theory. He replied: 'Then I would feel sorry for the good Lord. The theory is correct.' Such a reference to beauty is, at first sight, puzzling; but it makes sense once we realise that beauty and order are closely related concepts, and that a scientist's appeal to beauty is usually a reflection of his conviction that the universe is orderly.

The Einstein story shows that aesthetic considerations play a role in convincing scientists of the truth of their theories. However, two important points should be kept in mind. First, the kind of beauty scientists are thinking about is often of a mathematical nature and cannot be appreciated unless you have a training in mathematics. Second, beauty is no guarantee of truth. If Einstein's theory of relativity had been repeatedly contradicted by experimental results, he would eventually have had to abandon it and think again. For it is always possible that the universe operates with an aesthetic that is quite different from our own.

Discovered or invented?

One important difference between science and art would seem to be that while scientific laws are *discovered*, works of art are *invented*. But, as usual, things are not quite as simple as they appear. Many great artists have felt that their work is as much one of discovery as of invention – that the form is somehow already out there waiting to be unpacked. 'The pages are still blank', said the novelist Vladimir Nabokov (1899–1977), 'but there is a miraculous feeling of the words being there, written in invisible ink and clamoring to become visible.' This idea is nicely illustrated by Michelangelo's (1475–1564) famous unfinished sculptures known as *The Prisoners*. When we look at these figures, it is hard to avoid the feeling that they are already in the marble and are simply waiting to be released with the help of the sculptor's chisel.

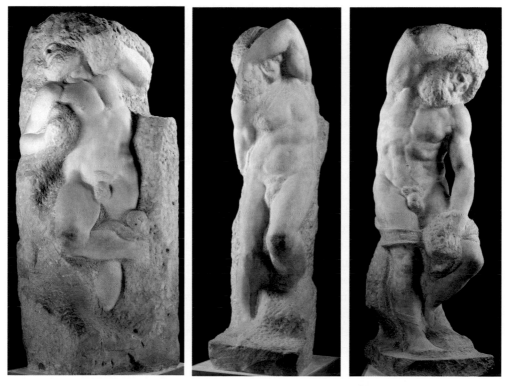

Figure 11.14 Michelangelo: *The Prisoners*

Just as some people have argued that art is as much discovery as invention, so others have argued that science is as much invention as discovery. To support this idea, they point out that even if a scientific law is useful and illuminating, it may eventually turn out to be false. That, after all, was the fate of Newtonian physics. So rather than think of scientific laws as eternal truths, we should perhaps see them as *useful fictions* which help us to make sense of reality.

Nevertheless, I think that it still makes sense to say that science is more discovered than invented, and that art is more invented than discovered. To see why, imagine the following situation. A building is on fire and the last surviving copy of Darwin's *The Origin of Species* is in one room and the last surviving copy of Shakespeare's *Hamlet* is in the other room. Ignoring the danger to yourself, you leap in to the building, but you only have time to rescue one of the books. Which should you rescue?

There is an argument for saying that you should go for *Hamlet* rather than *The Origin of Species*. Why? Because if Darwin's manuscript goes up in smoke, then sooner or later someone else will come up with the theory of evolution. (In fact, Alfred Russel Wallace, 1823–1913, came up with the theory around the same time as Darwin.) But if Shakespeare's manuscript meets a similar fate, no one else is going to write *Hamlet*. The play as we know it will be lost for ever.

What this example suggests is not that works of art are more precious than works of science, but that there is an impersonal aspect to scientific discoveries that is lacking in the case of the arts. And it is this which justifies our using the word 'discovery' more in the case of the former than in that of the latter.

Science and art as complements

Another way of thinking about the relation between the sciences and the arts is to say that they are complementary ways of making sense of the world and that for a balanced outlook we need both. Following this line of thought, it could be argued that while science looks at things from the outside, art looks at them from the inside. Einstein once said that science does not give the taste of the soup. What I think he meant by this is that while science can tell you what soup is made of and why it is good for you, it has nothing to say about what it feels like to drink soup on a cold day.

Admittedly, soup is not a major theme in the arts, but they do deal with other complex experiences. Think again of an emotion such as love. While science may be able to tell you what happens to your hormones and heart-beat when you fall in love, it is to the arts that many people instinctively turn to make sense of the *experience* of love. We are back to the idea of art as the language of the emotions. With this in mind, it could be argued that at the most general level the arts help to remind us that subjective experience is as much a part of the scheme of things as objective measurable facts.

The arts and truth

What, then, can we say about the relationship between the arts and truth? At the literal level, the Martians at the beginning of this chapter would seem to be right in saying that works of art are by definition untrue because they deal with fiction rather than fact. But at a deeper level we might speak of the **paradox of fiction** – the fact that fiction is sometimes able to reveal deep truths about the human condition. While it may seem strange that we human beings often turn to fiction in search of the truth, it also seems to be true!

1 What can science tell us about the nature of love that the arts cannot; and what can the arts tell us about the nature of love that science cannot?
2 Take any work of art, piece of music, or novel of your choice and explain how it has given you a deeper understanding of some aspect of the human condition.
3 According to Noam Chomsky (1930–), 'It is quite possible – overwhelmingly probable, one might guess – that we will always learn more about human life and human personality from novels than from scientific psychology.' What is your opinion about this?

We have drawn attention to the fact that the arts can help make sense of our experience of the world. Yet the kind of truth we find in them does seem to be different from that found in the sciences. If two scientific theories contradict one another, and one of them is true, then we must conclude that the other one is false. But when it comes to the arts, we may feel that two quite different works can be equally revealing of the truth. This suggests that when we look at a work of art, it may be more illuminating to ask, not 'Is it true?' but 'What has the artist seen?' Understood in this way, the arts might be said to contribute richness and depth to our experience of the world.

1 Do you think it makes sense to say that some works of art are 'truer' than others? Illustrate your answer with examples of your choice.
2 Do you think we can speak of artistic progress in the way we usually speak of scientific progress? What does this suggest to you about the similarities or differences between art and science?

Conclusion

We began this chapter with the story of Martians who have no understanding or appreciation of the arts. For human beings, however, a life without the arts is difficult to imagine and it would surely be a cold, grey, drab affair. (A single day without music would be more than some people could bear!) Since we derive great pleasure from the arts, that in itself is enough to justify them. But, as we have seen in this chapter, they can also be said to contribute to our knowledge of the world. Typically, great works of art make the familiar strange or make the strange familiar. At their best they can perhaps help us to recognise truths we were previously unaware of and reignite our sense of wonder at the world.

Further reading

Donald Palmer, *Does the Center Hold?* (Mayfield, 1991), Chapter 10: 'But is it art?'. This chapter gives a clear and readable account of some major theories of art, including those of Plato, Aristotle, Freud, Marx and Wittgenstein.

Ernst Gombrich, *Art and Illusion* (Phaidon, 1960). This classic book by a famous art critic explores the psychology underlying the visual arts. Gombrich likens the visual arts to a language and he explores the way in which artistic styles and conventions influence the way we see the world.

Linking questions

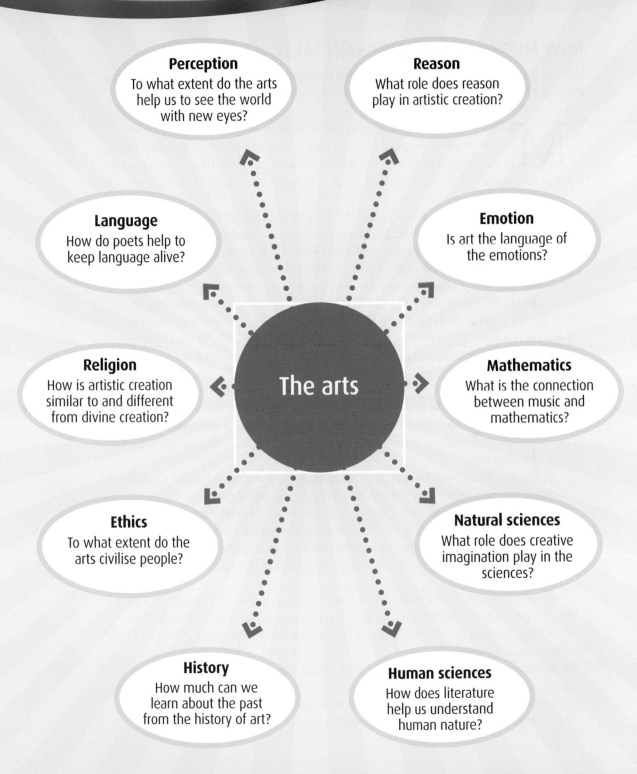

Perception
To what extent do the arts help us to see the world with new eyes?

Reason
What role does reason play in artistic creation?

Language
How do poets help to keep language alive?

Emotion
Is art the language of the emotions?

Religion
How is artistic creation similar to and different from divine creation?

The arts

Mathematics
What is the connection between music and mathematics?

Ethics
To what extent do the arts civilise people?

Natural sciences
What role does creative imagination play in the sciences?

History
How much can we learn about the past from the history of art?

Human sciences
How does literature help us understand human nature?

HOW MUCH ART CAN THE BRAIN TAKE?

Why do human beings lavish so much of their time and energy on what, from a biological point of view, might seem to be a frivolous activity, asks psychologist Steven Pinker.

Man does not live by bread alone, nor by know-how, safety, children, or sex. People everywhere spend as much time as they can afford on activities that, in the struggle to survive and reproduce, seem pointless. In all cultures, people tell stories and recite poetry. They joke, laugh, and tease. They sing and dance. They decorate surfaces.

As if that weren't enough of a puzzle, the more biologically frivolous and vain the activity, the more people exalt it. Art, literature, and music are thought to be not just pleasurable but noble. They are the mind's best work, what makes life worth living. Why do we pursue the biologically trivial and futile and experience them as sublime? To many educated people the question seems horribly philistine, even immoral. But it is unavoidable for anyone interested in the makeup of *Homo sapiens*. Members of our species do mad deeds like living for their art and (in India) selling their blood to buy movie tickets. Why? How might we understand the psychology of the arts within the modern understanding of the brain as a biological organ shaped by the forces of evolution?

Every university has a faculty of arts, which usually dominates the institution in numbers and in the public eye. But the tens of thousands of scholars and millions of pages of scholarship have shed almost no light on the question of why people pursue the arts at all. The function of the arts is almost defiantly obscure, and I think there are several reasons why.

One is that the arts engage not only the psychology of aesthetics but the psychology of status. The very uselessness of art that makes it so incomprehensible to the evolutionary biologist makes it all too comprehensible to the economist and social psychologist. What better proof that you have money to spare than your being able to spend it on doodads and stunts that don't fill the belly or keep the rain out but that require precious materials, years of practice, a command of obscure texts, or intimacy with the elite?

Thorstein Veblen's and Quentin Bell's classic analyses of taste and fashion, in which an elite's conspicuous displays of consumption, leisure, and outrage are emulated by the rabble, sending the elite off in search of new inimitable displays, nicely explain the otherwise inexplicable oddities of the arts. The grand styles of one century become tacky in the next, as we see in words that are both period labels and terms of abuse (*gothic, mannerist, baroque, rococo*). The steadfast patrons of the arts are the aristocracy and those who want to join them. Most people would lose their taste for a musical recording if they learned it was being sold at supermarket checkout counters or on late-night television, and even the work of relatively prestigious artists, such as Pierre Auguste Renoir and Claude Monet, draws derisive reviews when it is shown in a popular 'blockbuster' museum show. Modern and postmodern works are intended not to give pleasure but to confirm or confound the theories of a guild of critics and analysts, to *épater la bourgeoisie*, or to baffle the rubes in Peoria.

The banality that the psychology of the arts is partly the psychology of status has been repeatedly pointed out, not just by cynics and barbarians but by erudite social commentators such as Quentin Bell and Tom Wolfe. But in the modern university, it is unmentioned, indeed, unmentionable. Academics and intellectuals are culture vultures. In a gathering of today's elite, it is perfectly acceptable to laugh that you barely passed Physics for Poets and Rocks for Jocks and have remained ignorant of science ever since, despite the obvious importance of scientific literacy to informed choices about personal health and public policy. But saying that you have never heard of James Joyce or that you tried listening to Mozart once but prefer Andrew Lloyd Webber is as shocking as blowing your nose on your sleeve or announcing that you employ children in your sweatshop, despite the obvious [un]importance of your tastes in leisure-time activity to just about anything. The blending in people's minds of art, status, and virtue is an extension of Bell's principle of 'sartorial morality': people find dignity in the signs of an honorably futile existence removed from all menial necessities.

I mention these facts not to denigrate the arts but to clarify an important mystery in understanding ourselves. To understand the psychology of the arts, we have to look at the phenomena with the disinterested eye of an alien biologist trying to make sense of the human species rather than as a member of the species with a stake in how the arts are portrayed. OF COURSE we find pleasure and enlightenment in contemplating the products of the arts, and not all of it is a pride in sharing the tastes of the beautiful people. But to understand the psychology of the arts that remains when we subtract out the psychology of status, we must leave at the door our terror of being mistaken for the kind of person who prefers Andrew Lloyd Webber to Mozart. We need to begin with folk songs, pulp fiction, and paintings on black velvet, not Mahler, Eliot, and Kandinsky. And that does *not* mean compensating for our slumming by dressing up the lowly subject matter in highfalutin 'theory' (a semiotic analysis of *Peanuts*, a psychoanalytic exegesis of James Bond, a deconstruction of *Vogue*). It means asking a simple question: What is it about the mind that lets people take pleasure in shapes and colors and sounds and stories and myths?

That question might be answerable, whereas questions about Art in general are not. Theories of Art carry the seeds of their own destruction. In an age when any Joe can buy CDs, paintings, and novels, artists make their careers by finding ways to avoid the hackneyed, to challenge jaded tastes, to differentiate the cognoscenti from the dilettantes, and to flout the current wisdom about what art is (hence the fruitless attempts over the decades to define art). Any discussion that fails to recognize that dynamic is doomed to sterility. It can never explain why music pleases the ear, because 'music' will be defined to encompass atonal jazz, chromatic compositions, and other intellectual exercises. It will never understand the bawdy laughs and convivial banter that are so important in people's lives because it will define humor as the arch wit of an Oscar Wilde. Excellence and the avant-garde are designed for the sophisticated palate, a product of years of immersion in a genre and a familiarity with its conventions and clichés. They rely on one-upmanship and arcane allusions and displays of virtuosity. However fascinating and worthy of our support they are, they tend to obscure the psychology of aesthetics, not to illuminate it.

Another reason the psychology of the arts is obscure is that they are not adaptive in the biologist's sense of the word. I believe there is much insight to be gained in studying the adaptive design of the major components of the mind, but that does not mean that everything the mind does is biologically adaptive. The mind is a neural computer, fitted by natural selection with algorithms for reasoning about plants, animals, objects, and people. It is driven by goal states that served biological fitness in ancestral environments, such as food, sex, safety, parenthood, friendship, status, and knowledge. That toolbox, however, can be used to assemble Sunday afternoon projects of dubious biological value.

Some parts of the mind register the attainment of increments of fitness by giving us a sensation of pleasure. Other parts use a knowledge of cause and effect to bring about goals. Put them together and you get a mind that rises to a biologically pointless challenge: figuring out how to get at the pleasure circuits of the brain and deliver little jolts of enjoyment without the inconvenience of wringing bona fide fitness increments from the harsh world. When a rat has access to a lever that sends electrical impulses to an electrode implanted in its medial forebrain bundle, it presses the lever furiously until it drops of exhaustion, forgoing opportunities to eat, drink, and have sex. People don't yet undergo elective neurosurgery to have electrodes implanted in their pleasure centers, but they have found ways to stimulate them by other means. An obvious example is recreational drugs, which seep into the chemical junctions of the pleasure circuits.

Another route to the pleasure circuits is via the senses, which stimulate the circuits when they are in environments that would have led to fitness in past generations. Of course a fitness-promoting environment cannot announce itself directly. It gives off patterns of sounds, sights, smells, tastes, and feels that the senses are designed to register. Now, if the intellectual faculties could identify the pleasure-giving patterns, purify them, and concentrate them, the brain could stimulate itself without the messiness of electrodes or drugs. It could give itself intense artificial doses of the sights and sounds and smells that ordinarily are given off by healthful environments. We enjoy strawberry cheesecake, but not because we evolved a taste for it. We evolved circuits that gave us trickles of enjoyment from the sweet taste of ripe fruit, the creamy mouth feel of fats and oils from nuts and meat, and the coolness of fresh water. Cheesecake packs a sensual wallop unlike anything in the natural world because it is a brew of megadoses of agreeable stimuli which we concocted for the express purpose of pressing our pleasure buttons. Pornography is another pleasure technology. At least to some extent, art may be a third.

The visual arts are one example of a technology designed to defeat the locks that safeguard our pleasure buttons and to press the buttons in various combinations. Vision solves the unsolvable problem of recovering a description of the world from its projection onto the retina by making assumptions about how the world is put together. Optical illusions, including paintings, photographs, movies, and television, cunningly violate those assumptions and give off patterns of light that dupe our visual system into seeing scenes that aren't there. That's the lock-picking. The pleasure buttons are the content of the illusions. Everyday photographs and paintings (the ones that most people hang in their living rooms, though not necessarily the ones you would see in a museum) depict plants, animals, landscapes, and people. Many biologists believe that the geometry of beauty is the visible signal of adaptively valuable objects: safe, food-rich, explorable, learnable habitats, and fertile, healthy dates, mates, and offspring.

Fiction and drama may be a mixture of the non-adaptive and the adaptive. John Dryden defined a play as 'a just and lively image of human nature, representing its passions and humours, and the changes of fortune to which it is subject; for the delight and instruction of mankind.' It's helpful to distinguish the delight, perhaps the product of a useless technology for pressing our pleasure buttons, from the instruction, perhaps a product of a cognitive adaptation.

The technology of fiction delivers a simulation of life that an audience can enter in the comfort of their cave, couch, or theater seat. Words can evoke mental images, which can activate the parts of the brain that register the world when we actually perceive it. Other technologies violate the assumptions of our perceptual apparatus and trick us with illusions that partly duplicate the experience of seeing and hearing real events. They include costumes, makeup, sets, sound effects, cinematography, and animation. Perhaps in the near future we can add virtual reality to the list, and in the more distant future the feelies of *Brave New World*. When the illusions work, there is no mystery to the question 'Why do people enjoy fiction?' It is identical to the question 'Why do people enjoy life?' When we are absorbed in a book or a movie, we get to see breathtaking landscapes, hobnob with important people, fall in love with ravishing men and women, protect loved ones, attain impossible goals, and defeat wicked enemies. Not a bad deal for seven dollars and fifty cents!

Even following the foibles of ordinary virtual people as they live their lives can press a pleasure button, the one labeled 'gossip.' Gossip is a favorite pastime in all human societies because knowledge is power. Knowing who needs a favor and who is in a position to offer one, who is trustworthy and who is a liar, who is available (or soon to become available) and who is under the protection of a jealous spouse or family — all give obvious strategic advantages in the games of life. That is especially true when the information is not yet widely known and one can be the first to exploit an opportunity, the social equivalent of insider trading. In the small bands in which our minds evolved, everyone knew everyone else, so all gossip was useful. Today, when we peer into the private lives of fictitious characters, we are giving ourselves the same buzz.

Literature, of course, not only delights but instructs. Fictional narratives might work a bit like experiments. The author places a fictitious character in a hypothetical situation in an otherwise real world, and allows the reader to explore the consequences. Once the fictitious world is set up, the protagonist is given a goal and we watch as he or she pursues it in the face of obstacles. We watch what happens to them and mentally take notes on the outcomes of the strategies and tactics they use in pursuing their goals.

What are those goals? A Darwinian would say that ultimately organisms have only two: to survive and to reproduce. And those are precisely the goals that drive the human organisms in fiction. Most of the thirty-six plots in Georges Polti's catalogue 'The Thirty-Six Dramatic Situations' are defined by love or sex or a threat to the safety of the protagonist or his kin (for example, 'Mistaken jealousy,' 'Vengeance taken for kindred upon kindred,' and 'Discovery of the dishonor of a loved one'). The difference between fiction for children and fiction for adults is commonly summed up in two words: sex and violence. The American movie critic Pauline Kael got the title for one of her books from an Italian movie poster that she said contained 'the briefest statement imaginable of the basic appeal of the movies': Kiss Kiss Bang Bang.

Sex and violence are not just the obsessions of pulp fiction and trash TV. The writers Richard Lederer and Michael Gilleland present the following tabloid headlines:

- DOCTOR'S WIFE AND LOCAL MINISTER EXPOSED FOR CONCEIVING ILLEGITIMATE DAUGHTER
- TEENAGERS COMMIT DOUBLE SUICIDE; FAMILIES VOW TO END VENDETTA
- STUDENT CONFESSES TO AXE MURDER OF LOCAL PAWNBROKER AND ASSISTANT
- MADWOMAN LONG IMPRISONED IN ATTIC SETS HOUSE ON FIRE, THEN LEAPS TO DEATH
- PRINCE ACQUITTED OF KILLING MOTHER IN REVENGE FOR MURDER OF HIS FATHER

Sound familiar? They are the plots of *The Scarlet Letter, Romeo and Juliet, Crime and Punishment, Jane Eyre,* and *Eumenides*. The intrigues of people in conflict can multiply out in so many ways that no one could possibly play out the consequences of all courses of action in the mind's eye. Fictional narratives supply us with a mental catalogue of the fatal conundrums we might face someday and the outcomes of strategies we could deploy in them. The cliché that life imitates art is true because the function of some kinds of art may be for life to imitate it.

Of course, there is far more to the arts than pressing our pleasure buttons and playing out lurid scenarios. Art can help us see the world in new ways, give us a sense of harmony with the cosmos, and allow us to experience the sublime. But if we really want to understand this strange and eternally fascinating quirk of the human brain, we cannot just exalt the finest examples. We have to look at the typical examples, and the mixture of motives that draws people to them.

WHICH SIDE ARE YOU ON?

In this article, the biologist Lewis Wolpert draws attention to the differences between art and science and argues that, although art broadens our experience, it does not help us to understand how the world works.

The current vogue for believing that art and science should be brought together and share much is strongly promoted by the Wellcome Trust that gives many thousands of pounds to art/science projects... In the pack that goes with the Trust's new Science Museum exhibition bringing artists and neuroscientists together, Dr Raj Persaud says that understanding the universe might also need art, Baroness Greenfield that the two are merging, and James Lovelock expresses the belief that they have much in common. I completely disagree.

This obsession for showing that art – particularly the visual arts – is similar to science in content and the creative processes is bemusing. I detect in it an element of social snobbery – artists are envious of scientists and scientists want to be thought of as artists.

Early in the past century, the great German physicist Max Planck asserted that the scientist must work by using an essentially artistic imagination. More recently, Jacob Bronowski took a similar line: 'The discoveries of science, the works of art, are explorations – more, are explosions of a hidden likeness. The discoverer or the artist presents in them two aspects of nature and fuses them into one. This is the act of creation, in which an original act is born, and it is the same act in original science and original art.'

Science is about understanding how the world works, there being only one correct explanation for any observed phenomenon. Unlike the arts it is a collective endeavour in which the individual is ultimately irrelevant – geniuses merely speed up discovery. If Watson and Crick had not got the structure of DNA we know that Franklin and Klug would soon have had it. Indeed simultaneous discovery is a common feature of science. If one could rerun the history of science and start again it would have a different history but the end results would be the same: water would be H_2O and genes would code for proteins but the names would be different.

How different are all the arts. No Shakespeare – no *Hamlet*; no Picasso – no *Guernica*. Moreover a work of art is capable of many interpretations and has moral content. There is but one correct scientific explanation for any set of observations and reliable scientific understanding has no moral or ethical content. Art is a personal creation and contains the personal views of the artist but whatever the feelings of the scientist these are absent from the final understanding of a process.

Because science is a communal process a scientist has to be very aware of what is known about the problem being investigated. There are strict criteria about lack of contradiction and, of course, correspondence with reality. Science makes progress, we build on the work of our current and earlier colleagues. To talk about progress in art makes no sense, there is change but not progress. Art is not constrained by reality. It cannot be shown to be wrong.

Of all the arts, painting is the one least related to science as it does not deal with complex ideas or explanations, is the easiest to appreciate, and the response is often an emotional one. Ideas in art come from art critics and historians, not the works themselves. Unlike the second law of thermodynamics, population genetics or quantum mechanics, which require much basic knowledge to appreciate properly, the response to a painting needs no prior training – though it can increase appreciation and pleasure. I cannot understand what is being referred to when there is reference to critical thinking in art. In what sense can a painting be right or wrong? Anyone can have views about a painting and engage in art discussions. Non-scientists can thrill to scientific ideas but to make meaningful comments about them, and I exclude their application to technology, one actually has to have detailed knowledge. Science needs a much greater, and quite different, intellectual effort – I cannot conceal my own snobbery.

I challenge anyone who goes to Tate Modern to find in just one of the hundreds of paintings, sculptures and videos in this wonderful gallery anything that has a serious connection with science...

If the idea of creativity makes scientists want to be thought of as artists and vice versa, what about accountants, lawyers, engineers, small business managers, bankers, or even politicians? There may well be something similar in all human creativity, but that it is particularly similar in scientists and artists is without foundation. The similarity between art and science is even less than that between billiards and rugby both of which at least use a ball. Just think of the possibilities of waxing eloquent about the similarities between the Newtonian mechanics of golf, cricket and tennis...

Art does not explain, but it broadens our experience in ways that are not clearly understood. I value it in its own terms but it has nothing to do with understanding how the world works. To pretend that it does is to trivialise science and do nothing for art. We should stop pretending that the two disciplines are similar, and instead rejoice in the very different ways that they enrich our culture.

12 Ethics

'Broken promises don't upset me. I just think, "Why did they believe me?"'
Jack Handey, 1949–

'These are my principles and if you don't like them – I have others.'
Groucho Marx, 1890–1977

'Whenever I'm caught between two evils, I take the one I've never tried.'
Mae West, 1892–1980

'I am human and therefore indifferent to nothing done by humans.'
Terence, 186–159 BCE

'Everything has been figured out, except how to live.'
Jean-Paul Sartre, 1905–80

'Happiness is for idiots.'
Charles de Gaulle, 1890–1970

'Happiness is good health and a bad memory.'
Ingrid Bergman, 1915–82

'I cannot see how to refute the arguments for the subjectivity of ethical values, but I find myself incapable of believing that all that is wrong with wanton cruelty is that I don't like it.'
Bertrand Russell, 1872–1970

'There is no duty we so much underrated as the duty of being happy.'
Robert Louis Stevenson, 1850–94

'Man's brain lives in the twentieth century; the heart of most men still lives in the Stone Age.'
Erich Fromm, 1900–80

'Ethical axioms are found and tested not very differently from the axioms of science. Truth is what stands the test of experience.'
Albert Einstein, 1879–1955

'As I know more of mankind I expect less of them, and am ready now to call a man a good man, upon easier terms than I was formerly.'
Samuel Johnson, 1709–84

'On the whole, human beings want to be good, but not too good, and not quite all the time.'
George Orwell, 1903–50

'When a stupid man is doing something he is ashamed of, he always declares it is his duty.'
George Bernard Shaw, 1856–1950

Introduction

One of the ways in which dogs have an easier time of it than we do is that they never have to worry about ethics. We, by contrast, have to think about what is right and wrong and good and bad. This is because, unlike dogs, we are capable of asking the question 'What should I do?' Admittedly, we are not constantly troubled by this question, and much of our behaviour is guided by habit and custom. But from time to time we have to consider our options and think seriously about the best course of action. Should you keep your promise to help a friend when you are behind with your school work and need to revise for tomorrow's exam? Is it OK to make illegal copies of music? What should you do to help protect the environment? What should you do with your life?

We are also confronted by all kinds of controversial social questions which force us to think about our values:

- Is abortion ever justified?
- Should drugs be legalised?
- Are there limits to free speech?
- Is there such a thing as a just war?

The trouble with these kinds of question is that they do not always seem to have a straightforward answer. This may lead us to wonder how, if at all, we can justify our moral judgements and whether it makes sense to talk about 'moral knowledge'.

In this chapter, we will begin by looking at the nature and limitations of moral reasoning. We will then look at two threats to ethics – relativism and self-interest theory. The first claims that there is no such thing as moral knowledge, the second that, even if there is, we are incapable of acting on it. We will suggest that these threats are not as serious as they appear, and then go on to look at three different theories of ethics: religious ethics, duty ethics and utilitarianism. While none of these theories is entirely satisfactory, they are nevertheless useful tools for helping us to think about and make sense of our values.

Moral reasoning

Some people who are sceptical about the possibility of moral knowledge claim that moral values and judgements are simply matters of *taste*. This implies that statements like 'abortion is acceptable'/ 'abortion is unacceptable' are on a par with statements like 'I like spinach'/ 'I don't like spinach'. But the very making of the comparison suggests that this is not right. For we take values more seriously than tastes, and, while there is no arguing about tastes, we expect people to justify their **value-judgements** and support them with reasons.

A simple model

When we argue about ethics, we typically appeal to a commonly agreed **moral principle** and then try to show that a particular action falls under it. Consider, for example, the following argument:

> Cheating on a test is wrong.
> Tom cheated on the test.
> Therefore what Tom did was wrong.

Given that cheating on a test is wrong, then if Tom cheated on the test, it follows that what he did was wrong. This is the way we reason about many moral issues – although, in practice, we usually take the underlying principles for granted.

Activity 12.1

What moral principle is being assumed in each of the following arguments?

a Paula shouldn't have kept the money she found – it doesn't belong to her.

b James was caught bullying his classmates, so he deserves to be punished.

c Jenkins should be released from prison – he didn't receive a fair trial.

d Danny is malicious – he's been spreading false rumours about everyone.

e The president accepted bribes, therefore he should be thrown out of office.

f Simon shouldn't have told that joke – it wasn't funny, it was racist.

When we argue about ethical questions, there are two things we often look at: whether people are being consistent in their judgements, and whether the alleged facts on which those judgements are based are true.

Figure 12.1

Consistency

We expect people to be consistent in their moral judgements just as we expect them to be consistent in their judgements in other areas of knowledge. If, for example, you think it is wrong for Tom to cheat on a test, then it is surely as wrong for Dick and Harriet to cheat on a test. The belief that people should be consistent in their judgements is closely connected with the belief that they should be *impartial*. If Tom, Dick and Harriet are all caught cheating on a test, then, other things being equal, we expect them to receive a similar punishment.

Trying to decide whether or not someone is being consistent is complicated by the fact that they might not only apply moral rules inconsistently, but also hold inconsistent principles.

Activity 12.2

To what extent do you think the following individuals are morally inconsistent?
a   An anti-abortionist who supports the death penalty
b   A vegetarian who buys leather shoes
c   A socialist who educates his children at a private school
d   A politician who advocates family values and has an extra-marital affair
e   An environmental activist who drives an SUV (sports utility vehicle)
f   Someone who thinks stealing is wrong but makes illegal copies of computer software

Facts

All kinds of facts are likely to be relevant to our moral judgements, and many arguments that initially look like disputes about values turn out to be disputes about facts. For example, if we are arguing about whether or not Smith behaved badly at the party on Saturday night, our disagreement may turn on the question of whether or not Smith punched Jones on the nose. Similarly, if we are arguing about the pros and cons of capital punishment, our disagreement may turn on the question of whether or not it is an effective deterrent. In both cases, we can – in principle at least – settle our dispute by looking at the empirical evidence. This is not to say that all moral disagreements can be settled in this way. For there may be cases where we agree on all the facts but make different value-judgements. For example, we may both agree that capital punishment is an effective deterrent, and yet you might be in favour of it because you think it is good for society and I might be against it because I think that all life, including that of a criminal, is sacred.

Activity 12.3

What facts, if any, are relevant in assessing the following value-judgements?
a   Child labour should be outlawed
b   Cannabis should be legalised
c   Genetically modified food should be banned
d   Rich countries should give more financial aid to poor countries

Disagreements about moral principles

We began this section by setting up a simple model of moral reasoning: *moral principle – fact – value-judgement.* Our discussion has suggested that many arguments can be settled by looking at the background facts and at whether people are being consistent in their judgements. If we agree that cheating is wrong, and there is factual evidence to establish that Tom was cheating, then Tom himself may be willing to admit that what he did was wrong.

If we all share the same underlying moral principles, there is likely to be plenty of scope for moral reasoning. But what if we don't? What if Tom thinks there is nothing wrong with cheating? What if the president thinks it is OK to take bribes? What if Simon approves of racism? What if someone has a whole set of values that are diametrically opposed to our own? How, if at all, can we convince them that they are wrong? Perhaps we can't! Perhaps our values have no ultimate justification. Perhaps our moral rules are no more universal than the grammatical rules of the language we speak!

"We've got to draw a line on unethical behavior and then get as close to that line as possible."

Figure 12.2

Moral relativism

According to **moral relativism** our values are determined by the society we grow up in, and there are no universal values. Moral values are simply customs or conventions that vary from culture to culture. ('Ethics' and 'morality' are both derived from words that originally meant 'custom'.) Just as people drive on the left in some countries and on the right in others, so some cultures eat pork while others prohibit it, some are monogamous while others are polygamous, and some bury their dead while others burn them.

Arguments for moral relativism

There are two main arguments for moral relativism: the diversity argument and the lack of foundations argument.

The diversity argument

According to the diversity argument, the sheer variety of moral practices suggests that there are no objective moral values. The dietary, marriage and burial practices mentioned above might not seem to reflect any very serious differences in values. But you don't have to look very hard to find examples of more unsettling practices. According to anthropologists, there are, or have been, cultures which have permitted such things as: keeping slaves; female genital mutilation; killing adulterers; burning widows on the funeral pyres of their dead husbands; slaughtering prisoners by ripping the hearts out of their bodies; killing unproductive members of society; and cannibalism.

The sheer diversity of such practices has been enough to convince some people of the truth of moral relativism. Of course, given the way *we* have been brought up, we are likely to find such practices barbaric; but since the people engaging in them presumably saw nothing wrong with them, it is tempting to conclude that morality, like beauty, is in the eye of the beholder.

Activity 12.4

1   Do you think there is a difference between moral values and customs or conventions?
2   Which of the following would you say are morally wrong and which would you say are simply matters of convention?
    a   You should not burn your country's flag.
    b   A man should not go to work wearing a dress.
    c   You should not persecute minority groups.
    d   A woman should not have more than one husband.
    e   You should not torture the innocent.
    f   You should not have sex with an animal.
    g   You should not use dead people for dog food.
    h   You should not execute adulterers.
    i   You should not execute murderers.
    j   You should not eat meat.
3   To what extent do you think you can predict someone's moral beliefs from a knowledge of their cultural background?

The lack of foundations argument

The second argument for relativism is that moral values are somehow ungrounded or lacking in foundations; for there does not seem to be an independent 'moral reality' against which we can test our values to see if they are true or false; and this suggests that they are simply the result of the way we have been brought up and conditioned by society.

We usually settle disputes in other areas of knowledge by appealing to perception or reason, but neither of these appeals seems to work when we are arguing about values. We cannot appeal to perception because we cannot see values in the way that we can see shapes and sizes and colours. And we cannot appeal to reason because there does not seem to be any logical way of getting from an *is* statement to an *ought* statement. Consider, for example, the following argument:

> Some people in the world are starving.
> I have more food than I need.
> Therefore, I *ought* to give some of my food to the starving.

This argument may be emotionally appealing, but the conclusion does not follow from the premises. Indeed, from a purely logical point of view, it is no better than saying:

> Some people in the world are starving.
> I have more food than I need.
> Therefore, lucky old me!

The Scottish philosopher David Hume (1711–76) dramatised the gap between an 'is' and an 'ought' by observing that, ''tis not contrary to reason to prefer the destruction of the whole world to the scratching of my finger'. This may sound like an extreme example, but it is worth pointing out that most people worry more about their own minor problems than they do about world poverty.

We saw earlier that, *given* certain moral principles, we can use reason to derive a particular moral judgement (e.g. *given* that people with more food than they need ought to give some of it to the starving, and I have more food than I need, then it follows that I *ought* to give some of it to the starving). But if we cannot justify these principles themselves, then it might seem that we have no choice but to accept moral relativism.

Does relativism imply tolerance?

One of the things that attracts some people to moral relativism is that it seems to encourage a tolerant 'live and let live' attitude to other cultures. Since different cultures have different beliefs, it would surely be arrogant to assume that *our* culture's values are right and everyone else's are wrong. Such a dogmatic attitude can easily lead to **cultural imperialism** – i.e. to one culture imposing *its* values on other cultures. (History suggests that conquering nations have routinely given the vanquished the choice between conversion and death.) Surely it is more reasonable to say that we have our values and they have theirs, and we have no more right to condemn their values than they have to condemn our values.

Despite the value of tolerance as an antidote to cultural imperialism, we cannot in fact conjure tolerance out of moral relativism. To see why not, imagine that you come across a culture – let us call them the Thugs – imposing their values on another culture. As a good relativist, you remonstrate with them and insist that they have no right to impose their values on other people. But what if they turn to you and say, 'In our culture it is OK to impose our values on other people, and you have no right to impose your value that you-shouldn't-impose-your-values-on-other-people on us!' What the Thugs are, in effect, saying is that while tolerance may be a value in *your* culture, it is not a value in *their* culture. As a consistent relativist, you are obliged to say that their intolerant values are no worse than your tolerant values. If, on the other hand, you want to insist that *everyone* should be tolerant, you are implicitly saying that there is at least one universal value – namely, tolerance – and you cannot then call yourself a relativist. What comes out of this example is that *the belief in universal tolerance is not consistent with moral relativism.*

Once moral relativism is uncoupled from the belief in tolerance, it becomes a much less attractive position. A well-known – and some would say compelling – objection to it is that it seems to leave us with no way of answering the committed Nazi who says that in *his* value system genocide is acceptable. The he's-got-his-values-and-I've-got-mine-and-who-am-I-to-say-he's-wrong response seems completely inappropriate in this case. For we surely want to say that the Nazi really *is* wrong – as wrong as anyone could be about anything.

1 Imagine that you arrive in a 'democratic' country in which adult women have the vote but men have no political power. When you interview them, the men tell you that they are quite happy with the situation, that public life is for women, and a man's place is in the home. To what extent would you accept the situation, and to what extent would you try to 're-educate' the men and make them see the extent to which they have been indoctrinated?

2 Which of the following 'cultural practices' should we tolerate and which should we seek to have banned?

   a Punishing adultery by stoning to death

   b Punishing murder by lethal injection

   c Female genital mutilation

   d Infanticide

   e Imprisoning suspected terrorists without trial

   f Discriminating against minority groups

3 Read 'Relative values: a dialogue' in the Reading resources and answer the following questions.

   a According to Jack, our moral beliefs are simply the result of the way in which we have been brought up. Could the same be said about all of our beliefs?

   b Assess the exchange between Jill and Jack concerning Nazi values. Who do you think gets the better of this exchange?

   c If Jack is a relativist, then he must accept Jill's belief that values are objective as 'true for her'. To what extent does this weaken his own position?

Arguments against moral relativism

There are two ways of responding to the threat posed by moral relativism. First it could be argued that, despite appearances, there are in fact some core values that have been accepted by all cultures. Since human beings have broadly similar needs and are confronted by broadly similar problems, it is plausible to think that they will come up with broadly similar rules to regulate communal life. Perhaps not surprisingly there is evidence to suggest that every society has some kind of rules to limit violence, protect property and promote honesty. For it is difficult to imagine how a society could survive and flourish if it inflicted needless suffering on its members, encouraged theft, and honoured deception.

But the worrying fact is that, for much of history, people have had no moral concern for outsiders who do not belong to their community and they have sometimes treated them with the kind of indifference we might treat lobsters. For example, the Wari tribe of the Amazon grouped under the heading 'edible' anyone who was not a member of the tribe. And the Spanish Conquistadors managed to convince themselves that the people they encountered in the New World were sub-human – and then proceeded to butcher them with a clear conscience.

There are clearly some dark and disturbing chapters in the moral history of the human species. But if it is true that all communities have regulated themselves by some recognisably moral values, then it could be argued that their treatment of outsiders was in some sense a *factual error* which they could, in principle at least, be reasoned out of. The Wari were wrong to think that outsiders were nothing but potential meat; and the Conquistadors were wrong to think that American Indians were not fully human. The optimistic interpretation of our moral history is that we have gradually expanded the moral circle from the tribe to the nation to the race to the whole of mankind, as we have come to recognise our common humanity.

Activity 12.6

1 Compare and contrast the moral codes of some of the world's great religions. How much overlap is there between them?
2 Which five values would you say have the best claim to be universal and why?
3 We have clearly made scientific progress over the last three hundred years. Does it also make sense to speak of moral progress? Give reasons.

A second possible response to moral relativism is to say that we can in fact justify our values. For it could be argued that some core values – such as the belief that it is wrong to inflict needless suffering on other people – are intuitively obvious, and that scepticism about such values is no more justified than any other form of scepticism. Admittedly, we cannot prove that our basic moral intuitions are true; but if you can't just see that, for example, random torture is wrong, there is probably nothing I can do to convince you. Fortunately, I think the vast majority of people believe that the statement 'random torture is wrong' is at least as obvious as $2 + 2 = 4$.

We should, however, be careful about appealing to intuition as a *general* way of justifying our moral beliefs. For when it comes to detailed questions of right and wrong, there is no consensus about what is intuitively obvious. (You cannot, for example, resolve the abortion debate by appealing to intuition.) Nevertheless, if we could at least agree on a small number of core intuitions, these would establish boundary conditions that any viable theory of ethics must satisfy.

Activity 12.7

1 Just as a person who cannot distinguish red and green is said to be colour blind, can we say that a person who cannot distinguish right and wrong is values blind?
2 To what extent can immorality be seen as a form of mental illness? Do you, for example, think that serial killers are best described as 'bad' or 'mad'?

Self-interest theory

Having done something to defuse moral relativism, we now consider another idea that threatens to undermine our values. According to **self-interest theory**, human beings are always and everywhere selfish. Since selfish behaviour is usually seen as the opposite of moral behaviour, this theory suggests that, even if there are objective moral values, we are incapable of living up to them. We will consider four arguments for self-interest theory: the definitional argument, the evolutionary argument, the hidden benefits argument, and the fear of punishment argument. We will also look at criticisms of each of these arguments.

The definitional argument

According to the definitional argument it is true by definition – i.e. *necessarily* true – that everyone is selfish. The idea behind this argument is very simple: you are being selfish when you do what you want to do, and you always end up doing what you most want to do – otherwise you wouldn't do it.

You might object that we often find ourselves doing things that we don't want to do; but, according to self-interest theory, this is not true. Imagine that one afternoon you have a choice between playing tennis – which you enjoy – and visiting an old lady – which you feel obliged to do, but do not enjoy. What do you do? We would normally say that if you decide to play tennis you are being selfish, and if you decide to visit the old lady, you are being *un*selfish or **altruistic**. But according to the definitional argument, even if you visit the old lady, there is a sense in which you are *still* being selfish. For once we take into account the fact that you will feel *guilty* if you don't visit the old lady, it turns out that overall you would rather visit the old lady than play tennis.

This simple, but apparently powerful, argument seems to mean that genuine altruism is not merely difficult, but *impossible*. To see this, compare Donald Trump – the American property developer – with Mother Teresa – the Catholic nun who devoted her life to helping the poor. At first sight, the contrast between these two people could not be greater; for while Donald Trump spends his time making money, Mother Teresa spent hers helping the poor. However, according to self-interest theory they are both doing what they want but merely have different tastes. Donald Trump gets his buzz out of making money, Mother Teresa got hers out of helping the poor. And while Donald Trump would hate doing what Mother Teresa did, Mother Teresa would have hated doing what Donald Trump does. Since both of them are doing what they most like doing, we seem forced to conclude that they are both equally selfish.

Criticisms

The problem with the definitional argument is that it effectively robs the word 'selfish' of its meaning. For if people are selfish no matter what they do, then it can no longer be a criticism to describe someone as selfish. Since no evidence is allowed to stand against it, what initially looked like an interesting empirical claim collapses into an empty truism!

The Mother-Teresa–Donald-Trump example shows how counter-intuitive the definitional argument is. Even if we admit that people always do what they most want to do, common sense suggests that we should distinguish between **self-regarding desires** and **other-regarding desires** and use the word 'selfish' to describe only the former. We usually praise someone if they do nice things for other people, but not if they do nice things for themselves. If I buy myself an ice-cream, you are unlikely to think well of me, but if I buy *you* an ice-cream you might. The fact that I may get pleasure from buying you something does not mean that my action is selfish, but simply that I get pleasure from your pleasure. What could be nicer than a world in which everyone got pleasure from helping other people?

The evolutionary argument

The second argument for self-interest theory takes its inspiration from the theory of evolution, and claims that human beings are naturally selfish creatures who are programmed to pursue their own interests. To succeed in the struggle for survival and get our genes into the next generation, we inevitably spend a huge amount of time looking after 'number one', and other people's interests usually concern us only to the extent that they affect our own. According to this view, the reason capitalism is a more successful political system than socialism is that it taps into our natural self-interest and competitiveness.

Criticisms

The problem with this argument is that there is plenty of evidence to suggest that **empathy** and altruism are as much a part of our biological inheritance as selfishness. In one intriguing experiment, monkeys refused to pull a lever that would give them food if pulling it also gave an electric shock to one of their companions. They were, in other words, willing to sacrifice food to avoid causing pain to another monkey. With regard to our own species, empathy – which is the emotional basis for altruism – has been observed in babies as young as one year. For example, if a baby sees its mother crying, it may try to console her by giving her a security blanket, or a favourite toy. This suggests that empathy may be a natural part of our make-up. The bottom line is that traits such as empathy and helpfulness pay in evolutionary terms. As the biologist Edward O. Wilson observes: 'Cooperative individuals generally survive longer and leave more offspring.'

The hidden benefits argument

The third argument for self-interest theory is that we get various hidden benefits – such as gratitude, praise and a positive image of ourselves – from being kind to other people. Furthermore, if we help other people when they are in trouble, then we can ask for their help when we are in trouble. Admittedly, we sometimes help other people who will never be able to 'repay the debt', and we may do socially useful things such as donate blood. But such activities not only make us feel good about ourselves, but also enhance our reputation as 'good people' and this, too, can be socially advantageous.

Activity 12.8

1   If you went out of your way to help someone in trouble, would it bother you if they showed no gratitude?
2   If you helped a friend when she had a problem, would you be annoyed if she refused to help you when *you* had a problem?
3   If you gave a lot of money to charity, would you rather your friends knew what you had done, or would you rather they did not know?

Consider, for example, a mother's love for her child, which is sometimes held up as the highest example of altruism. A supporter of self-interest theory might argue that, since a mother loves only *her* children and not *all* children, such love is still self-interested. Many parents are competitive on behalf of their offspring and are anxious for them to do better than other people's children. Such natural competitiveness turned into murderous rivalry in 1991 when a Texas 'cheerleader Mom' plotted the murder of her daughter's rival for a place on the cheerleader team! Fortunately, most parents do not go quite so far in trying to further their children's prospects!

What, then, of a hero who lays down his life for his friends or a martyr who sacrifices it for a noble cause? Well, even heroes and martyrs could be said to get some kind of satisfaction from their sacrifice. They may, for example, think of the posthumous fame they will achieve, or the joys that await them in heaven. Perhaps as a young child, you occasionally thought to yourself, 'I wish I was dead!... And then they'd be sorry!' You may then have imagined your parents weeping at your grave, and saying: 'If only we had been kinder to our son when he was alive!' Such are the consolations of martyrdom!

Criticisms

The problem with the argument from hidden benefits is that, although we do often help other people expecting that they will at some point return the favour, there are some situations in which this cannot be our motive. Consider the everyday example of someone leaving a tip in a restaurant they will never visit again. From a self-interested point of view, this is hardly rational behaviour; but people do it all the time – from, it seems, a sense of fairness. You may, of course, feel good about yourself if you leave a tip, but this hardly justifies our calling it selfish.

There are other more dramatic examples of altruism. During the Second World War, the people of Chambon in France risked their lives to hide Jews fleeing from Nazi persecution. Similarly, a German Czech called Oskar Schindler (1908–74) took huge personal risks to save the lives of hundreds of Jews. Again, these people doubtless got satisfaction from what they did; but perhaps what really matters is not so much their motives – which are often obscure – as their actions. As one survivor rescued by Schindler observed: 'I don't know what his motives were... But I don't give a damn. What's important is that he saved our lives.'

The existence of 'ordinary heroes' who have other-regarding rather than self-regarding desires, and who are sometimes willing to take great personal risks to help other people, effectively takes the sting out of self-interest theory. As David Hume (1711–76) observed:

> I esteem the man whose self-love, by whatever means, is so directed as to give him a concern for others, and render him serviceable to society; as I hate or despise him who has no regard to anything beyond his own gratifications and enjoyments.

The fear of punishment argument

The fourth argument for self-interest theory says that the main thing that keeps us in line and prevents our doing wrong is fear of punishment. When people are thinking of doing something wrong, they usually ask themselves, 'What if I get caught?' The fear of a fine, imprisonment, or even death is enough to deter most people. In situations where law and order break down and there is no longer any fear of getting caught, things can quickly revert to the law of the jungle. Imagine, for example, that the police and security guards in your town went on strike for a day, or a week, or a month. What do you think would happen? If past evidence is anything to go by, there would be pandemonium. Here is a brief description of what happened during a one-day strike by the Montreal police back in 1969:

> At 8:00 AM on October 17, 1969... the Montreal police went on strike. By 11:20 AM the first bank was robbed. By noon most downtown stores had closed because of looting. Within a few more hours, taxi drivers burned down the garage of a limousine service that had competed with them for airport customers, a rooftop sniper killed a provincial police officer, rioters broke into several hotels and restaurants, and a doctor slew a burglar in his suburban home. By the end of the day, six banks had been robbed, a hundred shops had been looted, twelve fires had been set, forty carloads of storefront glass had been broken, and three million dollars in property damage had been inflicted, before city authorities had to call in the army... to restore order.

Criticisms

Although law enforcement plays an important role in ensuring social order, there is no reason to think that *all* good behaviour is motivated by fear. We cannot really explain the behaviour of people like Mother Teresa in this way. A cynic might argue that religious people are motivated primarily by the fear of being punished in the afterlife. But God would probably take a dim view of people who did good simply to avoid punishment; and most of the world's great religions – at least in their more sophisticated form – in fact teach that virtue is its own reward.

In one of his dialogues, the Greek philosopher Plato (428–348 BCE) wrote about a fabled ring called the **ring of Gyges**, which enabled its bearer to become invisible at will. If you found such a ring, you might be tempted to transgress; but there are surely things you would still be unwilling to do. I imagine that most people would not want to harm the weak, deprive the needy, persecute the oppressed, corrupt the innocent, betray their friends, or dishonour their families – even if there was no danger of being caught. And that is surely enough to suggest that not *all* good behaviour is motivated simply by fear of punishment.

Activity 12.9

1 If you discovered the ring of Gyges, how, if at all, would it affect your behaviour?
2 If the perfect crime existed, would you be tempted to commit it? (Imagine you could break into the computer of a major bank, shave a few cents off each customer's account, and end up with millions of dollars for yourself. Further imagine that no one will ever notice what has happened, let alone be able to trace the crime to you.)

How selfish are we?

We might conclude from our discussion that although we often pursue our own interests at the expense of other people, we are not *always* selfish and we *are* in fact capable of genuine altruism. However, this still leaves plenty of room for disagreement about the *extent* of altruism. According to one economist, 'the average human being is about 95 percent selfish in the narrow sense of the term'; but people who have experienced the kindness of strangers at first hand may well have a more positive view of human nature.

Activity 12.10

1 Do you think it makes more sense to say that people are basically good and corrupted by society, or that people are basically bad and must be kept in line by society?
2 Do you think society works best when each individual pursues his own best interest, or do you think this is a recipe for disaster?

Theories of ethics

Our discussion in the last two sections has done something to neutralise the threats posed by moral relativism and self-interest theory. While it may be that *some* values are relative and that people are *often* selfish, we do not have to conclude that *all* values are relative or that people are *always* selfish. This leaves space for the idea that there is such a thing as moral knowledge and that people are capable of acting on this knowledge. We should now perhaps look for a more systematic and coherent approach to ethics which enables us to make sense of our various moral beliefs and intuitions. In what follows, we will briefly consider religious ethics, and then look in more detail at duty ethics and utilitarianism.

Religious ethics

Perhaps the simplest approach to ethics would be to find an authoritative rule book which told us what moral principles to follow. Some people believe that such books are to be found in religion. The world's great religions have been, and continue to be, important sources of moral insight and guidance to millions of people. However, they do not settle all the questions, or free us from the responsibility of thinking about ethics. We still have to decide which sacred texts to follow and how to interpret and apply their rules. The Bible, for example, says that if anyone works on the Sabbath they should be put to death (Exodus 35:2). I imagine that no religious people would take this injunction seriously today, and they would doubtless point out that religious ideas change and develop over time. If we reject what some people have called the 'idolatry of literalism', this leads to the idea that we should follow the spirit rather than the letter of a moral code.

The Greek philosopher Plato (428–348 BCE) argued that we cannot derive ethics from religion. In one of his dialogues, he raised the following tantalising question: Is something good because God says it is good, or does God say that it is good because it *is* good? On the one hand, if something is good simply because God says it is good, then if God suddenly decided that murder was good, it would be good. Most people would reject this conclusion. On the other hand, if God says that something is good because it *is* good, then it seems that values are independent of God and we do not need to appeal to Him in order to justify them. This suggests that, rather than deriving our values from religion, we already have values by which we decide whether to accept or reject what religion tells us do. Since a religion based ethics is, in any case, not going to satisfy atheists, we will need to look at other ways of justifying our moral values.

"Jitters on Wall Street today over rumors that Alan Greenspan said, 'A rich man can as soon enter Heaven as a camel fit through the eye of a needle.'"

Figure 12.3

Activity 12.11

1 According to the New Testament, 'it is easier for a camel to go through the eye of a needle than for a rich man to enter the kingdom of God' (Matthew 19:24). How do you think this statement should be interpreted?

2 Since the Pope condemns birth control, can a person still be a good Catholic if they practise birth control?

3 Can religious texts give us moral guidance on the use of genetic engineering and other technologies that were unheard of when such texts were written?

4 The Russian novelist Fyodor Dostoevsky (1821–81) said that, 'if God is dead, everything is permitted'. What do you think he meant by this? Do you agree or disagree with him?

Duty ethics

According to some philosophers, ethics is fundamentally a matter of doing your duty and fulfilling your obligations. Since the word 'duty' has sometimes been associated with mindlessly obeying orders, it has not always had a good press. But we do take seriously the idea that people have duties. You would, for example, probably agree that a teacher has a duty to help you pass your exams and a doctor has a duty to try to cure you. Admittedly, most people would prefer to talk about their **rights** rather than their duties. But it is worth noting that *rights* and *duties are two different sides of the same coin*. If, for example, you have a duty not to steal, there must be a corresponding right to property; and if you have a right to life, there must be a corresponding duty not to kill.

1 Imagine that you and a group of colonists have just arrived on a fertile and uninhabited planet and decide to make a ten-point declaration of rights. What rights would you include in your declaration? How would you justify your choice?

2 What difference do you think it would make if we replaced the UN Declaration of Human Rights with a UN Declaration of Human Duties?

3 If everyone has the right to life, who exactly has a duty to keep alive the thousands of people that starve to death every day? Do you?

If duty ethics is to be viable, we will, of course, need to know what our duties are. One idea might be to consult a table of commandments which list all the *thou-shalt-nots*. But which table should we consult and how can the duties it imposes on us be *justified*? Perhaps we can appeal to intuition; but the problem is that people may have conflicting intuitions. Some people, for example, believe that we have a duty not to commit adultery; others do not. So if our list of duties is not to be arbitrary, we need to find a more compelling criterion for determining what they are.

According to the philosopher Immanuel Kant (1724–1804) our duties are not arbitrary and we can determine what they are in an objective way by appealing to *reason*. Since Kant's approach to ethics has been so influential, we will devote the rest of this section to an exploration of his ideas.

Kant's approach to ethics

Kant argued that the way to decide if something is your duty is to see whether or not you can consistently generalise it. Imagine that you are wondering whether or not it is OK to jump the lunch queue because you can't be bothered to wait in line. According to Kant, you should ask yourself what would happen if everyone did that. The answer is, of course, that there would be chaos. Indeed, if everyone jumped the queue, there would be no queue left to jump! So if you try to generalise the rule, 'Jump the queue whenever you feel like it', you end up with a contradiction. Therefore, it is your duty *not* to jump the queue whenever you feel like it.

Kant used a similar line of reasoning to argue that we should keep our promises and refrain from such things as stealing, murder and suicide. Consider promising. Imagine that you wish to break a promise because it is inconvenient to keep it. Using the generalisation test, you should ask yourself, 'What would happen if everyone broke their promises when they felt like it?' The result is again a contradiction. If you say to someone, 'I promise to do X unless I change my mind', then you have not made a promise at all. To promise to do X is to commit yourself to doing it even if it becomes inconvenient. That is *supposed* to be why people make marriage vows. After all, there would be little point in making a vow of the form, 'For richer and for poorer, in sickness and in health – unless someone better turns up'! Since you cannot consistently generalise the rule, 'Break your promises whenever you feel like it', it is your duty *not* to break your promises.

1 Using the above example as a model, construct arguments to show what our duty is with regard to each of the following:

   a Stealing

   b Cheating on tests

   c Polluting the environment

   d Voting in elections

   e Suicide

   f Writing honest references for university applications

2 How convincing are these arguments?

"Before we try assisted suicide, Mrs. Rose, let's give the aspirin a chance."

Figure 12.4

The reason Kant attached so much importance to the idea of consistency was, I think, because he was aware of the extent to which we engage in **special pleading** and make excuses to justify our own behaviour that we would not find acceptable if they came from someone else. Our natural egoism encourages us to think that while rules should *generally* be respected, we are special and they do not apply to *us*. Consider, for example, how some people casually lie to their friends without thinking anything of it, and yet are outraged if they discover that their friends have done the same thing to them. To counter this tendency, the great Muslim mystic Al Ghazali's (1058–1111) gave the following advice:

> If you want to know the foulness of lying for yourself, consider the lying of someone else and how you shun it and despise the man who lies and regard his communication as foul. Do the same with regard to all your own vices, for you do not realize the foulness of your vices from your own case, but from someone else's.

At the heart of Kant's approach to ethics is the idea that we should each adopt a dual conception of ourselves as not only *me* but also *one among others*. For reason demands that we should at least *try* to be impartial and look at things objectively without making exceptions in our own case. This idea lies behind the so-called **golden rule**, 'Do as you would be done by', versions of which can be found in all of the world's great religions.

"How would you feel if the mouse did that to you?"

Figure 12.5

A good way of trying to be objective is to imagine various situations through what philosophers have called a ***veil of ignorance***. Imagine, for example, that person X does action p to person Y, and that you are either person X or person Y, but you do not know which one. How do you feel about the action? Do you think it is acceptable or unacceptable? (A good way of getting two children to share a cake fairly is to suggest that one of them cut the cake and the other one choose which half to take.) This method – which is really a generalisation of Al Ghazali's advice – can be an effective way of getting us to think more objectively about ethics.

Values and dignity

Kant uses the dual conception of the self to argue not only that no individual should be given preferential treatment, but also that no individual should be discriminated against. For example, he claimed that it is never right to sacrifice one individual's life for the greater good. To explain why not, we can simply reverse the dual conception of the self. For an individual is not only *one among others* but also a *me*, and his life is the only one that he has. Therefore, he should never be treated as a mere means to some further end. In this respect, there is a crucial difference between objects and persons, which Kant marks by saying that, while the former have *value*, only the latter have *dignity*. To see the difference between value and dignity, compare the following two situations.

1   A friend borrows your portable computer and accidentally drops it. The computer is broken beyond repair and you are furious. Being a decent fellow, your friend immediately goes out and buys you an identical computer to replace the one he broke. Assuming that he also replaces the software and copies the files that were on your old machine, you will probably conclude that no great harm has been done. You no longer have your original computer, but you have a replacement that is in every respect as good as the one that was broken.

2   You are in hospital dying of an incurable disease. Your parents come to visit you every day and weep at your bedside. They are devastated by the thought of your impending death. But you are incredibly brave and do what you can to comfort them. One day they arrive looking a great deal more cheerful. 'We have some good news for you', they say. 'The doctor tells us that although you are going to die, we can clone you, so that after your death we will be able to replace you. Although your clone won't actually be you, he will look like you and in many ways behave like you. We can give him your bedroom and your old toys. Isn't it wonderful news?' I imagine that your jaw would drop if you heard this speech. How dare they imagine that they can replace *you*! You are a unique individual and, unlike a broken computer, you cannot simply be replaced by someone genetically identical to you.

According to Kant, if something has value it can be replaced by something else of equal value, but if it has dignity it is irreplaceable. Since individuals have dignity rather than merely value, it is never right to sacrifice their lives for the greater good.

The importance of motives

Another key aspect of Kant's ethics is that the moral value of an action is determined by the *motive* for which it is done rather than the *consequences* that follow from it. Many of our everyday moral judgements seem to reflect this principle. If you are trying to be helpful but things turn out badly, we do not usually blame you – after all, you meant well. On the other hand, if you intend to harm someone, but your efforts come to nothing, we will still think of you as a bad person. In practice, we tend to blame someone more for serious accidents than for minor ones; you are likely to be more annoyed if someone drops ten plates than if they break one plate – especially if they are *your* plates. But Kant would say that is an immature way of thinking, and insist that all that really matters is the motive for your action.

Kant not only focused on motives but also insisted that to be truly moral our actions should be motivated by *reason* rather than *feeling*. He had a low opinion of feelings because he thought that they are too unreliable to justify our values. If you only do good things when you *feel* like it, what happens if you feel like helping someone today but not tomorrow, or helping person A but not person B? Kant sought to avoid this problem by basing values on reason rather than feeling, and insisting that reason tells us that we have certain duties regardless of what we may feel.

We can in fact distinguish at least three different motives for doing good: (i) you expect something in return; (ii) sympathy; (iii) duty. According to Kant, your action has moral value only if you act on motive (iii). You might agree that if you help someone only on an 'I'll scratch your back if you scratch mine' basis, then, although this might make pragmatic sense, it does not deserve moral praise. But it is harder to understand why Kant thinks that being motivated by sympathy has no moral value. I think Kant would say that to the extent that someone is a *naturally* friendly and sympathetic person they do not deserve any praise for it. After all, they can't *help* being like that, any more than someone who is naturally anti-social can help being the way they are. Somewhat paradoxically, this suggests that a naturally anti-social person deserves more moral praise for being kind and friendly than a naturally sociable person.

"I told him it wouldn't kill him to try to be nice once in a while, but I was wrong."

Figure 12.6

Activity 12.14

1   If a cat jumps into a pram and attacks a baby, who deserves more praise for removing it: someone who likes cats, or someone who is frightened of cats?
2   Who deserves more praise: a person who helps another person because they like them, or a person who helps another person even though they don't like them?
3   How does Kant's view differ from the view attributed to Hume in our discussion of self-interest theory?

Criticisms of Kant

Despite its positive features, Kant's approach to ethics can be criticised on a number of grounds.

Rule worship

To start with, some critics have pointed out that it leads to **moral absolutism**. This is the belief that certain moral principles should *always* be followed irrespective of context. To see the problem, consider the ethics of lying. Using the universalisability test, Kant said that you cannot consistently will that people lie whenever they feel like it, because if they did, language would no longer be an effective means of communication. Kant concluded that it is *always* wrong to lie. This is, however, counter-intuitive. Imagine that an axe-wielding maniac rushes into your school screaming that he is going to kill your teacher, Mr Clark – who promptly hides in the cupboard. The maniac bursts in to your classroom and demands to know where Clark is. Reasoning that you should never lie, you calmly reply 'He's hiding in the cupboard!' Something has clearly gone wrong here, and no one is going to congratulate you for telling the truth. For in this situation you surely *ought* to lie to save the life of your teacher. Kant might say that you can avoid lying by refusing to answer the maniac's question. However, if I were the person in the cupboard, I would *want* you to lie and send the maniac off in the wrong direction!

The problem with Kant's approach to ethics, then, is that it seems to lead to **rule worship** – i.e. to blindly following a moral rule without regard to the consequences. Many people would say that rather than mechanically applying moral principles irrespective of the context, we should try to be sensitive to the details of a situation and make a *judgement* about when it is appropriate to make an exception to a generally agreed principle.

Activity 12.15

Which of the following is a special case that justifies breaking a generally accepted rule?

1a You should respect the highway code, but it's OK to drive through a red light if you are late for work.

1b You should respect the highway code, but it's OK to drive through a red light if you are taking a critically ill person to hospital.

2a You should keep your word, but it is OK to break a social engagement if something more interesting comes up.

2b You should keep your word, but it is OK to break a social engagement if you have just contracted an infectious disease.

3a You should pay your taxes, but it is OK not to pay them if you are short of money this year.

3b You should pay your taxes, but it is OK not to pay them if they are being spent on a nuclear arms programme.

4a Murder is wrong, but it would have been OK to assassinate Hitler in 1942.

4b Murder is wrong, but it would be OK to kill someone planning a terrorist attack.

Conflicts of duty

A related problem is that Kant's ethics leaves us no way of resolving conflicts of duty. Consider, for example, the following dilemmas:

- If a person has been unfaithful to their partner, should they confess and make their partner unhappy, or say nothing and deceive them?
- If your grandmother and a world-famous doctor are trapped in a burning building and you only have time to rescue one of them, should you save your grandmother because she is a family member, or the doctor because she is more useful to society?
- If your wife is dying of a rare disease and you cannot afford to buy the drugs that will cure her, are you justified in stealing the drugs?
- If a terrorist group takes a civilian hostage and threatens to kill them unless the government releases five convicted terrorists, should the government give in to their demands?

It is difficult to see how Kant's approach can help us to resolve these kinds of dilemma, for it seems to give us no criterion in accordance with which our duties can be ranked.

Activity 12.16

1 Explain which two moral principles are in conflict in each of the above dilemmas.
2 Take one of the above dilemmas and give as many arguments as you can for resolving it one way and then as many arguments as you can for resolving it the other way.

Moral coldness

A final problem with Kant's approach to ethics is that it seems to be too focused on reason at the expense of feelings. Allowing that we should try to be consistent in our moral judgements, what outrages most people about, say, Nazi war criminals, is not their *inconsistency* but their *inhumanity*. Kant is unable to accommodate this common-sense intuition because he refuses to give any place to feelings in his moral philosophy. As we saw above, he rejected feelings on the grounds that they are unreliable; but, in practice, appeals to reason might be equally ineffective. For just as you cannot appeal to people's sympathy if they have none, so you cannot appeal to their reason if they don't mind being called irrational. (It is, for example, hard to imagine a seasoned torturer being too bothered by such an accusation.) Furthermore, taking feelings out of moral consideration seems to lead to a cold and heartless ethics. Many people would say that it is better for a husband to help his wife because he *loves* her and *wants* to help her than because it is his *duty* to help her.

We might even reverse Kant's position and argue that feelings are what connect us with other people, and reason is what isolates us. When you see someone in distress, your natural impulse is to help them, but once reason kicks in you might start weighing costs and benefits. In reflecting on what motivated him, one of the inhabitants of Chambon who helped the Jews during the Second World War said: 'The hand of compassion was faster than the calculus of reason.' What I think he meant was that if he had stopped and thought too much about what he was doing, he would probably never have done it. This suggests that reason has its limits and that we would sometimes do better to follow our hearts.

1 'The advantage of following moral rules is that it helps to avoid special pleading; the disadvantage is that it leads to rule worship.' What role do you think rules should play in moral reasoning?

2 What relevance do the following two quotations from the Irish playwright George Bernard Shaw (1856–1950) have to our discussion of Kant's moral philosophy? Do you agree or disagree with them?

   a 'Don't do unto others as you would have them do to you – their tastes might be different.'

   b 'When a stupid man is doing something he is ashamed of, he always declares that it is his duty.'

3 'What if everyone did that?' 'But they don't!' To what extent does this response undermine Kant's approach to ethics?

Utilitarianism

Utilitarianism is a deceptively simple theory of ethics, which says that there is one and only one supreme moral principle – that we should seek *the greatest happiness of the greatest number*. This slogan can be reduced to two words: *Maximise happiness!*

The theory of utilitarianism was developed in the late eighteenth and early nineteenth century by Jeremy Bentham (1748–1832) and John Stuart Mill (1806–73), who wanted to establish ethics on a scientific foundation. Just as Newton had explained natural phenomena in terms of the principle of gravity, so Bentham and Mill tried to explain ethical phenomena in terms of the principle of utility. According to this principle, the only thing that is good in itself is happiness, and *actions are right in so far as they tend to increase happiness and wrong in so far as they tend to decrease it.* If we ask 'what is happiness?', Bentham tells us that it is the sum of pleasures, and that a happy life is one that maximises feelings of pleasure and minimises feelings of pain.

To get a sense of how utilitarianism might work in practice, imagine that you are living at the beginning of the twenty-second century. While people still wear wrist-watches on their left arms, on their right arms they now wear something called a *utilitometer*. This has a needle and a dial going from 0 to +100 on half of its face and from zero to –100 on the other half. The details of how a utilitometer works need not concern us, but it plugs in to your central nervous system and measures your pleasure. If, for example, you are at a party and want to know how good you are feeling, you can consult your utilitometer: 'Wow! Plus 92 – ecstasy.' And if you are bored in class on a Friday afternoon, you can determine just how bad things are: 'Minus 70 – seriously dull'.

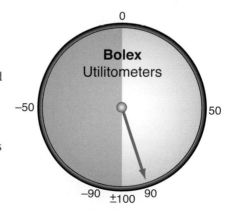

Figure 12.7

Your utilitometer also has a little button on the right which you can press to find your total net happiness for the day (sum of pleasures minus sum of displeasures). And at the end of each day, it automatically sends this figure to a central computer which calculates the total for the whole country – the *gross national happiness*, or GNH. We can now say that utilitarianism comes down to the claim that a higher GNH means a morally better world and a lower GNH means a morally worse world.

Arguments in favour of utilitarianism

As a moral theory, utilitarianism has a number of attractive features:

1   Utilitarianism is a simple and coherent theory which is able to explain all of our beliefs about right and wrong in terms of the greatest happiness principle. This gives us a simple way of solving moral dilemmas which are such a problem in duty ethics. If you are faced with a conflict of duties, all you need to do is see which course of action has the greatest effect on GNH.

2   Utilitarianism is a democratic theory because each individual is considered to be the best judge of what makes him or her happy, and every individual's happiness is taken into account in determining GNH.

3   Utilitarianism is a rational theory because it encourages us to take into account not only the short-term but also the long-term consequences of our actions. For example, although smoking gives some people short-term pleasure, a utilitarian might argue that you shouldn't smoke because in the long term it is likely to give you more pain than pleasure.

4   Finally, it could be argued that utilitarianism is an egalitarian theory because it can, for example, justify redistributing money from the rich to the poor. Since a dollar means more to a poor person than to a rich person, a progressive system of taxation which takes some money from the rich and gives it to the poor will increase GNH.

Activity 12.18

1   How might a utilitarian try to justify or criticise the following actions?
    a   Eating ice-cream every day
    b   Wearing seat-belts in cars
    c   Forcing a reluctant child to learn the piano
    d   Voluntary euthanasia
2   How do you think a utilitarian would try to resolve the various moral dilemmas on page 384? What problems arise in trying to use the greatest happiness principle to resolve them?
3   Take any moral dilemma from a novel or play that you have studied and explain how a utilitarian and a Kantian would analyse it.
4   When calculating GNH, do you think the happiness and suffering of animals as well as human beings should be included in the calculation?

Practical objections to utilitarianism

Despite the theoretical attractions of utilitarianism, it is not so easy to put into practice. To start with, how do we measure happiness? Although Bentham defines happiness as the sum of pleasures, it is difficult to see how different pleasures can be measured on a common scale. Imagine, for example, that someone gets pleasure from eating ice cream, listening to opera, and spending time with their friends. How can we attach numbers to such pleasures and compare them with one another? 20 scoops of ice-cream = $\frac{1}{2}$ an opera = 1 afternoon spent with friends? An economist might say that we can measure different pleasures by seeing how much people are willing to pay for them. But is it really possible to put a price, or a 'happiness value', on such things as health or love or friendship?

Furthermore, we might question the idea that a constant stream of pleasures makes for a happy life. You only have to think of the lives of some of the idle rich to see that someone can have a great deal of pleasure at their disposal and still be bored and unhappy. Although we all want to be happy, the strange fact is that most of us are unable to say what it is that we really want; and it sometimes seems as if, the more we actively pursue happiness, the more difficult it is to find.

Activity 12.19

1 What do you think is the relationship between pleasure and happiness? Is happiness just the sum of pleasures, or can you have many pleasures and still be unhappy?

2 What connection, if any, do you think there is between money and happiness?

3 Which of the following two situations would you prefer? A world in which you earn $50,000 a year and all your friends earn $25,000, or a world in which you earn $100,000 a year and all your friends earn $250,000? What does this suggest to you about the nature of happiness?

4 'I thought I was happy at the time, but now I realise that I was wrong.' Do you think that we are always the best judges of whether or not we are happy? Could the men in the 'democratic' country described on page 370 be wrong in thinking they are happy?

5 According to Bertrand Russell (1872–1970), 'To be without some of the things you want is an indispensable part of happiness.' What do you think he meant by this? Do you agree with him?

A final practical problem concerns how we can predict the consequences of our actions. Imagine that a married woman falls passionately in love with a colleague at work and is wondering whether or not to leave her husband. What should she do? In theory, utilitarianism gives a straightforward solution to the problem. The woman should compare the consequences of staying with her husband with the consequences of leaving him and do whatever maximises the happiness of the people involved. The trouble is that, in practice, it is very difficult to know what the consequences of our actions will be. A utilitarian might say that we usually have some idea of the consequences of our actions, but they may still be difficult to predict in any detail. To take an extreme example, in a short story by Roald Dahl, called *Genesis and Catastrophe*, a doctor saves a mother and child in a difficult birth. The story ends with the doctor saying 'You'll be alright now, Mrs Hitler.'

"It's a new anti-depressant — instead of swallowing it, you throw it at anyone who appears to be having a good time."

Figure 12.8

Theoretical objections to utilitarianism

As well as practical objections, utilitarianism is also open to a number of theoretical objections. Three common criticisms are: that pleasure or happiness is not always a good thing; that actions should be judged by their motives rather than their consequences; and that utilitarianism is incompatible with the belief that we have moral obligations and individual rights.

Bad pleasures

As we have seen, utilitarianism is based on the assumption that the only things that are good in themselves are pleasure and happiness. But a critic might argue that there are in fact many bad pleasures – such as *malicious pleasures* and *empty pleasures*.

a *Malicious pleasures* are pleasures that are derived from the suffering of other people. Imagine, for example, that a sadist meets a masochist (someone who wants to be hurt) and obligingly beats him up. On utilitarian principles, the world has become a better place because GNH has gone up. But many people would argue that, far from the world becoming a better place, the world has in fact become a worse place, and that any well-adjusted human being ought not to get pleasure from sado-masochism.

To take another example: imagine a mugger who assaults someone in the street and gets a buzz out of doing it. A utilitarian would no doubt say that the mugger's action is wrong because it has a negative effect on GNH. However, he would seem committed to saying that the more pleasure the mugger gets from his action the less serious his crime because the smaller its negative effect on GNH. Against this, many people would say that the fact that a criminal enjoys his crime and gets pleasure from it makes it worse not better.

b *Empty pleasures* are pleasures that do not help us to develop our potential, or flourish as human beings. While pleasures such as shopping or eating chocolate may have their place, a critic would say that a life devoted exclusively to their pursuit is unworthy of a human being.

In the novel *Brave New World*, the writer Aldous Huxley (1894–1963) imagined a world where people are genetically engineered and conditioned to be happy and where a drug called soma is freely available so that everyone can live on a permanent high. If you are familiar with this novel you might agree that what Huxley describes is not so much a perfect world, or utopia, as a perfectly awful world, or dystopia. A world of happy junkies does not seem like the best of all possible worlds.

Activity 12.20

1 What problems does the idea that some pleasures are better than others create for utilitarianism? How might a utilitarian try to respond to these problems?
2 Do you think that there are other things apart from pleasure and happiness that are good in themselves?

"I think the dosage needs adjusting. I'm not nearly as happy as the people in the ads."

Figure 12.9

Judging actions

According to utilitarianism, the rightness or wrongness of an action depends on its consequences: an action is right if it increases happiness and wrong if it decreases it. But, as we saw in our discussion of Kant's ethics, it could be argued that actions should be judged by their motives rather than their consequences, and that we should praise a well-intentioned bungler whose clumsy efforts accidentally reduce general happiness, and condemn a malicious person whose evil intentions accidentally increase it.

Activity 12.21

1 Most legal systems punish attempted murder less severely than actual murder. Do you think this is right? What would a Kantian say? What would a utilitarian say?
2 What good utilitarian reasons might there be for generally praising people who have good motives and condemning people who have bad motives?

Obligations and rights

A final criticism of utilitarianism is that it does not seem to leave any room for respecting moral obligations or human rights. When we discussed Kant's ethics we saw that it is too inflexible in its approach, but critics of utilitarianism argue that it suffers from the opposite weakness and is too unprincipled. For example, while Kant said you should *never* lie, utilitarianism would seem to justify lying to people whenever it makes them happy. However, many people would feel uncomfortable with the idea of shamelessly flattering or systematically deceiving someone just to make them happy.

Activity 12.22

1 Imagine that you are at a dinner party and the food is awful. Your host asks you if you are enjoying your meal. What would you reply?
2 If someone asks you what you think of them, how honest would you be in your response? How honest *should* you be?

Furthermore, since utilitarianism is only concerned with maximising happiness, it does not seem to pay sufficient attention to individuals' rights. To see the problem, imagine that Smith, who is an orphan with no family and few friends, is in hospital for a cataract operation, and that the man in the bed on his left is dying of kidney failure, and the man in the bed on his right is dying of heart failure.

Activity 12.23

1 What do you think a utilitarian would say you should do in this situation, and what difficulties does this create for utilitarianism?
2 What response, if any, could a utilitarian give to these difficulties?

Here is another example. Jones is a malicious individual who devotes his time to making life as difficult as possible for everyone in your community. You are a good utilitarian and one day you decide that it is time to do something to increase happiness. You hide behind the door and when Jones comes in you hit him on the head with a baseball bat and throw his unconscious body in the river. Good-bye Jones, hello happiness!

What is troubling about each of the above examples is that utilitarianism seems to justify sacrificing an individual to increase general happiness. A utilitarian doctor pillages a healthy body for 'spare parts'; and a community kills an individual whom everyone hates. In reality, of course, the doctor and the community would probably feel *guilty* about killing someone, and such feelings might reduce general happiness. Nevertheless, on purely utilitarian grounds, such guilt would seem to be irrational. If you are sure that you have done the right thing, why feel bad about it?

Despite appearances, a utilitarian is not obliged to say that the above killings are justified. In practice, there may be good utilitarian reasons why it is a bad idea to kill innocent people. If you live in a society where people who go into hospital with minor ailments are sometimes killed and used for spare parts, you will probably keep postponing that cataract operation! And if in your community unpopular people are sometimes killed, you may begin to worry if you get the impression that people don't like you any more. The point in both cases is that killing innocent people is likely to create an atmosphere of *fear* and this is likely to have a negative effect on GNH. In practice, then, there are probably good utilitarian reasons for protecting people's rights.

The place of rules

The above line of thinking has led some people to adopt a position known as **rule utilitarianism**. According to this we should judge the rightness or wrongness of an action not by whether it promotes general happiness but by whether it conforms to a rule that promotes general happiness. Since it is impossible to calculate the consequences of each individual action, rule utilitarianism says that in practice it makes more sense to let our actions be guided by rules which experience has shown tend to promote happiness. So with respect to something like promising, the question is no longer 'what will the effect on the general happiness be if I break this particular promise?' but rather 'what will the effect on general happiness be if we abandon the rule that people should keep their promises?'. On this approach, it is not difficult to see that the world will generally be a happier place if we have rules against such things as lying, theft and murder, and we are likely to end up with the kinds of rules that can be found in many moral codes.

This emphasis on rules pushes utilitarianism closer to duty ethics – with the advantage that the rules can be more flexible than allowed by Kant. For example, rather than say 'never tell lies', we could instead adopt the rule, 'Never tell lies unless you can save a great deal of suffering by doing so.' This rule is admittedly rather vague, but it enables us to deal with the axe-wielding murderer example considered earlier (page 383), and is more in keeping with the way we normally think about ethics. Thus rule utilitarianism might seem to be a good compromise between rule worship on the one hand and unprincipled behaviour on the other. However, we might still wonder why on a particular occasion we should follow a rule if we can increase GNH by breaking it. But perhaps this just shows that we must sometimes weigh the negative effects on happiness of following a rule against the dangers of weakening respect for the rule. There is, it seems, no substitute for good judgement.

1 Imagine that you are the sole heir to your great-uncle's fortune of $5 million. On his deathbed, he makes you swear to use the money to establish a butterfly farm. After his death, and without telling anyone, you decide to ignore your promise and give the money to an AIDS charity. Is your action right or wrong?

2 People sometimes talk about the ends justifying the means. When, if ever, do you think that this is true?

3 What light can the moral theories we have looked at in this chapter shed on the questions we raised at the beginning?

   a Is abortion ever justified?   c Are there limits to free speech?

   b Should drugs be legalised?   d Is there such a thing as a just war?

www.CartoonStock.com

"But on the positive side, money can't buy happiness – so who cares?"

Figure 12.10

Conclusion

Since we are, during the course of our lives, bound to be confronted by all kinds of moral dilemma, there is a sense in which ethics is inescapable; and, since we can never be sure that we are doing the right thing, there is a sense in which ethics is insoluble. Such dilemmas are typically the stuff of novels and films. For example, in a film called *The Bridges of Madison County*, an unfulfilled Iowa housewife meets the man of her dreams while her husband is out of town. He asks her to go away with him, but in the end she refuses. Did she make the right decision or not? What would a Kantian say? What would a utilitarian say? How much use are such theories in practice? Perhaps they do help to illuminate things; but in the end we cannot pass the moral buck, and no matter how thick our rule book is, we have to make our own decisions about what to do. The fact that we can never be sure that we have done the right thing, or that we are painfully aware that we could have done better, is perhaps part of the tragedy of the human condition.

- When we argue about ethics we typically appeal to various moral principles, but we might wonder how these principles can be justified.

- According to moral relativism, our values are determined by the society we grow up in, but it could be argued that some core values are universal.

- Some people claim that human beings are always and everywhere selfish, but since this robs the word 'selfish' of its meaning, it makes more sense to say that we are sometimes capable of altruism.

- We might try to derive moral values from religion, but Plato put forward an argument against this, and such an approach is in any case not going to satisfy an atheist.

- According to Immanuel Kant, ethics is a matter of doing your duty, and the test of whether something is your duty is whether or not it can be consistently generalised.

- Despite its attractions, Kant's approach to ethics is too absolutist and leaves us with no way of resolving moral dilemmas.

- According to utilitarianism, happiness is the only thing that is good in itself and we should seek 'the greatest happiness of the greatest number'.

- Two objections to utilitarianism are that some pleasures seem to be bad, and that the greatest happiness principle is inconsistent with our belief in human rights and moral obligations.

- Some form of rule utilitarianism might be a good compromise between the extremes of duty ethics on the one hand and act utilitarianism on the other.

- In ethics, as in other areas of knowledge, there is in the end no substitute for good judgement.

Terms to remember

altruism	moral principle	self-interest theory
cultural imperialism	moral relativism	self-regarding desires
duty ethics	other-regarding desires	special pleading
egoism	relativism	utilitarianism
golden rule	rights	value-judgement
moral absolutism	rule worship	veil of ignorance

Further reading

Simon Blackburn, *Being Good* (Oxford University Press, 2001). This is an excellent short introduction to ethics. After considering various sceptical threats to ethics, Blackburn insists that it still makes sense to speak of moral knowledge. There are short, clear discussions of a wide range of topics including relativism, egoism, utilitarianism and human rights.

Matt Ridley, *The Origins of Virtue* (Penguin, 1997). This engaging and provocative book asks why naturally competitive human beings cooperate with one another. A zoologist by training, Ridley takes an interdisciplinary approach to his subject and brings insights from anthropology, biology, economics and history to bear on his thesis that it pays to cooperate.

Linking questions

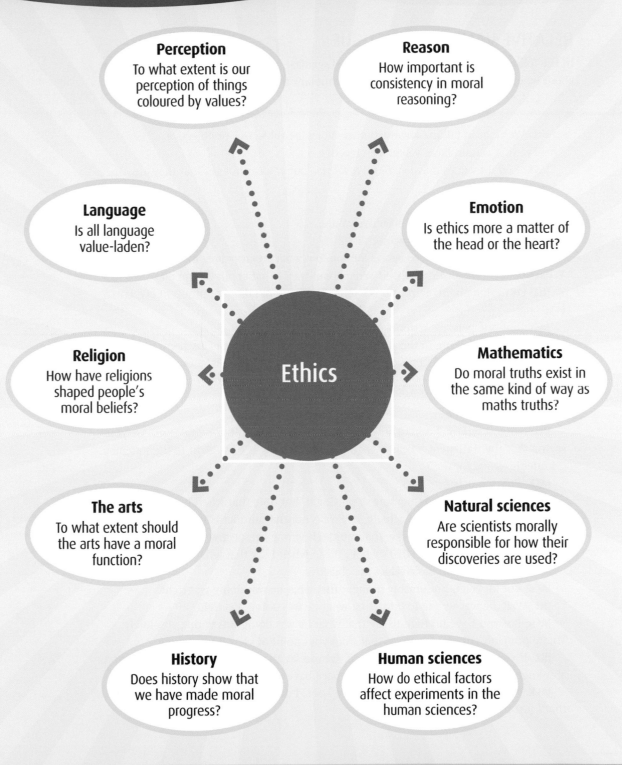

Perception
To what extent is our perception of things coloured by values?

Reason
How important is consistency in moral reasoning?

Language
Is all language value-laden?

Emotion
Is ethics more a matter of the head or the heart?

Religion
How have religions shaped people's moral beliefs?

Ethics

Mathematics
Do moral truths exist in the same kind of way as maths truths?

The arts
To what extent should the arts have a moral function?

Natural sciences
Are scientists morally responsible for how their discoveries are used?

History
Does history show that we have made moral progress?

Human sciences
How do ethical factors affect experiments in the human sciences?

RELATIVE VALUES: A DIALOGUE

In the following dialogue by Richard van de Lagemaat, two characters, Jack and Jill, argue about whether or not there are any objective moral values.

JILL: We've been talking about whether values are subjective or objective. I believe that certain basic values are objective.

JACK: Certain values may be objective *for you*, but you cannot say that they are objective period.

JILL: I don't see why not.

JACK: Well, name me some objective values.

JILL: How about: Murder is wrong!

JACK: Well, murder may be wrong for you, but what about people for whom it is OK? What about cannibalistic societies? What about war? What about capital punishment?

JILL: OK. What about: Terrorism is wrong! The random killing of innocent civilians is wrong!

JACK: But one person's terrorist is another person's freedom fighter.

JILL: Let's stop talking in the abstract. Look, take the Oklahoma City bombing in 1995. Timothy McVeigh bombs a government building in downtown Oklahoma City, killing 168 people and injuring 400 others. 19 of the victims are children. What McVeigh did was wrong.

JACK: Wrong *for you*.

JILL: No, just wrong. I don't know what you mean by all this 'for you' stuff. Are you saying that the statement 'I believe that murder is wrong' is equivalent to the statement 'Murder is wrong for me'?

JACK: Pretty much.

JILL: OK, that's an interesting way of putting it. But note that when I say 'I believe that murder is wrong', what I actually believe is not that murder-is-wrong-for-me, but that murder-is-wrong-period – i.e. that murder is wrong irrespective of what I or anyone else happens to believe. And that's what I mean when I say that what McVeigh did was wrong, and that certain basic values are objective.

JACK: But McVeigh presumably thought that what he was doing was right.

JILL: Well, he was wrong to think that what he was doing was right.

JACK: But you have no right to say that what he was doing was wrong absolutely. You're not God. All you can say is that from your point of view it was wrong.

JILL: If you're telling me that I have no right to say that what McVeigh did was wrong absolutely, then you have no right to say that I have no right to say that!

JACK: Now you're just trying to be clever. Look, I don't like what McVeigh did, but that's just my personal feeling.

JILL: But there must be more to it than personal feelings. After all, we incarcerate murderers and terrorists. What if at his trial McVeigh's defence was that as far as he was concerned, what he did was OK. So he thinks he did the right thing in blowing up the government building in Oklahoma City, and the jury thinks he did the wrong thing. If there's no way of arbitrating between these two views, then we surely have no right to lock McVeigh up.

JACK: Well, we have to protect society.

JILL: So it's right to protect the innocent?

JACK: Yes. Right *for us*.

JILL: What you appear to be saying is that there is no real difference between morality and tastes, that we just *happen* to feel that what McVeigh did was wrong and that we just *happen* to feel that innocent people should be protected.

JACK: Yes, that's pretty much what I think.

JILL: But that's absurd. We don't just *happen* to have the moral beliefs that we have. They are the reflective product of an entire cultural tradition. I don't just wake up one day and suddenly feel that murder and terrorism are wrong.

JACK: We have the beliefs that we have because of the way in which we've been brought up. If we'd all grown up in a society that approved of acts of terrorism, then we probably wouldn't object to what McVeigh did.

JILL: I'm not sure I can imagine that kind of society.

JACK: Try thinking about how countries act in times of war. That should give you a reasonable approximation.

JILL: Well, I believe that there are such things as war crimes, and I also believe that if a society seriously approved of random acts of terrorism, then it would be a sick society.

JACK: But if you grew up in such a society you wouldn't think the way you do now.

JILL: Maybe not, but then I'd be horribly deluded. If I had grown up in a society that believed that the earth was flat, then I would believe that the earth was flat. But that would do nothing to show that the earth *is* flat.

JACK: That just shows that there is a difference between scientific facts and moral values. We can, after all, prove that the earth is round. But you can't *prove* that murder is wrong.

JILL: I agree that there is *some* difference between science and morality, but that doesn't mean that all our values are merely subjective. Let me take the most extreme case that I can think of: random torture – torturing other people just because one feels like it. That is absolutely wrong.

JACK: My point is that you cannot prove that it's wrong. It's just your personal feeling that it's wrong – a feeling with which I happen to agree. After all, there may be some people in the world who see nothing wrong with random torture.

JILL: I agree with you. I can't prove that random torture is wrong, but that is simply because it is self-evident. It doesn't need any further proof. You can't *prove* that $2 + 2 = 4$, but that doesn't mean that it's just your personal feeling that it's true. And the fact that there may be a few rationally challenged people in the world who don't believe that 2 + 2 = 4 is irrelevant to the truth of the matter. It simply shows that when it comes to mathematics some people are morons. In the same way, I also believe that some people are ethical morons.

JACK: That's not a good analogy. I *can* prove that 2 + 2 = 4. I get two apples and another two apples and then make you count them.

JILL: In that case, I can prove that random torture is wrong. I take you some place where innocent people are being tortured and make you watch.

JACK: But that doesn't prove that it's wrong. It simply 'proves' that you have a feeling of revulsion when you see innocent people being tortured.

JILL: Well, you haven't proved that 2 + 2 = 4. All that you have proved – assuming that your eyes are not deceiving you and that you are not dreaming – is that *in this particular case* 2 + 2 = 4. You have done nothing to prove the general truth that two plus two is always equal to four.

JACK: You're making a very good debating point, but only by appealing to the topsy-turvy world of philosophy, which, as everyone knows, has no relation to the real world. However, for the sake of the argument, I shall let that pass. Given what you have just said, it seems to me that you are now implicitly admitting that there are no absolute moral values. For if nothing – not even arithmetic – is certain, then there can be no absolutes in any area, least of all in morality.

JILL: Absolutely not! You clearly aren't getting my point. I'm not arguing for radical scepticism – I'm simply saying that *by your standards* we can't be certain of anything.

JACK: But we can't, can we? I mean, you can't even prove that the whole of your life isn't just some weird dream and that we are all simply figments of your imagination.

JILL: That kind of blanket scepticism just isn't interesting and does nothing to illuminate experience.

JACK: Maybe not. But you can't disprove it, can you?

JILL: It depends what you mean by *proof*. If your model for proof is mathematics, then I cannot disprove that life isn't a dream. The fact, however, remains that it isn't a dream.

JACK: But how do you know?

JILL: It's intuitively obvious that life isn't a dream; just as it is intuitively obvious that 2 + 2 = 4 and intuitively obvious that random torture is wrong. I'm not interested in arguing about some kind of blanket idiot scepticism. My claim is that there are a few basic moral insights which are as certain as anything is certain.

JACK: But who are you to say that your basic moral insights are the correct ones? And how come there has been so little agreement about what these insights are?

JILL: Actually, I think there has been quite a lot of agreement. But in any case I am not claiming that my beliefs are *necessarily* true. That, indeed, would be to claim the status of God. The possibility of error is built into all our beliefs; but, in the absence of error, if you have a belief about something, then you believe that it is true independent of the fact that you happen to believe it.

JACK: If, as you say, the possibility of error is always present, that surely means that you can never be certain about anything. It follows that you can say only that something is true *for you* – which is exactly what I have been arguing all along.

JILL: You seem to think that if we cannot achieve certainty, then any opinion is as good as any other – and that is a big mistake. It is a dangerous and misguided democratic prejudice to believe that all moral beliefs are of equal value, and such a belief flies in the face of common sense.

JACK: So, according to you, some beliefs are inherently better than others! Hmm, that's the kind of arrogance that led to Western imperialism. That's how the Europeans thought when they arrived in Africa and the Americas and forcibly converted the indigenous peoples to Christianity. That's the kind of arrogance that rides roughshod over other cultures and thinks it has nothing to learn from them.

JILL: It's hardly appropriate for you to adopt that condemnatory tone. After all, you are the one who is a relativist – not me.

JACK: What do you mean?

JILL: Well, your position commits you to saying that what the European imperialists did was right for them, and that there is no higher standard according to which we can judge and condemn them. Of course, what they did was wrong for the indigenous people, but the Europeans were the ones with the guns, so they triumphed. Since, on your view, there is no truth of the matter and hence nothing to argue about, moral disagreement amounts to nothing more than a power struggle. Might is right.

JACK: No, you're the one who's in error. You believe in moral absolutes and that commits you to saying that some cultures are better than others, in the sense that some cultures are closer to the absolute moral truth. That's cultural racism.

JILL: You, on the other hand, are saying that, independent of the evidence, all cultures' ethical beliefs are of equal value. Now, that may, at first glance, sound open-minded and tolerant, but in reality it is the result of some very confused thinking. Consider a culture based on Nazi values. You would surely agree that it is in some sense worse than a culture based on the principles of human rights and tolerance?

JACK: You use the word tolerance, but your own position is a very intolerant one, and your reference to Nazism is simply muddying the waters. We can, I'm sure, both agree that Nazism is loathsome and odious; but with respect to our disagreement, this leads us nowhere. What I object to in your position is the presumptuous belief that, in a multi-cultural world, we have the right to dismiss some belief systems without a second thought. Do you honestly think that we have nothing to learn from other cultures?

JILL: That is not what I meant at all. Such an automatic and thoughtless dismissal of an alien way of life would, I agree, be quite unacceptable. What I would advocate is thoughtful dialogue between cultures; but I would want to keep in play the idea that at the end of this process we might come to the conclusion that some cultures are in some respects better than others.

JACK: But that would be a conversation of condescension. In any such conversation you would be bound to believe from the start that your own views were better than those of your interlocutor. You wouldn't truly believe that you had anything to learn from them.

JILL: On the contrary, it is you who is committed to saying that we have nothing to learn from other cultures.

JACK: I don't see how.

JILL: Well, if you know from the start that all cultures and all opinions are of equal value, then no one has anything to learn from anyone at all. Conversation – *all* conversation – then ceases to have any kind of educative function and it becomes nothing more than a way of passing
the time.

JACK: Well, this has been an interesting conversation, and it has indeed passed the time; but you've done nothing to convince me of the falsity of relativism.

JILL: All I can say is that relativism may be true for you, but it is certainly not true for me!

AGAINST HAPPINESS

How important is happiness? In the following article, Jim Holt suggests that the pursuit of happiness may have undesirable consequences and discourage critical thinking.

Sad people are nice. Angry people are nasty. And, oddly enough, happy people tend to be nasty, too.

Such (allowing for a little journalistic caricature) were the findings reported in last month's issue of *Psychological Science*. Researchers found that angry people are more likely to make negative evaluations when judging members of other social groups. That, perhaps, will not come as a great surprise. But the same seems to be true of happy people, the researchers noted. The happier your mood, the more liable you are to make bigoted judgments – like deciding that someone is guilty of a crime simply because he's a member of a minority group. Why? Nobody's sure. One interesting hypothesis, though, is that happy people have an "everything is fine" attitude that reduces the motivation for analytical thought. So they fall back on stereotypes – including malicious ones.

The news that a little evil lurks inside happiness is disquieting. After all, we live in a nation whose founding document holds the pursuit of happiness to be a God-given right. True to that principle, the United States consistently ranks near the top in international surveys of happiness. In a 1994 survey of 41 countries, only the supposedly dour Swedes surpassed us in "positive affect." (Elaborate scales have been invented to measure individual happiness, but researchers admit that difficulties remain; for example, a person is more likely to express satisfaction with his life on a sunny day than on a cloudy one.) Of course, happiness has always had its skeptics. Thinkers like Aleksandr Solzhenitsyn have criticized it as a shallow and selfish goal. But the discovery that happiness is linked to prejudice suggests a different kind of case against it. Does happiness, whether desirable or not in itself, lead to undesirable consequences? In other words, could it be bad for you, and for society?

The burgeoning new science of happiness hasn't paid a lot of attention to this question. Its practitioners are more concerned with the causes of happiness than with its effects. Defining happiness as "well-feeling" – being satisfied with life, having episodes of joy – they have discovered some interesting things: a large part of happiness seems to be genetic; marriage fosters it, but having children doesn't; men become happier with age, women less happy; money does little to boost happiness; religious people are happier, possibly because of the social support they get from church; and so forth.

As to the consequences of being happy, they are widely presumed to be positive. Happiness is held to lengthen life, buffer stress and make people more productive on the job. Some of these notions appear to be justified. A Dutch study in the 1980's, for example, found that a happy 70-year-old man can expect to live 20 months longer than his less happy counterpart. But an earlier American study found that children who are cheerful and optimistic end up having shorter life spans (perhaps because they take more risky chances).

Some have worried that happy people tend to be apathetic and easily manipulated by political leaders – contented cows, so to speak. In Aldous Huxley's dystopian novel, "Brave New World," the working classes are kept in docile submission by a diet of drugs that render them universally happy. In the real world, however, there is little evidence that happiness creates complacent citizens; in fact, studies show that happy people are more likely than alienated people to get politically involved, not less.

There is one bit of the world that happy people do see in an irrationally rosy light: themselves. As the British psychologist Richard P. Bentall has observed, "There is consistent evidence that happy people overestimate their control over environmental events (often to the point of perceiving completely random events as subject to their will), give unrealistically positive evaluations of their own achievements, believe that others share their unrealistic opinions about themselves and show a general lack of evenhandedness when comparing themselves to others." Indeed, Bentall has proposed that happiness be classified as a psychiatric disorder.

That may be going a bit far. But the evidence he cites, along with the newfound link between "well-feeling" and prejudice, might at least shake our belief in happiness as the *summum bonum*. Over the last few decades, it is precisely the groups that have made the most social progress in the United States – women and educated African-Americans – that have reported declines in their level of happiness. On reflection, this is not surprising. As education and freedom increase, desires – and unmet desires – inevitably multiply; our well-feeling may decrease, even as life becomes fuller and more meaningful. In Eastern nations like China, where happiness as a goal is less highly rated, people report lower levels of life satisfaction, but they also have lower suicide rates.

The very idea that happiness could harm a person's character – that it could be associated with prejudice, for example – would have been unthinkable to ancient philosophers. They believed in an indissoluble bond between happiness and virtue. The virtuous man, they held, was bound to be happy, since he knew himself to be in possession of the highest good, a good that could not be taken away from him even when he was being tortured on the rack. With modern times, however, came the subjective "well-feeling" definition of happiness: when the fellow in the white coat asks you if you're happy, just check your mood, compare your circumstances with those of the people around you, then tell him how contented you feel.

Ambrose Bierce, in "The Devil's Dictionary," offered the following definition: "Happiness, n. An agreeable sensation arising from contemplating the misery of another." Well, there's no need to be that cynical. But, given some of the things we've learned about happiness, let's be grateful that we merely have a right to pursue it, not a duty.

13 Religion (optional)

'I believe in God, only I spell it Nature.'
Frank Lloyd Wright, 1867–1939

'Religion is as much a human universal as language.'
Talcott Parsons, 1902–79

'To live at all is miracle enough.'
Mervyn Peake, 1911–68

'Some piously record "In the beginning God", but I say "In the beginning hydrogen".'
Harlow Shapley, 1885–1972

'You must abandon your reason, know nothing of it, annihilate it completely, or you will never enter heaven.'
Martin Luther, 1483–1546

'The Tao that can be talked about is not the Eternal Tao. The name that can be named is not the Eternal Name.'
Lao Tzu, c. 600 BCE

'When men cease to believe in God, they don't then believe in nothing – they believe in anything.'
G. K. Chesterton, 1874–1936

'A religion which declares war on reason will not in the long run be able to hold out against it.'
Immanuel Kant, 1724–1804

'What is it: is man only a blunder of God's, or God only a blunder of man's?'
Friedrich Nietzsche, 1844–1900

'Men never do evil so completely and cheerfully as when they do it from religious conviction.'
Blaise Pascal, 1623–62

'Those who try to prove that God exists a priori are guilty of impious curiosity. For to do that is tantamount to making oneself the god of God, thereby denying the God one seeks.'
Giovanni Vico, 1668–1744

'All sects deserve reverence for one reason or another. By thus acting, a man exalts his own sect and at the same time does service to the sects of other people.'
Ashoka, d. 238 BCE

'The religious geniuses of all ages have been distinguished by the kind of religious feeling, which knows no dogma.'
Albert Einstein, 1879–1955

'There is only one religion, though there are a thousand different versions of it.'
George Bernard Shaw, 1856–1950

Introduction

Important note: religion is not an IB Area of Knowledge.

We devote a great deal of time and energy to our material needs, but when we have finally satisfied them, we are still troubled by questions about the meaning and purpose of our lives. Since we naturally ask questions like 'what is the meaning of life?', 'why do innocent people suffer?' and is death the end?' we might describe human beings as 'religious animals'. For many people turn to religion in seeking the answers to such questions, and some kind of religious dimension has been found in every culture that has been studied by anthropologists. The trouble is that different religions give different answers to these questions, and some people are not satisfied with any of the answers that are on offer.

Since many cultures have organised their understanding of the world around their religious beliefs, our exploration of the various areas of knowledge would be incomplete if we did not include a discussion of religion. Having said that, it remains an open question whether it makes sense to speak of 'knowledge' in relation to religion. Much of the discussion in this chapter will focus on the extent to which it is possible for human reason to penetrate the mysteries of religion. Perhaps we should take our cue from Thomas Jefferson (1743–1826) who advised that we 'Question with boldness even the existence of God; because if there be one, he must more approve of the homage of reason than that of blindfolded fear.' Although it is no easy matter to discuss our deepest convictions in an objective and dispassionate way, it could be argued that as 'global citizens' we have an obligation – at least occasionally – to ask how our own beliefs relate to those of people from different cultures and backgrounds.

Without Making a Big Deal Out of It, Dogs Often Question the Existence of an Almighty.

Figure 13.1

Activity 13.1

Suggest ways in which a person's religious beliefs may affect their understanding of the following areas of knowledge:

a science   c the arts

b history   d ethics

Some preliminary distinctions

We begin by distinguishing three broad views about religion: theism, pantheism and atheism. (*Theos* is Greek for 'God', *pan* for 'all', and *a* for 'not'.)

1   ***Theism***   A theist believes that the universe is governed by an eternal, all-powerful, all-knowing, all-loving creator, God (Judaism, Christianity and Islam are examples of theistic religions).

2   ***Pantheism***   A pantheist believes that God is everything and everything is part of God, and that reality is spiritual in nature and the everyday world is an illusion (Hinduism, Taoism and Buddhism are examples of pantheistic religions).

3   ***Atheism***   An atheist denies the existence of a creator God and believes that the universe is material in nature and has no spiritual dimension.

Theists, pantheists and atheists have strikingly different beliefs about the meaning of life, the universe and everything. Since these beliefs are **metaphysical** in nature, we cannot determine whether they are true or false on the basis of experience alone. Given this, it is perhaps not surprising that some people have adopted a fourth position, known as **agnosticism**, which neither asserts nor denies the existence of God or some higher reality, but keeps an open – albeit sceptical – mind about these things. You might dismiss agnostics as people who 'sit on the fence', unable to commit themselves; or you might welcome their admission of ignorance about some of the deeper questions that confront us.

The nature of God

Since we have only a single chapter in which to consider religion, we will focus mainly on theistic religions and spend some time looking at various arguments for and against the existence of God. To start with, we must say something about the meaning of the word 'God'. For we need to know what it is that people are claiming when they say 'I believe in God' or 'I do not believe in God'. However, in trying to describe God in human language, there is a danger that we either reduce Him to something less than God or run into insoluble paradoxes.

The danger of anthropomorphism

Since we are human beings, it is natural to think of God in human terms by, for example, speaking of him as a father or thinking of His love as similar to human love. The tendency to picture God in this way is known as **anthropomorphism** (literally 'in the form of man') and it is particularly apparent in the religion of the ancient Greeks where the gods are portrayed as glorified human beings. This led the philosopher Xenophanes (*c.* 580–478 BCE) to say that if oxen or horses or lions could draw they would give their gods the same bodily shapes as themselves. Some atheist philosophers argue that, rather than God creating man in His own image, as the Bible claims, man created God in *his* own image and that we continue to project human qualities onto Him.

However, many people would claim that we have outgrown such childish ways of thinking about God. Michelangelo may have painted Him as an old man with a beard (see Figure 13.2) but we do not take such images seriously. And, although religious people continue to speak of God as a father, they would say that they are simply making an *analogy* between God and human beings and a father and his children. Indeed, it could be argued that all religious language is based on analogy. Even when you say 'God *exists*', you are not using the word 'exists' in its normal sense. After all, if you take off in a spaceship, you might one day find another planet or star that is believed to exist, but you will never find God, no matter how far you travel.

Activity 13.2

1 Do you think of God as a 'he' or a 'she' or an 'it'? What difference, if any, do these different words make to the way you think about God?
2 Do you think that God exists – or is supposed to exist – as a thing, or a force, or in an entirely different way?

Figure 13.2 Michelangelo: *The Creation of Adam*

The God of the philosophers

Some philosophers argue that the best way to avoid the taint of anthropomorphism is to describe God in abstract language. According to the so-called **God of the philosophers**, God is the eternal, all-powerful (**omnipotent**), all-knowing (**omniscient**), all-loving (**omniamorous**) creator of the universe. This may strike you as a very cold and impersonal definition, but it does seem to capture the key elements of what most people mean by the word 'God'. The trouble is that, when we look at this definition more closely, we run into all kinds of paradoxes. Here are four:

1 ***The paradox of omnipotence*** Consider the question 'Could God create a being that he could not subsequently control?' If He couldn't, then there is at least one thing He can't do and therefore He is not omnipotent; and if He could, then as soon as He creates such a being He ceases to be omnipotent. This suggests that the idea of an omnipotent being is self-contradictory.

2 ***The paradox of change*** This paradox arises when we ask how a God who is perfect can intervene in human history as He has traditionally been thought to do. The problem is that being perfect is like being at the top of a mountain in that if you move at all you can only go in one direction: down. So it seems that, if God takes any action, He will inevitably become imperfect which contradicts our assumption that He is a perfect being.

3 ***The paradox of suffering*** This troubling paradox arises from the twin assumptions that 'God is all-loving and does not want us to suffer' and that 'God is all-powerful and is able to prevent us from suffering'. Why then is there so much suffering in the world? We will discuss the problem of suffering in more detail later in this chapter (see p. 417).

4 ***The paradox of free-will*** If God is all-knowing, then He knows not only the past and the present, but also the future. This means that He knows not only everything we have done in the past, but also everything we will do in the future. This would seem to make human free-will an illusion and reduce us to nothing more than characters in a divinely predetermined script.

A believer might be undisturbed by the above paradoxes and simply argue that human reason is unable to comprehend the infinite. Since we are finite beings, it could be argued that we can no more understand God than a worm can understand a human being. Faced with the difficulty of talking about God without running into paradoxes, some mystics have claimed that the highest religious truths lie beyond language and are to be found only in silence.

Is religious language meaningless?

At this point, an atheist may become impatient and insist that if religion cannot tell us anything about the nature of God, then believers are not really saying anything when they claim that God exists. This was the line taken by a group of philosophers, known as the **logical positivists**, who were active in the middle of the twentieth century. They argued that a statement is genuinely meaningful only if it can be empirically verified or falsified. Since they thought that religious statements do not satisfy this requirement they concluded that they are meaningless. If we accept this position, then so-called religious statements are *not even false* and they have no more significance than the sound of the wind on a stormy night or the baying of a dog at the moon.

"You're kidding! You count S.A.T.s?"

Figure 13.3

Fortunately, we are not obliged to accept the logical positivists' theory of meaning and most philosophers are unconvinced by the arguments put forward to support it. At a common-sense level, we might agree that religious language is sometimes difficult to understand, but still insist that we have some idea what people are talking about when they discuss the existence of God.

Furthermore, although 'God exists' is a metaphysical rather than an empirical proposition, there may be evidence that is at least *relevant* to determining its truth or falsity. Indeed, if it turns out that there is life after death, we will presumably be able to verify the truth of religious propositions in the next life, even if we are unable to do so in this one. (On the other hand, if death really is the end, we will never be able to *falsify* religious propositions. So if atheists are right, they will never have the satisfaction of being able to say, 'I told you so!')

Activity 13.3

1 Which, if any, of the following would convince you that God exists?
   a A world littered with pieces of granite stamped with the words 'Made by God'
   b Scientific evidence that people who pray are more likely to survive heart surgery than people who do not
   c A thousand people at an atheist convention having a religious experience which makes them believe in God
   d An earthquake which destroys a city, killing all of the atheists but none of the believers
   e Surviving completely unharmed in a plane crash in which everyone else is killed
   f A declaration by the world's five hundred most intelligent people saying that they believe in God

2 What evidence, if any, would convince you that God does not exist?

FIRST CONTACT

Figure 13.4

The argument from religious experience

We saw above that difficulties arise when we try to define God, and some theologians have pointed out that there is a big difference between the so-called 'God of the philosophers' and the 'God of Abraham, Isaac and Jacob'. Since the biblical patriarchs claimed to be directly acquainted with God, they would have felt no more need to define Him than you feel the need to define your mother or father. This draws attention to the fact that all religions are founded on a bedrock of intense personal experiences. Indeed, if no one had ever claimed to have had a religious experience, religion might not exist.

Despite their importance, religious experiences are, of course, very different from everyday experiences, and they are difficult, if not impossible, to verify. This has led sceptics to try to give natural or scientific explanations of such experiences. Thus when a mystic claims that God spoke to him in a dream, a sceptic might say that this is no different from saying that the mystic dreamt that God spoke to him. A sceptic might also point out that, since mystics frequently deprive themselves of food and sleep for long periods of time, it is not surprising that they end up having strange experiences. As the philosopher Bertrand Russell (1872–1970) wryly observed: 'From a scientific point of view, we can make no distinction between the man who eats little and sees heaven and the man who drinks much and sees snakes.' More recently, neuroscientists have observed that epileptic seizures can result in intense religious experiences, and this has led some people to speculate that St Paul and Joan of Arc may have been epileptics. A Canadian neuroscientist called Michael Persinger has even claimed that by stimulating the temporal lobes of the brain he can artificially induce religious experiences in people.

How should we respond to natural explanations for alleged religious phenomena? A religious person might begin by pointing out that *to explain something is not necessarily to explain it away*. Since we are – in part at least – material beings, it is not surprising that religious experiences can be correlated with various states of the brain. But it does not necessarily follow that they are illusions. After all, your experience of colour is also correlated with various states of the brain, but you would probably not conclude that colours are therefore unreal. Nor does the claim that epileptics are particularly prone to religious experiences prove anything one way or another. For it is possible that God has chosen to communicate to humanity primarily through such people. Perhaps, as the neuroscientist V. S. Ramachandran says:

> God has vouchsafed for us 'normal' people only occasional glimpses of a deeper truth... but these patients [epileptics] enjoy the unique privilege of gazing directly into God's eyes every time they have a seizure. Who is to say whether such experiences are 'genuine' (whatever that might mean) or 'pathological'?

There is, however, still the question of how religious experiences should be interpreted. The fact that people tend to interpret them in terms of their own cultural traditions – Buddhists do not have visions of the Virgin Mary, and Catholics do not have visions of the Buddha – suggests that they cannot simply be taken at face value. Moreover, since no one accepts *all* such experiences as valid, there is also the question of how to distinguish revelations from delusions. For example, David Koresh, the leader of an American religious cult called the Branch Davidians, claimed that he was the reincarnation of Jesus Christ; but most orthodox Christians would dismiss such a claim as blasphemy.

Miracles

While on the subject of religious experience, we should also say something about miracles. A miracle can be defined as an extraordinary event which is brought about by God's intervention in the natural order of things.

If, for example, you survived a plane crash that killed everyone else on board, you might say 'It was a miracle that I survived.' This is because there was an extremely low probability that anyone would survive. However, it is worth noting that extremely unlikely events happen surprisingly often if you look at a large enough population. For example, in a country of 300 million people, you should expect 300 chances-in-a-million to happen every day! So we should occasionally expect someone to survive a tragedy against the odds.

Perhaps we should adopt a more robust definition of a miracle and say that it is not merely an extremely unusual event, but one that contravenes the laws of nature. Think, for example, of biblical miracles such as the parting of the Red Sea, the turning of water into wine, or the raising of Lazarus. Such events, if they happened, would seem to provide compelling evidence for the existence of God. What are we to make of them?

Hume's argument against miracles

The Scottish philosopher David Hume (1711–76) was in no doubt about what we should think. He denied the existence of miracles and argued that it is never rational to believe in them because the weight of evidence must always be against them. Imagine a workman telling you that while he was working on a tenth-floor scaffolding yesterday he accidentally dropped a large brick. Since the street below was crowded with people, the brick could easily have killed someone. However, instead of falling to the ground, the brick miraculously stopped midway through its fall and then floated upwards into the heavens. Should you believe the workman? Hume says that you should not. Since there is a uniform body of evidence to show that when bricks are dropped they fall to the ground, it is surely more likely that the workman is deluded or lying than that the law of gravity has been broken. According to Hume, the same line of argument can be used against any alleged miracle. In short, it is always more likely that the witnesses to an alleged miracle are mistaken than that the laws of nature should suddenly stop working.

1 What, if anything, would convince you that a miracle had occurred? To what extent would you take into account the following factors?

   a The nature of the alleged miracle

   b The number of witnesses

   c The reliability of the witnesses

   d How long ago it happened

2 Do you think that Hume's argument against miracles would carry any conviction with someone who claimed to have witnessed a miracle herself?

3 We sometimes speak of 'the miracle of birth'. Is this just a metaphor, or do you think there is a sense in which birth really is a miracle?

4 G. K. Chesterton (1874–1936) once asked: 'Do you know why a pumpkin goes on being a pumpkin? If you don't, then you can't know whether sooner or later it won't turn into a coach?' What do you think Chesterton is getting at here?

5 Look back on our discussion of the problem of induction in Chapter 8 (p. 233). If we take the problem seriously, does it make belief in miracles more or less reasonable?

Does Hume's argument prove too much?

Hume's argument against miracles might be said to prove too much; for it implies that it is irrational to believe not only in miracles, but also in *any* observations that do not fit in with our current understanding of the world. However, in our discussion of natural science in Chapter 8, we saw that anomalous observations – ones that do not fit in with current ways of thinking – can play an important role in helping to bring about scientific revolutions. When nineteenth-century astronomers found that Mercury was deviating from the path predicted by Newton's laws of motion, Hume would presumably have said that they should reject the observation on the grounds that it was more likely that they were mistaken than that Newton's laws were wrong. But if they had done that, Einstein might never have come up with the theory of relativity. The problem, then, is that if we adopted Hume's approach, not only would miracles be outlawed but scientific progress would also grind to a halt.

   This suggests that we should not simply dismiss unusual or extraordinary events out of hand, but be willing to take them seriously. At the same time, we should keep in mind Carl Sagan's (1934–96) point that 'extraordinary claims require extraordinary evidence' (see Chapter 1, p. 15). And even if we accept that an event contradicts the laws of nature, we are not obliged to say that it is a miracle. For it might simply show the limitations of our current understanding of the world. As science progresses, what seems miraculous to one generation may be normal to the next. After all, a great deal of modern technology would seem miraculous to someone living two thousand years ago. This suggests that whether or not something is interpreted as a miracle depends, in part at least, on the state of scientific knowledge and our understanding of how the universe normally works.

We said above that a miracle is something that contradicts the laws of nature, but perhaps we should understand the word 'miracle' in a broader sense. For it could be argued that the underlying order and harmony of the universe – which makes the discovery of laws of nature possible – is itself a miracle. Some scientists claim to experience a feeling of wonder and awe bordering on the religious when they survey the universe. But, sadly, most people are so habituated to the world that they have lost whatever sense of wonder they might once have had. The result, in the words of a Jewish Sabbath prayer, is that, 'Days pass, years vanish, and we walk sightless among miracles.'

The idea that everything is a miracle is in some ways an attractive one; but whether or not the word 'miracle' has at this point become so broad as to lose its meaning, I leave for you to decide.

The argument from design

According to the argument from design, the order and harmony of the universe could not have come about by chance, but must have been made by an intelligent creator. The eighteenth-century theologian William Paley (1743–1805) made a famous analogy between a watch and a watchmaker on the one hand and God and the world on the other. If you discovered an old watch on a beach, opened up the back and saw the intricate mechanism that drives it, you would naturally conclude that it had been made by a skilled watchmaker. Similarly, when you look at the order and harmony of the natural world, you can see the fingerprints of an intelligent designer on everything. As evidence, a biologist might point to the exquisite design of the eye, and a physicist to the majestic harmony of the heavens. According to Isaac Newton (1642–1727): 'This most beautiful system of the sun, planets and comets, could only proceed from the counsel and dominion of an intelligent and powerful Being.' The evidence from biology and physics was enough to convince most eighteenth-century scientists that the universe had indeed been designed.

"Sorry — He's changed His mind again. Stripes on the zebra, spots on the giraffe, no stars on the lion and make the elephant bigger and the amoebae smaller."

Figure 13.5

Activity 13.5

1 How does the 'hypothesis' of a divine creator to explain the order and harmony of the universe resemble a scientific hypothesis?

2 How good is the analogy of the watch and the watchmaker? How does the universe resemble a watch and how does it differ from it?

Hume's criticisms of the argument from design

There were, however, dissenting voices, and once again David Hume was foremost among the critics. According to Hume:

1   Paley's analogy is a poor one because there is in fact little resemblance between the world and a machine.

2   The most the argument from design can prove is the existence of an *architect* god – not a creator god. After all, a watchmaker does not create his parts out of nothing, but fashions them out of pre-existing material.

3   If we look at the universe objectively, it is far from clear that it was designed by an omnipotent and benevolent God. Indeed, for all we know, says Hume, the world 'is very faulty and imperfect, compared to a superior standard, and was only the first rude essay of some infant deity who afterwards abandoned it, ashamed of his lame performance'. As an anonymous wit once said, 'Don't worry, God is alive and well and now working on a less ambitious project.'

Does the theory of evolution make design unnecessary?

The theory of evolution would seem to cast further doubt on the argument from design. For it gives us a way of explaining the complexity and harmony of nature without having to appeal to a designer God. According to biologists, such complex and apparently well-designed features as a human eye or a bird's wing have developed through random changes over long periods of time. And the so-called 'balance of nature' can be explained by the fact that species evolved to fit in with their environment. As the scientist Paul Davies (1946–) summarises it:

> Darwin's theory of evolution demonstrated decisively that complex organization efficiently adapted to the environment could arise as a result of random mutations and natural selection. No designer is needed to produce an eye or a wing.

Since everything we see around us can be explained in terms of natural processes, it would seem, echoing Paley, that nature itself is the watchmaker – but, unlike God, a blind rather than prescient watchmaker.

Physics and the new argument from design

Recently, a new version of the argument has emerged which focuses more on physics than biology, and the laws underlying the universe rather than the things within it. Some physicists have drawn attention to the mysterious fact that the universe is not only orderly, but orderly in such a way that it can be understood by human beings. To the religiously inclined, this suggests that there is some kind of rational plan behind the universe.

The mystery deepens when we ask ourselves why the laws of physics are the way they are. For it almost looks as if some of the key values, such as the speed of light, the force of gravity and the charge carried by electrons, have been fine-tuned to guarantee the emergence of life in the universe. Take, for example, gravity, which determines how much things are attracted to each other. If it was any stronger, things would be crushed together; and if it was any weaker, they would fly apart. The other laws are equally fine-tuned, and if their values had been even slightly different, then life would never have appeared in the universe. Yet scientists have no explanation for these astonishing coincidences. How, then, should we interpret them? According to Paul Davies,

> If it is the case that the existence of life requires the laws of physics and the initial conditions of the universe to be fine-tuned to high precision, and that fine-tuning does in fact obtain, then the suggestion of design seems compelling.

A different possibility, which is taken seriously by some physicists, and which avoids invoking a creator God, is that we inhabit a 'multiverse', and our universe is only one of an infinite number of universes. Since every conceivable value for the laws of physics is explored in one universe or another, the values that hold in our universe were bound to turn up somewhere. So the multiverse hypothesis explains the coincidence of fine-tuning, but only at what might seem the exorbitant price of an infinite number of universes. This hypothesis is, of course, highly speculative, and, on our current understanding at least, there is no way we could prove the existence of these other universes.

We seem to be left with a choice between two metaphysical hypotheses: a universe designed by an intelligent creator, or an infinity of universes. If you do not like either of these options, you might say that the laws of nature are simply brute facts about the universe that we will never be able to explain. Yet brute facts sit uncomfortably with the human intellect, and it is hard for us to resist the itch to make sense of things.

Activity 13.6

Read the following piece by Douglas Adams (1952–2001). How does it affect your view of the argument from design?

'Imagine a puddle waking up one morning and thinking, "This is an interesting world I find myself in – an interesting hole I find myself in – fits me rather neatly, doesn't it? In fact it fits me staggeringly well, must have been made to have me in it!" This is such a powerful idea that as the sun rises in the sky and the air heats up and as, gradually, the puddle gets smaller and smaller, it's still frantically hanging on to the notion that everything's going to be alright, because this world was meant to have him in it, was built to have him in it; so the moment he disappears catches him rather by surprise. I think this may be something we need to be on the watch out for.'

The cosmological argument

The cosmological argument for the existence of God is based not on the order of the universe but on the fact that it exists at all. Science can trace the history of the universe all the way back to the Big Bang fifteen billion years ago, but at that point it reaches an impasse. It is unable to answer the ultimate question, 'What caused the Big Bang?' Yet there must be an explanation. After all, the universe could not have sprung into existence out of nothing. Nothing can come from nothing. So the only possible explanation is that the universe was created by God. God, we might say, lit the fuse that set off the Big Bang.

How convincing do you find the cosmological argument? What criticisms, if any, would you make of it?

Some alternatives

Many arguments for the existence of God come down to the feeling that 'there must be something'. This may explain the popularity of the cosmological argument. But the question remains, Do we really need a creator God to explain the existence of the universe? At least two other alternatives suggest themselves:

1   ***The universe has always existed***   Although cosmologists believe that the universe originated in the Big Bang, some are willing to entertain as a speculative possibility the idea that the Big Bang is itself the result of a Big Crunch, and that the universe has been expanding and contracting for ever in an endless series of cycles. Interestingly, a similar idea can be found in Hindu philosophy, which traditionally had a much better grasp of the vast extent of cosmic time than the West. (The basic cycle in Hinduism is known as a 'day of Brahma' and lasts 4,200 million years. This is a far cry from Archbishop Ussher, a seventeenth-century Irish cleric, who calculated that the world was created on the evening of 22 October 4004 BCE!)

Activity 13.8

Do you think it makes sense to say that the universe is eternal and goes back infinitely far in time?

2   ***The Big Bang was the uncaused first cause***   A second alternative to a creator God is to deny that everything has a cause and to argue that the Big Bang was an uncaused event – the ultimate brute fact. Perhaps the universe was born by chance from a wrinkle in the fabric of nothingness. The idea of something coming from nothing is, admittedly, as difficult to understand as the idea that the universe is eternal; for we tend naturally to believe that everything has a cause and that nothing can come into existence out of pure nothingness. But perhaps our belief in the causal principle is simply a metaphysical prejudice, perhaps it is simply wrong to think that every event has a cause.

To many people the idea that God created the universe makes more sense than the idea that it has always existed or that it appeared by chance. But this solution invites the question that children sometimes ask: 'And who made God?' The answer is, of course, that God is the *uncreated* creator and requires no cause; but this answer contradicts our initial assumption that everything has a cause. For we are now saying that everything *except God* has a cause. As the philosopher Arthur Schopenhauer (1788–1860) observed, supporters of the cosmological argument treat the causal principle like a hired cab which they dismiss when they have reached their destination. So we seem to be faced with the following dilemma: either everything has a cause, in which case God must have a cause; or it is not the case that everything has a cause, in which case the universe could have come into existence by chance. Neither of these options gives us an uncreated creator.

1 When you create something new, such as a piece of music or a novel or a painting, the whole is greater than the sum of the parts. Does this show that something can come from nothing? What has this got to do with our discussion?

2 Imagine finding a sandcastle on the beach. When you ask someone who made it, they reply 'The Unknown Builder'. How does this differ from saying 'I don't know'? What has this got to do with our discussion?

3 What distinguishes a good explanation from a bad explanation? Do you think the claim that God created the universe is a good explanation or a bad one? Give reasons.

Perhaps the reason that a believer finds the idea of a creator God a satisfying explanation is not so much that it solves the problem of where the universe came from as that it guarantees that the universe has a meaning and that our lives have significance. Most people would rather believe that we are part of a divine plan than that we are simply a cosmic accident in a meaningless universe. However, an atheist might say that it is a category mistake to ascribe meaning to the universe in the same way that it is a category mistake to ascribe weight to a dream. If that is the case, then it makes no more sense to say that the universe is meaningless than that it is meaningful – just as it makes no more sense to say that dreams are light than that they are heavy. On this view, meaning is not so much something we discover in the universe as something we create in our lives. At this point in the argument we reach an impasse, with a believer asserting, and a non-believer denying, that the universe must have some kind of deeper meaning.

Whether or not you believe in God, the existence of the universe remains a highly puzzling fact. If you are a believer, you might wonder why God bothered creating the universe. Was He lonely, or bored, or somehow incomplete? If you are not a believer, you might wonder why the universe goes to all the bother of existing, why anything at all exists rather than nothing. This is surely a mystery that will always lie beyond the reach of science.

"This is a little embarrassing to admit, but everything that happens happens for no real reason."

Figure 13.6

The problem of suffering

We now need to consider one of the main arguments against the existence of God – the problem of suffering. As we saw earlier, the problem arises from the fact that God is supposed to be not only all-powerful, but also all-loving. For it would seem that if He is all-powerful, He is able to prevent our suffering; and if He is all-loving, He does not want us to suffer. So why is there so much suffering in the world? We seem forced to conclude either that God is not all-powerful and that suffering is the result of circumstances beyond His control, or that He is not all-loving and that He doesn't care about our plight. Perhaps God created the universe, but it didn't turn out the way He had planned; or perhaps He created it and then lost interest in it. Neither of these options is very attractive. If God is an incompetent bungler, or a heartless dictator, then He hardly seems worthy of worship.

The free-will defence

One standard response to the problem of suffering is known as the **free-will defence**. As the name suggests, this says that God gave human beings free-will, and that we have misused our freedom to inflict suffering on one another. If you look at the raw statistics, there would seem to be something in this argument. Take war, for example. Since 1500, an estimated 142 million people have died in more than 600 wars around the world. During the same period, there have been at least 36 genocides, leading one commentator to bleakly observe that 'Genocide is as human as art and prayer.' Now look at poverty. Something like 24,000 people starve to death every day; yet the United States and Europe spend more money on pet food every year than it would take to feed the one billion undernourished people on the planet. With these uncomfortable facts in mind, we clearly have a lot to answer for in terms of our contribution to world suffering.

Does the free-will defence 'let God off the hook' when it comes to responsibility for suffering? Some critics have argued that it does not. We might, for example, ask why God could not have made the universe with slightly different laws of physics so that we could not develop weapons of mass destruction. Indeed, why could He not have made us in such a way that we are free, yet always freely choose to do what is good? Well, perhaps always 'freely' choosing to do what is good is no different from not being free at all. A believer might argue that, if we are to have genuine freedom, then the freedom to sin must be a real option.

However, even if the free-will defence resolves one paradox, it seems to do so only at the expense of creating another. For if the problem of suffering is explained by the fact that human beings have free-will, we might now ask how we can reconcile human free-will with divine omniscience. The problem is that, if God knows everything, then He must know our future as well as our past – indeed, He must have known our entire life stories from the beginning of time. This would seem to reduce us to little more than characters in a divine novel, or computer simulation. However, in response to this it could be said that, since God does not *force* us to make the choices that we make, divine foreknowledge is perfectly compatible with human free-will. Whether or not the two really are compatible is something that different people have different intuitions about.

Natural suffering

Another problem with the free-will defence is that it only addresses the suffering which is brought about by human beings. What are we to say about all of the 'natural' suffering in the world? The argument from design suggests that God's goodness can be read out of His creation; but you might well disagree with that. For while some religious believers wax lyrical about the beauty and harmony of nature, one could just as easily point to its ugliness and cruelty. Think, for example, of such things as earthquakes, tornadoes, sharks, scorpions, cancer and malaria. Such examples of nature's cruelty would seem to be difficult to reconcile with the existence of a benevolent creator.

One possible response to the existence of natural suffering is to argue that, despite appearances, we live in *the best of all possible worlds*. The key idea here is that the world comes as a 'package deal', and it would be impossible to have a perfectly good world without any suffering, just as it would be impossible to have a mountain without a valley. Advocates of this view generally argue that the best possible world is not necessarily the happiest, but the one that brings the most opportunity for growth and development. With this in mind, it could be argued that the apparent cruelty of nature contributes to the greater good and that 'good cometh out of evil'. This was a line taken by the philosopher Immanuel Kant (1724–1804). He claimed that the reason God created mosquitoes was 'to urge... primitive men to drain the marshes and bring light into the dense forests that shut out the air, and, by so doing... to render their abodes more sanitary'.

This line of argument is connected with the idea that suffering has an educative value. When parents punish their children, they sometimes speak of being 'cruel to be kind'. And sports coaches are fond of the expression, 'No pain, no gain.' So perhaps natural suffering helps us to grow and develop as individuals. Despite the havoc caused by such things as earthquakes, forest fires and tsunamis, one might point out that they sometimes bring out the best in people, and give rise to acts of heroism, self-sacrifice and simple generosity. They may also give survivors a new sense of perspective and help them to see that what really matters in life are not material possessions, but personal relationships.

1 Give some examples of the apparent goodness and kindness of nature.
2 Give some examples of where the apparent cruelty of nature turns out to be beneficial.
3 Do you think that on balance nature is more cruel than kind, or more kind than cruel?

All Things Bright and Beautiful	*All Things Dull and Ugly*
All things bright and beautiful,	*All things dull and ugly,*
All creatures great and small,	*All creatures short and squat,*
All things wise and wonderful,	*All things rude and nasty,*
The Lord God made them all.	*The Lord God made the lot.*
Each little flower that opens,	*Each little snake that poisons,*
Each little bird that sings –	*Each little wasp that stings,*
He made their glowing colours,	*He made their brutish venom,*
He made their tiny wings.	*He made their horrid wings.*
From a hymn by Cecil Frances Alexander	A parody of the Alexander hymn by Monty Python

There are two main problems with the above defence of suffering. First, it is far from clear that the alleged benefits of natural suffering outweigh the costs in terms of death and destruction. Second, even if they do, this does not explain the *distribution* of suffering. If good people prospered and only bad people were struck down, we might claim to see the working of divine justice in the distribution of suffering. But it seems that the good suffer as much as the bad, the innocent as much as the guilty. The suffering of little children seems particularly difficult to reconcile with the belief in an all-loving God. For it is hard to see how anything could justify the death of thousands of innocent children in an earthquake or a tsunami.

1 Given that God is omnipotent, do you think that He could have created the world with less suffering in it?
2 To what extent do natural disasters bring out the best in people, and to what extent do they bring out the worst in people?
3 In the novel *The Brothers Karamazov*, by Fyodor Dostoevsky (1821–81), one of the characters, Ivan, gives his brother, Alyosha, the following challenge:
'"Imagine that you are creating a fabric of human destiny with the object of making men happy in the end, giving them peace and rest at last, but that it was essential and inevitable to torture to death only one tiny creature – that baby beating its breast with its fist, for

instance – and to found the edifice on its unavenged tears, would you consent to be the architect on those conditions? Tell me and tell me the truth."

"No, I wouldn't consent", said Alyosha softly.'

Do you agree or disagree with Alyosha's response to Ivan's challenge? Give reasons.

4 To what extent could it be argued that so-called 'natural disasters' are the result of our interfering with the balance of nature, and are therefore our responsibility?

While an atheist sees the existence of natural suffering as evidence against the existence of God, a believer might say that it is foolish to try to comprehend the will of God in any detail. For religion is based more on faith than reason – in this case faith that there is a divine plan and that everything is for the best. Perhaps it is time to look more closely at the relation between reason and faith.

Reason versus faith

We have looked at various arguments for and against the existence of God, but we have not arrived at any definite conclusion. This is hardly surprising – since certainty cannot be found in any other area of knowledge, we should not expect to find it in an area as difficult and controversial as religion. Indeed, since human understanding is limited and cannot comprehend the infinite, many believers would say that it is absurd to try to prove the existence of God. If God wished, then presumably He could reveal Himself in a way that left us in no doubt about His existence; but then we would have no choice about what to believe. So perhaps the lack of proof gives us the freedom to decide for ourselves and the lack of knowledge leaves room for faith.

What is faith?

The word 'faith' is difficult to define in a neutral way. On the positive side, St Paul defined it as 'the conviction of things hoped for and the assurance of things not seen'. On the negative side, Sigmund Freud (1856–1939) dismissed it as 'the believing of propositions upon insufficient evidence'. More neutrally, we might say that faith is a kind of belief which is held with a strong emotional commitment and concerns things that have great significance to the believer.

1 In which of the following cases does it make sense to say, 'I have faith that...'? Give reasons.

   a 2 + 2 = 4.
   b God exists.
   c John is in the washroom.
   d There is life after death.
   e My friends will be there when I need them.
   f I will pass the IB.
   g I will fail the IB.
   h The universe is orderly.
   i Janet hates me.
   j Life is meaningful.
   k I will be in a car crash.
   l Manchester United will win the European Champions League.

2 What role, if any, does evidence play in the statements where it makes sense to say 'I have faith that...'?

Is faith rational?

As Freud's definition of faith suggests, most atheists would say that, while scientific belief is rational, religious faith is irrational and amounts to little more than **wish fulfilment**. Since you are keen to believe that something is true, you convince yourself, on the basis of little or no evidence, that it really is true.

An atheist might point out that, as our scientific knowledge of the universe has expanded, the role played by God has contracted. Thus while primitive people explained thunder and lightning as the anger of the gods, we can now explain them in terms of build-up of electricity in the atmosphere. And while people once attributed complex organs such as eyes and wings to a designer God, we can now explain them in terms of Darwin's theory of evolution. Extrapolating from this, an atheist might argue we will eventually be able to explain everything that is worth knowing in terms of science, and that religion, which Freud saw as a childish form of escapism, will eventually wither away.

Despite Freud's belief that faith and reason are opposed to one another, many religious traditions emphasise the rationality of faith. For example, in Islam, the prophet Muhammad said that 'God has not created anything better than reason'; and, in Christianity, the philosopher Thomas Aquinas (1225–74) argued that reason and faith are complementary ways of seeking the truth. As we have seen, there are several rational arguments for the existence of God, and even though none of them is conclusive, taken together they might be said to provide a rational foundation for faith.

Thomas Aquinas claimed that once we have acquired faith we look at the world differently, and begin to see God's fingerprints on everything. This, I think, is what he meant when he said: 'The light of faith makes us see what we believe.' We might then think of religious faith as a kind of **paradigm** through which we interpret our experience and make sense of the world. But this line of argument cuts both ways: perhaps if you commit yourself to atheism, you will see signs of God's non-existence wherever you look!

Science and religion

When it comes to the relation between science and religion, most religious believers would claim that they are quite consistent with one another. After all, many famous scientists have believed in God, and they seem to have had no difficulty in reconciling their scientific beliefs with their religious beliefs. One way of trying to do this is to say that while science is concerned with the *how* of the universe, religion is concerned with its *why*, and that problems arise only when religion gets involved with *how* questions, or science with *why* questions. If religion tries to answer scientific questions by, for example, insisting that the sun goes round the earth, or that each species is uniquely created by God, then it will find itself having to retreat before the forward march of science. (The Catholic Church belatedly acquitted Galileo of heresy in 1993; and it finally accepted evolution 'as an effectively proven fact' in 1996.) And if science tries to answer religious questions by pontificating about ultimate reality or human destiny, then it effectively ceases to be science and becomes a kind of religion. (You might like to look back at our discussion of the difference between science and scientism in Chapter 8, p. 246.)

A religious apologist might also point out that there is a sense in which not only religion but also science is based on faith. For a scientist must have faith that the universe is orderly, and that human beings are capable of discovering that order. (Since we can never be certain of anything, it could, indeed, be argued that there is an element of faith built into *all* knowledge claims.) However, an atheist might argue that the faith of a scientist is quite different from that of a religious person, and that while our belief in an orderly universe is confirmed by experience every day, we struggle to find consistent signs of God's love for us.

Activity 13.14

1 How is the faith of a scientist similar to the faith of a religious believer? How is it different?
2 Do you think that having faith in something necessarily means that one is religious?

Pascal's wager

The philosopher Blaise Pascal (1623–62) argued that a rational person ought to bet on the existence of God. The argument runs as follows. Since we do not know whether or not God exists, let us assume that the odds are 50–50. Now consider the gains and losses of betting on God's existence or non-existence. If you bet that God exists and you are right, you hit the jackpot – heaven. And if you are wrong – well, you haven't really lost anything. If you bet that God does not exist and you are right, you win nothing. But if you are wrong, it's bad news – hell. Given this distribution of potential gains and losses, Pascal concluded that a rational gambler ought to bet on the existence of God.

	God exists	God does not exist
You bet that God exists	You win everything	You lose nothing
You bet that God does not exist	You lose everything	You win nothing

Despite its ingenuity, most people have been unconvinced by **Pascal's wager** and there are many arguments against it. In fairness to Pascal, he saw his wager as being only the first step in pushing a wavering atheist towards religion. His idea seems to have been that religion is ultimately a matter of *practice*, and that if you begin leading a religious life you will end up genuinely believing in God.

Activity 13.15

1 Do you think it is possible to make yourself believe in God if you have not previously believed in Him?
2 Assuming that God exists, how do you think He would feel about someone who cynically gambles on His existence as a kind of insurance policy?
3 Would you agree that you lose nothing if you bet that God exists and it turns out that He does not?
4 If you don't believe in God, but have led a good life, do you think that you would still lose everything and go to hell if it turns out that God exists?
5 Since there are many different religions in the world, does Pascal's wager apply to all of them? Does this mean that you should sign up for every religion?

Is faith irrational?

Some religious believers have taken a different approach to the relation between faith and reason and have argued that faith is indeed irrational, but that faith without evidence is superior to faith based on evidence. When in the Christian tradition the apostle Thomas refused to believe that Jesus had risen from the dead until he had the evidence of his own eyes, Jesus then said to him: 'Because you have seen me, you have believed; blessed are those who have not seen and yet have believed.'

One way of trying to make sense of this appeal to the irrationality of faith is by seeing that there are limits to reason. Pascal once said that reason's last and greatest step is to recognise that there are many things that lie beyond it. His point was that reason can take us only so far, and that when it comes to our **core intuitions** about the nature of reality, we have no choice but to appeal to faith. As we saw in our discussion of such intuitions in Chapter 6, there is no way we can prove any of the following beliefs, and yet we remain committed to their truth:

- Life is not a dream.
- Other people have minds.
- The laws of physics will not break down tomorrow.
- The past really happened.

So rather than say that faith is as rational as our other beliefs, we might say that faith is indeed irrational but so are our other core beliefs. In this situation, what is required is not so much a proof as a decision – a **leap of faith**. To believe or not to believe, that is the question!

The varieties of religion

For much of this chapter we have spoken as if there is some one thing called religion; but there are, of course, many different religions in the world. The four biggest in terms of numbers of adherents are: Christianity (2,000 million), Islam (1,300 million), Hinduism (900 million) and Buddhism (360 million). Other major world religions include Confucianism, Shintoism, Taoism, Judaism, Sikhism, and the Baha'i faith. The question that we must now consider is how these different religions are related to one another.

"We're thinking maybe it's time you started getting some religious instruction. There's Catholic, Protestant, and Jewish — any of those sound good to you?"

Figure 13.7

If we take what different religions say at face value, then they clearly contradict one another. For there are many different views about such things as the nature of God, what happens when you die, and which prophets and holy books contain the truth.

Activity 13.16

Compare and contrast the beliefs of two different religions about the following topics:
a How the universe came into existence
b The existence of suffering
c What happens when you die

"You picked the wrong religion, period. I'm not going to argue about it."

Figure 13.8

There are three possible ways of responding to the fact that different religions contradict one another.

1 One religion is true and all the rest are false

This approach has the attraction of simplicity, but it raises the question of how we should determine which religion is true and which are false. The problem is complicated by the fact that within each religion there are many different sects each claiming that *it* is the sole guardian of the truth. For example, in North America, there are more than a thousand different Christian groups, many of which believe that they alone are the one true church.

Activity 13.17

1 What reasons, if any, are there for believing that some religions are superior to others?
2 If it does turn out that one religion is true and all the rest are false, what do you think the consequences will be for good people who happen to have followed the wrong religion?

---

2 All religions are false

The second option, favoured by atheists, is to take the variety of religious beliefs as evidence for their all being false. Several related points can be made here.

a   Since any evidence in support of one religion counts as evidence *against* every other religion, and since every religion puts forward evidence in support of its own doctrines, the balance of evidence and counter-evidence for any particular religion would seem to cancel out.

b   We cannot appeal to the passion of the faithful to decide between different religions because the faithful of different religions hold their beliefs with equal passion.

c   The fact that, in practice, the vast majority of religious people follow the beliefs of the community they grow up in might suggest that they are simply culturally conditioned beliefs.

Christianity
Islam
Hinduism
Buddhism
Judaism
Chinese
Others

Figure 13.9 Map of world religions

3 All religions point towards the same underlying truth

A third possible response to the fact that different religions contradict one another is to argue that, despite superficial differences, they are all pointing towards the same underlying truth. An analogy that is sometimes used to illustrate this idea is that of the blind men and the elephant. One blind man holds the elephant's leg and thinks that an elephant is like a big tree; a second grabs its trunk and insists that it is like a large snake; a third touches its side and concludes it is like a huge wall. While each of the blind men is convinced that he is right and the others are wrong, they are, of course, all touching the same elephant. Perhaps in a similar way, different religions have captured different aspects of the same underlying truth.

This option, which is sometimes known as **religious pluralism**, is an attractive one for at least three reasons. First, it takes seriously the religious beliefs of millions of people. Second, while admitting that the world's religions are culturally conditioned, it nevertheless holds that they are genuine responses to the same underlying religious truth. Third, if widely embraced, it might do something to reduce religious conflicts in the world. However, as noted elsewhere, the mere attractiveness of an option does not guarantee that it is true.

Despite the analogy of the blind men and the elephant, the biggest obstacle to religious pluralism remains the fact that different religions appear to contradict one another. One way of trying to get round this problem is to argue that many religious statements are not literally true, but only metaphorically true. The Bible, for example, says that God created the world in seven days, but many Christians are comfortable with the idea that this is not literally true.

The idea that some religious statements should be interpreted metaphorically rather than literally is an interesting one, but it solves one problem only by creating another. For the question now is: which statements should we interpret literally and which metaphorically? A Christian, for example, might be happy to take the idea that God created the world in seven days metaphorically, but what about the virgin birth or the resurrection?

As attractive as religious pluralism is, it is hard to avoid the conclusion that the explicit beliefs of different religions contradict one another. And yet the similarities that can be found in the mystical experiences of people from many different traditions continue to nourish the belief that, at the deepest level, all religions point towards the same underlying truth.

Pantheism

There are many people who do not subscribe to any organised religion, and yet experience a sense of wonder when they contemplate starry skies, or stormy seas or snow-covered mountains. Since such feelings engender a sense of being part of something greater than ourselves, they, too, might loosely be described as religious.

Perhaps not surprisingly, pantheism – the belief that God and nature are one – seems to be particularly popular among scientists. For example, although Einstein (1879–1955) explicitly denied that he believed in a God 'who concerns himself with the fate and actions of human beings', he often spoke of his sense of awe in contemplating the universe, and he once wrote to a colleague: 'I have found no better expression than "religious" for confidence in the rational nature of reality, insofar as it is accessible to human reason.'

Such a 'nature religion' seems to be very different from theistic religions which speak of a creator God and an immortal soul, and heaven and hell, and miracles and prayer. So perhaps it is misleading to use the word 'religion' to cover both sets of beliefs. Indeed, since pantheism claims that God and nature are one, we might be tempted to agree with Schopenhauer (1788–1860) that it is simply a polite form of atheism. For it is difficult to see the difference between saying that everything is God and nothing is God. There does, however, seem to be at least a difference in *flavour* between pantheism's reverence for nature and some cruder forms of atheistic materialism which lack any sense of wonder at the world and see nature as merely something to be exploited for human ends.

1   Do some research on the Internet and read the Pantheist Credo drawn up by the World Pantheist Movement. Which points in the Credo do you agree with and which do you disagree with?
2   What arguments can be made for and against Schopenhauer's claim that pantheism is simply a polite form of atheism?

Conclusion

Our discussion in this chapter has raised many of the big questions about the meaning and purpose of life. While some people turn to religion to find the answers to these questions, others believe that religion raises more questions than it answers. If anything has come out of our discussion, it is that there are no easy options in this area. Perhaps religious believers and atheists can at least agree that we are not gods and that – in this life at least – we will never have the answers to the deepest mysteries. And perhaps if we can learn to hold even our deepest beliefs with a degree of humility, we will be less likely to kill one another in the name of things we do not fully understand.

Key points

- Religions are concerned with questions of meaning and purpose which trouble all human beings.
- If we try to define God, we are in danger of falling into anthropomorphism or running into paradoxes, but this does not mean that religious language is meaningless.
- All religions are founded on a bedrock of intense personal experiences, but opinions differ about how such experiences should be interpreted.
- The argument from design sees the order and harmony of the universe as evidence for the existence of God, but critics argue that there are natural explanations for such order.
- The cosmological argument says that, since everything has a cause, the universe must have been created by God; but we might then ask 'who created God?'
- Some see the existence of suffering as incompatible with an all-powerful and all-loving God; but it could be replied that much of the suffering in the world is a consequence of human free-will.
- Faith plays an important role in religion, but people have different views about what faith is and whether or not it is rational.
- The fact that there are many different religions in the world raises the question of whether they all contradict one another or whether they all point towards the same underlying truth.
- Some people are attracted by the pantheistic belief that God and nature are one; but critics argue that pantheism is simply a polite form of atheism.
- Since we will never have the answers to the deepest mysteries, it may be wise to hold our religious beliefs with a degree of humility.

Terms to remember

agnosticism	God of the philosophers	pantheism
anthropomorphism	leap of faith	paradox of omnipotence
argument from design	logical positivism	Pascal's wager
atheism	metaphysics	problem of suffering
core intuitions	omniamorous	religious pluralism
cosmological argument	omnipotent	theism
free-will defence	omniscient	wish fulfilment

Further reading

Richard H. Popkin and Avrum Stroll, *Philosophy Made Simple* (Heinemann, 1986), Chapter 4: 'Philosophy of religion'. This chapter gives a very clear and easy-to-follow account of some of the main arguments for and against the existence of God.

Todd C. Moody, *Does God Exist?: A Dialogue* (Hackett Publishing, 1996). This short and accessible book explores the question of the existence of God through a series of dialogues. It is worth reading a couple of them to get a sense of how arguments and counter-arguments can be developed in this area.

Linking questions

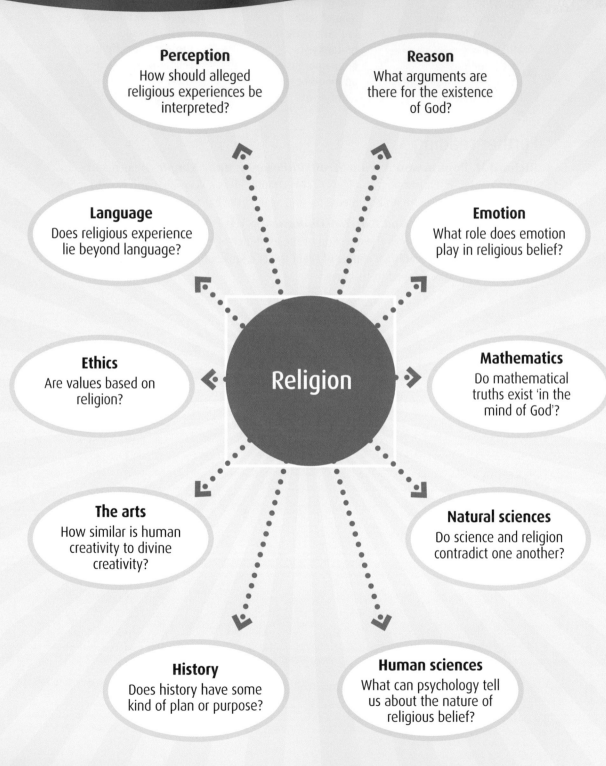

Perception
How should alleged religious experiences be interpreted?

Reason
What arguments are there for the existence of God?

Language
Does religious experience lie beyond language?

Emotion
What role does emotion play in religious belief?

Religion

Ethics
Are values based on religion?

Mathematics
Do mathematical truths exist 'in the mind of God'?

The arts
How similar is human creativity to divine creativity?

Natural sciences
Do science and religion contradict one another?

History
Does history have some kind of plan or purpose?

Human sciences
What can psychology tell us about the nature of religious belief?

TESTS OF FAITH

Religion may be a survival mechanism. So are we born to believe? Ian Sample reports in this article from the *Guardian* (24 February 2005).

First for some figures. Last year, an ICM poll found 85% of Americans believe that God created the universe. In Nigeria, 98% claimed always to have believed in God, while nine out of 10 Indonesians said they would die for their God or religious beliefs. Last month, a survey by the market research bureau of Ireland found 87% of the population believe in God. Rather than rocking their faith, 19% said tragedies such as the Asian tsunami, which killed 300,000 people, bolstered their belief. Polls have their faults, but if the figures are even remotely right they illustrate the prevalence of faith in the modern world.

Faith has long been a puzzle for science, and it's no surprise why. By definition, faith demands belief without a need for supporting evidence, a concept that could not be more opposed to the principles of scientific inquiry. In the eyes of the scientist, an absence of evidence reduces belief to a hunch. It places the assumptions at the heart of many religions on the rockiest of ground.

So why do so many people believe? And why has belief proved so resilient as scientific progress unravels the mysteries of plagues, floods, earthquakes and our understanding of the universe? By injecting nuns with radioactive chemicals, by scanning the brains of people with epilepsy and studying naughty children, scientists are now working out why. When the evidence is pieced together, it seems that evolution prepared what society later moulded: a brain to believe.

One factor in the development of religious belief was the rapid expansion of our brains as we emerged as a species, says Todd Murphy, a behavioural neuroscientist at Laurentian University in Canada. As the frontal and temporal lobes grew larger, our ability to extrapolate into the future and form memories developed. 'When this happened, we acquired some very new and dramatic cognitive skills. For example, we could see a dead body and see ourselves in that position one day. We could think "That's going to be me", he says. That awareness of impending death prompted questions: why are we here? What happens when we die? Answers were needed.

As well as providing succour for those troubled by the existential dilemma, religion, or at least a primitive spirituality, would have played another important role as human societies developed. By providing contexts for a moral code, religious beliefs encouraged bonding within groups, which in turn bolstered the group's chances of survival, says Pascal Boyer, an anthropologist turned psychologist at Washington University in St Louis, Missouri. Some believe that religion was so successful in improving group survival that a tendency to believe was positively selected for in our evolutionary history. Others maintain that religious belief is too modern to have made any difference.

'What I find more plausible is that rather than religion itself offering any advantage in evolutionary terms, it's a byproduct of other cognitive capacities we evolved, which did have advantages,' says Boyer.

Psychological tests Boyer has run on children go some way to proving our natural tendency to believe. 'If you look at three- to five-year-olds, when they do something naughty, they have an intuition that everyone knows they've been naughty, regardless of whether they have seen or heard what they've done. It's a false belief, but it's good preparation for belief in an entity that is moral and knows everything,' he says. 'The idea of invisible agents with a moral dimension who are watching you is highly attention-grabbing to us.'

Childish belief is one thing, but religious belief is embraced by people of all ages and is by no means the preserve of the uneducated. According to Boyer, the persistence of belief into adulthood is at least in part down to a presumption. 'When you're in a belief system, it's not that you stop asking questions, it's that they become irrelevant. Why don't you ask yourself about the existence of gravity? It's because a lot of the stuff you do every day presupposes it and it seems to work, so where's the motivation to question it?' he says. 'In belief systems, you tend to enter this strange state where you start thinking there must be something to it because everybody around you is committed to it. The general question of whether it's true is relegated.'

While some continue to tease out the reasons for the emergence of religion and its persistent appeal, others are delving into the neuroscience of belief in the hope of finding a biological basis for religious experience. As a starting point, many studies focused on people with particular neural conditions that made them prone to experiences so intense, they considered them to be visions of God.

At the University of California in San Diego, neuroscientist VS Ramachandran noticed that a disproportionate number of patients – around a quarter – with a condition called temporal lobe epilepsy reported having deeply moving religious experiences. 'They'd tell me they felt a presence or suddenly felt they got the meaning of the whole cosmos. And these could be life-changing experiences,' says Ramachandran. The feelings always came during seizures, even if the seizures were so mild, they could only be detected by sensitive electroencephalograms (EEGs). Between the seizures, some patients became preoccupied with thoughts about God.

Ramachandran drew up three explanations he thought might explain why the patients with epilepsy seemed so spiritual. First, he considered that the upwelling of emotion caused by the seizure might simply overwhelm, and patients made sense of it by believing that something extremely spiritual was going on. Second, the seizure might prompt the left hemisphere to make up yarns to account for seemingly inexplicable emotions. The ability of the brain's left hemisphere to 'confabulate' like this is well known to neuroscientists. Third, he wondered whether seizures disrupted the function of part of the brain called the amygdala which, among other tasks, helps us focus on what is significant while allowing us to ignore the trivial.

Ramachandran decided to test a couple of patients using what is called the galvanic skin response. Two electrodes are used to measure tiny changes in the skin's electrical conductivity, an indirect measure of sweating. In most people, conductivity goes up when they are shown violent or sexual pictures, or similarly loaded words. In the test, Ramachandran found that patients with temporal lobe epilepsy responded very differently from others. Violent words such as 'beat' and sexual words produced not a flicker, but religious icons and the word 'God' evoked a big response.

With only two patients involved in the study, Ramachandran says it is impossible to draw any conclusions, but if the results stand up to future testing, it might indicate that seizures in the temporal lobe strengthen certain neural pathways connected to the amygdala, meaning we attribute significance to banal objects and occurrences. 'If those pathways all strengthen indiscriminately, everything and anything acquires a deep significance, and when that happens, it starts resembling a religious experience,' he says. 'And if we can selectively enhance religious sentiments, then that seems to imply there is neural circuitry whose activity is conducive to religious belief. It's not that we have some God module in our brains, but we may have specialised circuits for belief.'

At the University of Pennsylvania, radiologist Andrew Newberg has cast a wider net to scan the brains of people performing all manner of spiritual activities. By injecting radioactive tracers into the veins of nuns, Buddhists and others, he has constructed brain maps that show how different practices affect neural processing. 'What comes out is there's a complex network in the brain and depending on what you do, it is activated in different ways,' says Newberg. 'If someone does Tibetan Buddhist meditation they'll activate certain parts of their brain, but if you have a nun praying they'll activate slightly different parts, with someone doing transcendental meditation activating other areas again.'

Newberg uncovered the neural processing behind the religious experience of 'oneness' with the universe. Blood flow drops off in the parietal lobe, a brain structure that helps us orient ourselves by giving us a sense of ourselves. 'We think this latter step is critical,' says Newberg. 'What seems to be happening is that as you block sensory information getting into the parietal lobe, it keeps trying to give you a sense of self, but it no longer has the information to do so. If that happens completely, you might get this absolute feeling of oneness.'

Newberg has been criticised for his investigations into the essence of spiritual experience – the most vehement attacks coming from atheists. 'Some people want me to say whether God is there or not, but these experiments can't answer that. If I scan a nun and she has the experience of being in the presence of God, I can tell you what's going on in her brain, but I can't tell you whether or not God is there,' he says. Religious groups point out that there is more to religion than extreme experiences. It is a criticism Newberg acknowledges. 'The problem is, the people who have these experiences are so much easier to study,' he says.

As neuroscientists unpick the biological mechanisms behind religious experience, others are considering what to do with the information. At Laurentian University, Todd Murphy and Michael Persinger are developing devices they think can stimulate parts of the brain to enhance spiritual experiences. Others see the possibility for drugs designed to boost spirituality. Newberg says this would be underpinning a practice that has existed for hundreds of years with scientific understanding. 'If you talk to a shaman who takes a substance so they can enter into the spirit world, they don't think that diminishes the experience in any way,' he says.

Intriguingly, many scientists, while stressing that they have set out to explore religion rather than disprove its basis, say that no matter what they uncover about the nature of spiritual experiences, mass religious belief will continue. The fastest growing religions in the US are the Mormon church and Scientology, both popular, according to Boyer largely because they are new. In other parts of the world, more fundamentalist religions succeed because they give a clear vision of the world.

'For two centuries, there's been competition between churches and in the free market of religion, the products get better and better as people want different things,' says Boyer. 'Will science be the death of religion? As neuroscience, it's interesting to see how brains can create very strange states of consciousness, but in terms of threatening religion, I think it'll have absolutely no effect.'

DIALOGUE ON THE COSMOLOGICAL ARGUMENT

Does the existence of the universe imply a creator God? The physicist Paul Davies looks at some of the arguments for and against in the following dialogue.

ATHEIST: At one time, gods were used as an explanation for all sorts of physical phenomena, such as the wind and the rain and the motion of the planets. As science progressed, so supernatural agents were found to be superfluous as an explanation for natural events. Why do you insist on invoking God to explain the big bang?

THEIST: Your science cannot explain everything. The world is full of mystery. For example, even the most optimistic biologists admit that they are baffled by the origin of life.

ATHEIST: I agree that science hasn't explained everything, but that doesn't mean it can't. Theists have always been tempted to seize on any process that science could not at the time explain and claim that God was still needed to explain it. Then as science progressed, God got squeezed out. You should learn the lesson that this 'God of the gaps' is an unreliable hypothesis. As time goes on, there are fewer and fewer gaps for him to inhabit. I personally see no problem in science explaining all natural phenomena, including the origin of life. I concede that the origin of the universe is a tougher nut to crack. But if, as it seems, we have now reached the stage where the only remaining gap is the big bang, it is highly unsatisfying to invoke the concept of a supernatural being who has been displaced from all else, in this 'last-ditch' capacity.

THEIST: I don't see why. Even if you reject the idea that God can act directly in the physical world once it has been created, the problem of the ultimate origin of the world is in a different category altogether from the problem of explaining natural phenomena once that world exists.

ATHEIST: But unless you have other reasons to believe in God's existence, then merely proclaiming 'God created the universe' is totally ad hoc. It is no explanation at all. Indeed, the statement is essentially devoid of meaning, for you are merely defining God to be that agency which creates the universe. My understanding is no further advanced by this device. One mystery (the origin of the universe) is explained only in terms of another (God). As a scientist I appeal to Occam's razor, which then dictates that the God hypothesis be rejected as an unnecessary complication. After all, I am bound to ask, what created God?

THEIST: God needs no creator. He is a necessary being – he must exist. There is no choice in the matter.

ATHEIST: But one might as well assert that the universe needs no creator. Whatever logic is used to justify God's necessary existence could equally well, and with an advantageous gain in simplicity, be applied to the universe.

THEIST: Surely scientists often follow the same reasoning as I have. Why does a body fall? Because gravity acts on it. Why does gravity act on it? Because there is a gravitational field. Why? Because space-time is curved. And so on. You are replacing one description with another, deeper description, the sole purpose of which is to explain the thing you started with, namely, falling bodies. Why do you then object when I invoke God as a deeper and more satisfying explanation of the universe?

ATHEIST: Ah, but that's different! A scientific theory should amount to much more than the facts it is trying to explain. Good theories provide a simplifying picture of nature by establishing connections between hitherto disconnected phenomena. Newton's gravitational theory, for example, demonstrated a connection between the ocean tides and the motion of the moon. In addition, good theories suggest observational tests, such as predicting the existence of new phenomena. They also provide detailed mechanistic accounts of precisely how the physical processes of interest happen in terms of the concepts of the theory. In the case of gravitation, this is through a set of equations that connect the strength of the gravitational field with the nature of the gravitating sources. This theory gives you a precise mechanism for how things work. By contrast, a God who is invoked only to explain the big bang fails in all three criteria. Far from simplifying our view of the world, a Creator introduces an additional complicating feature, itself without explanation. Second, there is no way we can test the hypothesis experimentally. There is only one place where such a God is manifested – namely, the big bang – and that is over and done with. Finally, the bald statement 'God created the universe' fails to provide any real explanation unless it is accompanied by a detailed mechanism. One wants to know, for example, what properties to assign to this God, and precisely how he goes about creating the universe, why the universe has the form it does, and so on. In short, unless you can either provide evidence in some other way that such a God exists, or else give a detailed account of how he made the universe that even an atheist like me would regard as deeper, simpler, and more satisfying, I see no reason to believe in such a being.

THEIST: Nevertheless, your own position is highly unsatisfactory, for you admit that the reason for the big bang lies outside the scope of science. You are forced to accept the origin of the universe as a brute fact, with no deeper level of explanation.

ATHEIST: I would rather accept the existence of the universe as a brute fact than accept God as a brute fact. After all, there has to be a universe for us to be here and argue about these things!

PART 4

Conclusion

14 Truth and wisdom

'There are no whole truths: all truths are half-truths.'
Alfred North Whitehead, 1861–1947

'All truth is a species of revelation.'
Samuel Taylor Coleridge, 1772–1834

'Truth is what stands the test of time.'
Albert Einstein, 1879–1955

'Knowledge is an unending adventure at the edge of uncertainty.'
Jacob Bronowski, 1908–74

'Keep the company of those who seek the truth, and run away from those who have found it.'
Václav Havel, 1936–

'When we believe with every fibre of our being that we have reached the truth, we must know that we believe, and not believe that we know.'
Jules Lequier, 1814–62

'What is truth but to live for an idea?... It is a question of discovering a truth which is truth for me, of finding the idea for which I am willing to live and die.'
Søren Kierkegaard, 1813–55

'Men stumble over the truth from time to time, but most pick themselves up and hurry off as if nothing had happened.'
Winston Churchill, 1874–1965

'There are many kinds of eyes... and consequently there are many kinds of "truths", and consequently there is no truth.'
Friedrich Nietzsche, 1844–1900

'We may be learned with another man's learning, but we can only be wise with wisdom of our own.'
Michel de Montaigne, 1533–92

'There are only two ways to live your life. One is as though nothing is a miracle. The other is as though everything is a miracle.'
Albert Einstein, 1879–1955

'If you wish to strive for peace of soul and pleasure, then believe; if you wish to be a devotee of truth, then inquire.'
Friedrich Nietzsche, 1844–1900

Introduction

Since we have been engaged in an investigation into the nature and limits of knowledge, there is a sense in which truth, like a ghost, has haunted the pages of this book. We cannot understand the nature of knowledge without some reference to the truth; and yet when we turn to examine it explicitly it seems to vanish before our eyes. The question 'What is truth?' looks innocent enough, but we can easily tie ourselves up in knots in trying to answer it.

We begin this chapter by looking at three different theories of truth: **the correspondence theory**, **the coherence theory** and **the pragmatic theory**. Although none of them is entirely satisfactory, each of them seems to capture a fragment of the 'truth about truth'. We then ask how, if at all, we can know the truth, and whether it makes sense to say that we are getting closer to the truth. Perhaps we can steer between the extremes of dogmatism – the belief that you possess the absolute truth – and relativism – the belief that there is no such truth to possess – by adopting what I call a cubist theory of truth. The thought here is that although absolute truth may lie beyond our grasp, we still need to keep hold of some concept of truth if we are to distinguish between reality and fantasy. There is, after all, a difference between *wishing* that something were true and its actually being true.

The habit of truth may help to discipline our thinking and encourage us to be objective, but disturbing questions remain about whether we should seek the truth at any price. Should we, for example, pursue the truth if it makes people unhappy, or if it can be exploited by the unscrupulous for evil and destructive ends? Since we live in a world of rapid and accelerating technological growth, such questions are of obvious relevance to us.

As we hurtle towards the future, we will need to think very carefully about how to use the knowledge we possess and the extent to which we should pursue it further. Given this, it is perhaps appropriate that we conclude this chapter with a discussion about the nature and value of wisdom.

Correspondence theory

According to the correspondence theory, a statement is true if it corresponds to a fact. For example, the statement 'Grass is green' is true if and only if grass is green; and the statement 'Violets are blue' is true if and only if violets are blue.

At first sight, this 'theory' may strike you as completely trivial. For it appears to be saying nothing more than that a statement is true if and only if it is true. Didn't we already know that? But one of the strengths of the correspondence theory is that it insists that truth depends on how things are in the world, and that a statement is true not because an authority said it was true, or because you happen to feel that it is true, but because it corresponds to something in reality. This belief was a powerful impetus behind the scientific revolution of the seventeenth century which helped to bring about the modern way of looking at the world.

Criticisms

1 Problems with facts

The correspondence theory says that a statement is true if it corresponds to a fact, but we might ask what it means for a fact to exist. The more you think about this question, the more puzzling it becomes. You may feel comfortable about the existence of particular facts, such as 'Paris is the capital of France'. But do you want to say that general facts, such as 'All metals expand when heated', or negative facts, such as 'There are no donkeys on Mars' also exist? If so, *where* do they exist? Does a catalogue of all true facts exist 'out there' or in the mind of God? What about the fundamental laws of physics? Do they exist in addition to the phenomena they describe? Did they exist before the Big Bang? Philosophers spend a lot of time puzzling over these kinds of questions. You may get a better sense of some of the problems we have touched on here from the 'Ghosts' reading at the end of this chapter.

2 Correspondence is never perfect

Since there is a gap between language and the world, correspondence can never be perfect. To see the point, look back at the picture in Chapter 1, 'The Treason of Images' (page 7). What does the picture show? A pipe! So why did Magritte write underneath it 'Ceci n'est pas une pipe' ('This is not a pipe')? Well, because it is not really a pipe, but only a picture of a pipe. You can't smoke the picture! As we saw in Chapter 3, what is true of pictures is equally true of language. You can describe something in as much detail as you like, but the truth described can never match up to the truth experienced, and the map of true propositions can never capture the underlying richness of the world.

Given this, perhaps we should abandon the idea that truth is an all-or-nothing concept – either a statement corresponds to reality or it does not – and think instead of there being *degrees of truth*. For, although there can never be a perfect correspondence, some statements, pictures and maps are surely more accurate than others. And if they are accurate enough for the purposes we have in mind, we might reasonably call them 'true'.

3 Truth cannot be determined in isolation

A final criticism of the correspondence theory is that it is not possible to determine the truth or falsity of a proposition in isolation from other propositions. You might say, 'Surely I can test the truth of a proposition such as "There is a snake in the cellar" by simply going down to the cellar and looking?' But it is always possible that your eyes are deceiving you. As we saw in our discussion of perception in Chapter 4, the only way of determining whether or not something is an illusion is to see how what you think you see fits in with other things that you believe to be true.

How, if at all, might the following propositions be said to correspond to facts about reality? What problems are there with them?

a The cat is on the mat.

b All metals expand when heated.

c Pigs do not have wings.

d Archduke Franz Ferdinand of Austria was assassinated in August 1914.

e Random torture is wrong.

f The *Mona Lisa* is a beautiful painting.

Coherence theory

According to the coherence theory of truth, a proposition is true if it fits in with our overall set of beliefs. In contrast to the correspondence theory, the focus here is not so much on *going and looking* as on *sitting and thinking*. Such an approach is particularly appropriate in the case of knowledge by testimony. In a criminal trial, for example, there is no question of checking up on what the various witnesses say by literally 'going and looking' – for the events to which they relate are in the past. All you can do is to see how coherent the evidence is, and whether or not it all points in the same direction. If at the end of a trial you are willing to say that the accused is guilty, then you presumably think the evidence is compelling enough to establish the truth.

As we saw above, coherence also plays a role in establishing the truth of empirical propositions. If, for example, someone claims to have seen a shark in Lake Geneva, you might reason that this has to be false because sharks live in salt water and Lake Geneva is a fresh-water lake. As this example shows, coherence is particularly effective as a negative test of truth and means that we don't have to waste time checking up on every wild belief we come across. If, for example, someone told me that Elvis Presley is alive and well and living in Scunthorpe, I would reject this claim on the grounds that there is documentary evidence to show that he died in August 1977. Elvis may live on in the hearts of his fans, but he is not living on in Scunthorpe.

Criticisms

1 Coherence is not sufficient for truth

Although coherence may be a good negative test of truth, it does not seem to be such a good positive test. More formally, we can say that, while coherence may be a necessary condition for truth, it does not seem to be a *sufficient* one. For example, although a work of fiction may be coherent, that does not make it true. Shakespeare's play *Richard III*, loosely based on the English king of that name, makes perfect sense, but it is not the historical truth. The same can be said of Oliver Stone's movie, *JFK*, about the assassination of President Kennedy in 1963.

2 Coherence cannot exclude crazy beliefs

If you use a bit of ingenuity, it is possible to make even the most outlandish theory seem coherent. You could, for example, make the flat earth theory consistent with the fact that the Apollo astronauts saw that the earth was round by simply claiming that the space missions were faked in a Hollywood studio. (This is precisely what the International Flat Earth Research Society does!)

Activity 14.2

Devise absurd but coherent explanations for each of the following.
a The movement of the sun across the sky
b Insomnia
c The price of stocks and shares
d The assassination of John F. Kennedy
e Global warming
f The variety of species on the planet

3 Coherence can lead to complacency

The coherence theory can lead to a kind of intellectual complacency which leads you to reject anything that does not fit in with your way of looking at things. But just because something does not fit in with your way of looking at things does not mean that it is false – for it may be your way of looking that needs to be changed. If, for example, a racist comes across evidence which contradicts his prejudice that immigrants are lazy, he should not – as the coherence theory appears to suggest – reject the evidence; rather he should change his world view. The point is that, painful as it may be, we sometimes need to question our assumptions and change our way of looking at the world.

Activity 14.3

How might our discussion in Chapter 8 (pages 226–8), of the role played by anomalies in bringing about scientific revolutions, count against the coherence theory of truth?

Pragmatic theory

According to the pragmatic theory of truth, a proposition is true if it is *useful* or *works in practice*. This theory takes a down-to-earth approach to truth and might seem to cut through a lot of nonsense. Rather than worry about whether ghostly negative facts exist or how to deal with coherent fictions, all that is required to see if an idea is true is to put it to work in the world. Pragmatists often speak of the 'cash value' of a statement, and what interests them is the difference a statement's being true or false makes in practice. You might think of this as an engineer's approach to truth: if the bridge does not fall down, then the principles on which it was built must be true!

Since people are often convinced of the truth of something if it works in practice, the pragmatic theory would seem to be on the right track. While scientists have enabled us to put men on the moon, build computers and cure diseases, astrologers, witch-doctors and faith-healers have been much less successful in helping us to achieve our goals. According to William James (1842–1910), one of the founders of the pragmatic theory, 'an idea is true so long as to believe it is profitable to our lives'. With reference to religious belief, James argued that 'if the hypothesis of God works satisfactorily in the widest sense of the word, it is true'.

Activity 14.4

1 How would you try to test whether the 'hypothesis of God' works in practice? What do you think it would mean for such a belief to work?
2 What would (a) the correspondence theory, and (b) the coherence theory say must be the case for the proposition 'God exists' to be true?

Criticisms

1 A statement can be useful but not true and true but not useful

There are many examples of statements that are useful but not true:

- There are all kinds of 'rules of thumb' in mathematics and science which are useful but not true. For example, Newton's laws of motion are useful for making day-to-day calculations, but since they only approximate to Einstein's theory of relativity a physicist will tell you that they are not strictly speaking true.
- It is often socially useful to hold beliefs that match those of other people. If, for example, you had grown up in Nazi Germany it would have been 'useful' to have racist beliefs. But the fact that such beliefs might have been good for your 'career' would not justify our calling them true!
- At a personal level, there are many statements that would be useful to believe in the sense that they would make us happy but which are not true. My belief that I am a deeply misunderstood genius may make me happy, but the sad reality might be that I am simply a deeply deluded mediocrity.

On the other side of the coin, there are also many examples of statements that we want to say are true but which are not useful.

- At an abstract level, a great deal of mathematics is useless in the sense that it has no practical application. (The mathematician G. H. Hardy, 1877–1947, proudly boasted that he had 'never done anything useful'.)
- More prosaically, there are literally millions of trivial facts which do not seem to do any useful work. For example, how useful is it to know that Sweden came 10th in the 1965 Eurovision Song Contest with a song called 'Absent Friends', or that David Beckham's father-in-law is called Tony Adams? Such gobbets of useless information are good only for trivia quizzes and game shows – but they are still true.
- There are also many 'inconvenient truths' about ourselves and other people which may not be very useful to believe, but which are nevertheless true.

1 Classify each of the following beliefs according to whether you think they are: (i) true and useful; (ii) true but not useful; (iii) useful but not true; (iv) not useful and not true. What does this suggest about the pragmatic theory of truth?

  a John Lennon's first girlfriend was called Thelma Pickles.

  b If a French noun ends with the suffix '-ion', then it is feminine.

  c I am a very sociable person with a good sense of humour.

  d John Smith has exactly 113,574 hairs on his head.

  e After we are dead we will soon be forgotten.

  f You should never talk to strangers.

  g 2 + 2 = 4.

  h Santa Claus is watching you to see if you are good or bad.

  i Human beings have free-will.

  j If you take cocaine your teeth will drop out.

  k I am surrounded by people who love and care for me.

  l We are fighting a just war and have God on our side.

  m We were all put on the earth for a reason and each of us has a special talent that makes us unique.

  n Anyone can make it in this country if they work hard enough.

2 Imagine you are an astronomer and that you have just discovered that a meteorite will hit the earth in twelve hours' time, wiping out life as we know it. How useful is this truth? Would you announce it to the world or keep this information to yourself?

2 The pragmatic theory implies that two contradictory beliefs could both be true

For example, while a Buddhist believes that the Buddha is the highest source of spiritual authority, a Christian believes that role is played by Jesus. Since these beliefs contradict one another they cannot both be true, but if they make their respective adherents happy, a pragmatist seems committed to saying that they are *both* true.

3 'Useful' and 'works in practice' are too vague to give us a workable theory of truth

A final criticism of the pragmatic theory is that it is not clear what it means to say that something is 'useful' or 'works in practice'. Perhaps a belief is useful if it gives us a feeling of power or security, or makes us feel happy. But then, as we saw above, many statements we naturally want to call true do not seem to be useful in this sense.

You might try to defend the pragmatic theory by pointing out that a statement which is useful in the short-run might not be useful in the long-run. If, for example, you have an exaggerated belief in your own abilities, it might be good for your self-esteem in the short-run but it will not ultimately help you to cope with reality. The most useful thing in the long-run is surely to have a realistic grasp of your own strengths and weaknesses.

The trouble with adopting this broader sense of 'useful' is that it seems to rob the pragmatic theory of its value. We said that a statement is useful if it enables us to cope with reality; but if we then ask what kinds of statement enable us to cope with reality, we naturally want to say: statements that are true. This is surely an example of **circular reasoning** – explaining A in terms of B, and B in terms of C, and C in terms of A. The pragmatic theory now seems to come down to little more than sticking the label 'useful' on statements that we have decided for independent reasons are true, and 'not useful' on ones that we have decided are false.

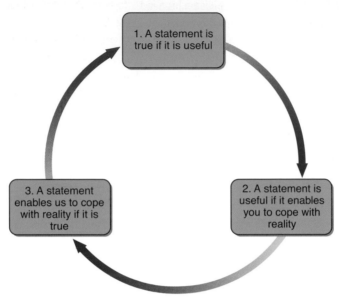

Figure 14.1 Circular reasoning

The common-sense conclusion which fits the way we naturally think is that it is not usefulness that makes a statement true, but truth that makes a statement useful. In other words, *usefulness is not a criterion of truth as the pragmatic theory claims, but a consequence of it.*

Activity 14.6

1 Give some examples of statements that might be useful in the short-run, but not in the long-run.
2 Do you think that someone could inhabit a comfortable illusion for their whole life without ever being let down by it? What are the implications of this for our discussion?
3 What are the benefits and drawbacks of modern technology? What do you think a Buddhist monk would say about its usefulness? What, if anything, does this imply about the truth of the scientific theories on which technology is based?
4 When a religious person says 'God exists' do you think they are saying any more than 'It is useful to believe that God exists'? If so, what?

Summary of theories

We have now looked at three different theories of truth and have found that, despite their attractions, they each have various weaknesses. These can be summarised in the table below.

Theory	Criticisms
Correspondence A proposition is true if it corresponds to a fact	1 The correspondence theory requires the existence of all kinds of ghostly facts to which true statements are supposed to correspond. 2 Since there is a gap between language and the world, correspondence can never be perfect. 3 We cannot determine the truth or falsity of a proposition in isolation from other propositions.
Coherence A proposition is true if it fits in with our overall set of beliefs	1 Coherence is not sufficient for truth. A fairy tale may be perfectly coherent, but it is still a fairy tale. 2 With a little ingenuity, any crazy belief can be made to appear coherent. 3 A knowledge claim that does not fit in with your way of thinking might still be true.
Pragmatic A proposition is true if it is useful or works in practice	1 A proposition can be true but not useful, and useful but not true. 2 The pragmatic theory implies that two contradictory beliefs could both be true. 3 The words 'useful' and 'works in practice' are too vague to get us very far.

Perhaps we should try to combine the above theories to make a three-part test of truth. We might then say that a theory is true if it reflects the facts, is coherent, and works in practice by, for example, enabling us to make good predictions.

Can we know the truth?

The three-part test of truth suggested above may be an effective way of distinguishing between truth and falsity in everyday life; but at a deeper level you might still have doubts about whether we can know the truth. When we think about truth, it is hard to avoid the idea that a true proposition must correspond to reality. The trouble is that, since we can never escape from our own distinctively human way of looking at things, we can in practice never compare our picture of reality with reality itself to see if our picture is true. The point in short is that *our picture of the world is always an interpretation and we can never be sure that our interpretation is true.*

The limitations of our knowledge tools

The idea that we are in some sense trapped inside our own interpretation of reality would seem to be supported by our discussion in Part 2 of the four knowledge tools: perception, language, reason and emotion. As we saw, these knowledge tools play an important role in helping us to construct a workable map of reality, but it could be argued that they also limit our ability to know the truth. Consider, for example, the following points:

- *Perception* If our senses had evolved differently, we would have a very different experience of reality.
- *Language* Since the map is not the territory, there will always be aspects of reality that lie beyond our best attempts to describe them.
- *Reason* Just as a rat cannot solve a differential equation, so there may be truths about the universe that lie beyond our intellectual abilities.
- *Emotion* The fact that you passionately believe something is no guarantee that it is true.

Perhaps if intelligent aliens exist in some far-flung galaxy they will have a very different picture of reality from our own, and understand some of the deeper truths of the universe that lie beyond our more limited grasp!

Activity 14.7

What does the following passage by Albert Einstein (1879–1955) imply about our ability to discover the truth?

'In our endeavour to understand reality we are somewhat like a man trying to understand the mechanism of a closed watch. He sees the face and the moving hands, even hears its ticking, but he has no way of opening the case. If he is ingenious he may form some picture of a mechanism which could be responsible for all the things he observes, but he may never be quite sure his picture is the only one which could explain his observations. He will never be able to compare his picture with the real mechanism and he cannot even imagine the possibility of the meaning of such a comparison.'

Are we getting closer to the truth?

Despite the above comments, you might insist that knowledge progresses over time, and that we are at least getting *closer* to the truth. Perhaps! But the success of the quest for knowledge in the past is no guarantee that it will continue to be successful in the future. Indeed, if we take the **problem of induction** seriously, perhaps the laws of nature will inexplicably break down one day and the world dissolve into chaos. Admittedly, these laws have worked well enough up until now, but how can we be sure that they will continue to do so in the future? Perhaps the 'great truths' we have discovered will turn out to be nothing more than local anomalies in the tangled fabric of the universe!

What confidence can we then have that our way of looking at things is the right one? If you are religious, you may say that 'God made man in his own image' and designed us so that if we use our faculties correctly we can discover the truth. However, you would probably agree that there is still a gulf between the truth as grasped by us and the truth as it is known to God. If you are not religious, you might argue that since we have evolved to cope with reality, our faculties are likely to be generally trustworthy – for otherwise we would not have survived. However, the father of evolutionary theory, Charles Darwin (1809–82), was not so sure about this, and once mournfully confessed: 'With me the horrid doubt always arises whether the convictions of man's mind, which has been developed from the mind of the lower animals, are of any value or at all trustworthy.'

The upshot of our discussion seems to be that at the most fundamental level there is an unbridgeable gap between our picture of reality and reality itself. This might suggest that while we can continue to talk about truth in an ordinary, everyday sense – truth with a small 't' – we may need to abandon the belief that we can ever achieve THE TRUTH.

Beyond dogmatism and relativism

Perhaps it is a good thing if we abandon the thirst for absolute truth; for it brings with it the danger that if you think you are in possession of such a truth, you seek to impose it on other people. You only have to glance at history to see the damage done by various kinds of **dogmatism**. The world might be a better place if people held their beliefs with a degree of humility.

Activity 14.8

1 Give some examples from history of the damage done by dogmatists and fanatics who are convinced that they are in possession of the truth.
2 Do you think the conviction that one has discovered the truth is always harmful, or can it sometimes be beneficial?
3 What practical difference would it make if we abandoned our belief in 'the truth' and concluded that truth is relative?

Figure 14.2

The lure of relativism

Since we do not have an absolute God's-eye view of the universe and can only know the-universe-as-it-is-for-us, you might think that our only choice is to embrace **relativism** and say that truth is relative. There is *my* truth, and there is *your* truth, and there is *Mervyn the Martian's* truth – but there is no absolute truth. We should, however, be careful here. For to say that we can never know the truth is not the same as saying that no such truth exists. You might say that a truth that can never be known has no practical value, but that does not make it any less true. If Jones is murdered and all the evidence is destroyed in a fire, we may never know who killed him, but there is still a truth of the matter.

You might still find relativism an attractive position on the grounds that it encourages a tolerant 'live and let live' attitude, which is appropriate in a multi-cultural world. But, as we saw in Chapter 1, relativism is also open to the objection that it is self-contradictory. The statement 'There is no truth' seems to refute itself as soon as you ask if it is true. If it is true, then there is at least one truth; and if it is false then it is *not* the case that there is no truth. A sophisticated relativist might try to avoid this problem by suggesting that we should simply abandon all talk of truth. But the concept of 'truth' seems to play too important a role in our thinking for us to be able to dispense with it completely.

Whether or not relativism encourages tolerance is debatable; but I think that in practice the drawbacks of embracing it outweigh the benefits. For if you abandon the belief that the truth is 'out there' independent of us, you no longer have any objective grounds for evaluating beliefs and distinguishing wishful thinking from 'facts'. And if your beliefs are no

"Do you swear to tell the truth, the whole truth, and nothing but the truth, and not in some sneaky relativistic way?"

Figure 14.3

longer disciplined by the truth, they are likely to end up being determined by nothing more than *prejudice*, or *persuasion*, or *power*. The danger is that you will then believe something simply because it fits in with your prejudices, or because someone has *persuaded* you to believe it, or because you have been *bullied* or *indoctrinated* into believing it. This is clearly not a desirable state of affairs.

Arguments against relativism
1   The fact that we cannot know something to be true does not mean there is no truth of the matter.
2   Statements such as 'There is no truth' are self-refuting.
3   Relativism reduces truth to such things as personal preferences, persuasion and power.

Degrees of truth

If we reject both dogmatism and relativism, and distrust not only those who claim to have found the truth, but also those who say that there is no truth, you might wonder what options are left to us. One possibility is to think of truth as an *ideal*, which – like all ideals – is unattainable, but which nevertheless gives direction to the quest for knowledge and which we can be nearer to or further away from.

Activity 14.9

1   In a US justice system you must swear to tell 'the truth, the whole truth, and nothing but the truth'. To what extent do you think it is possible to do this? How would you rephrase the demand to make it more realistic?

2   What does it mean to call something a 'half-truth'? Give some examples of statements that you consider to be half-truths.

3   What difference do you think it would make if, instead of thinking of a statement as 'true' or 'false', we thought of it as having a truth-value between 0 and 10?

4   T. S. Eliot (1888–1965) once said that if a person takes hold of a truth too hard it transforms itself into a falsehood. What do you think he meant by this?

What, then, does it mean to say that something is nearer to the truth than something else? Well, it is surely nearer the truth to say that a Labrador is a 'dog' than to say that it is an 'animal'; and it is nearer the truth to say that the earth is round than to say that it is flat; and Einstein's theory of relativity is nearer the truth than Newtonian mechanics. Admittedly, our current 'truths' may be replaced in the future by other truths, but at least until now it has made sense to think of each revolution in thought as bringing us closer to the truth.

The cubist theory of truth

Another way to understand 'nearness to truth' is to say that you are nearer to the truth about something the more perspectives you have on it. Imagine, for example, that you are trying to find out what someone – let us call him Henry – is 'really like'. His mother describes him in one way, his brother in another, his teachers in a third, and his friends in a fourth. While there may be some overlap between these perspectives, each one captures only some aspects of Henry, and, in a sense, gives us only *half-truths* but not the *whole truth* about him. (This may explain why if a child gets into trouble at school his surprised parents say 'But he's never like that at home!') According to what l call the **cubist theory of truth**, we get closer to the truth about Henry the more perspectives we have on him.

The cubist theory of truth should not be confused with relativism, and it is worth emphasising that, just because the truth varies with your perspective, this does not mean that there is no truth at all. To see that this is an error, imagine four people are looking at Mount Everest, and one is standing to the north, one to the south, one to the east, and one to the west; the fact that they have different perspectives on the mountain and describe it in different ways does not mean that truth is relative. For there can be more and less accurate descriptions of Mount Everest as seen from north, south, east and west, and there is a sense in which they all point to the same underlying truth.

One of the attractions of this way of thinking about truth is that it seems to avoid the errors of both dogmatism and relativism. *The error of dogmatism is to mistake a half-truth for the whole truth. And the error of relativism is to think that, since the truth varies with your perspective, there is no truth at all.* The theory also enables us to go beyond an 'I-am-right-and-you-are-wrong' approach to truth; for it suggests that when we come across someone with a different view from our own, it might be more illuminating to ask not 'Is she right or is she wrong?', but rather 'What has she seen?' and 'How does her perspective enrich my understanding of the truth?'

What price truth?

During the course of this book, we have generally assumed that seeking the truth is a 'good thing'. At the beginning of the Western tradition, Aristotle (384–322 BCE) claimed that human beings naturally desire to know the truth, and Socrates (470?–399 BCE) famously identified knowledge with happiness and virtue. As we come to the end of our enquiry, we should perhaps examine these optimistic pronouncements and ask whether the costs of the quest for knowledge and truth sometimes outweigh the benefits.

Activity 14.10

Many traditions have myths about the dangers of curiosity and wanting to know too much. Give two examples and explain what relevance, if any, they have to us today.

Do we naturally seek the truth?

The idea that we naturally seek the truth might seem to be supported by the observation that children are naturally curious and are constantly asking 'why?' However, it is worth pointing out that children are not only naturally curious but also naturally *credulous*. This trait seems to persist into adult life; for, despite the enormous growth of knowledge in the last hundred years, we do not seem to be any less superstitious than our ancestors.

There is a wealth of evidence to suggest that *people often engage in wishful thinking and believe what they want to believe rather than what is justified by the evidence.* Some people are reluctant to disturb their peace of mind by questioning their fundamental assumptions and prefer to inhabit their own comfortable illusions rather than face up to harsh and unsettling truths. To protect their beliefs, they may use a variety of **defence mechanisms**, such as **selective attention** (seeing what they want to see), **rationalisation** (manufacturing bad reasons to justify their prejudices) and **communal reinforcement** (mixing exclusively with people who hold similar beliefs).

Sadly, there is no reason to believe that if we are confronted with the truth it will make us happy, and there would seem to be something in the well-known saying that 'ignorance is bliss'. Perhaps there are things about ourselves, and other people, and the world we live in that it would be better not to know. We might, for example, be happier if we never discovered that we are not as smart as we like to think, or that our friends gossip about us behind our backs, or that there is untold suffering in the world.

Nevertheless, it is probably not a good idea to disengage completely from reality and retreat into a fool's paradise. For, if we are to adapt successfully to the world, we need accurate feedback, and the longer we harbour comforting illusions, the more difficult it will be to make the necessary adjustments. Zak may dream of being the next Einstein, but at some point he will have to face up to his low grades in physics and rethink his career plans. The truth may not make us happy in the short-run, but perhaps confronting it is the best strategy for avoiding unpleasant surprises in the long-run.

Figure 14.4

1 To what extent do you agree or disagree with the following quotations?
   a 'There is nothing I would not rather know than not know' (Samuel Johnson, 1709–84).
   b 'For in much wisdom is much grief and he who increases knowledge increases sorrow' (The Bible).
   c 'Mankind cannot bear too much reality' (T. S. Eliot, 1888–1965).

2 If there was a completely objective way of measuring intelligence on a scale of 1 to 100, would you want to know your score? Would there be any disadvantages in knowing it?

3 Imagine a parallel world identical to this one except that each individual is born with a 'sell by' date stamped on their left buttock which accurately states the day they will die. Would you prefer to live in our world or the parallel world? Why?

4 To what extent should you tell other people the truth if you know that it will hurt them?

5 Imagine that a manufacturer develops a portable lie-detector which can be integrated into your mobile phone and is 100% accurate. Whenever someone you are talking to face-to-face or by phone tells you a lie, the lie-detector beeps. What would be the pros and cons of such a machine being generally available?

6 What do you think a utilitarian would say about the extent to which we should pursue the truth?

Ought we to seek the truth?

Since the task of any area of knowledge is surely to tell us what *is* the case rather than what we would *like* to be the case, some people insist that we should seek the truth whether or not it makes us happy, and that the truth has value simply because it is the truth. Some of the great thinkers of the past – such as Socrates or Copernicus or Darwin – were willing to follow the truth wherever it led; they seem to have believed that truth is more important than happiness.

There are nevertheless two problems with the belief that the search for truth has some kind of intrinsic value. First, knowledge does not come free, and the time and money we invest in it could be spent on other things. Some people have, for example, questioned how we can justify spending vast amounts of money on space exploration when millions of people in the world lack basic necessities such as food, clean drinking water and shelter.

A second problem is that, even if we think that knowledge has intrinsic value, we also need to take account of the fact that it is a double-edged commodity which can be used for both good and bad ends. Thus nuclear physics can be used to develop a cheap and safe source of energy or to make bombs of huge destructive power. And genetic engineering can be used to eradicate hereditary disease or to breed the master race. Similarly, the human sciences can be used to alleviate the suffering of the mentally ill or to manipulate and control people's behaviour. History can be used to promote truth and reconciliation or to keep alive past grievances and fan the flames of hatred. And the arts can be used to illuminate the human condition and extend the bonds of empathy or to celebrate gratuitous violence.

But the greatest danger in the unregulated pursuit of knowledge lies in science and its foster-child, technology. If there was a moment in history when the search for truth lost its innocence, it was surely 8:15 a.m. on 6 August 1945 when a B-29 bomber called the *Enola Gay* dropped an atomic bomb on Hiroshima. We are now condemned to live with the fact that we are in possession of knowledge that could be used to bring about our own destruction.

Some people have argued that in itself knowledge is always a good thing and that we should distinguish between the *possession* of knowledge and the *use* to which it is put. This might suggest the following neat division of labour: the responsibility of scientists and academics is to seek knowledge, and the responsibility of politicians – who are (or claim to be) the representatives of the people – is to decide how such knowledge should be used.

The trouble with this argument is that it is in practice difficult to distinguish between the possession and the use of knowledge; for once the genie of knowledge is out of the bottle, it may be difficult to control. Some new technologies, such as *genetic engineering* and *nanotechnology* (building tiny machines from the bottom up, molecule by molecule), which do not require large facilities and can be developed in small laboratories using knowledge that is readily available, may be impossible to regulate. That is why some observers see them as a greater long-term threat to our survival than nuclear weapons.

At the same time we should not forget the potential benefits of new technologies that could, for example, lead to the elimination of genetically inherited diseases thereby improving the quality of life of millions of people. According to James Watson (1928–), one of the co-discoverers of DNA, 'you should never put off doing something useful for fear of evil that may never arrive', for 'we can react rationally only to real (as opposed to hypothetical) risks'. Ideally, we should perhaps do a cost–benefit analysis before deciding whether or not to adopt a new technology, but in practice this may be difficult to do – not least because the relevant costs and benefits are very difficult to estimate.

THE SCIENTIFIC COMMUNITY IS DIVIDED. SOME SAY THIS STUFF IS DANGEROUS, SOME SAY IT ISN'T.

Figure 14.5

1 Make a list of the potential benefits and drawbacks of any technology of your choice. Do you think that on balance the benefits outweigh the drawbacks, or vice versa?
2 How seriously should we take the claim that technological developments may make it easier for future terrorists to commit massively destructive acts?
3 Do some research into something called the 'precautionary principle'. What are the pros and cons of using this principle to guide scientific research?
4 According to the science fiction writer Brian Aldiss, 'Man has the power to invent but not control.' Do you think that it is possible to control scientific research in areas such as genetics?

Wisdom

The poet T. S. Eliot once lamented 'Where is the wisdom we have lost in knowledge?/ Where is the knowledge we have lost in information?' We said something about the difference between knowledge and information in the first part of this book (page 29), and it is perhaps appropriate if we finish it by saying something about the difference between wisdom and knowledge. So I shall briefly look at what I think are five key features of wisdom: good judgement, breadth of vision, self-knowledge, responsibility and intellectual humility.

"I think I've acquired some wisdom over the years, but there doesn't seem to be much demand for it."

Figure 14.6

© The New Yorker Collection 1999 J.B. Handelsman from cartoonbank.com. All Rights Reserved.

Who would you describe as a wise person? What characteristics do they possess which make them wise?

Good judgement

Human beings are fallible creatures, and if one thing has come out of this book it is that the dream of certainty is an impossible dream. But, as we have also seen, just because we cannot achieve certainty, it does not follow that any opinion is as good as any other. We are surely right to take more seriously opinions that are informed, coherent and insightful than those which are not. And we are surely justified in saying that we *know* something if we have enough evidence for it. If we ask 'how much evidence is enough evidence?', there is no definite answer and we can only say that it is a matter of judgement.

Since every situation that confronts us is unique, we must also use our judgement when we apply knowledge to the world. The relevance of good judgement in areas such as history, ethics and the arts is clear, but it also plays a role in something as seemingly objective as measurement. For example, to say that 'X is exactly 5 cm long' is based on the judgement that it has been measured to the appropriate number of decimal places for the task at hand.

How can we develop good judgement? Sadly, it is not something that can be learnt from books but only from experience and practical engagement with the world. This may be why we tend to associate wisdom with old people rather than young people. In fact, it is not experience as such that matters, but *reflection on experience* and the ability to learn from it. That is why you can be old without being wise!

Breadth of vision

Wisdom requires not only good judgement, but also breadth of vision. We live in an increasingly specialised world in which there are said to be more than 8,000 definable fields of knowledge. Such an intellectual division of labour has doubtless helped to fuel the explosive growth of knowledge over the last hundred years, but it has also resulted in a fragmented picture of reality. If you want to succeed in the modern world, you need to specialise, but if you are *too* specialised, you may end up becoming what the Germans call a *Fachidiot* – a person who is very brilliant in a narrow area but who has no real understanding of the world.

To understand the world, it makes sense to take it apart and examine the pieces. This is why we divide knowledge into different subjects. But the world does not arrive in neat packages labelled 'physics', 'biology', 'economics', 'ethics', etc.; and at some point we have to put the separate pieces together again. That is why we put so much emphasis in TOK on comparing and contrasting knowledge claims in different subjects. The ideal is surely to have both depth and breadth, to have specialists with a sense of the whole.

This is of more than theoretical interest. If we are to solve some of the urgent problems that confront us in the modern world – such as the destruction of the natural environment, or poverty, or the spread of infectious diseases – we will need an interdisciplinary approach that goes beyond the one-eyed vision of a *Fachidiot* and integrates the perspectives of many different subjects.

"I'm on the verge of a major breakthrough, but I'm also at that point where chemistry leaves off and physics begins, so I'll have to drop the whole thing."

Figure 14.7

Self-knowledge

A third ingredient of wisdom is self-knowledge. Among other things, the quest for self-knowledge encourages us to question our beliefs and motives and to become aware of our underlying prejudices. As we saw in our discussion of paradigms (page 181), our prejudices can be likened to a pair of tinted glasses that colour the way we see and think about the world. And just as we look through *but rarely see* the glasses that are on the end of our nose, so the underlying prejudices through which we make sense of reality usually remain invisible to us.

We like to think that we are rational beings, but we sometimes find it easier to comfortably inhabit our prejudices than to question them. There is doubtless an element of vanity in this, and it seems that we are often attached to our beliefs for no better reason than that they are *ours*. So perhaps what is needed – at least occasionally – is the courage to question our convictions and to ask ourselves why we believe what we believe and how far our beliefs are justified by the evidence. If we can develop self-knowledge and become aware of some of the prejudices that underlie our beliefs, then we have taken a step towards overcoming them and moving towards a more inclusive picture of the world.

Responsibility

A wise person is aware of the relation between knowledge and values. Since the search for knowledge is as much a communal as an individual enterprise, there is a sense in which values are built into it from the beginning. You may be attracted by the heroic image of the lonely thinker struggling with the truth, but the reality is that almost any statement you accept as true requires that you are willing to believe a great many people. You cannot conduct every biology experiment yourself, or personally check all the documentary evidence on which a book on the Second World War is based; so you have to trust that the biologists are not faking their results and the historians are not making it up as they go along. Indeed, if you had not trusted other people, you could never have learnt language in the first place and so would be unable to express your doubt. Trust, then, is the glue that holds the enterprise of knowledge together, and doubt only makes sense in a broader context of trust.

If knowledge is based on trust, then each of us must exercise responsibility in our knowledge claims. There are certain things we *ought* to do before we say that we know something. For example, we *ought* to look at the evidence, we *ought* to be consistent and we *ought* to be open to criticism. We are accustomed to make a sharp distinction between facts and values, but perhaps, at a deep level, facts depend on values. How, after all, can there be knowledge without such **intellectual virtues** as honesty, perseverance, courage, humility and tolerance?

As we saw in the last section, we must exercise responsibility not only in the *production* of knowledge but also in its *use*. You can be clever if you know many things, but you can be wise only if you have also thought about the use to which knowledge should be put. Perhaps one of the problems in the modern era is that we have plenty of clever people with know-how, but few wise ones with what might be called know-why.

Intellectual humility

The last aspect of wisdom I wish to mention is intellectual humility. Since we are not gods but finite beings with limited minds we can never achieve absolute knowledge. Such knowledge lies beyond our reach because we interpret the world through *our* senses and *our* reason and *our* concepts – and these can never give us the whole picture. We can perhaps be proud of our achievements and confident that we are making progress, but it seems that as our knowledge expands so does our ignorance and that every answer breeds new questions. In view of this, it is unlikely that we will ever know all there is to know about even a single grain of sand. At the limit, some of the big questions about life, the universe and everything may lie permanently beyond our grasp – mysteries to be contemplated rather than problems to be solved.

Some of the great minds of the past have been profoundly aware of the limits of knowledge. Socrates (470?–399 BCE) famously observed that all he knew was that he knew nothing, and Isaac Newton (1642–1727) compared himself to 'a little boy playing on the sea-shore, and diverting myself in now and then finding a smoother pebble or a prettier shell than ordinary, while the great ocean of truth lay all undiscovered before me'. Such **learned ignorance** – achieved after a lifetime of thought – is very different from the empty ignorance of the know-nothing who would short-circuit the search for knowledge by abandoning it at the first step.

The intellectual humility of a Socrates or a Newton is, I think, connected with a sense of wonder. (That may be why dogmatists, who think they already have all the answers, never seem to experience it.) Wonder is common among children who come to the world with new eyes and see everything as a miracle; but as we grow older we tend to get habituated to the mystery of things and can end up finding the world dull and uninteresting – *boring*. Perhaps it is the inability to find wonder in the ordinary and the normal that drives people to seek it in the extraordinary and the para-normal, and to experiment with such things as hallucinogenic drugs, pseudo-science and new-age cults. My hope is that if we could see knowledge as 'an unending adventure at the edge of uncertainty' (Jacob Bronowski, 1908–74) rather than a dull catalogue of facts to be swotted up for exams, we could reignite our sense of wonder in the everyday world.

Perhaps you will agree with me that in the end we should try to make sense of the world we live in not so much to reach a destination – for we will never have all the answers – as to travel with a different and altogether richer point of view. I hope you have a good journey!

Figure 14.8

- There are three main theories of truth: the correspondence theory, the coherence theory and the pragmatic theory.

- The correspondence theory says that a statement is true if it corresponds to a fact; but it is not clear in what sense facts exist, and the language in which we describe things will always fall short of reality.

- The coherence theory of truth says that a proposition is true if it fits in with our overall set of beliefs; but a set of beliefs can be coherent and yet untrue.

- The pragmatic theory of truth says that a proposition is true if it is useful or works in practice; but a proposition can be true but not useful, and useful but not true.

- We could try to combine the above theories and make a three-part test of truth, but there is still a gap between our picture of reality and reality itself.

- We cannot, however, dispense with the idea of truth, and it could be argued that the more perspectives we have on something the closer we get to the truth about it.

- Although it is generally considered good to seek the truth, it does not always make us happy, and the growth of modern technology, in particular, may make us wonder whether the costs sometimes outweigh the benefits.

- Beyond knowledge lies wisdom which might be said to consist of: good judgement, breadth of vision, self-knowledge, responsibility and intellectual humility.

- Perhaps the ultimate point of trying to make sense of the world is not so much to reach a destination as to travel with a different point of view.

Terms to remember

circular reasoning	cubist theory of truth	pragmatic theory of truth
coherence theory of truth	defence mechanisms	rationalisation
communal reinforcement	dogmatism	relativism
correspondence theory of truth	intellectual virtues	selective attention
	learned ignorance	

Further reading

Roger Shattuck, **_Forbidden Knowledge_** (St Martin's Press, 1996). Written by a literary critic, this book explores the question of whether we should pursue the truth at any price by exploring various myths and literary texts, such as *Faust* and *Frankenstein*. You might enjoy dipping into some of the chapters.

André Comte-Sponville, **_The Little Book of Philosophy_** (Heinemann, 2004), Chapter 12: 'Wisdom'. This short chapter contains many thoughtful insights on the nature of wisdom which, says Comte-Sponville, is best understood as 'the knowledge of how to live'.

Linking questions

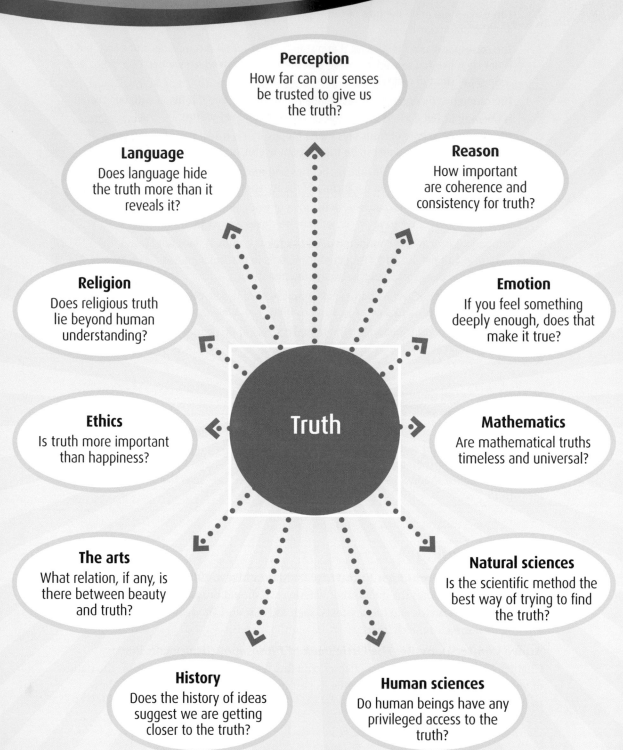

Perception
How far can our senses be trusted to give us the truth?

Language
Does language hide the truth more than it reveals it?

Reason
How important are coherence and consistency for truth?

Religion
Does religious truth lie beyond human understanding?

Emotion
If you feel something deeply enough, does that make it true?

Ethics
Is truth more important than happiness?

Truth

Mathematics
Are mathematical truths timeless and universal?

The arts
What relation, if any, is there between beauty and truth?

Natural sciences
Is the scientific method the best way of trying to find the truth?

History
Does the history of ideas suggest we are getting closer to the truth?

Human sciences
Do human beings have any privileged access to the truth?

GHOSTS

In the following extract from Robert Pirsig's novel *Zen and the Art of Motorcycle Maintenance*, the narrator argues that there is a sense in which the laws of nature do not exist because there is nothing in reality to which they correspond. They are, he provocatively suggests, simply human inventions – like ghosts.

'It is completely natural,' I say, 'to think of Europeans who believed in ghosts or Indians who believed in ghosts as ignorant. The scientific point of view has wiped out every other view to a point where they all seem primitive, so that if a person today talks about ghosts or spirits he is considered ignorant or maybe nutty. It's just all but completely impossible to imagine a world where ghosts can actually exist.'

John nods affirmatively and I continue.

'My own opinion is that the intellect of modern man isn't that superior. IQs aren't that much different. Those Indians and medieval men were just as intelligent as we are, but the context in which they thought was completely different. Within that context of thought, ghosts and spirits are quite as real as atoms, particles, photons and quanta are to a modern man. In that sense I believe in ghosts. Modern man has his ghosts and spirits too, you know.'

'What?'

'Oh, the laws of physics and of logic – the number system – the principle of algebraic substitution. These are ghosts. We just believe in them so thoroughly they seem real.'

'They seem real to me,' John says.

'I don't get it,' says Chris.

So I go on. 'For example, it seems completely natural to presume that gravitation and the law of gravitation existed before Isaac Newton. It would sound nutty to think that until the seventeenth century there was no gravity.'

'Of course.'

'So when did this law start? Has it always existed?'

John is frowning, wondering what I am getting at.

'What I'm driving at,' I say, 'is the notion that before the beginning of the earth, before the sun and the stars were formed, before the primal generation of anything, the law of gravity existed.'

'Sure.'

'Sitting there, having no mass of its own, no energy of its own, not in anyone's mind because there wasn't anyone, not in space because there was no space either, not anywhere... this law of gravity still existed?'

Now John seems not so sure.

'If that law of gravity existed,' I say, 'I honestly don't know what a thing has to do to be nonexistent. It seems to me that law of gravity has passed every test of nonexistence there is. You cannot think of a single attribute of nonexistence that that law of gravity didn't have.

Or a single scientific attribute of existence it did have. And yet it is still "common sense" to believe that it existed.'

John says, 'I guess I'd have to think about it.'

'Well, I predict that if you think about it long enough you will find yourself going round and round and round and round until you finally reach only one possible, rational, intelligent conclusion. The law of gravity and gravity itself did not exist before Isaac Newton. No other conclusion makes sense.

'And what that means,' I say before he can interrupt, 'and what that means is that that law of gravity exists nowhere except in people's heads! It's a ghost! We are all of us very arrogant and conceited about running down other people's ghosts but just as ignorant and barbaric and superstitious about our own.'

'Why does everybody believe in the law of gravity then?'

'Mass hypnosis. In a very orthodox form known as "education."'

'You mean the teacher is hypnotizing the kids into believing the law of gravity?'

'Sure.'

'That's absurd.'

'You've heard of the importance of eye contact in the classroom? Every educationist emphasizes it. No educationist explains it.'

John shakes his head and pours me another drink. He puts his hand over his mouth and in a mock aside says to Sylvia, 'You know, most of the time he seems like such a normal guy.'

I counter, 'That's the first normal thing I've said in weeks. The rest of the time I'm feigning twentieth-century lunacy just like you are. So as not to draw attention to myself.

'But I'll repeat it for you,' I say. 'We believe the disembodied words of Sir Isaac Newton were sitting in the middle of nowhere billions of years before he was born and that magically he discovered these words. They were always there, even when they applied to nothing. Gradually the world came into being and then they applied to it. In fact, those words themselves were what formed the world. That, John, is ridiculous.'

They are just looking at me so I continue: 'The problem, the contradiction the scientists are stuck with, is that of mind. Mind has no matter or energy but they can't escape its predominance over everything they do. Logic exists in the mind. Numbers exist only in the mind. I don't get upset when scientists say that ghosts exist in the mind. It's that only that gets me. Science is only in your mind too; it's just that that doesn't make it bad. Or ghosts either.

'Laws of nature are human inventions, like ghosts. Laws of logic, of mathematics are also human inventions, like ghosts. The whole blessed thing is a human invention, including the idea that it isn't a human invention. The world has no existence whatsoever outside the human imagination. It's all a ghost, and in antiquity was so recognized as a ghost, the whole blessed world we live in. It's run by ghosts. We see what we see because these ghosts show it to us, ghosts of Moses and Christ and the Buddha, and Plato, and Descartes, and Rousseau and Jefferson and Lincoln, on and on and on. Isaac Newton is a very good ghost. One of the best. Your common sense is nothing more than the voices of thousands and thousands of these ghosts from the past. Ghosts and more ghosts. Ghosts trying to find their place among the living.'

INTEGRITY

In the following extract from his book *True to Life: Why Truth Matters* the philosopher Michael P. Lynch discusses the importance of intellectual integrity.

How many times has this happened to you: you are sitting on a bus, or talking to your in-laws, or chatting at a party, and someone says something racist, or homophobic, or just plain mean. There is a momentary pause. You know that what was said was wrong and hurtful, and you want to say something about it, something that politely but firmly indicates that you thought the remark inappropriate. But you don't, and the moment passes. Later, thinking back on it, you think of all the things you might have said. You feel bad. You feel you've let yourself down.

Context matters, of course. In such situations, tact is often called for, and you must pick your battles. Nonetheless, we don't always stand up for what we think is right, even when we could. When that happens, we lack what we might call intellectual integrity.

Intellectual integrity is an aspect or part of integrity proper. It requires being willing to stand up for your best judgment of the truth, by being willing to act in accordance with that judgment when the need arises. Like other intellectual virtues, intellectual integrity is a character trait. This means that you can have intellectual integrity even if you are never called on to stand up for what you believe, and even if you are prevented from standing up for what you believe. What matters is that you are *willing* to do so, that you are disposed, other things being equal, to try.

You don't lack intellectual integrity simply because you've done something wrong. Nor is it the same as not having self-control ... Intellectual integrity requires caring for the truth for its own sake. This reveals itself in several important ways in our ordinary life. First, people who run around loudly defending whatever view they happen to land on, whether or not they've bothered to examine whether it is true, lack intellectual integrity. Willingness to stand for anything amounts to standing for nothing.

Second, a person with intellectual integrity is someone who is willing to *pursue* the truth. This means they are willing, as much as possible, to figure things out for themselves, to form their own opinion, to not just go along with the crowd or whatever happens to be fashionable or expedient. Consider, for example, a tobacco company executive who claims he is concerned about the safety of cigarette smoke. In forming his opinion that smoking does not cause cancer, he might consult several scientific studies. But intuitively, if he consults only those studies conducted by scientists on the company pay-roll, and ignores all the evidence amassed by those who are not, he lacks intellectual integrity – precisely because he has not really bothered to pursue the truth about the matter. If he is honest with himself, he cannot say that he is standing for his own best judgment on the matter, that is for the judgment most likely to be true. He has not really bothered to determine what that judgment is. He is rather standing for what is most expedient for him to believe given his position.

Third, a person of intellectual integrity stands for what she thinks is true *precisely because she thinks it is true*. Martin Luther King, Jr., implicitly makes this point in his "Letter from a Birmingham Jail." In the letter, King responds to some leading clergymen who, while claiming that they agreed with the substance of King's view on race, derided King's protest movement against segregation in Alabama as "unwise and untimely." During his impassioned reply, King writes:

I have heard numerous southern religious leaders admonish their worshipers to comply with a desegregation decision because it is the law, but I have longed to hear white ministers declare: "Follow this decree because integration is morally right and because the Negro is your brother." In the midst of blatant injustices inflicted upon the Negro, I have heard white churchmen stand on the sideline and mouth pious irrelevancies and sanctimonious trivialities ... Where were their voices of support when bruised and weary Negro men and women decided to rise from the dark dungeons of complacency to the bright hills of creative protest?

King believed his "moderate" critics were lacking integrity because while they said they wanted integration, they would encourage it insofar as it was already legal. When the chips were down – when the law and what they said they believed were inconsistent – they went with the law. But as King reminds them elsewhere in the letter, legality is not morality. Just because something is legal is not any reason to think it is the right thing to do, and just because something is illegal doesn't mean it is wrong. What distresses King is that if the white preachers really thought that African Americans have civil rights, they should say just that. Further, they should support the peaceful protest of any laws that were inconsistent with such rights. But rather than standing up for what they said they believed was true, they stood up instead for what was legal.

Fourth, intellectual integrity also requires being open to the truth just because it is the truth. To be open to the truth is to be willing to admit that you are wrong. A good example of this is the actions of Governor Ryan, former Republican governor of Illinois. When elected to office, Ryan was a staunch defender of the death penalty. But in January 2000, after it was revealed that since 1977 thirteen people convicted of the death penalty were subsequently exonerated (while twelve others were executed), Ryan placed a controversial moratorium on executions in the state. He would not, he said, approve any more executions until a thorough examination of the state's procedures for state executions was implemented and the process found to be neither arbitrary nor capricious. Some criticized Ryan's actions as lacking intellectual integrity because he had changed his mind. But to say this is to betray a lack of understanding of what intellectual integrity is. Intellectual integrity is not simply a matter of being consistent. Gritting your teeth and holding to what you've said in the past in the face of new evidence is not intellectual integrity, but stupidity. Thus, far from lacking in integrity, Ryan's actions, on this matter at least, were a paradigmatic instance of it, precisely because he was open to his view on the matter being mistaken, and he was willing to pursue the question until he felt confident that he had formed the best judgment possible about the matter.

Persons with intellectual integrity, it is worth emphasizing, don't care about truth selectively, whenever it suits them. Indeed, that's part of the point: to have intellectual integrity is to be willing to stand for one's own best judgment on any matter of importance – not just when it is convenient to do so. And since, as far as we know, almost any matter could be important at some point or other, to have integrity means caring about the truth in general. To have it, one must be open to having true beliefs in general, and pursuing the truth in general, on those questions that come before you, whatever those may be.

Index

a priori / a posteriori knowledge, 197–8, 200–2
absolutism, moral, 383
abstraction, 40–1
  and maths, 188, 189, 199, 217–18
ad hominem fallacy, 125, 129
Adams, Douglas, 275, 414
Adler, Alfred, 235–6
advertising, and language, 63, 72
aesthetics, 331, 339–42
agnosia, visual, 91, 108–10
agnosticism, 405
altruism, 372, 373–4, 376
ambiguity
  in language, 56–7, 59, 126, 182
  visual, 88–9, 182
analogy
  false, 128, 129
  and religious language, 406, 412–13
analytic propositions, 174, 176–7,
  197–8, 200
animals
  and emotions, 149
  and language, 79–82
  and self-consciousness, 257
anomalies, 227, 229, 238, 239, 411
anthropology, 262, 263, 276, 277
anthropomorphism, of God, 405–6
apathy, 154
Apollonius of Perga, 208–9
appearance and reality, 95–6
Aquinas, Thomas, 421
argument ad ignorantiam, 14, 127, 129
Aristotle, 43, 156–7, 161, 243, 348–9
art, 329–30
  and aesthetic judgement, 338–44
  as discovered or invented, 351–2
  effect on emotions, 348–9
  as imitation, 344–6
  and intention criterion, 331–3
  as means of communication, 346–7
  moral and educative role of, 347–8
  nature and scope of, 330–8
  and quality criterion, 333–6
  and science, 349–53, 361–2
  and spectator response, 336–8
  and universal standards, 340–4
assumptions, background, 232
atheism, 405, 421, 427–8, 435–6
attention, selectivity of, 91–2, 105–7,
  189, 453
authority worship, 30
avant garde, in art, 346, 358
axioms, 190, 205

bad news bias, 34
beauty
  and art, 333–4
  and science and mathematics, 195,
  233, 350

behaviour
  and history, 306–7
  irrational, 154, 157, 169–71
belief, 11–16
  belief bias, 116
  coherence of, 14–15
  and emotion, 149–50, 156
  and faith, 420, 431–4
  and judgement, 12
  justified, 26–8, 178–9, 233, 244
  and knowledge, 25–6
  and perception, 93–4
  and truth, 10–11, 24, 36, 448
Bentham, Jeremy, 385, 387
bias
  bad news, 34
  confirmation, 14, 34–5, 122, 230–1,
  313, 314
  cultural, 6–7
  hindsight, 313
  in history, 309, 312, 313–15
  in human sciences, 278
  national, 314
  social, 309
  in topic choice, 313, 314
Big Bang, 414–15, 435–6
biology
  and measurement, 284–5
  and religious belief, 432–4
  and subject-specific intuitions, 162
body language, 49–50
Bomberg, David, 340–1
Boyer, Pascal, 431–2, 434
Brecht, Bertolt, 42–4
Buffon's needle problem, 209–10
Butler, Samuel, 308

capital punishment, 124, 297, 366
Capra, Fritjof, 40–1
causation
  and cosmological argument, 414–16
  of events, 291–2
  and free-will, 289–91
  and history, 315–16, 318
  versus correlation, 124, 272
certainty, 8–10
  and mathematics, 188, 197–201, 205,
  208, 209
  and reason, 112, 131–4
  and science, 21–2, 221
chance, and history, 319
change blindness, 105–7
chemistry, 238, 284
Chesterton, G. K., 133, 135, 411
Chomsky, Noam, 84, 183, 353
circular reasoning, 125–6, 129, 446
coherence, 14–15, 95, 123
coherence theory of truth, 442–3, 447
Collingwood, R. G., 317, 347

colour, 97–8
common sense, 4–7, 161
  realism, 87, 99, 101
compatibilism, 294–6
confirmation bias, 14, 34–5, 122, 230–1,
  313, 314
conjectures
  and proofs, 192–4
  and refutations, 236–7
connotation, 57, 178
consciousness, measurement of, 264–5
consistency
  in mathematics, 207
  in moral judgements, 366, 378–9
  versus lateral thinking, 135
context
  and knowledge, 27, 37
  and meaning, 55, 57, 58, 59, 61, 277
  and perception, 88
  and reasoning, 143–4
conventions, 6–7, 367, 368
Copernicus, Nicolaus, 184, 226–7, 232, 233,
  236, 244
copy theory of art, 344–5
correspondence theory of truth, 440–1, 447
cosmological argument, 414–17, 435–6
creativity, 258
  mathematical, 163–4, 195–6
  in science, 362
culture
  and aesthetic judgement, 342, 343–4
  of critique, 141–2
  and emotion, 147
  and knowledge, 30, 31
  as maps of meaning, 181
  perceptual biases, 6–7
  and relativism, 143–4, 218, 367–71

Darwin, Charles, 183, 230, 238, 413, 449
Davies, Paul, 413–14, 435–6
Davis, Wade, 263
Dawkins, Richard, 127, 250–2
De Bono, Edward, 135–6
decision-making
  and emotions, 155
  and free-will, 292–3, 294–6
deduction, 114–19, 133, 143
  deductive system, paradigms, 180
  and induction, 121
  in mathematics, 191, 217–18
definition theory of meaning, 52–3
definitional truths, 174
denotation, 57
denotation theory of meaning, 53
Descartes, René, 9–10, 113, 137, 201
design, argument from, 412–14, 418
desires
  control of, 294–5
  self and other-regarding, 373

determinism
  economic, 318–19
  and ethics, 296–8
  and free-will, 289–96
  linguistic, 68–71
  and rationality, 299
Diamond, Jared, 283–5, 316
dilemmas
  false, 128, 129
  moral, 384, 386, 392
discovery versus invention, 202–3, 216–17, 351–2
disinterest, and aesthetic judgement, 339–40
disputes, factual and verbal, 176–7
diversity argument, moral relativism, 367–8
dogmatism, 449, 452
doubt *see* scepticism
Duchamp, Marcel, 337, 338
duty ethics, 377–85

economic determinism, 318–19
economics
  as a science, 286–7
  and experiment, 268, 287
  and historical change, 318
  and holism, 275–6
  and the observer effect, 263
  and prediction, 279, 286
  and reason, 169–71, 263
  and trends, 272
education
  and aesthetic judgements, 339
  art as, 347–8
  and intuitions, 161, 163–4, 196
  as source of knowledge, 4, 32, 464
  versus indoctrination, 32
Einstein, Albert, 125, 183
  on language and thought, 70
  and mathematics, 209
  and religion, 427
  and science, 234, 246, 254, 352
  theory of relativity, 214, 229, 236, 239, 243, 350
  and truth, 448, 451
ellipses and planetary motion, 208–9, 213, 233
Elton, G. R., 308
Emin, Tracey, 332–3
emotion, 9, 146
  and art, 347, 348–9, 352
  and beliefs, 149–50, 156
  emotional energy, 150–1
  and ethics, 381–2, 384
  and irrational behaviour, 154, 157
  James-Lange theory, 148
  and language, 73, 151, 153
  and love, 151, 172–3, 352
  as obstacle to knowledge, 151–4
  and perception, 92–3
  primary, 147, 148
  and rationalisation, 152–4, 157
  and reason, 156–8
  social emotions, 150
  as source of knowledge, 155–7
  see also intuition

empathy
  and the arts, 348
  and emotion, 148–9
  and ethics, 373
  and history, 317
empirical propositions, 175, 176, 178–9, 198–9
empiricism
  and mathematics, 198–9
  and perception, 86, 100, 101
  and science, 234–5, 239–40
enthymemes, 119
equivocation, 126, 129
ethics, 364
  and art, 347–8
  and determinism, 296–8
  duty ethics, Kant, 377–85
  free-will assumption, 288
  and intuition, 162, 371, 378
  moral absolutism, 383
  moral reasoning, 364–7
  moral relativism, 367–71, 396–400
  religious, 376–7
  self-interest theory, 372–6
  utilitarianism, 385–92
Euclid, 180, 189–91, 200–1, 205, 208, 209
euphemisms, 57, 73
evidence, 14, 457, 459
  historical, 302–3, 308–10
  and religious belief, 420, 421, 423, 431
  see also facts
evolutionary theory, 238, 449
  and argument from design, 413, 421, 422
  and religious belief, 431–2
  and self-interest theory, 373
excluded middle, law of, 132, 133
existence of God, 405–8
  argument from design, 412–14
  argument from religious experience, 409–12
  and the cosmological argument, 414–17, 435–6
  and free-will, 407
  and Pascal's wager, 422–3
  and pragmatic theory of truth, 444, 446
  and suffering, 407, 417–20
existence of mathematical entities, 202–3
expectations
  and illusion, 90, 107
  and observation, 229, 231
  predicting behaviour, 263
  self-realising, 307
experience
  mystical, 41
  religious, 409–12, 432–4
  and wisdom, 457
experiment
  in human sciences, 268–70, 287
  in the natural sciences, 226
experts / expertise
  in art, 336–7
  fallibility of, 33
  and intuition, 163–4
  as knowledge source, 8, 33–4
  in scientific observation, 229

explanation
  and history, 304, 315
  and religion, 409, 416
eye-witness testimony, 36, 94, 107, 309–10
Eysenck, Hans, 125

facts
  historical, 309–10
  and knowledge, 29
  problems with, 441
  scientific, 253–4
  and values, 178, 366, 367, 459
faith, 420–1
  and reason, 133, 420–3
  tests of, 431–4
  see also religion
fallacies, 113, 124–31, 177–8, 272, 275
fallibility of experts, 33
falsification, 230, 235–40, 242, 245
Farb, Peter, 69–70
feelings *see* emotion
Festinger, Leon, 153
Feynman, Richard, 34, 245
fiction and history, 325–7
figure-ground phenomenon, 88–9, 91–2
forgery, and art, 334–6
formalism, and mathematics, 201, 202, 204
free-will, 270, 288
  and causation, 291–4
  and compatibilism, 294–6
  and determinism, 289–96
  as illusion, 293, 296–9, 407
  and problem of suffering, 417–18
  and punishment, 297–8
Freud, Sigmund, 183, 235, 420, 421

Galileo Galilei, 42–4, 221, 227, 232
  and the Church, 184, 229, 254, 422
  and mathematics, 188, 208
generalisations, 120–3, 129, 133–4
  ethical rules, 378
  in mathematics, 196, 198
  in science, 234
geometry
  Euclidean, 180, 189–90, 200–1, 208
  non-Euclidean, 205–8
  Riemannian, 205–7
Al Ghazali, 379–80
ghosts, 463–4
God
  and anthropomorphism, 405–6
  of the philosophers, 406–7, 409
  see also existence of God
Goldbach's conjecture, 193–4, 200
golden rule, 380
'great person' theory of history, 316–18
gullibility, 12, 250–1
Gödel, Kurt, incompleteness theorem, 208

Haney, William, 122
happiness
  pursuit of, 401–2
  and truth, 454
  utilitarianism, 385–91
Harrison, Edward, 21–2